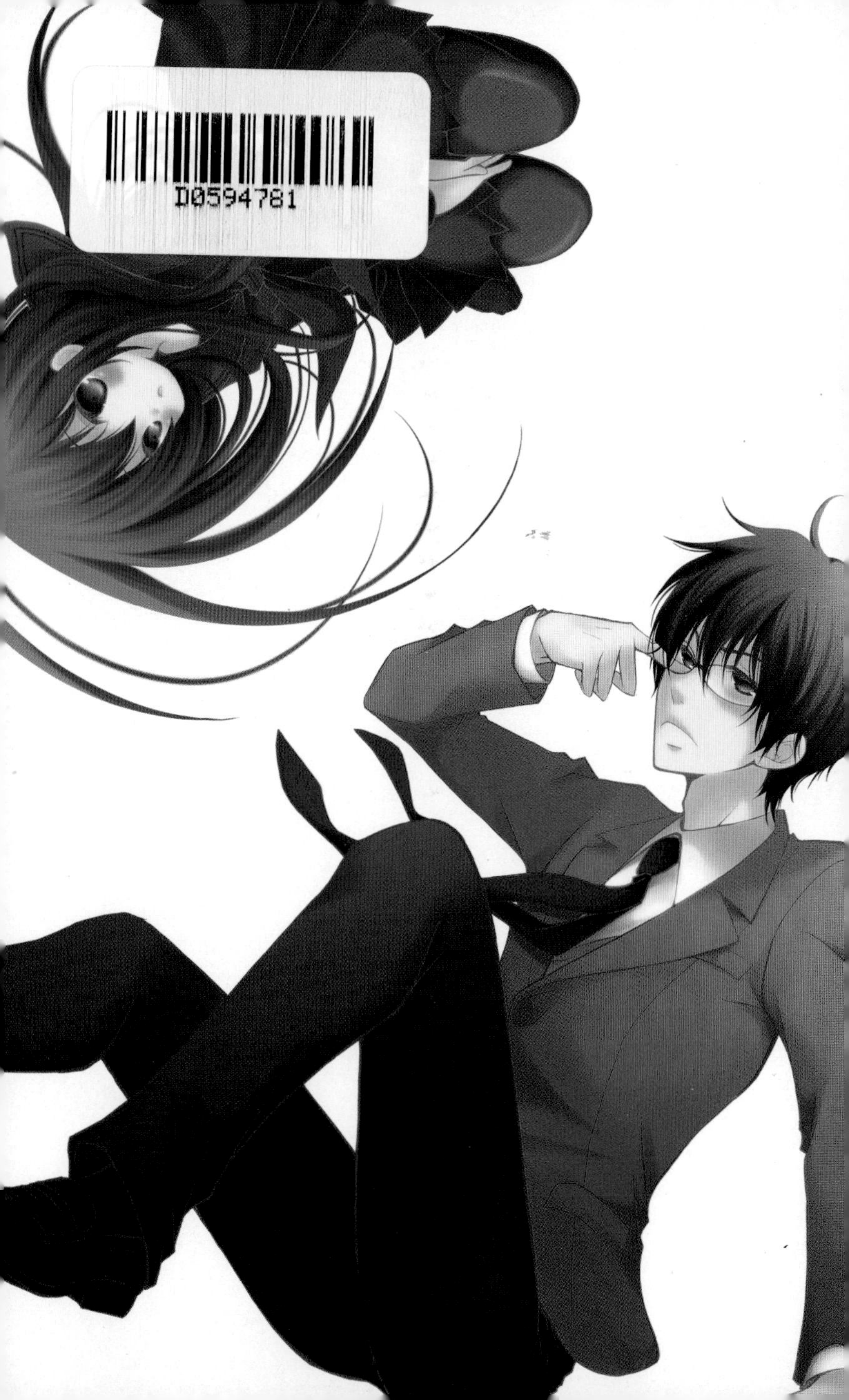

[Ani-Imo]

Big Brother becomes Little Sister;
Little Sister becomes Big Brother.

Ani-Imo

(1)

[Ani-Imo]
**Big Brother becomes
Little Sister;
Little Sister becomes
Big Brother.**

**Haruko
Kurumatani**

CONTENTS

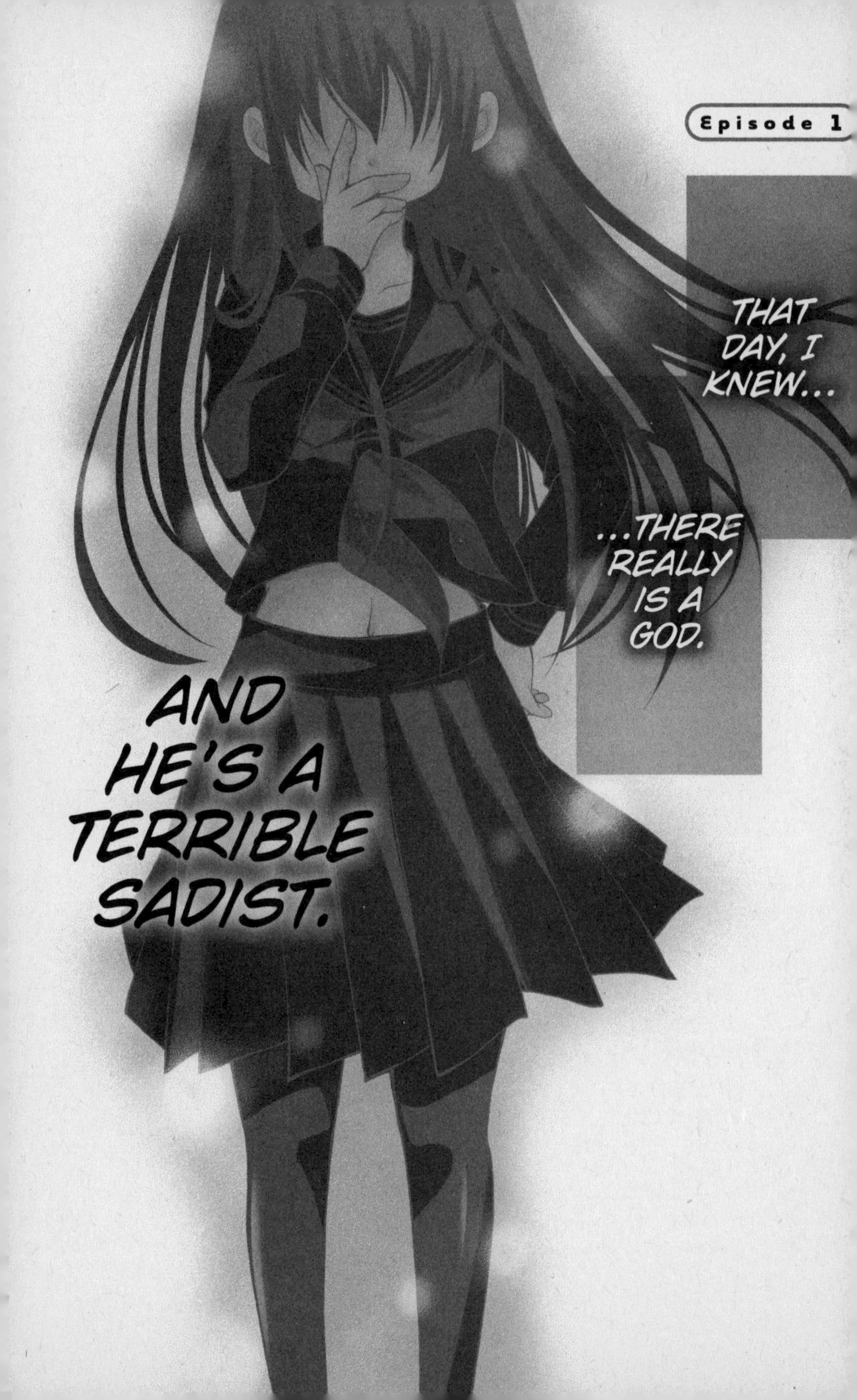
Episode 1
THAT DAY, I KNEW...
...THERE REALLY IS A GOD.
AND HE'S A TERRIBLE SADIST.

Episode 1

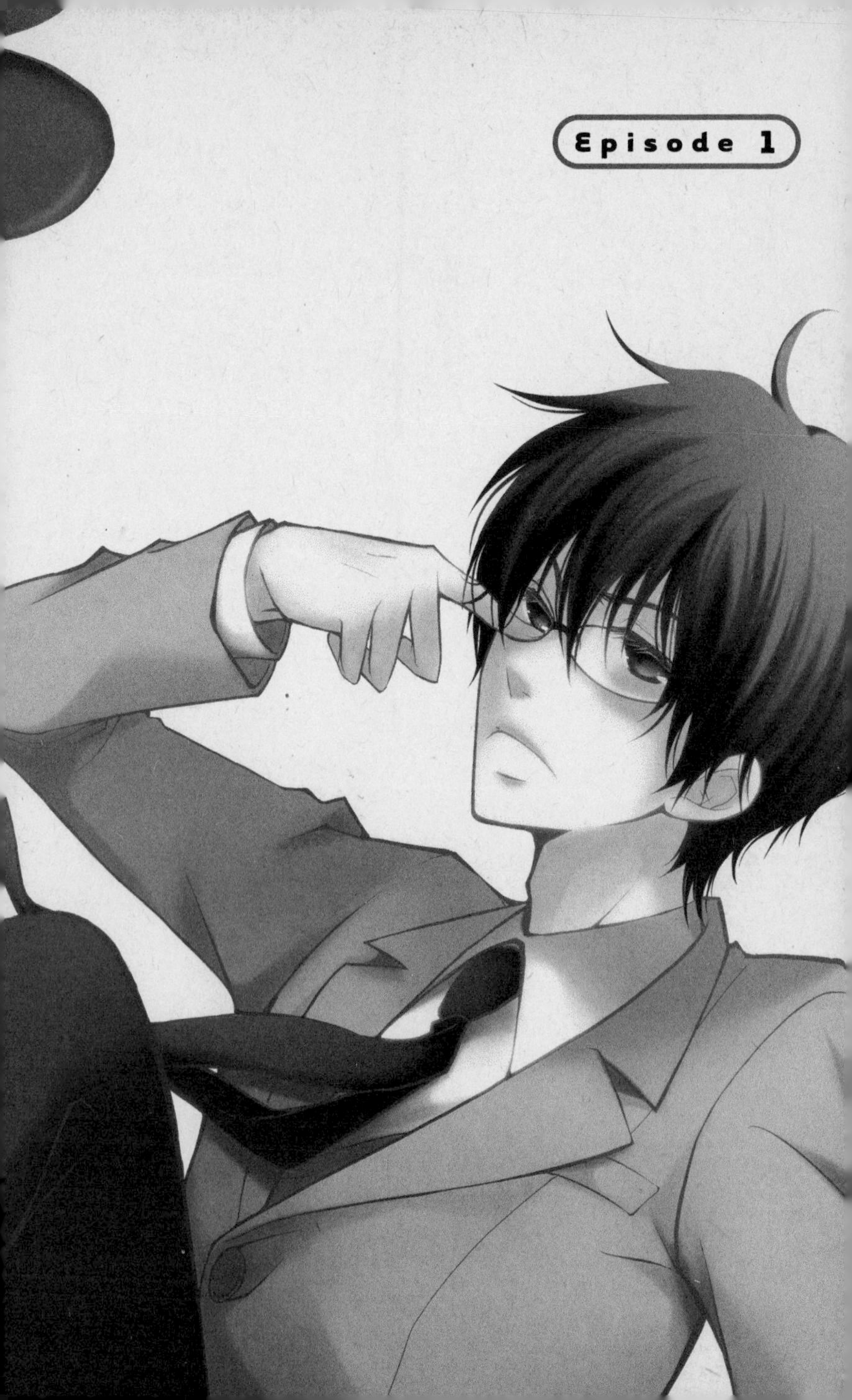

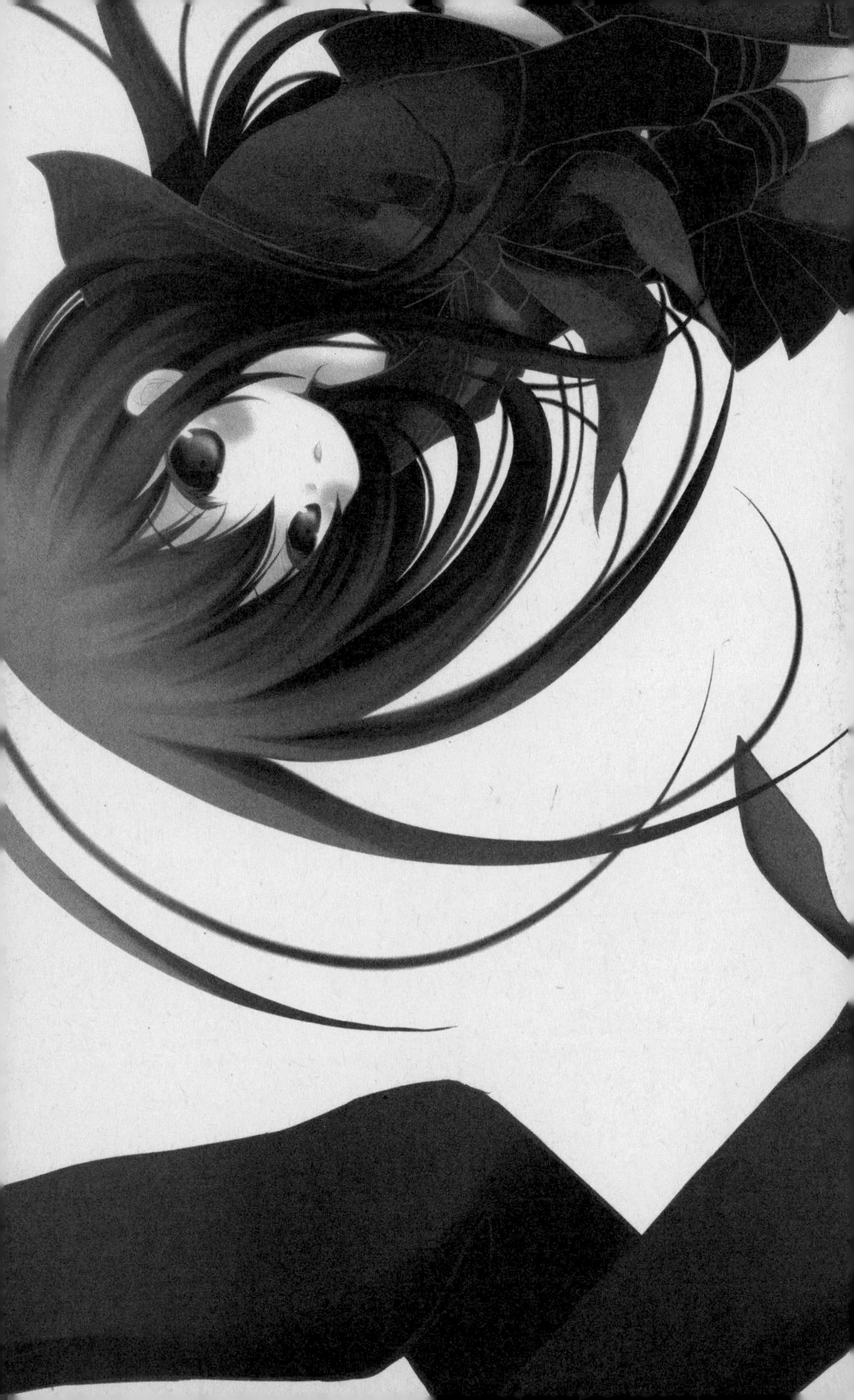

[Ani-Imo]

Big Brother becomes Little Sister;
Little Sister becomes Big Brother.

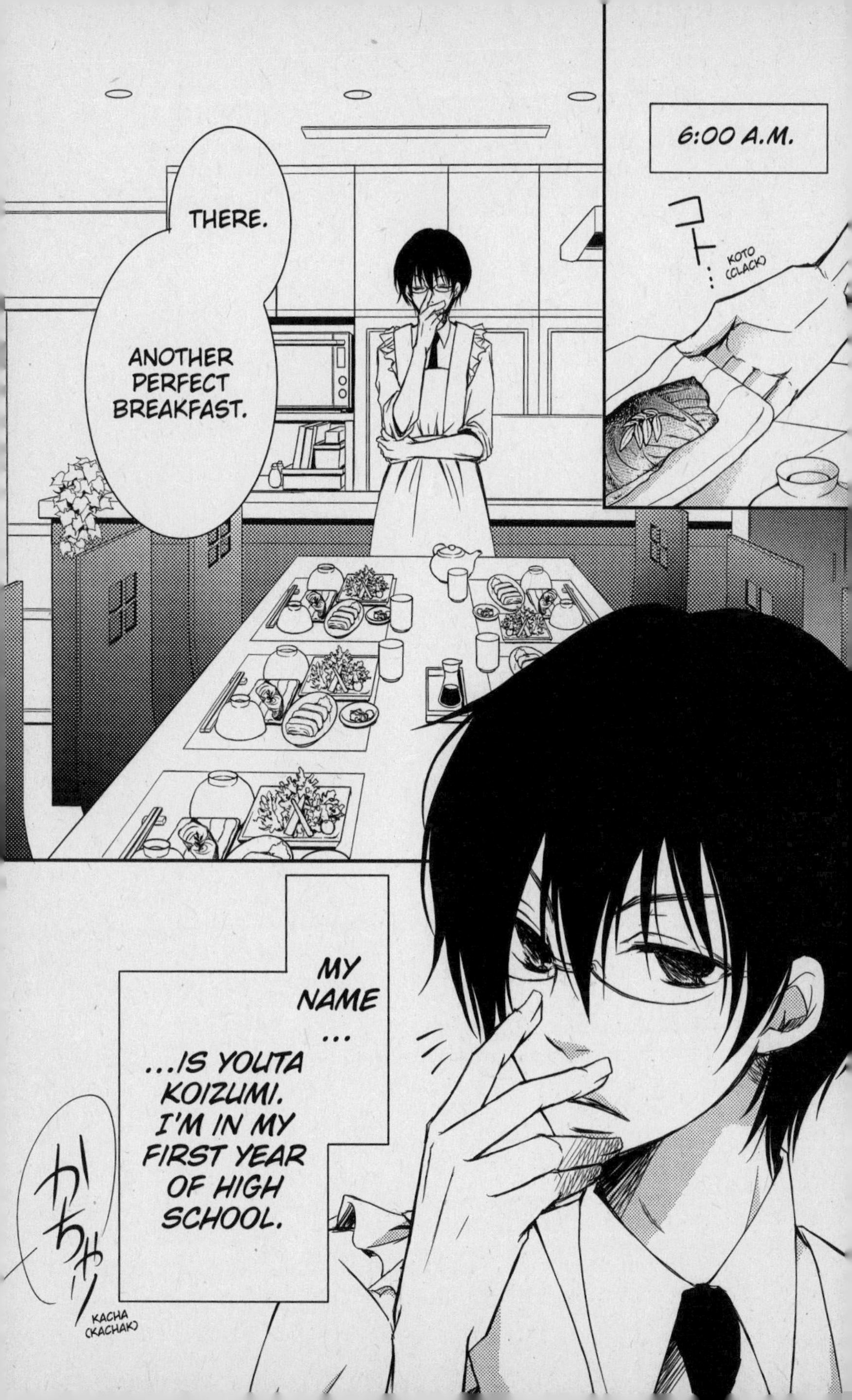
6:00 A.M.
コト…
KOTO (CLACK)
THERE.
ANOTHER PERFECT BREAKFAST.
MY NAME…
…IS YOUTA KOIZUMI. I'M IN MY FIRST YEAR OF HIGH SCHOOL.
KACHA (KACHAK)

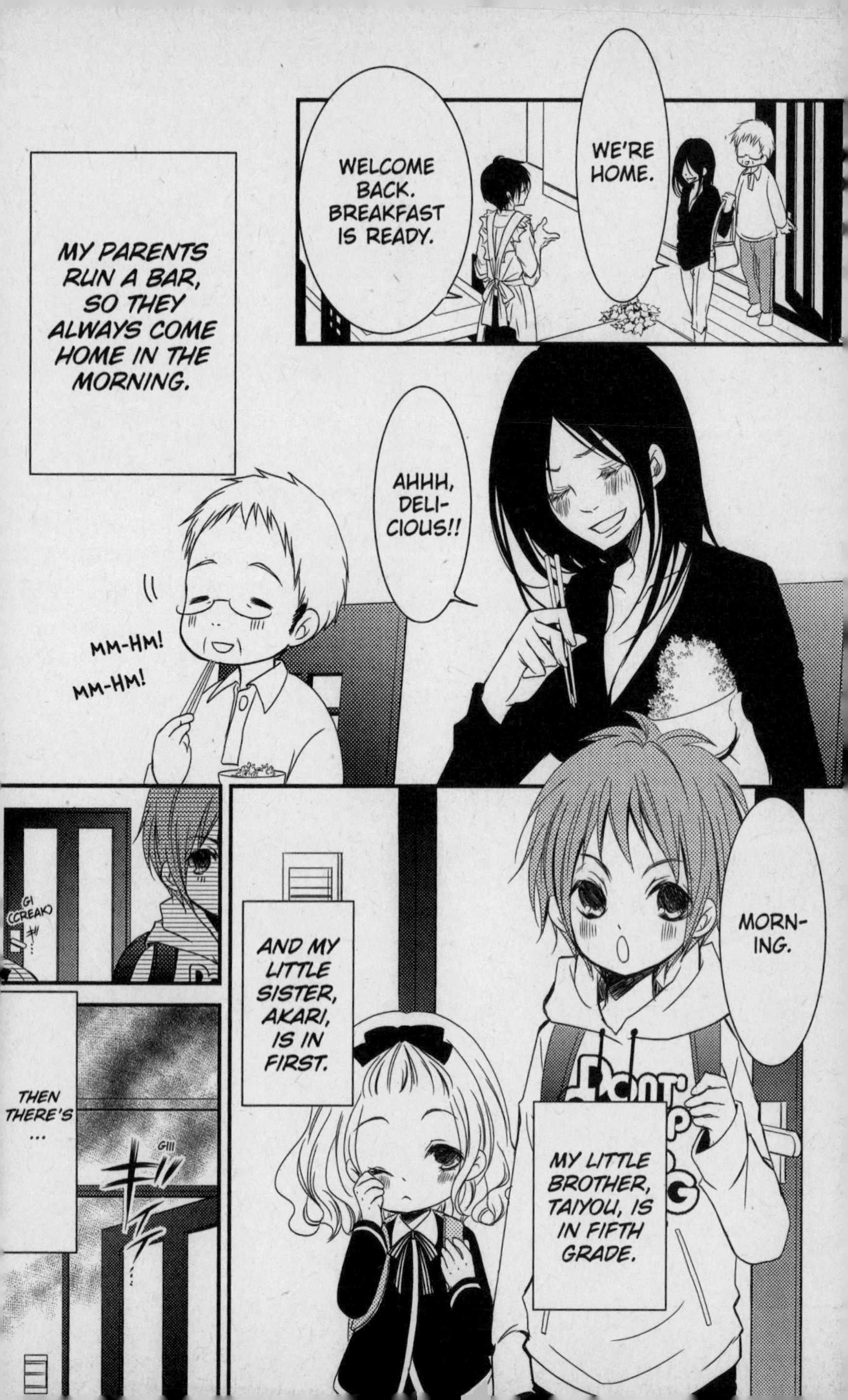
WE'RE HOME.
WELCOME BACK. BREAKFAST IS READY.
MY PARENTS RUN A BAR, SO THEY ALWAYS COME HOME IN THE MORNING.
AHHH, DELICIOUS!!
MM-HM!
MM-HM!
MORN-ING.
MY LITTLE BROTHER, TAIYOU, IS IN FIFTH GRADE.
AND MY LITTLE SISTER, AKARI, IS IN FIRST.
GI (CREAK)
THEN THERE'S...
GIII

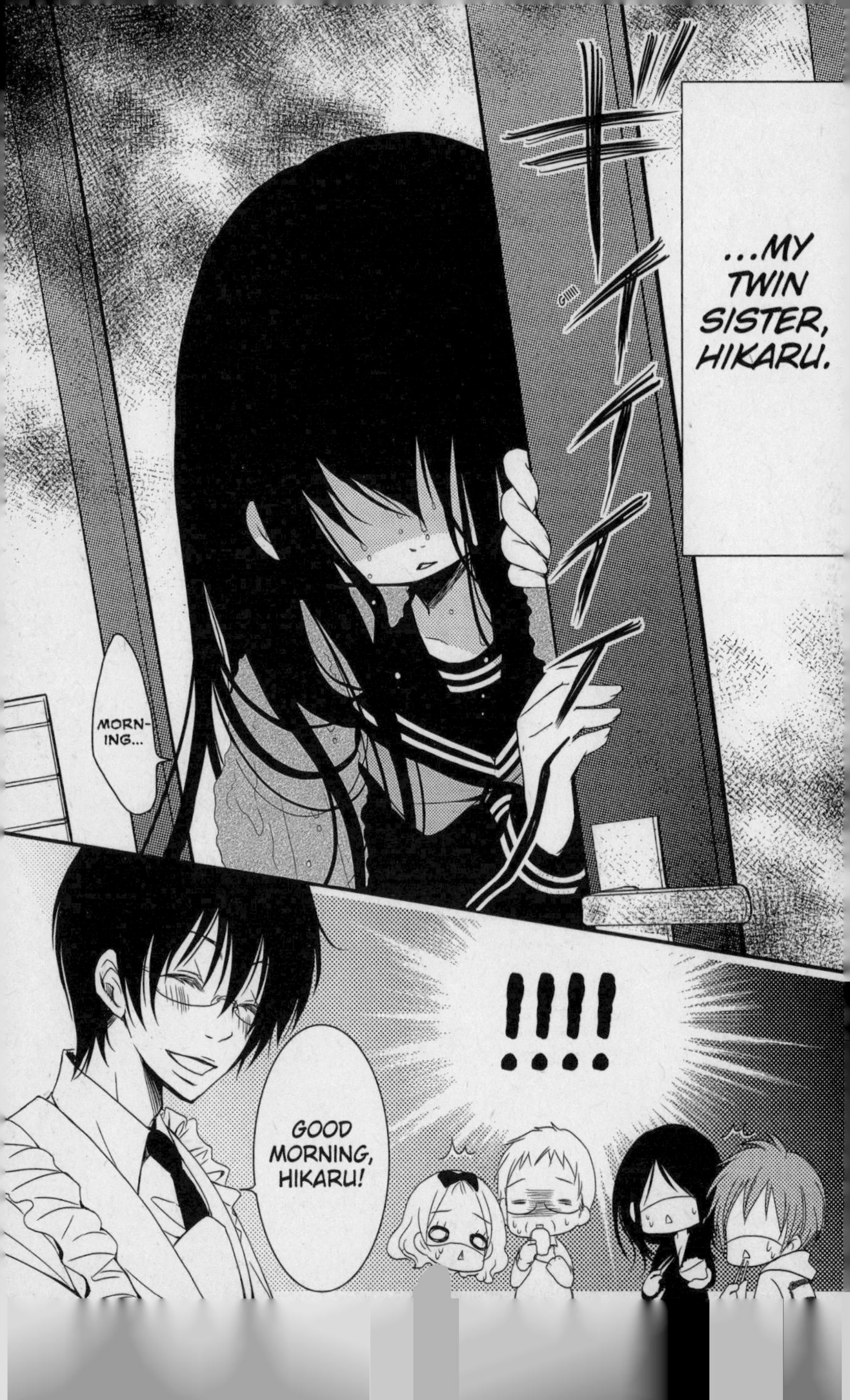
...MY TWIN SISTER, HIKARU.
GIIIII
MORNING...
!!!!
GOOD MORNING, HIKARU!

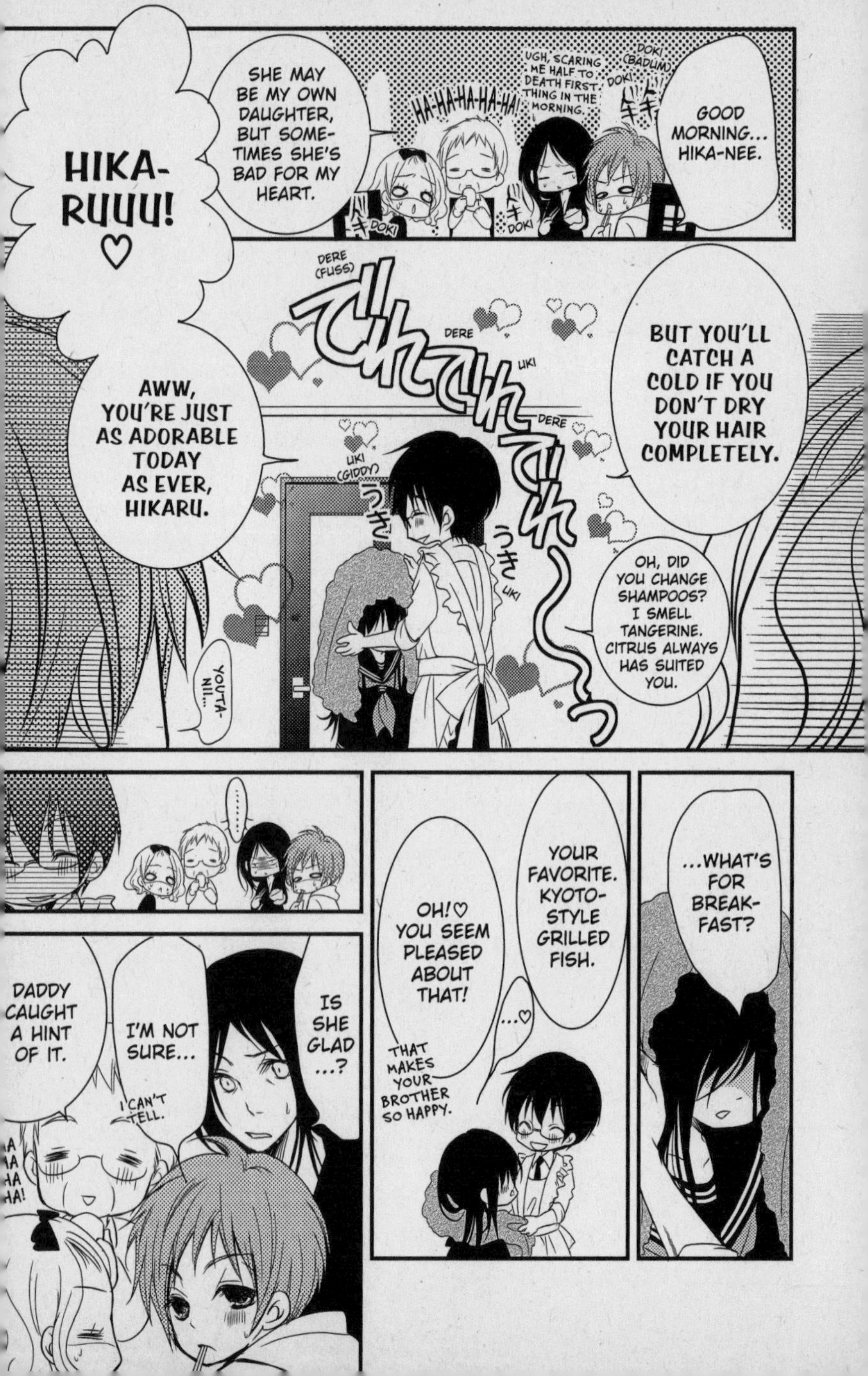
GOOD MORNING... HIKA-NEE.
DOKI (BADUM) DOKI
ドキ
UGH, SCARING ME HALF TO DEATH FIRST THING IN THE MORNING.
HA-HA-HA-HA-HA!
DOKI
SHE MAY BE MY OWN DAUGHTER, BUT SOMETIMES SHE'S BAD FOR MY HEART.
DOKI
HIKA-RUUU! ♡
BUT YOU'LL CATCH A COLD IF YOU DON'T DRY YOUR HAIR COMPLETELY.
DERE (FUSS)
でれでれでれでれ〜っ
DERE
DERE
UKI
OH, DID YOU CHANGE SHAMPOOS? I SMELL TANGERINE. CITRUS ALWAYS HAS SUITED YOU.
うき
UKI
うき
UKI (GIDDY)
AWW, YOU'RE JUST AS ADORABLE TODAY AS EVER, HIKARU.
YOUTA-NII...
...WHAT'S FOR BREAKFAST?
YOUR FAVORITE. KYOTO-STYLE GRILLED FISH.
...♡
OH!♡ YOU SEEM PLEASED ABOUT THAT!
THAT MAKES YOUR BROTHER SO HAPPY.
......
IS SHE GLAD...?
I'M NOT SURE...
I CAN'T TELL.
DADDY CAUGHT A HINT OF IT.

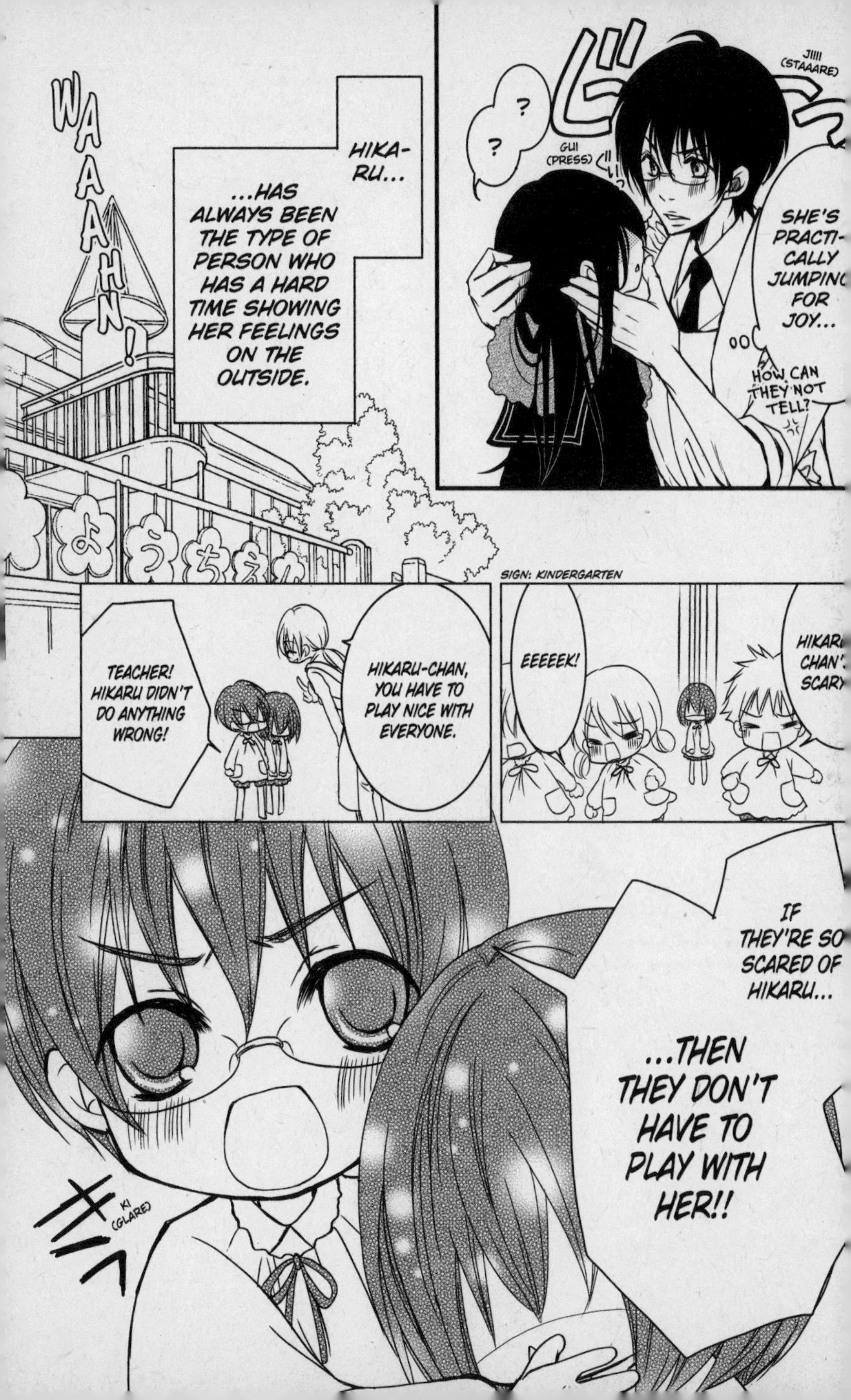
JIIII (STAAARE)
SHE'S PRACTICALLY JUMPING FOR JOY...
HOW CAN THEY NOT TELL?
GUI (PRESS)
? ?
HIKARU...
...HAS ALWAYS BEEN THE TYPE OF PERSON WHO HAS A HARD TIME SHOWING HER FEELINGS ON THE OUTSIDE.
WAAAAHN!
SIGN: KINDERGARTEN
HIKAR CHAN' SCAR
EEEEEK!
HIKARU-CHAN, YOU HAVE TO PLAY NICE WITH EVERYONE.
TEACHER! HIKARU DIDN'T DO ANYTHING WRONG!
IF THEY'RE SO SCARED OF HIKARU...
...THEN THEY DON'T HAVE TO PLAY WITH HER!!
KI (GLARE)

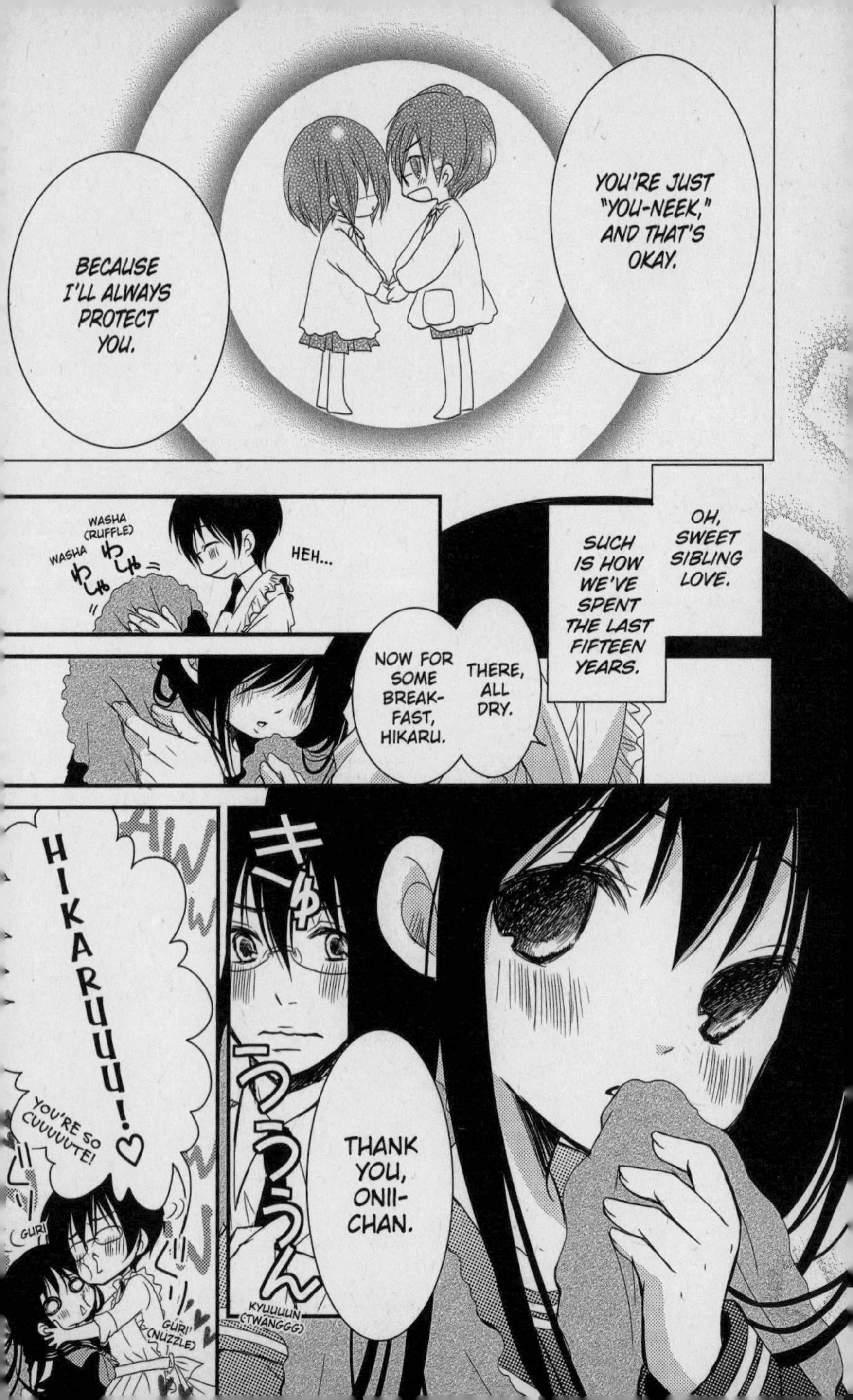
YOU'RE JUST "YOU-NEEK," AND THAT'S OKAY.
BECAUSE I'LL ALWAYS PROTECT YOU.
OH, SWEET SIBLING LOVE.
SUCH IS HOW WE'VE SPENT THE LAST FIFTEEN YEARS.
HEH...
WASHA (RUFFLE)
WASHA
THERE, ALL DRY.
NOW FOR SOME BREAKFAST, HIKARU.
THANK YOU, ONII-CHAN.
KYUUUUN (TWANGGG)
HIKARUUUU!♡
YOU'RE SO CUUUUUTE!
GURI
GURI (NUZZLE)

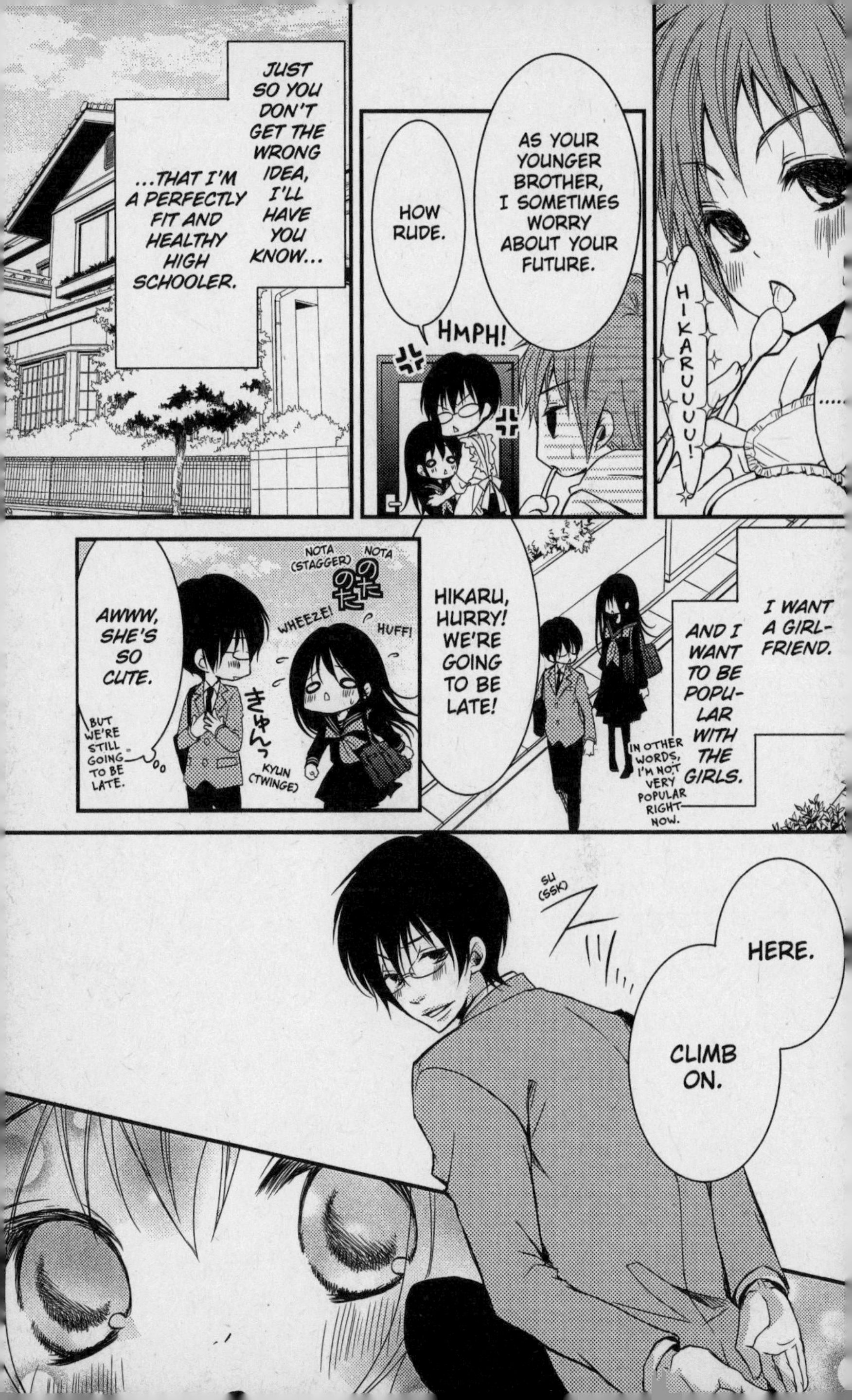
HIKARUUUU!
.....
AS YOUR YOUNGER BROTHER, I SOMETIMES WORRY ABOUT YOUR FUTURE.
HOW RUDE.
HMPH!
JUST SO YOU DON'T GET THE WRONG IDEA, I'LL HAVE YOU KNOW...
...THAT I'M A PERFECTLY FIT AND HEALTHY HIGH SCHOOLER.
I WANT A GIRL-FRIEND.
AND I WANT TO BE POPU-LAR WITH THE GIRLS.
IN OTHER WORDS, I'M NOT VERY POPULAR RIGHT NOW.
HIKARU, HURRY! WE'RE GOING TO BE LATE!
のたのた
NOTA NOTA (STAGGER)
HUFF!
WHEEZE!
きゅんっ
KYUN (TWINGE)
AWWW, SHE'S SO CUTE.
BUT WE'RE STILL GOING TO BE LATE.
SU (SSK)
HERE.
CLIMB ON.

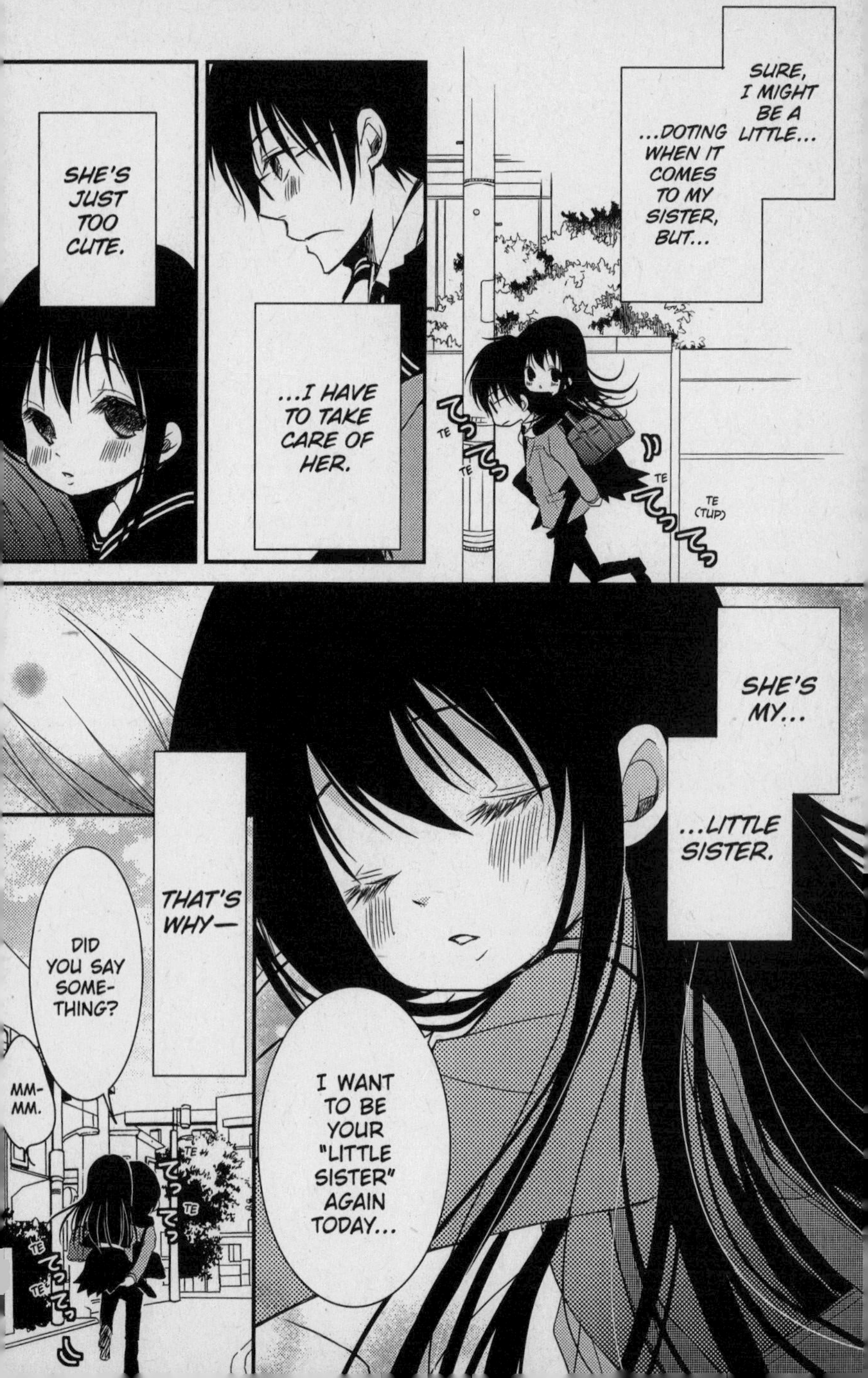
SURE, I MIGHT BE A LITTLE...
...DOTING WHEN IT COMES TO MY SISTER, BUT...
TE
TE
TE
TE (TUP)
...I HAVE TO TAKE CARE OF HER.
SHE'S JUST TOO CUTE.
SHE'S MY...
...LITTLE SISTER.
THAT'S WHY—
I WANT TO BE YOUR "LITTLE SISTER" AGAIN TODAY...
DID YOU SAY SOMETHING?
MM-MM.
TE
TE
TE
TE

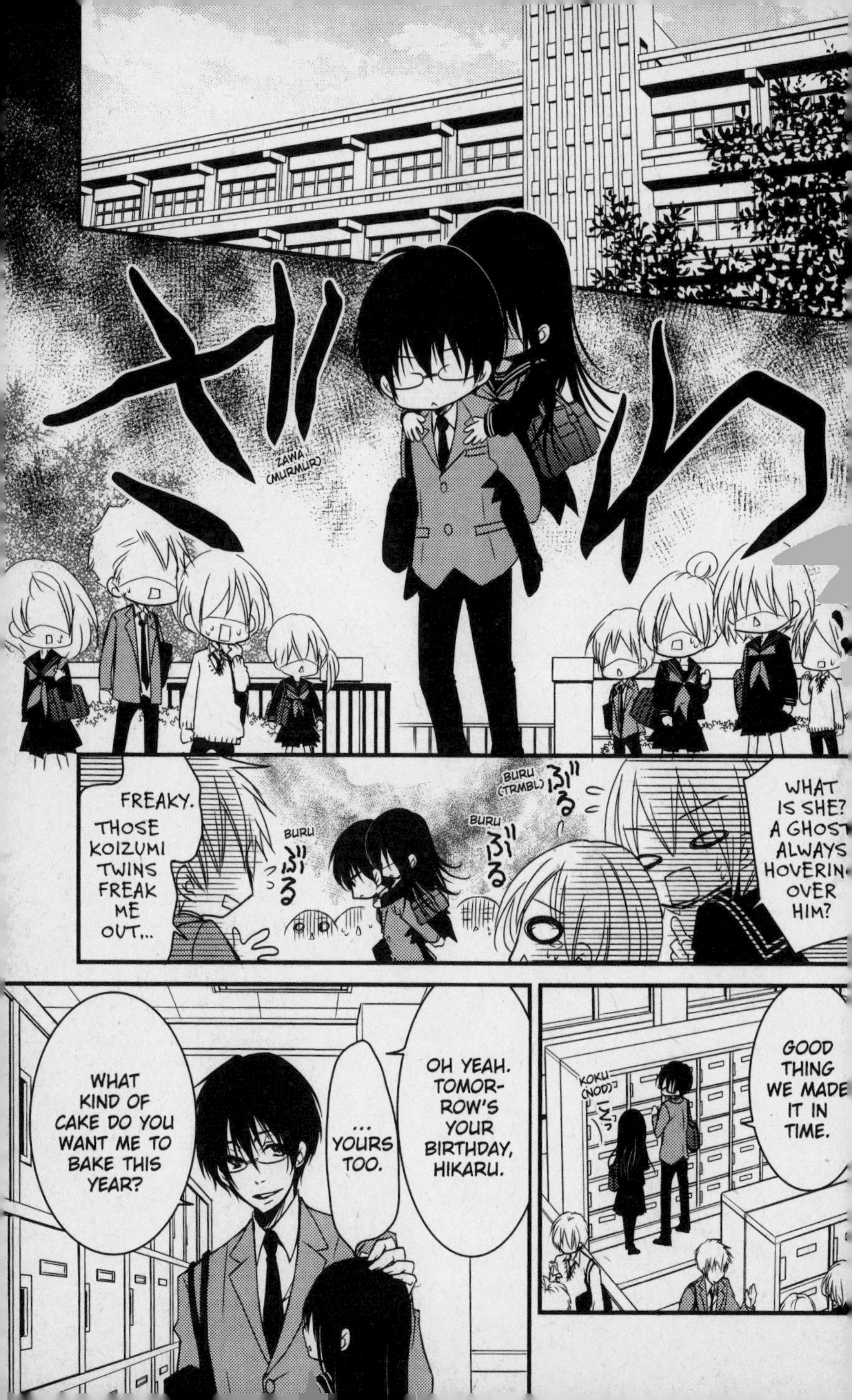
ZAWA (MURMUR)
WHAT IS SHE? A GHOST ALWAYS HOVERIN OVER HIM?
BURU (TRMBL) ぶる
BURU ぶる
BURU ぶる
FREAKY. THOSE KOIZUMI TWINS FREAK ME OUT...
GOOD THING WE MADE IT IN TIME.
KOKU (NOD) こく
OH YEAH. TOMOR-ROW'S YOUR BIRTHDAY, HIKARU.
... YOURS TOO.
WHAT KIND OF CAKE DO YOU WANT ME TO BAKE THIS YEAR?

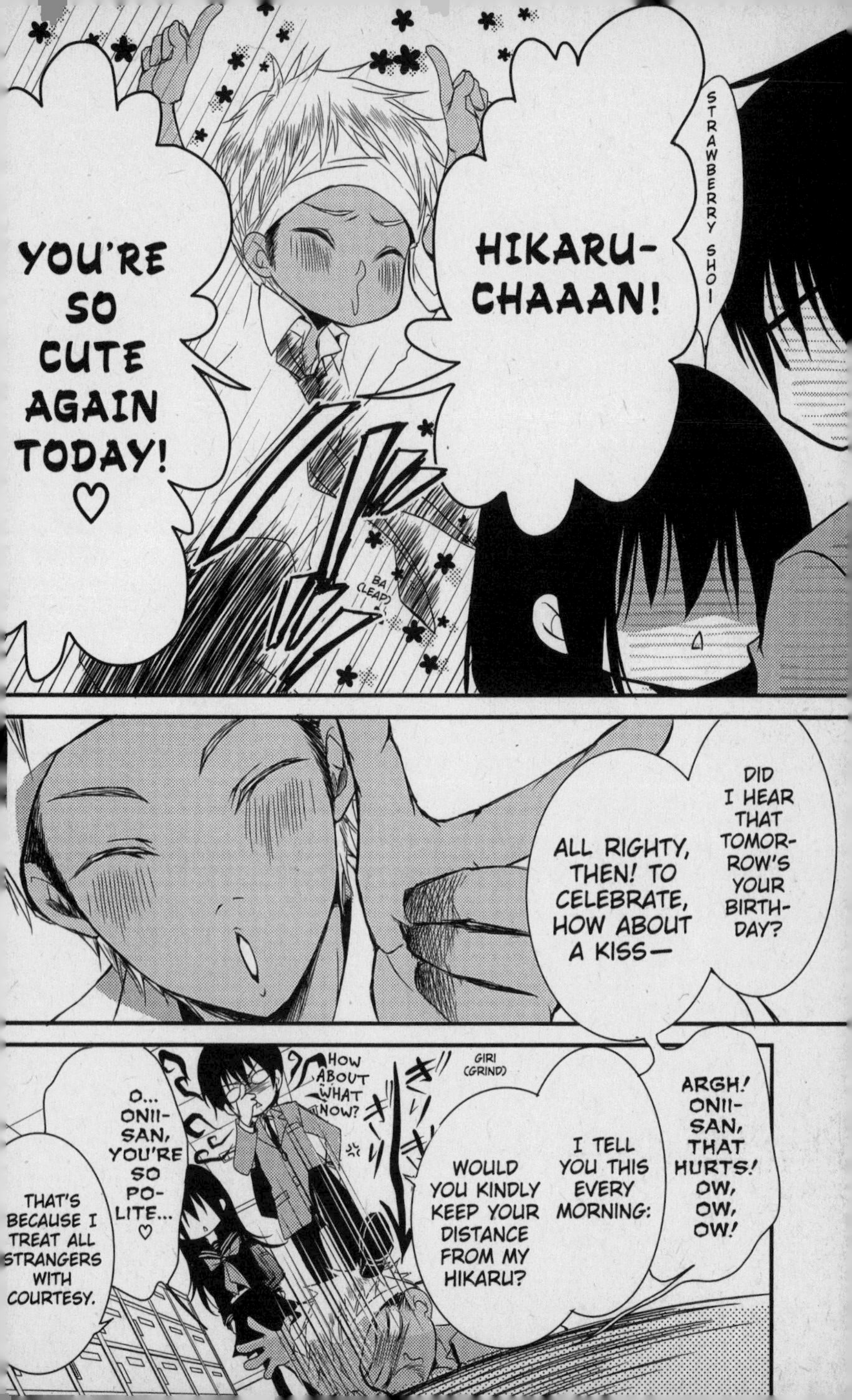
STRAWBERRY SHOOT
HIKARU-CHAAAN!
YOU'RE SO CUTE AGAIN TODAY! ♡
BA (LEAP)
DID I HEAR THAT TOMORROW'S YOUR BIRTHDAY?
ALL RIGHTY, THEN! TO CELEBRATE, HOW ABOUT A KISS—
ARGH! ONII-SAN, THAT HURTS! OW, OW, OW!
I TELL YOU THIS EVERY MORNING:
WOULD YOU KINDLY KEEP YOUR DISTANCE FROM MY HIKARU?
GIRI (GRIND)
HOW ABOUT WHAT NOW?
O... ONII-SAN, YOU'RE SO POLITE... ♡
THAT'S BECAUSE I TREAT ALL STRANGERS WITH COURTESY.

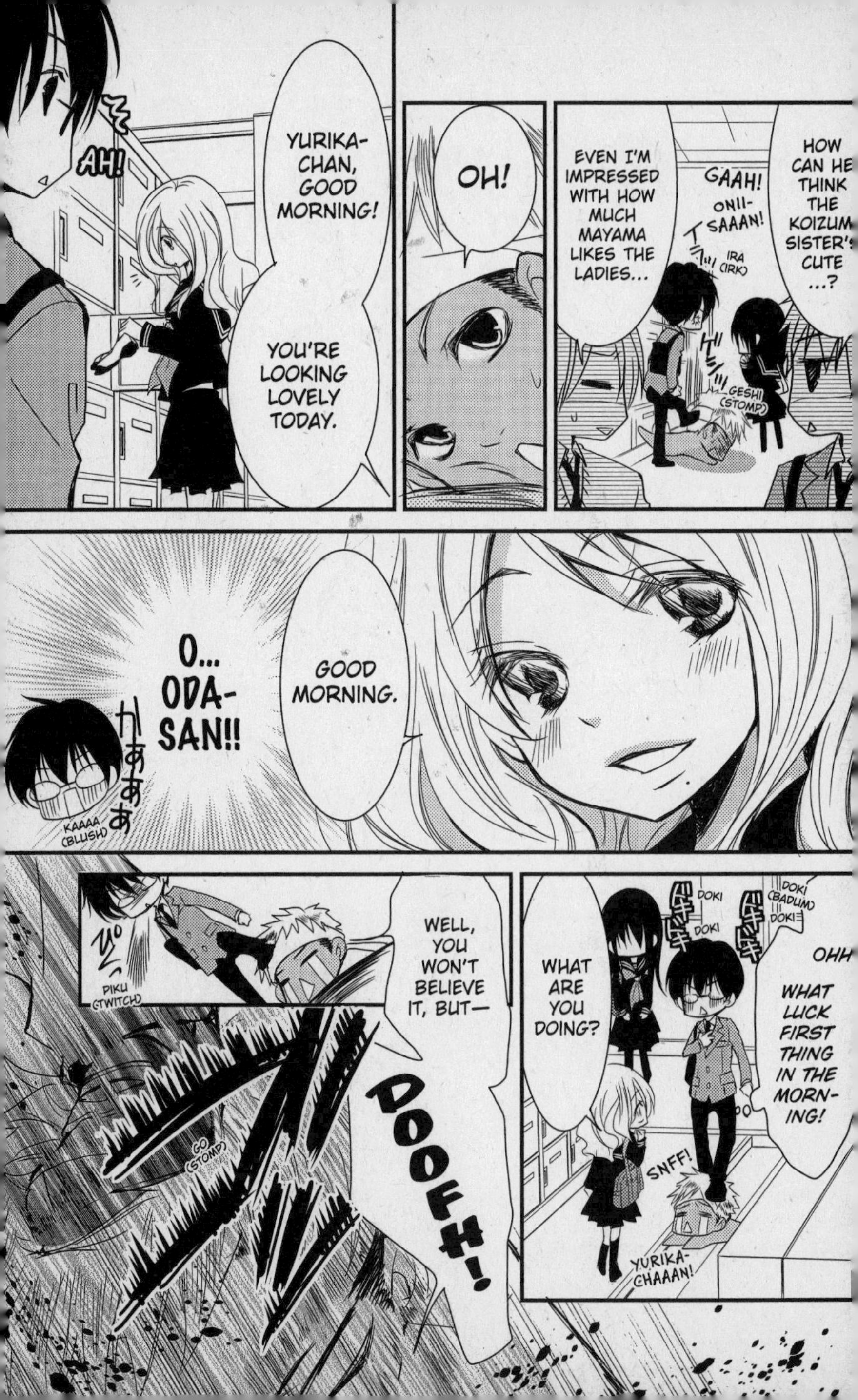
HOW CAN HE THINK THE KOIZUM SISTER'S CUTE ...?
EVEN I'M IMPRESSED WITH HOW MUCH MAYAMA LIKES THE LADIES...
GAAH! ONII-SAAAN!
IRA (IRK)
GESHI (STOMP)
OH!
YURIKA-CHAN, GOOD MORNING!
YOU'RE LOOKING LOVELY TODAY.
AH!
GOOD MORNING.
O... ODA-SAN!!
かあああ
KAAAA (BLUSH)
DOKI (BADUM) DOKI
DOKI
DOKI
OHH
WHAT LUCK FIRST THING IN THE MORN-ING!
WHAT ARE YOU DOING?
SNFF!
YURIKA-CHAAAN!
WELL, YOU WON'T BELIEVE IT, BUT—
PIKU (TWITCH)
DOOFH!
GO (STOMP)

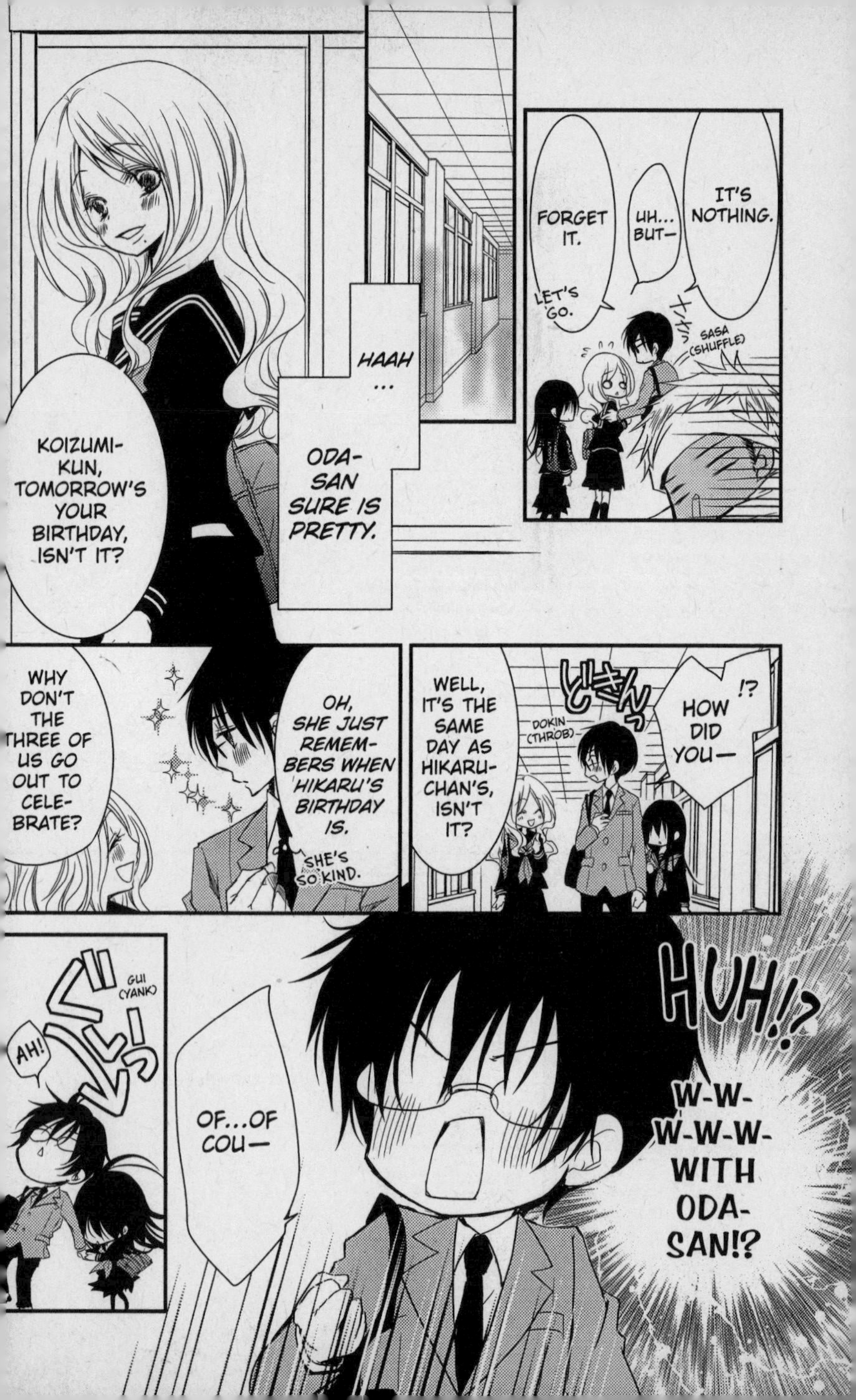
IT'S NOTHING.
UH... BUT—
FORGET IT.
LET'S GO.
SASA (SHUFFLE)
HAAH ...
ODA-SAN SURE IS PRETTY.
KOIZUMI-KUN, TOMORROW'S YOUR BIRTHDAY, ISN'T IT?
HOW DID YOU— !?
DOKIN (THROB)
WELL, IT'S THE SAME DAY AS HIKARU-CHAN'S, ISN'T IT?
OH, SHE JUST REMEMBERS WHEN HIKARU'S BIRTHDAY IS.
SHE'S SO KIND.
WHY DON'T THE THREE OF US GO OUT TO CELEBRATE?
HUH!?
W-W-W-W-W-WITH ODA-SAN!?
OF...OF COU—
GUI (YANK)
AH!

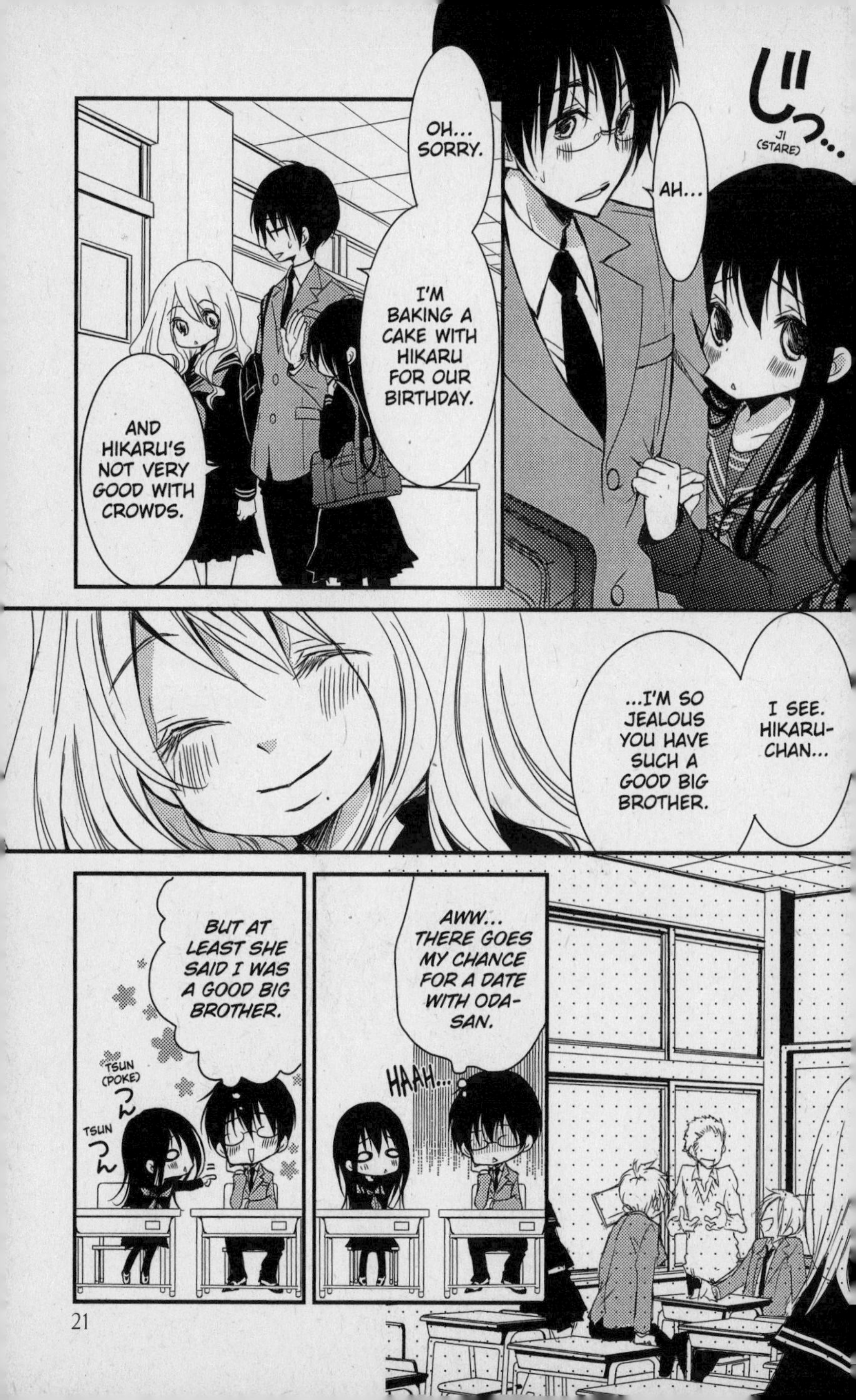
じっ...
JI (STARE)
AH...
OH... SORRY.
I'M BAKING A CAKE WITH HIKARU FOR OUR BIRTHDAY.
AND HIKARU'S NOT VERY GOOD WITH CROWDS.
I SEE. HIKARU-CHAN...
...I'M SO JEALOUS YOU HAVE SUCH A GOOD BIG BROTHER.
AWW... THERE GOES MY CHANCE FOR A DATE WITH ODA-SAN.
HAAH...
BUT AT LEAST SHE SAID I WAS A GOOD BIG BROTHER.
TSUN (POKE) つん
TSUN つん

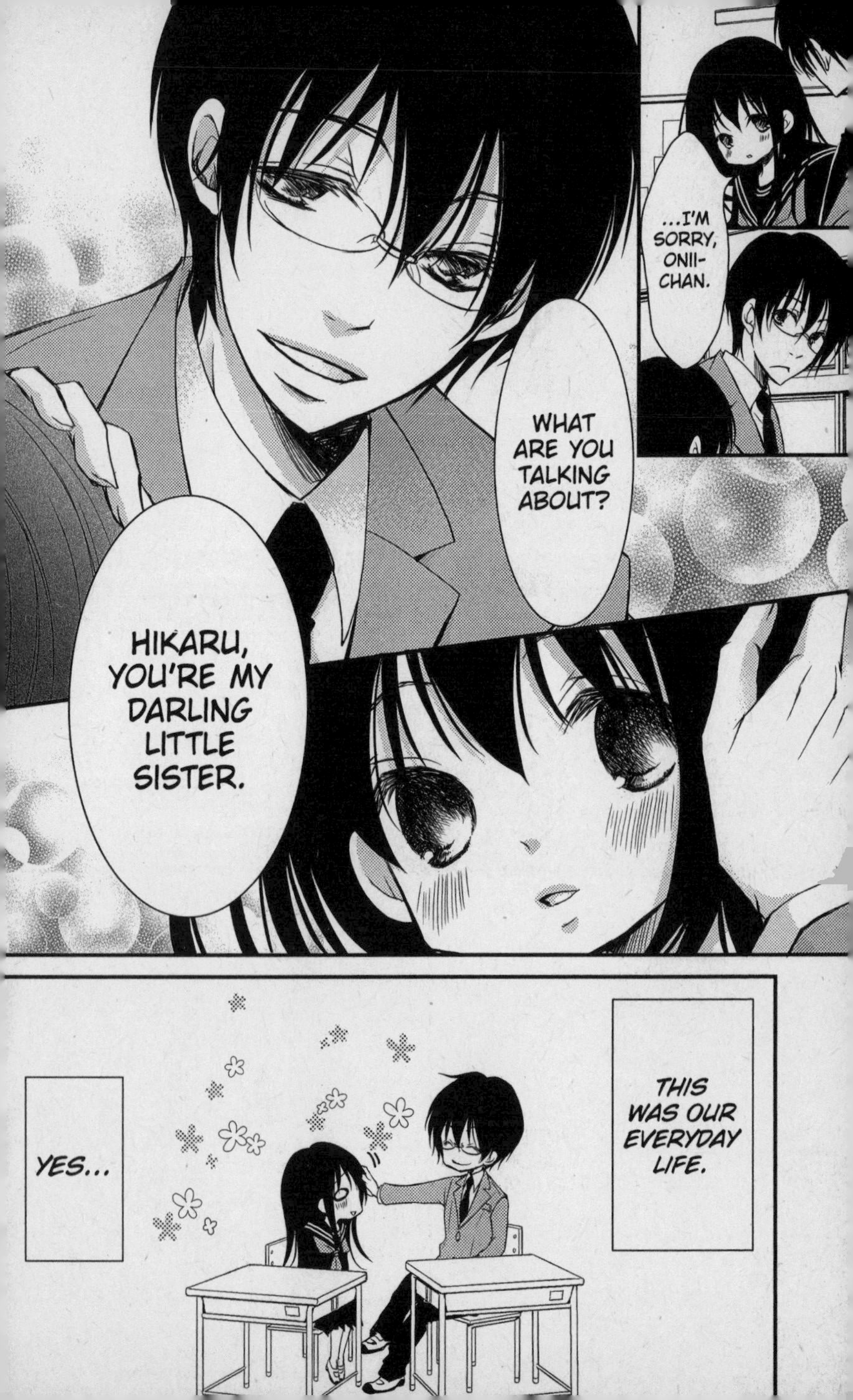
...I'M SORRY, ONII-CHAN.
WHAT ARE YOU TALKING ABOUT?
HIKARU, YOU'RE MY DARLING LITTLE SISTER.
THIS WAS OUR EVERYDAY LIFE.
YES...

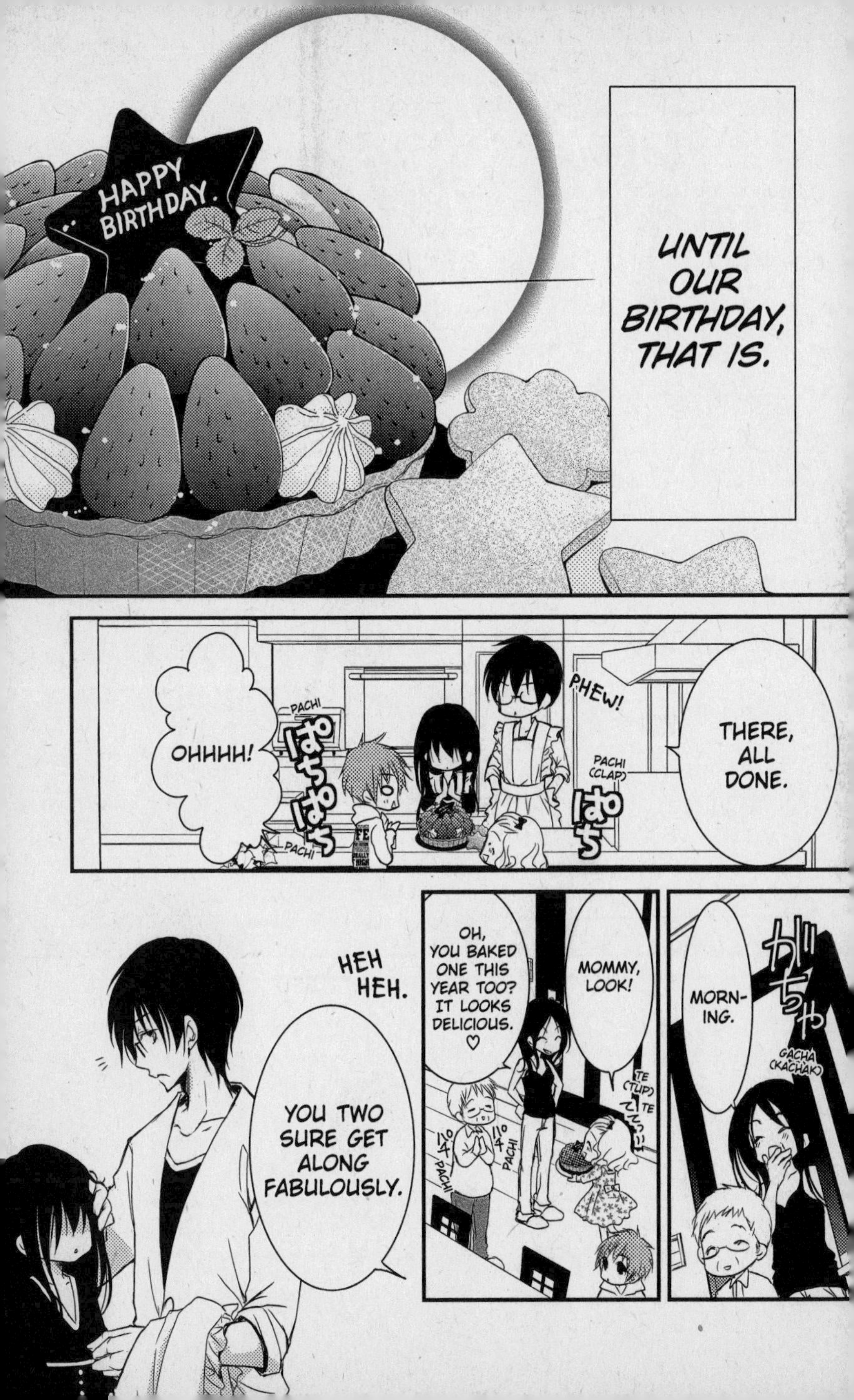
HAPPY BIRTHDAY
UNTIL OUR BIRTHDAY, THAT IS.
THERE, ALL DONE.
PHEW!
PACHI (CLAP)
ぱち
PACHI
ぱちぱち
PACHI
OHHHH!
がちゃ
GACHA (KACHAK)
MORNING.
MOMMY, LOOK!
TE (TUP) TE
OH, YOU BAKED ONE THIS YEAR TOO? IT LOOKS DELICIOUS. ♡
パチ PACHI
パチ PACHI
HEH HEH.
YOU TWO SURE GET ALONG FABULOUSLY.

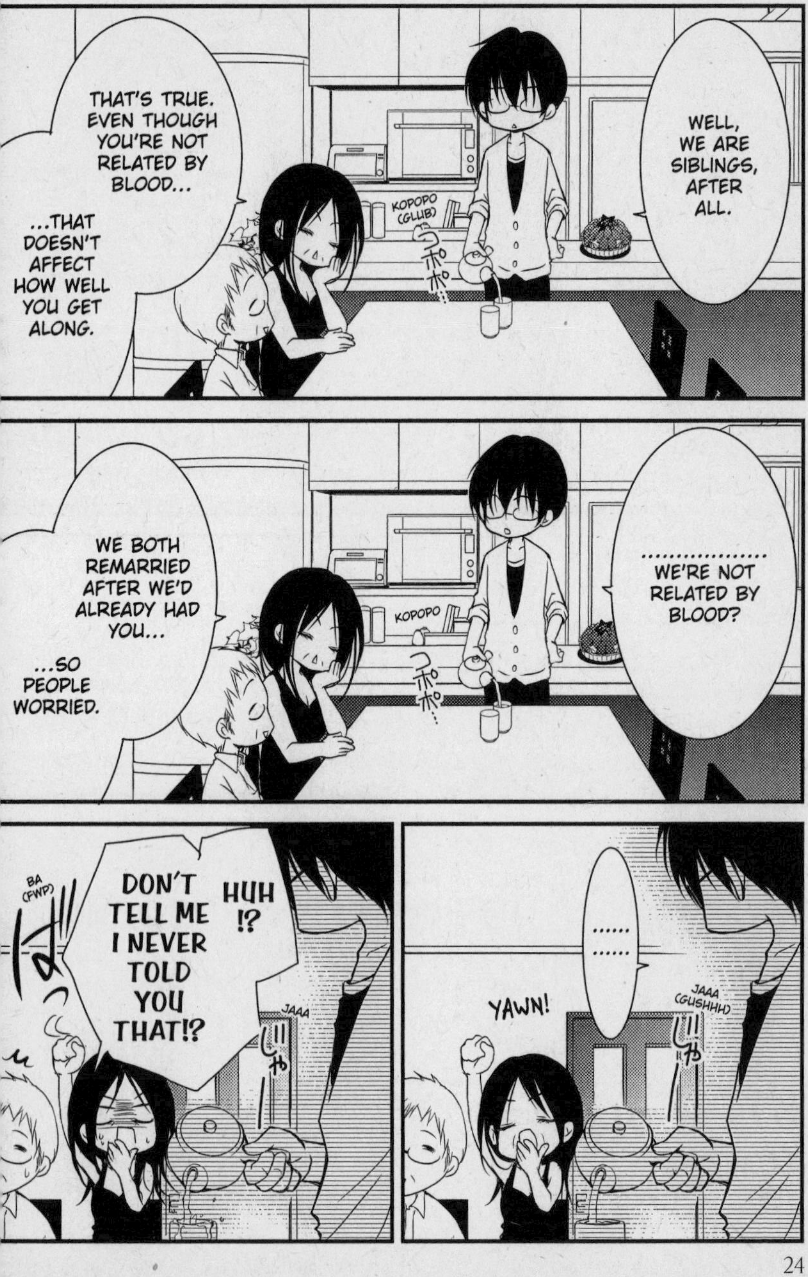

WELL, WE ARE SIBLINGS, AFTER ALL.
KOPOPO (GLUB)
THAT'S TRUE. EVEN THOUGH YOU'RE NOT RELATED BY BLOOD...
...THAT DOESN'T AFFECT HOW WELL YOU GET ALONG.
.... WE'RE NOT RELATED BY BLOOD?
KOPOPO
WE BOTH REMARRIED AFTER WE'D ALREADY HAD YOU...
...SO PEOPLE WORRIED.
....
JAAA (GUSHHH)
YAWN!
HUH!?
DON'T TELL ME I NEVER TOLD YOU THAT!?
JAAA
BA (FWP)

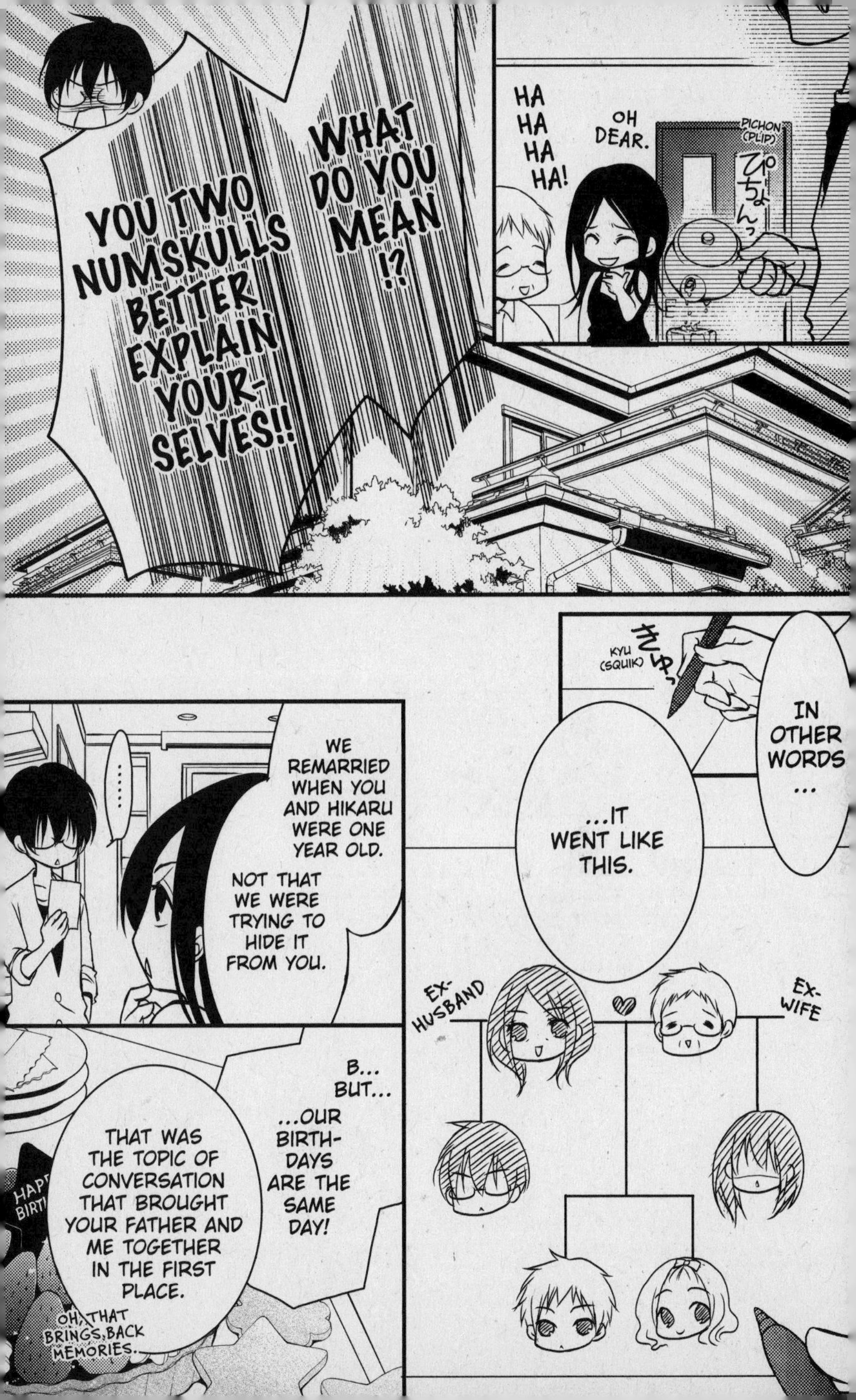
HA HA HA HA!
OH DEAR.
PICHON (PLIP)
ぴちょんっ
WHAT DO YOU MEAN!?
YOU TWO NUMSKULLS BETTER EXPLAIN YOUR-SELVES!!
KYU (SQUIK)
きゅっ
IN OTHER WORDS...
...IT WENT LIKE THIS.
EX-WIFE
EX-HUSBAND
WE REMARRIED WHEN YOU AND HIKARU WERE ONE YEAR OLD.
NOT THAT WE WERE TRYING TO HIDE IT FROM YOU.
......
B... BUT...
...OUR BIRTH-DAYS ARE THE SAME DAY!
THAT WAS THE TOPIC OF CONVERSATION THAT BROUGHT YOUR FATHER AND ME TOGETHER IN THE FIRST PLACE.
OH, THAT BRINGS BACK MEMORIES.

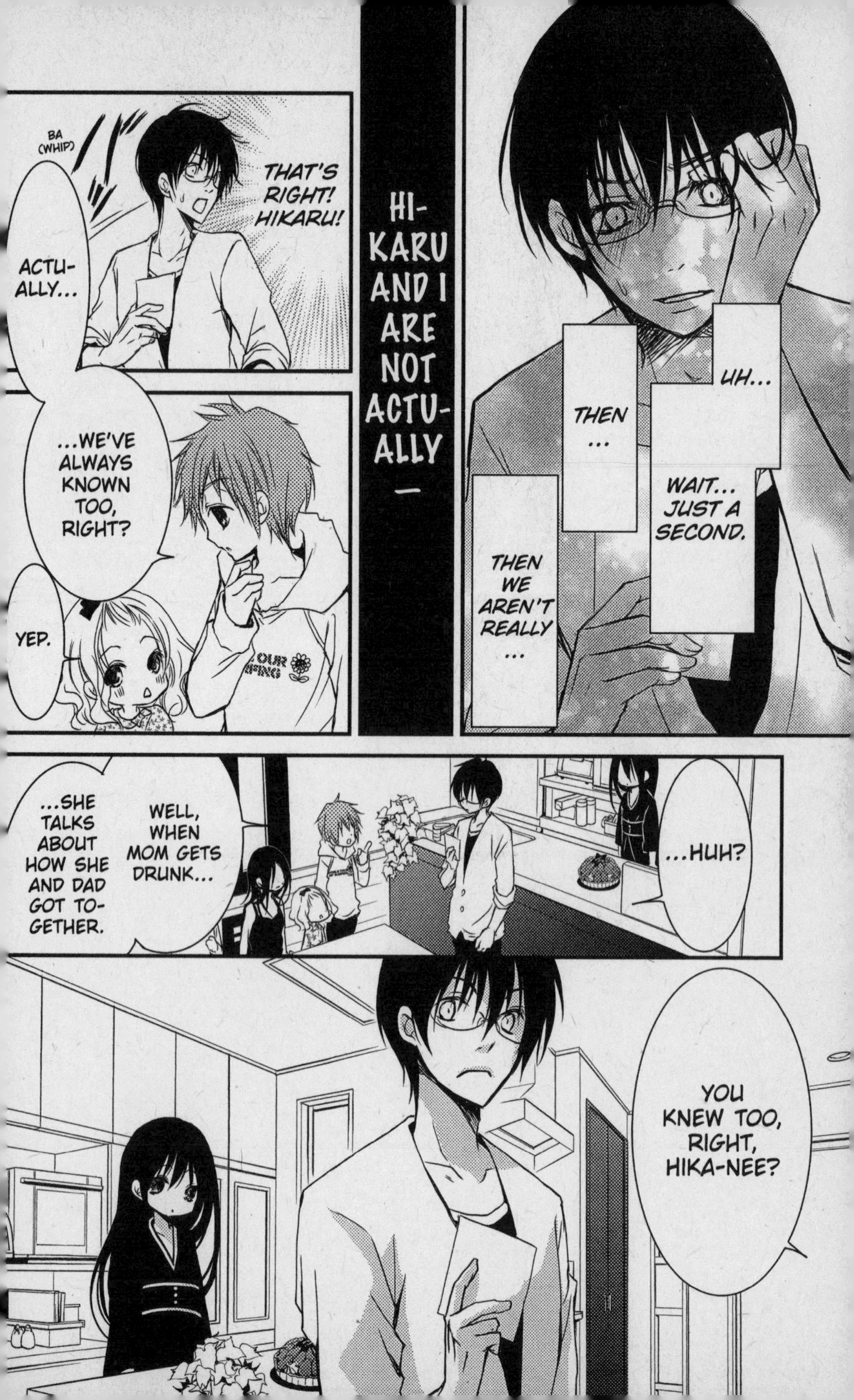
UH...
WAIT... JUST A SECOND.
THEN ...
THEN WE AREN'T REALLY ...
HI-KARU AND I ARE NOT ACTU-ALLY —
BA (WHIP)
THAT'S RIGHT! HIKARU!
ACTU-ALLY...
...WE'VE ALWAYS KNOWN TOO, RIGHT?
YEP.
...HUH?
WELL, WHEN MOM GETS DRUNK...
...SHE TALKS ABOUT HOW SHE AND DAD GOT TO-GETHER.
YOU KNEW TOO, RIGHT, HIKA-NEE?

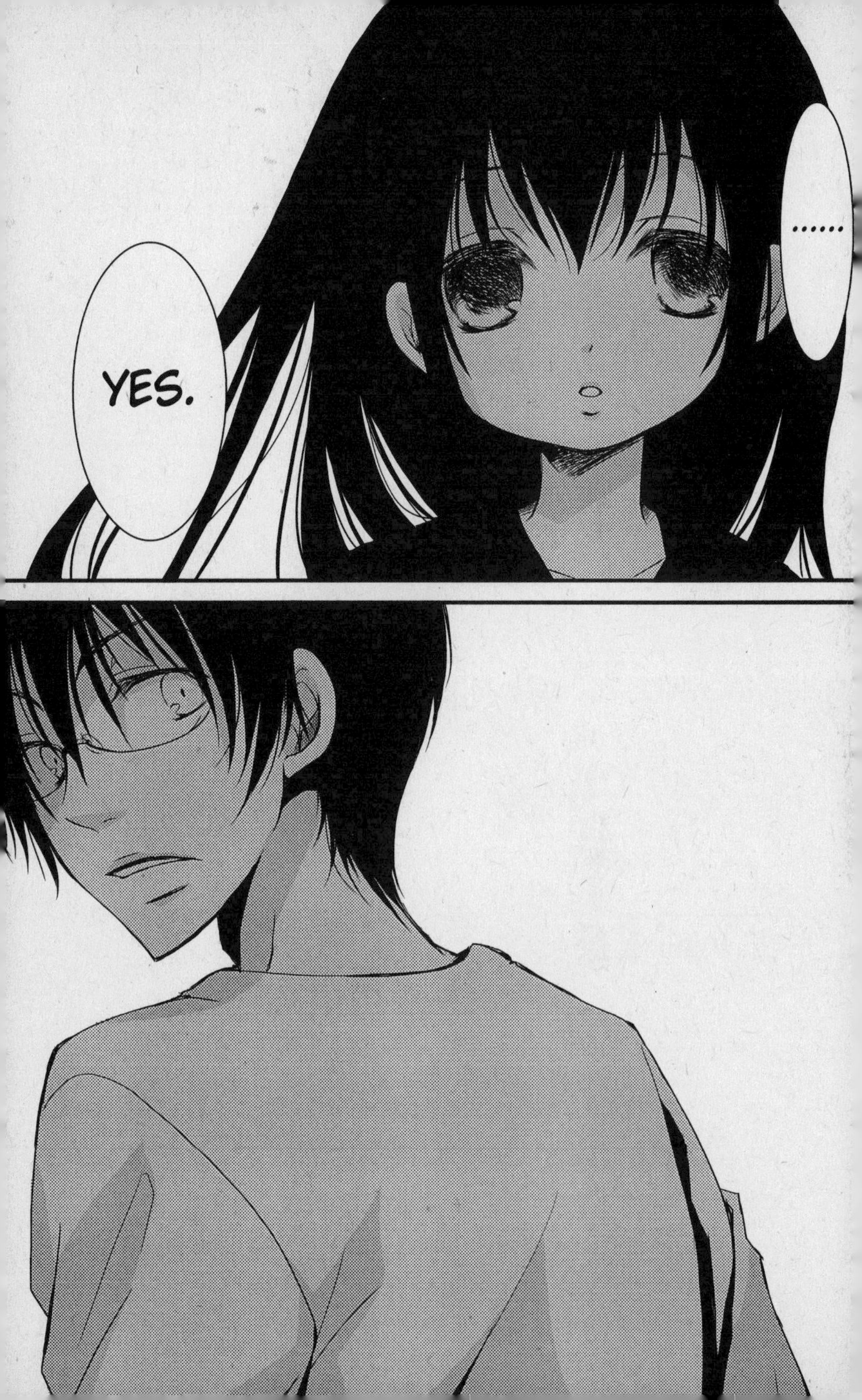
......
YES.

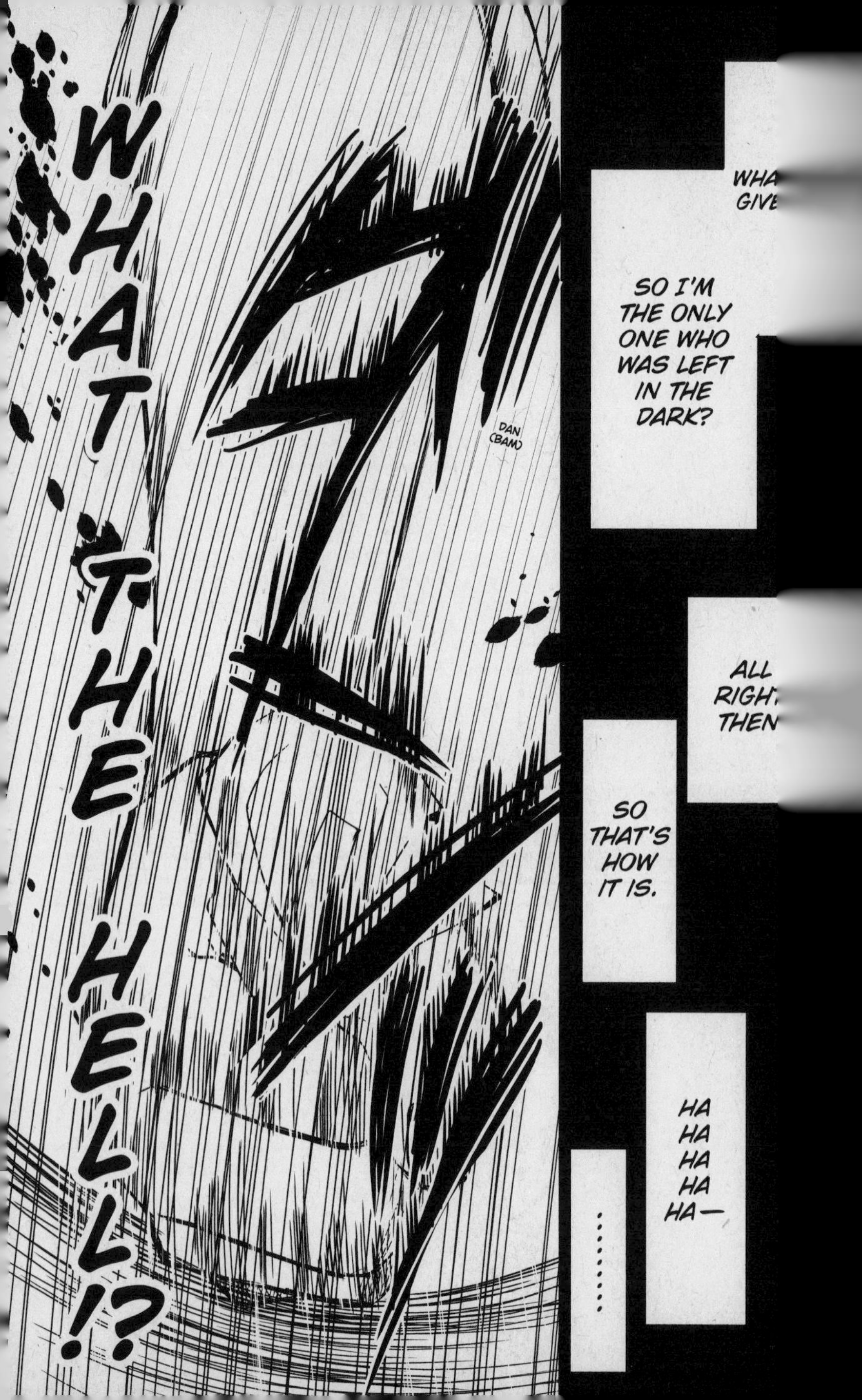
SO I'M THE ONLY ONE WHO WAS LEFT IN THE DARK?
ALL RIGHT THEN
SO THAT'S HOW IT IS.
HA HA HA HA HA—
......
DAN (BAM)
WHAT THE HELL!?

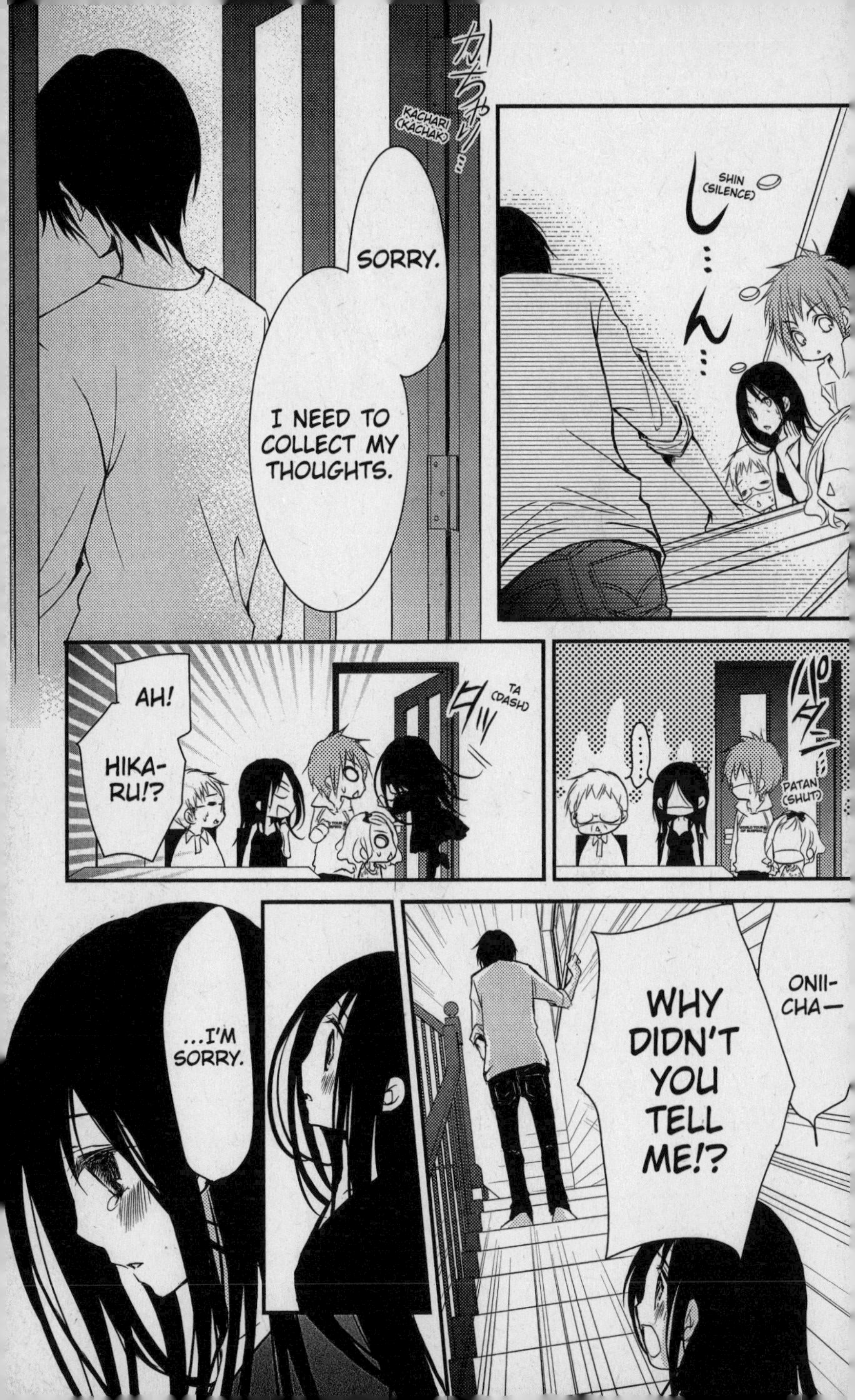
SHIN (SILENCE)
KACHARI (KACHAK)
SORRY.
I NEED TO COLLECT MY THOUGHTS.
...
PATAN (SHUT)
TA (DASH)
AH!
HIKA-RU!?
ONII-CHA—
WHY DIDN'T YOU TELL ME!?
...I'M SORRY.

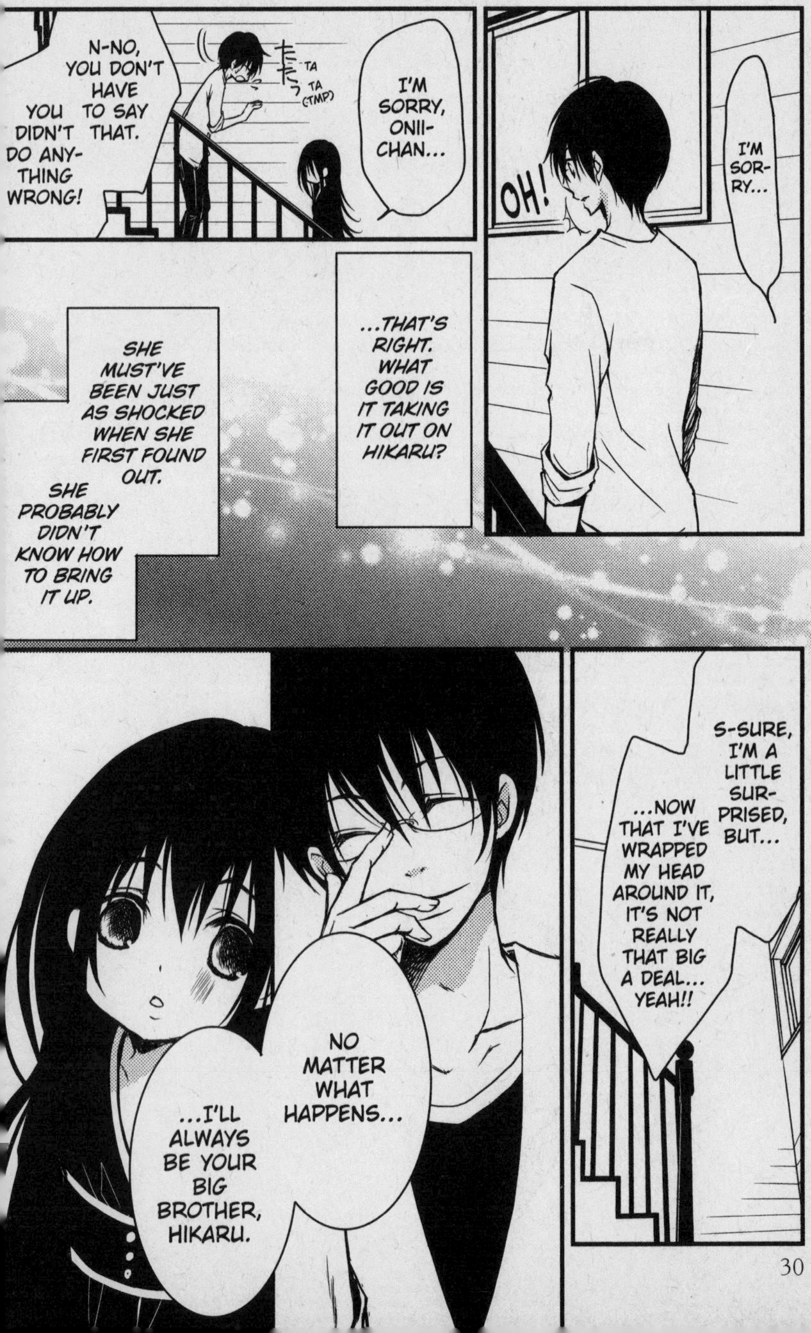
I'M SORRY...
OH!
I'M SORRY, ONII-CHAN...
TA TA (TMP)
N-NO, YOU DON'T HAVE TO SAY THAT.
YOU DIDN'T DO ANY-THING WRONG!
...THAT'S RIGHT. WHAT GOOD IS IT TAKING IT OUT ON HIKARU?
SHE MUST'VE BEEN JUST AS SHOCKED WHEN SHE FIRST FOUND OUT.
SHE PROBABLY DIDN'T KNOW HOW TO BRING IT UP.
S-SURE, I'M A LITTLE SUR-PRISED, BUT...
...NOW THAT I'VE WRAPPED MY HEAD AROUND IT, IT'S NOT REALLY THAT BIG A DEAL... YEAH!!
NO MATTER WHAT HAPPENS...
...I'LL ALWAYS BE YOUR BIG BROTHER, HIKARU.

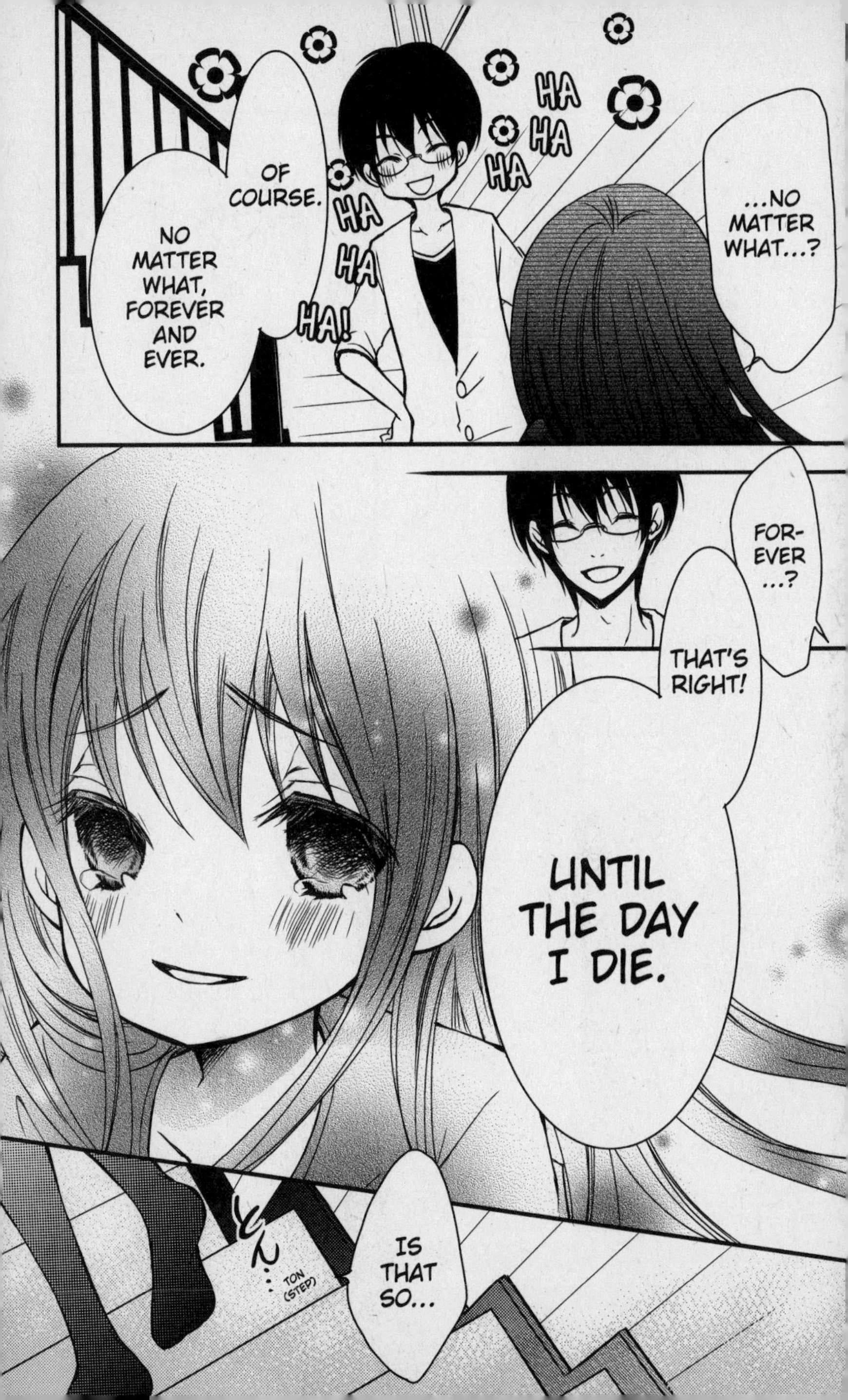
...NO MATTER WHAT...?
HA HA HA
OF COURSE.
NO MATTER WHAT, FOREVER AND EVER.
HA HA HA!
FOR-EVER...?
THAT'S RIGHT!
UNTIL THE DAY I DIE.
IS THAT SO...
とん… TON (STEP)

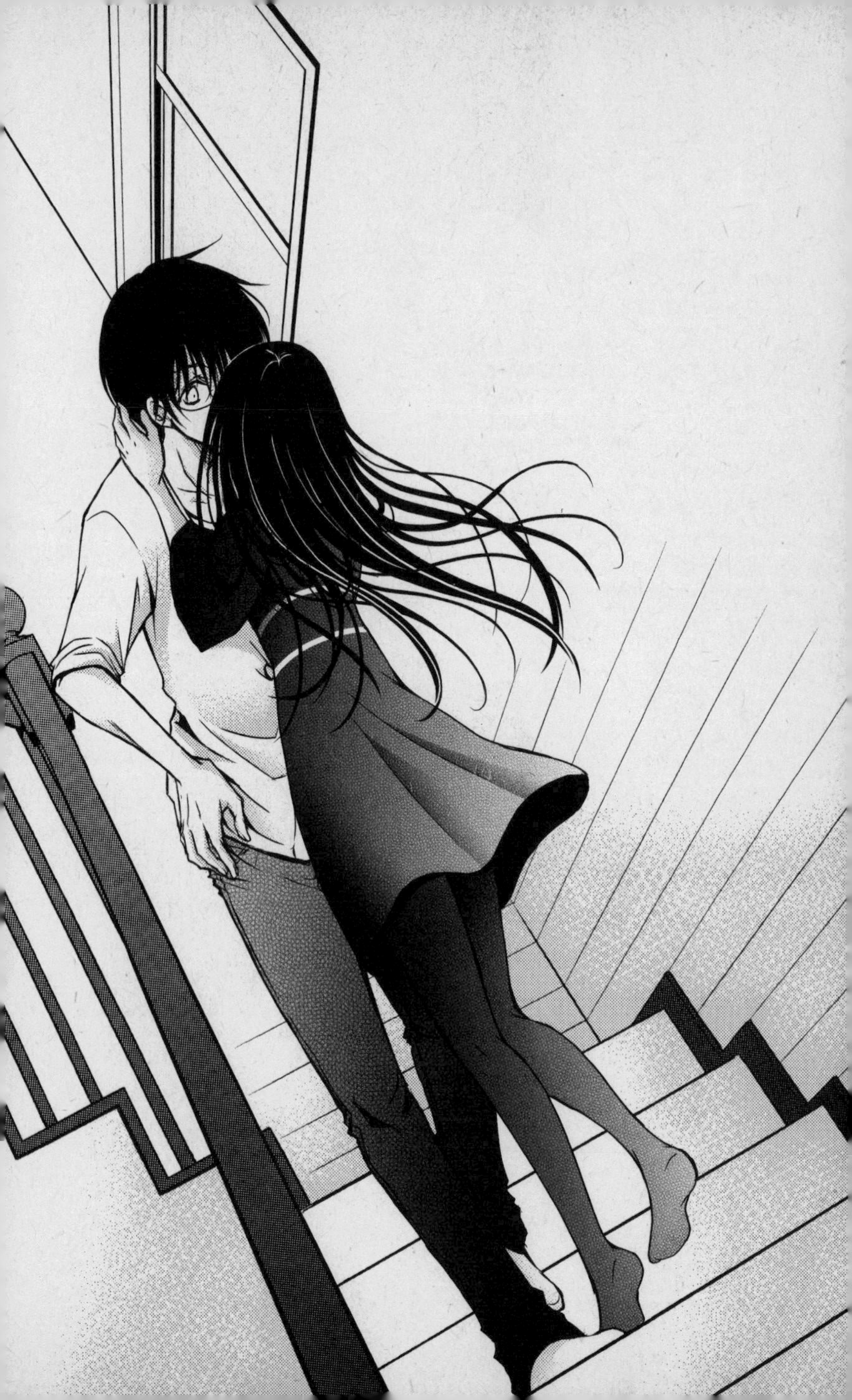

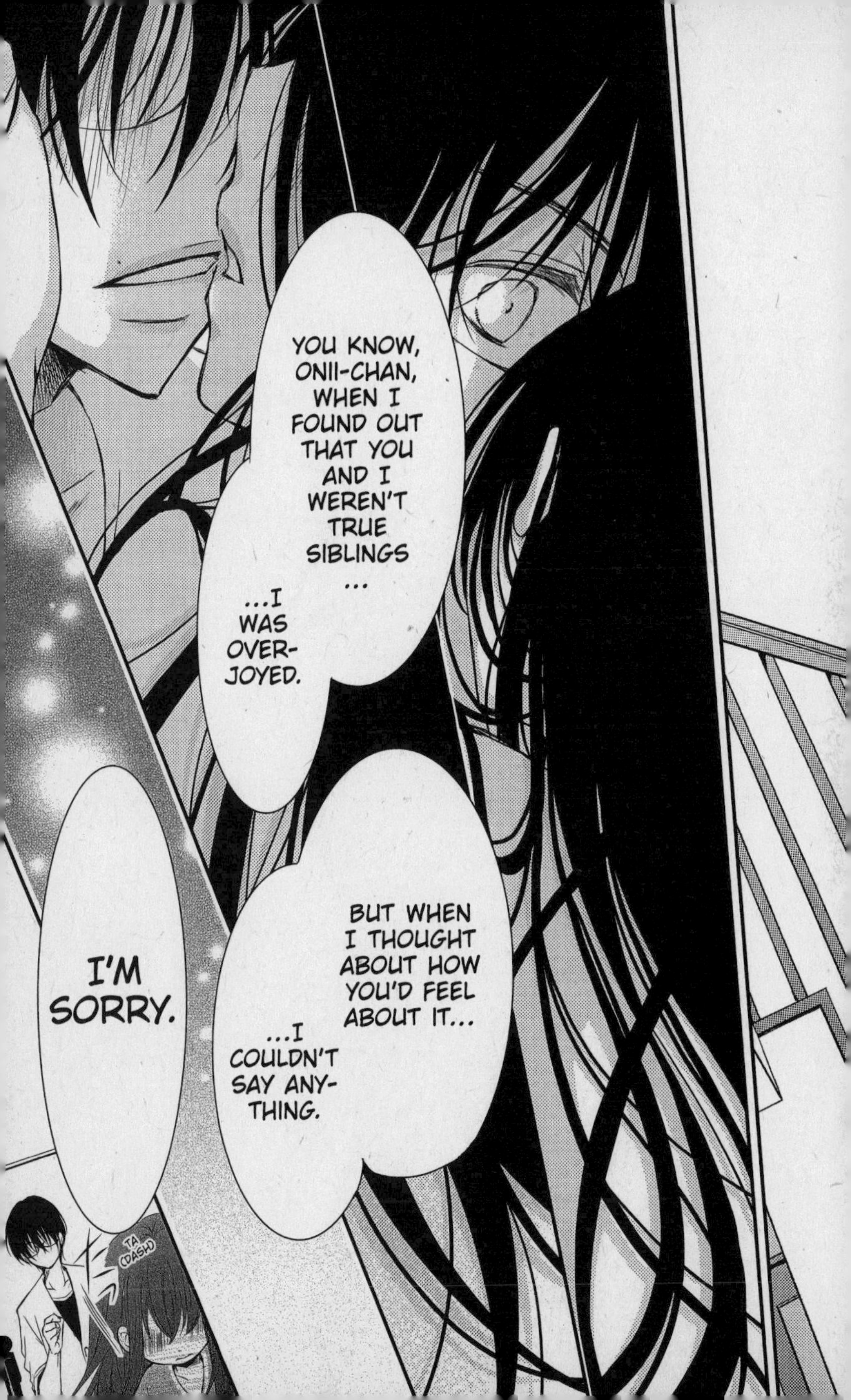
YOU KNOW, ONII-CHAN, WHEN I FOUND OUT THAT YOU AND I WEREN'T TRUE SIBLINGS...
...I WAS OVER-JOYED.
BUT WHEN I THOUGHT ABOUT HOW YOU'D FEEL ABOUT IT...
...I COULDN'T SAY ANY-THING.
I'M SORRY.
TA (DASH)

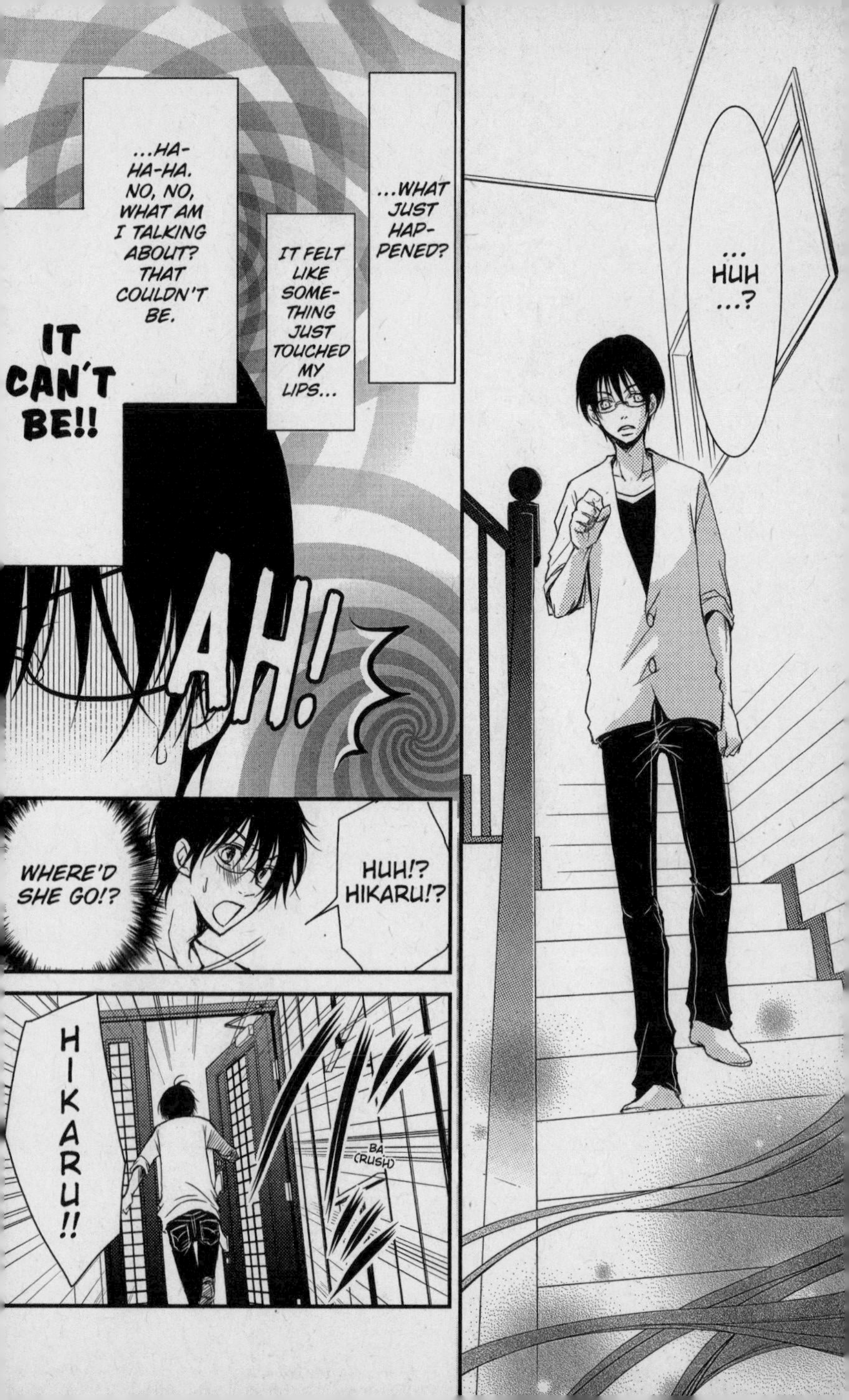
...HUH...?
...WHAT JUST HAP-PENED?
IT FELT LIKE SOME-THING JUST TOUCHED MY LIPS...
...HA-HA-HA. NO, NO, WHAT AM I TALKING ABOUT? THAT COULDN'T BE.
IT CAN'T BE!!
AH!
HUH!? HIKARU!?
WHERE'D SHE GO!?
HIKARU!!
BA (RUSH)

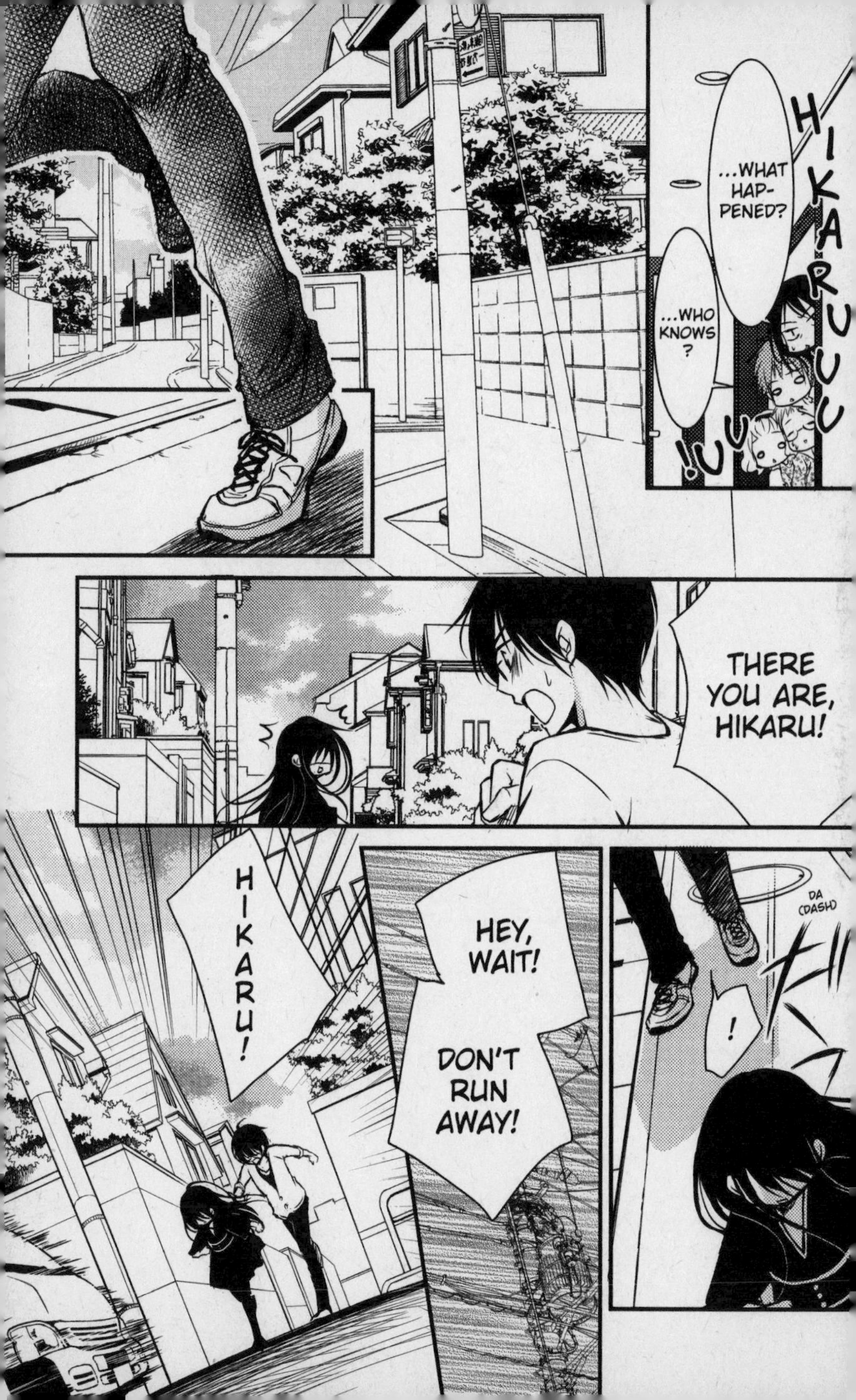
HIKARUUUUUU!
...WHAT HAPPENED?
...WHO KNOWS?
THERE YOU ARE, HIKARU!
DA (DASH)
!
HEY, WAIT!
DON'T RUN AWAY!
HIKARU!

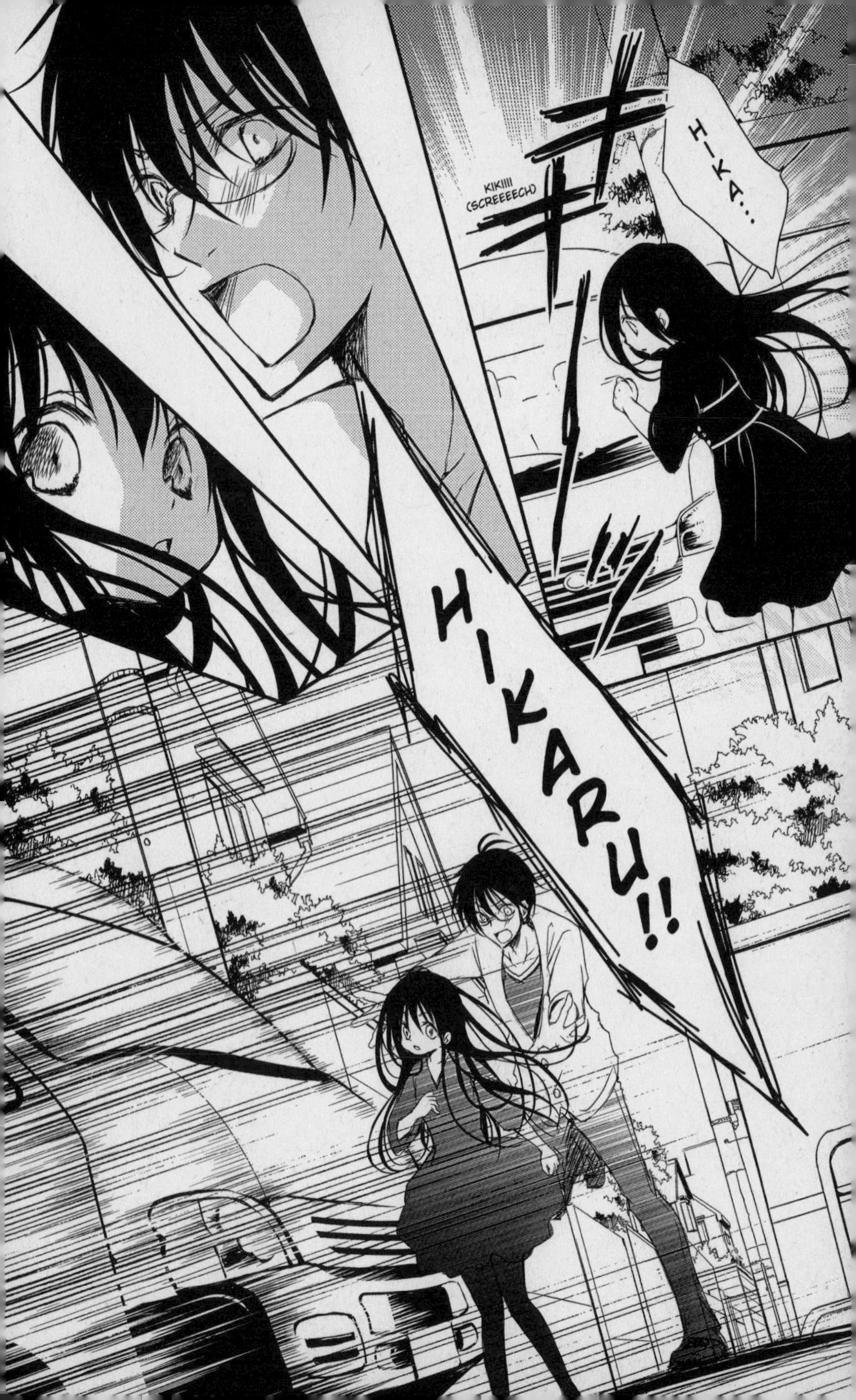
HIKA...
KIKIIII (SCREEEECH)
HIKARU!!

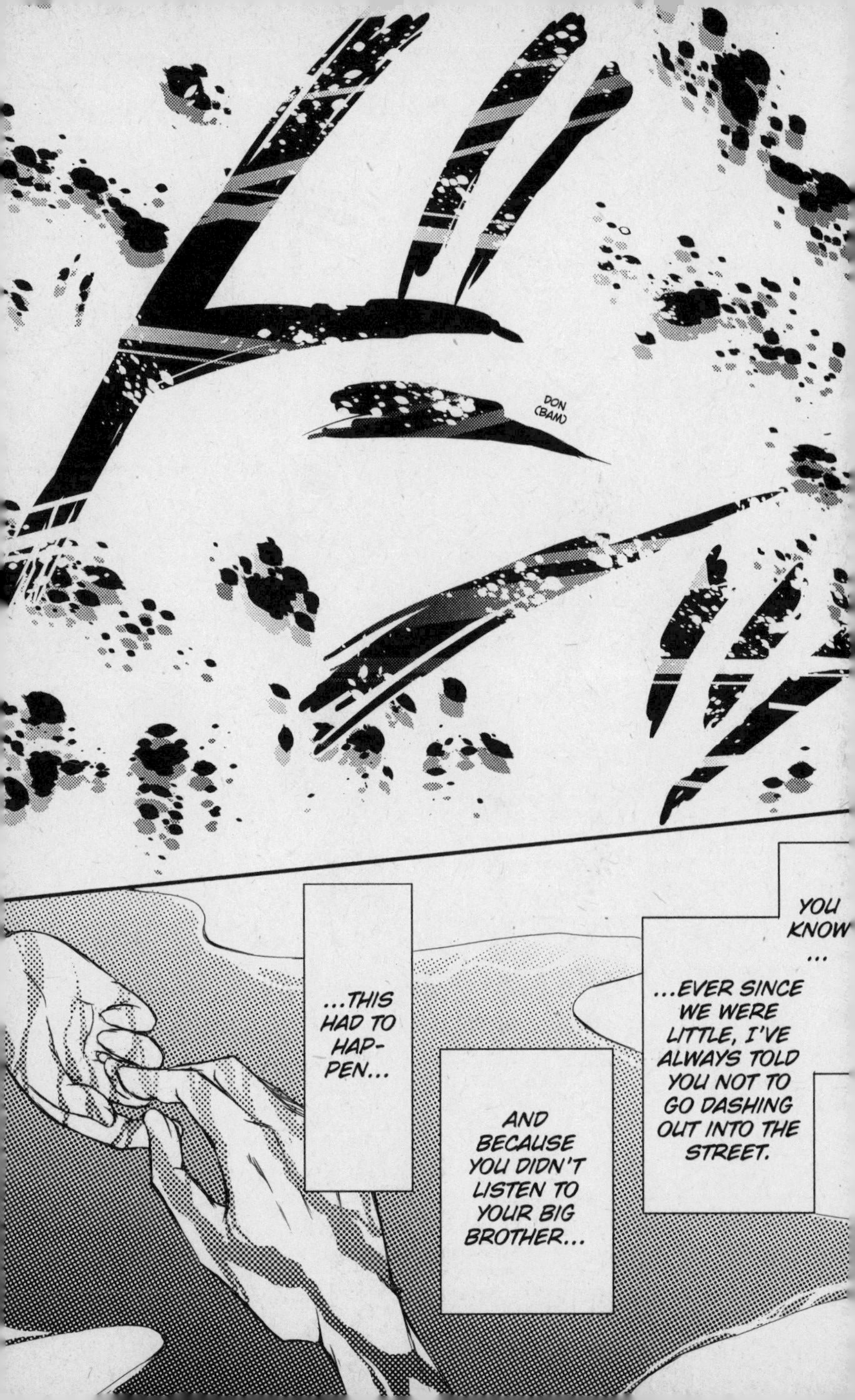
DON (BAM)
YOU KNOW ...
...EVER SINCE WE WERE LITTLE, I'VE ALWAYS TOLD YOU NOT TO GO DASHING OUT INTO THE STREET.
AND BECAUSE YOU DIDN'T LISTEN TO YOUR BIG BROTHER...
...THIS HAD TO HAP-PEN...

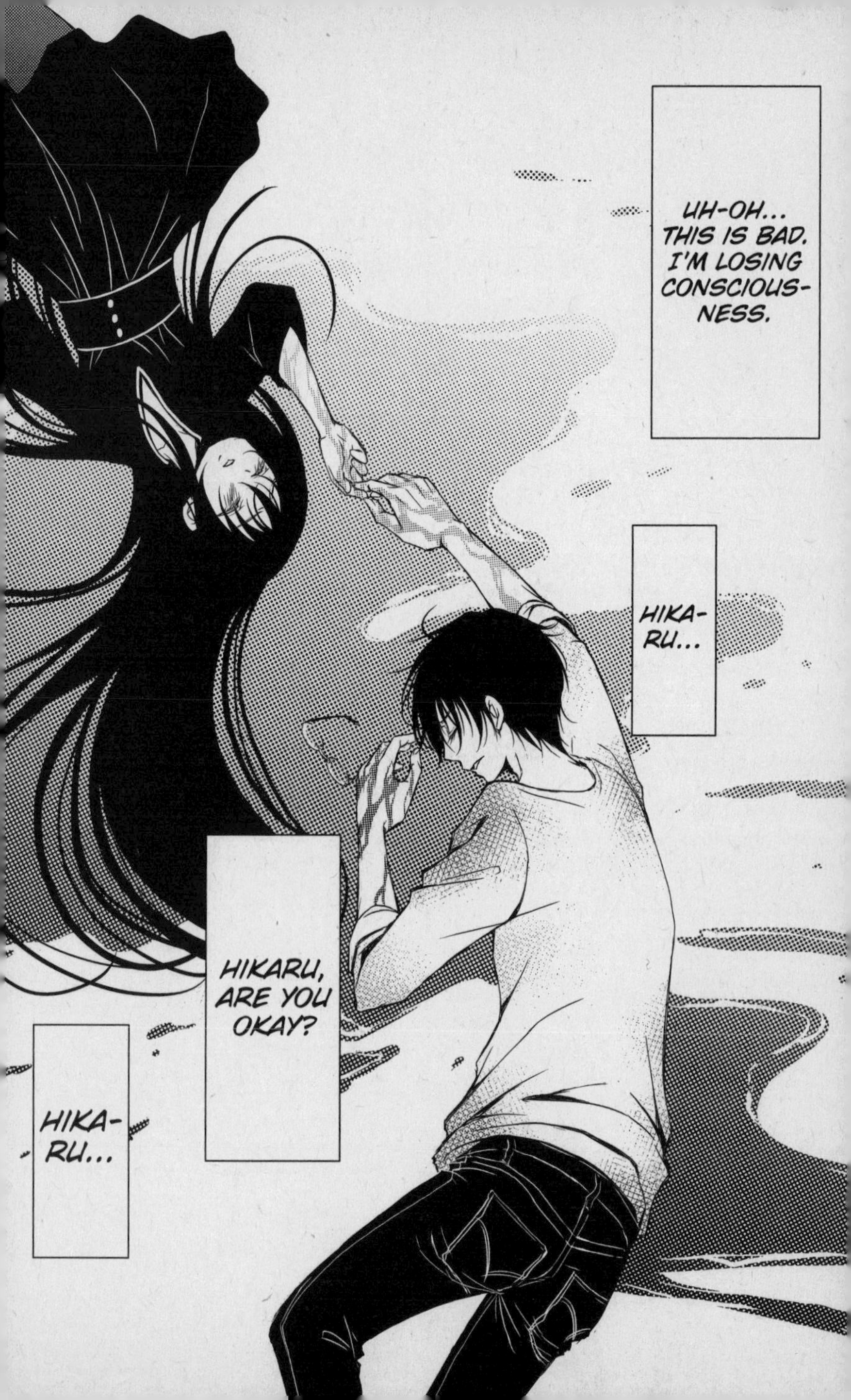
UH-OH... THIS IS BAD. I'M LOSING CONSCIOUS-NESS.
HIKA-RU...
HIKARU, ARE YOU OKAY?
HIKA-RU...

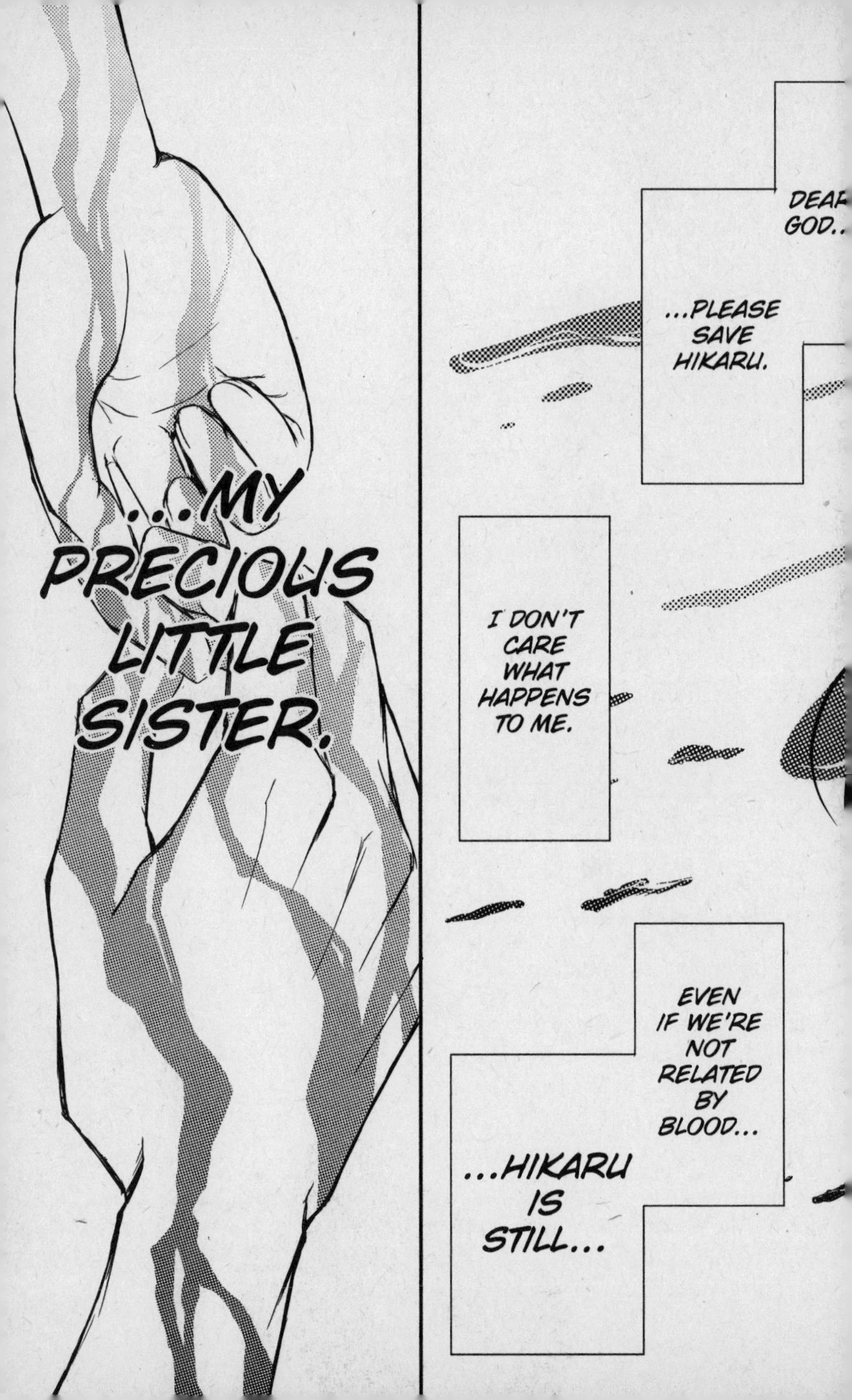
DEAR GOD..
...PLEASE SAVE HIKARU.
I DON'T CARE WHAT HAPPENS TO ME.
EVEN IF WE'RE NOT RELATED BY BLOOD...
...HIKARU IS STILL...
...MY PRECIOUS LITTLE SISTER.

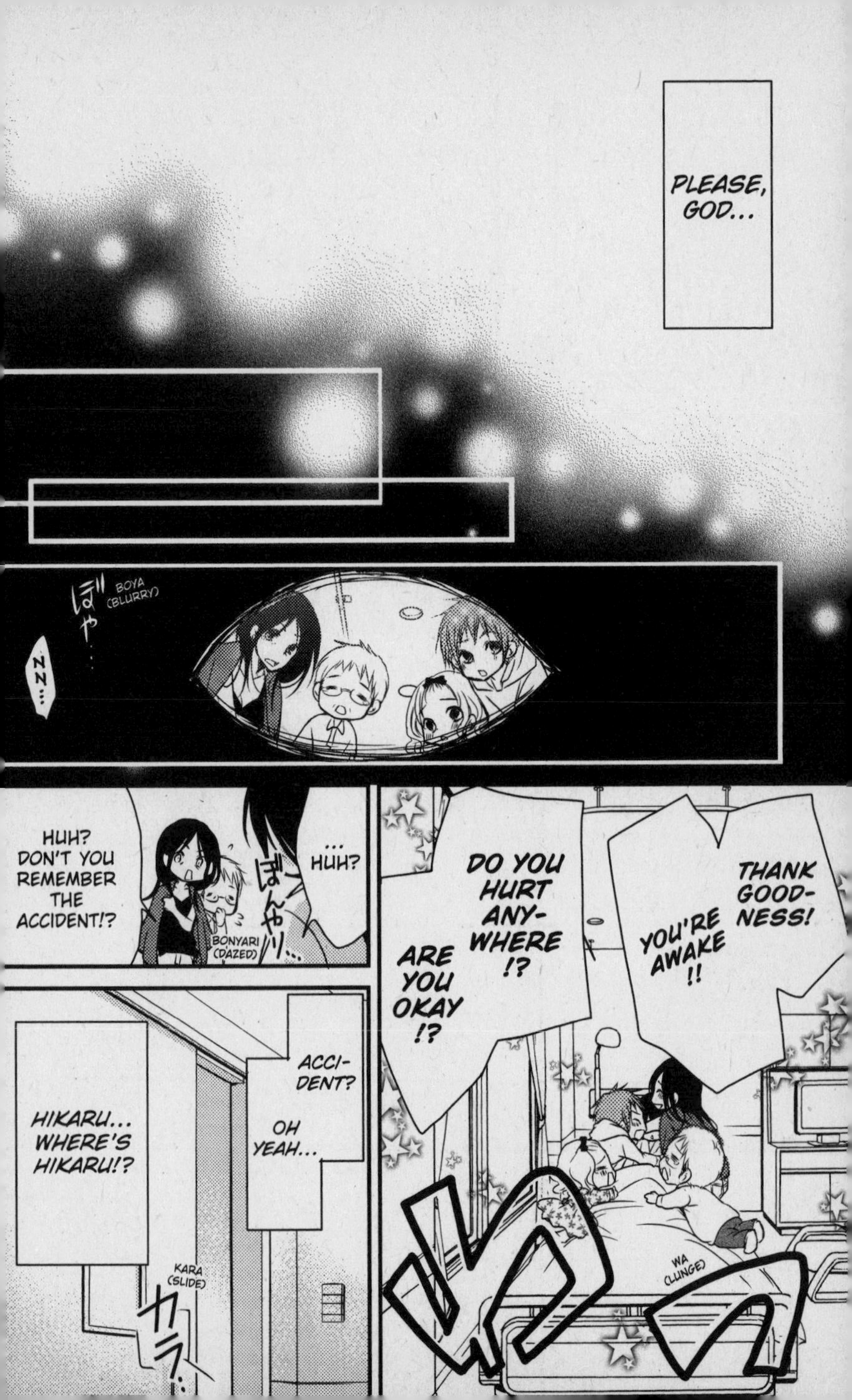
PLEASE, GOD...
ぼや‥
BOYA (BLURRY)
NN...
THANK GOODNESS! YOU'RE AWAKE!!
DO YOU HURT ANYWHERE!?
ARE YOU OKAY!?
WA (LUNGE)
...HUH?
ぼんやり...
BONYARI (DAZED)
HUH? DON'T YOU REMEMBER THE ACCIDENT!?
ACCIDENT?
OH YEAH...
HIKARU... WHERE'S HIKARU!?
カラ‥
KARA (SLIDE)

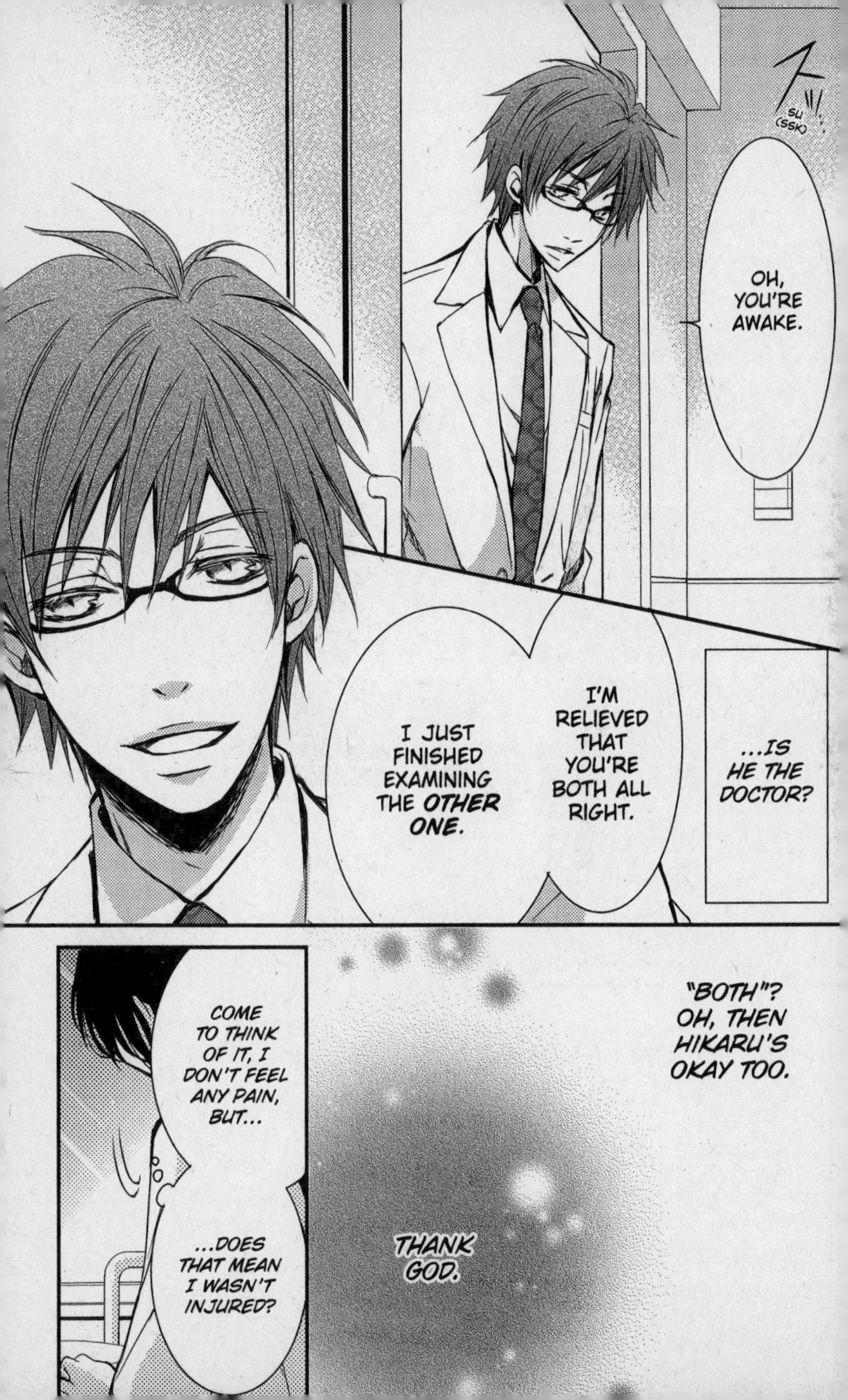
SU (SSK)
OH, YOU'RE AWAKE.
...IS HE THE DOCTOR?
I'M RELIEVED THAT YOU'RE BOTH ALL RIGHT.
I JUST FINISHED EXAMINING THE OTHER ONE.
"BOTH"? OH, THEN HIKARU'S OKAY TOO.
THANK GOD.
COME TO THINK OF IT, I DON'T FEEL ANY PAIN, BUT...
...DOES THAT MEAN I WASN'T INJURED?

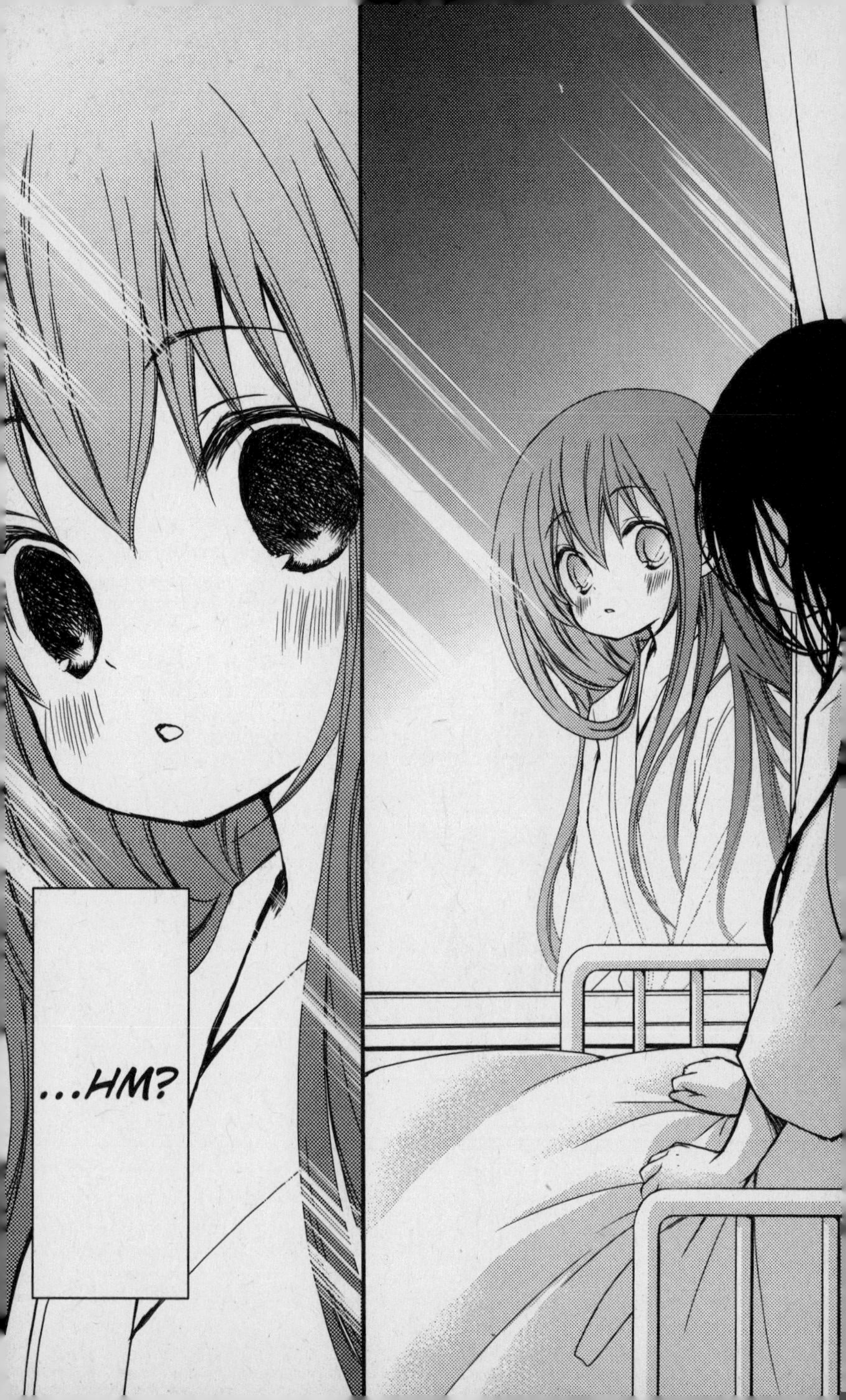
...HM?

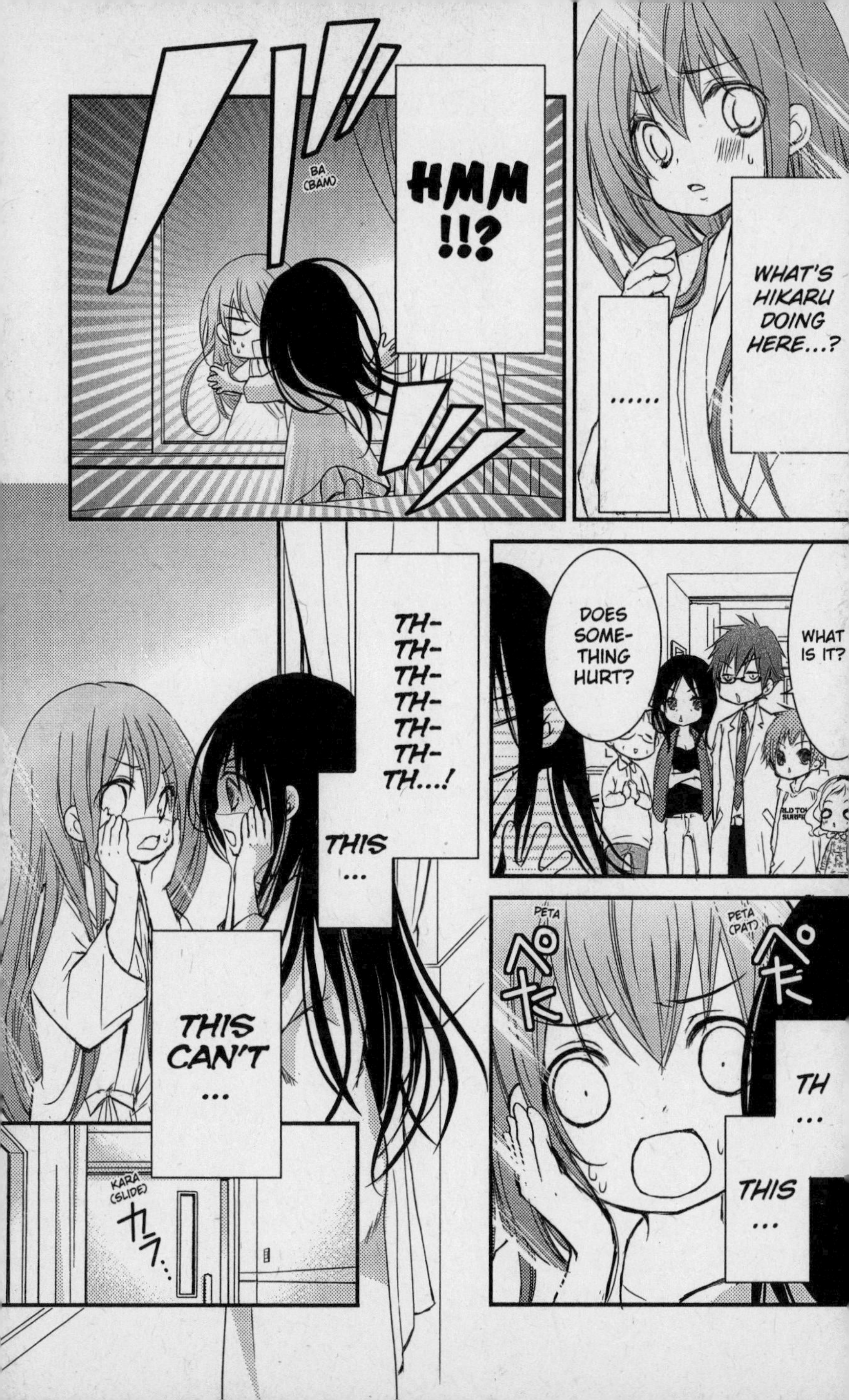
WHAT'S HIKARU DOING HERE...?
......
BA (BAM)
HMM !!?
WHAT IS IT?
DOES SOMETHING HURT?
PETA (PAT)
PETA
TH ...
THIS ...
TH-TH-TH-TH-TH-TH-TH...!
THIS ...
THIS CAN'T ...
KARA (SLIDE)

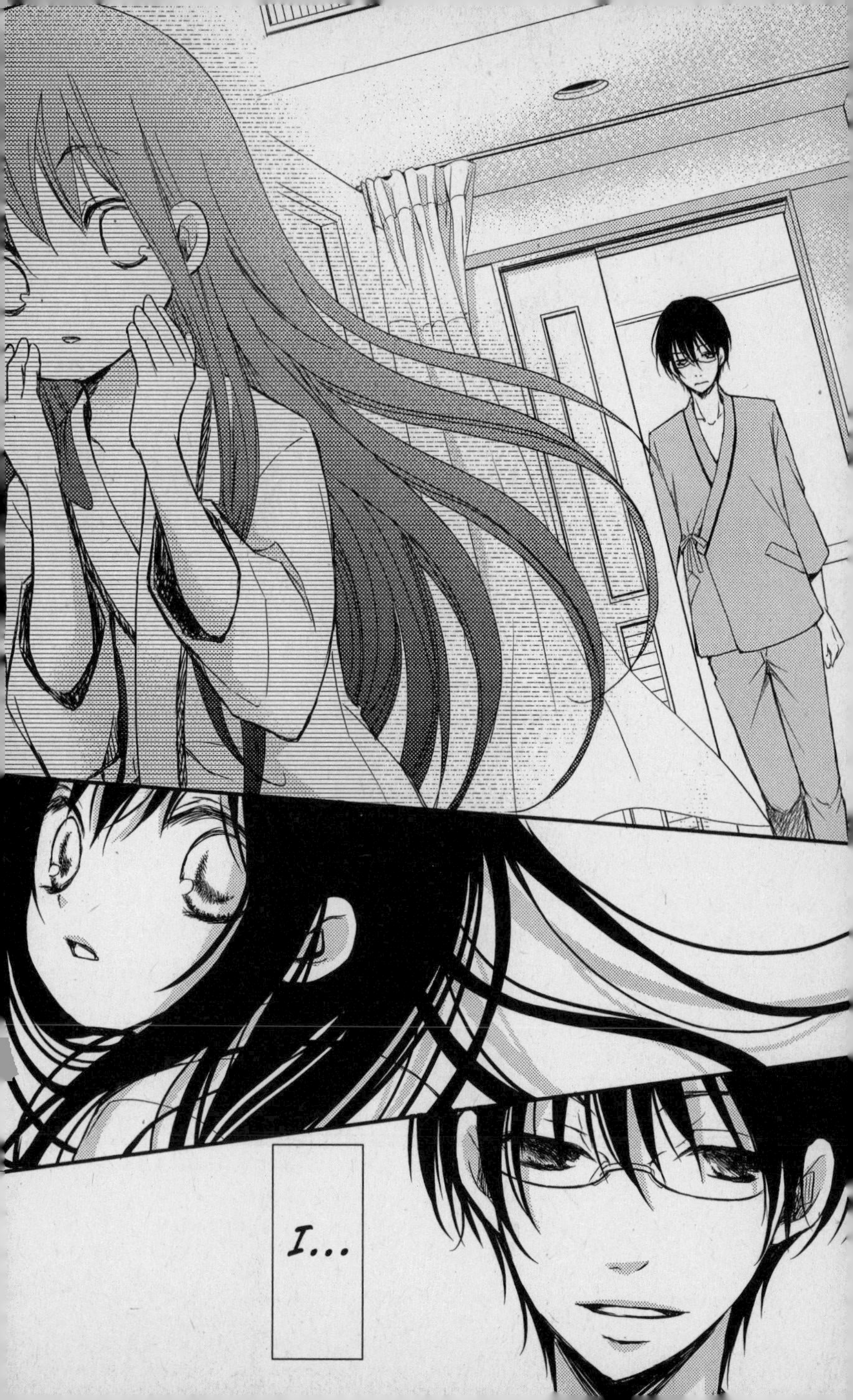
I...

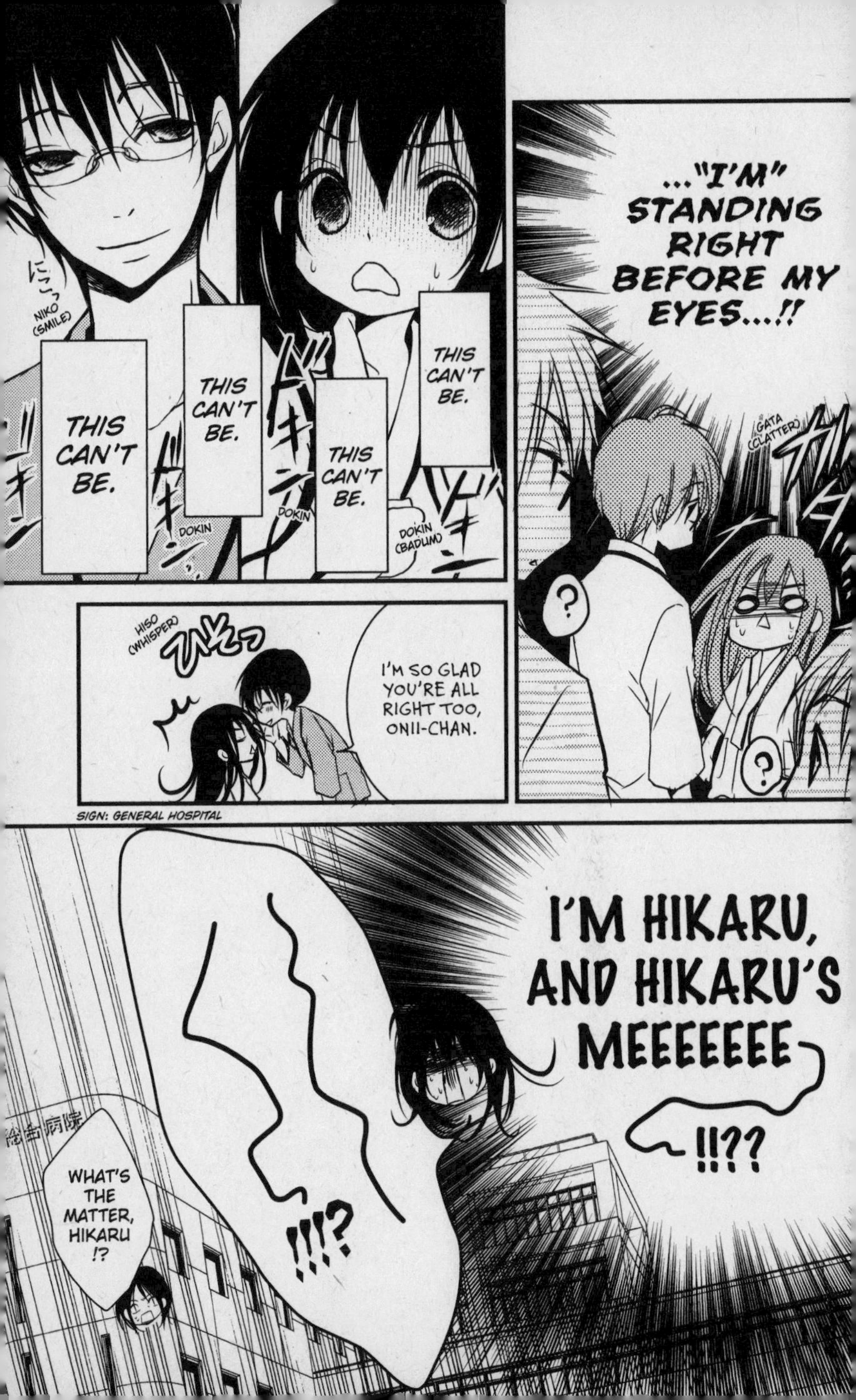
..."I'M" STANDING RIGHT BEFORE MY EYES...!!
GATA (CLATTER)
?
?
THIS CAN'T BE.
DOKIN (BADUM)
THIS CAN'T BE.
DOKIN
THIS CAN'T BE.
DOKIN
THIS CAN'T BE.
にこっ
NIKO (SMILE)
HISO (WHISPER)
ひそっ
I'M SO GLAD YOU'RE ALL RIGHT TOO, ONII-CHAN.
SIGN: GENERAL HOSPITAL
I'M HIKARU, AND HIKARU'S MEEEEEEE
!!??
!!!?
総合病院
WHAT'S THE MATTER, HIKARU !?

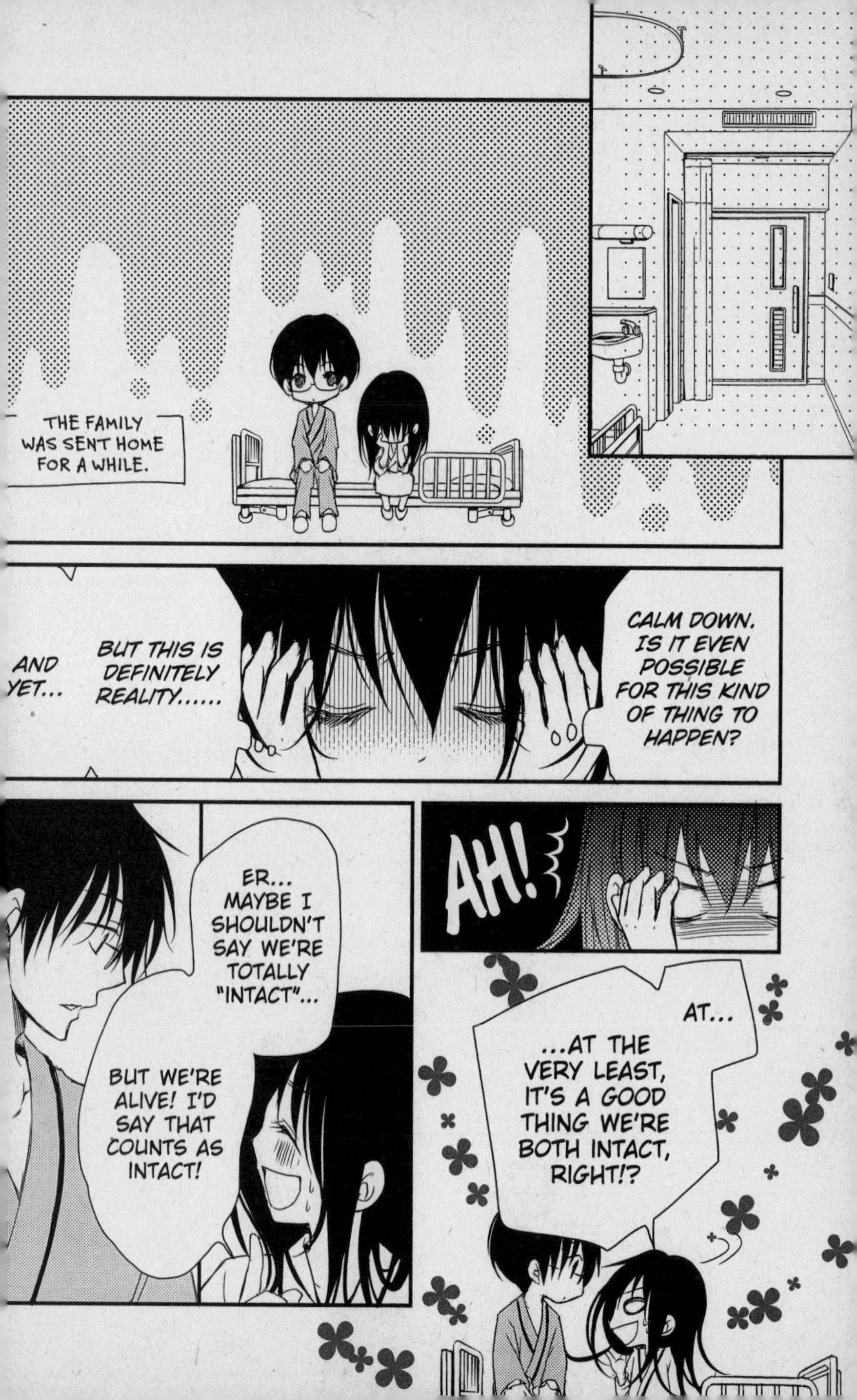

THE FAMILY WAS SENT HOME FOR A WHILE.
CALM DOWN. IS IT EVEN POSSIBLE FOR THIS KIND OF THING TO HAPPEN?
BUT THIS IS DEFINITELY REALITY......
AND YET...
AH!
AT...
...AT THE VERY LEAST, IT'S A GOOD THING WE'RE BOTH INTACT, RIGHT!?
ER... MAYBE I SHOULDN'T SAY WE'RE TOTALLY "INTACT"...
BUT WE'RE ALIVE! I'D SAY THAT COUNTS AS INTACT!

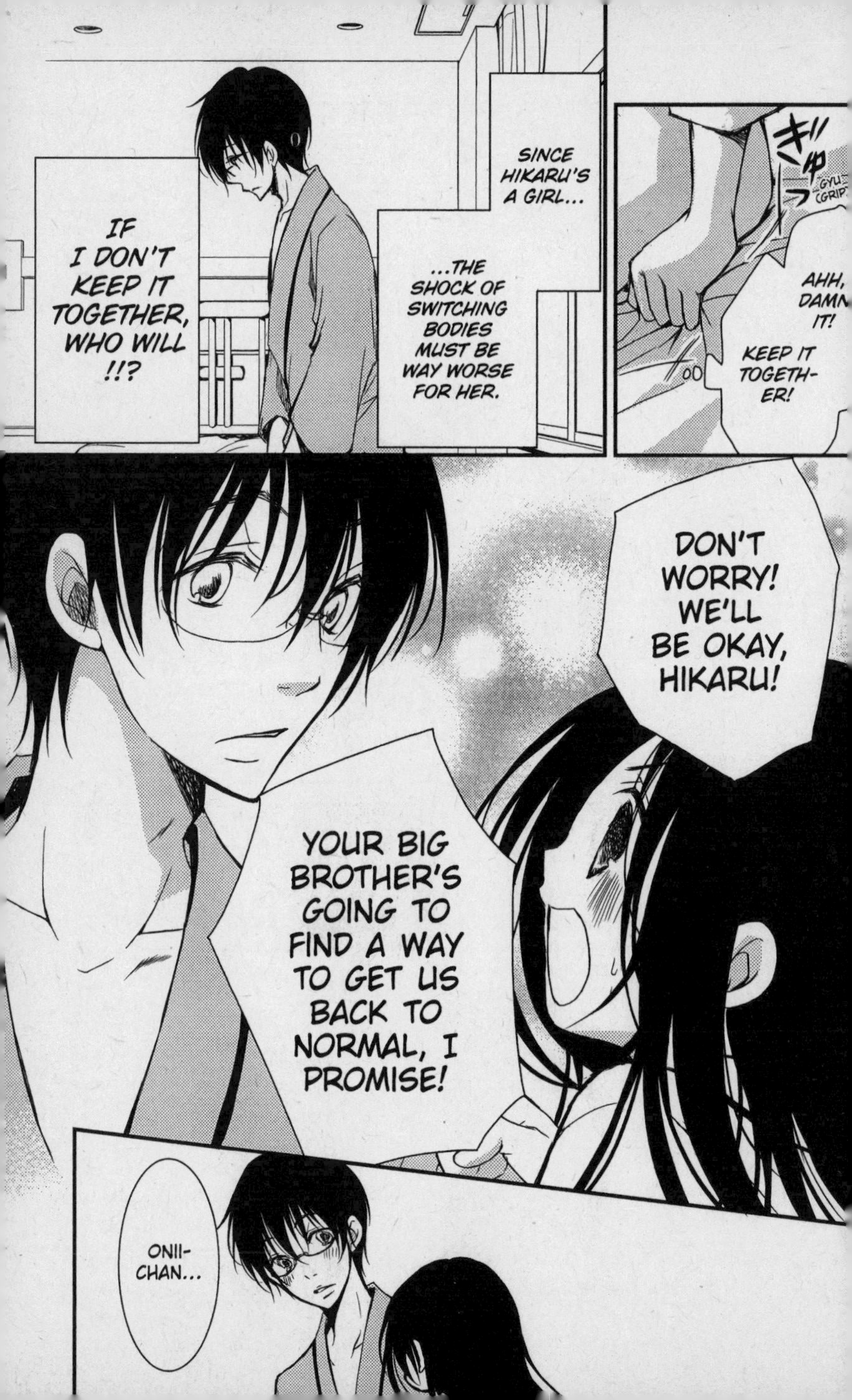

ギュッ
GYU (GRIP)
AHH, DAMN IT!
KEEP IT TOGETH-ER!
SINCE HIKARU'S A GIRL...
...THE SHOCK OF SWITCHING BODIES MUST BE WAY WORSE FOR HER.
IF I DON'T KEEP IT TOGETHER, WHO WILL !!?
DON'T WORRY! WE'LL BE OKAY, HIKARU!
YOUR BIG BROTHER'S GOING TO FIND A WAY TO GET US BACK TO NORMAL, I PROMISE!
ONII-CHAN...

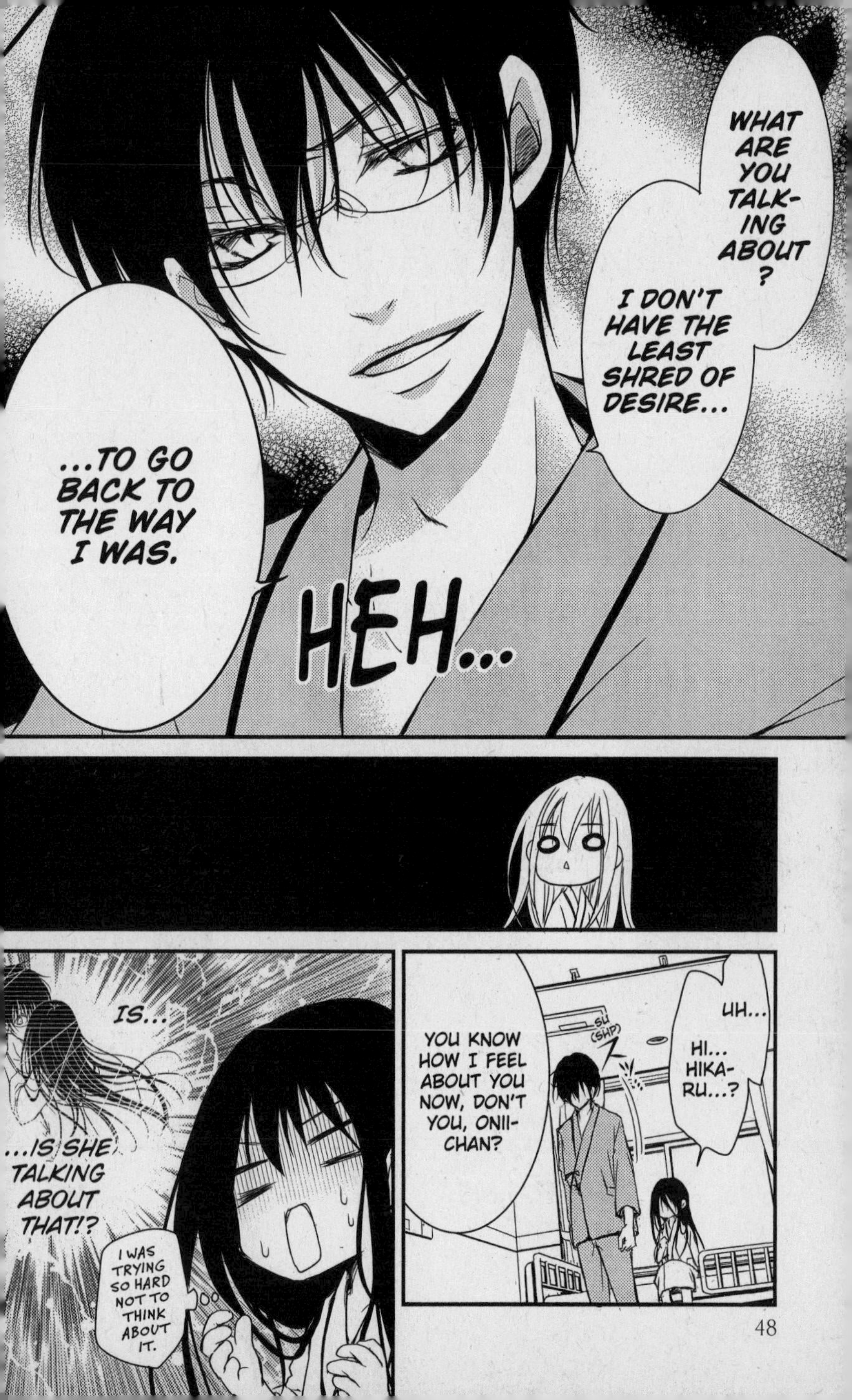
WHAT ARE YOU TALKING ABOUT?
I DON'T HAVE THE LEAST SHRED OF DESIRE...
...TO GO BACK TO THE WAY I WAS.
HEH...
UH...
HI... HIKARU...?
SU (SHP)
YOU KNOW HOW I FEEL ABOUT YOU NOW, DON'T YOU, ONII-CHAN?
IS...
...IS SHE TALKING ABOUT THAT!?
I WAS TRYING SO HARD NOT TO THINK ABOUT IT.

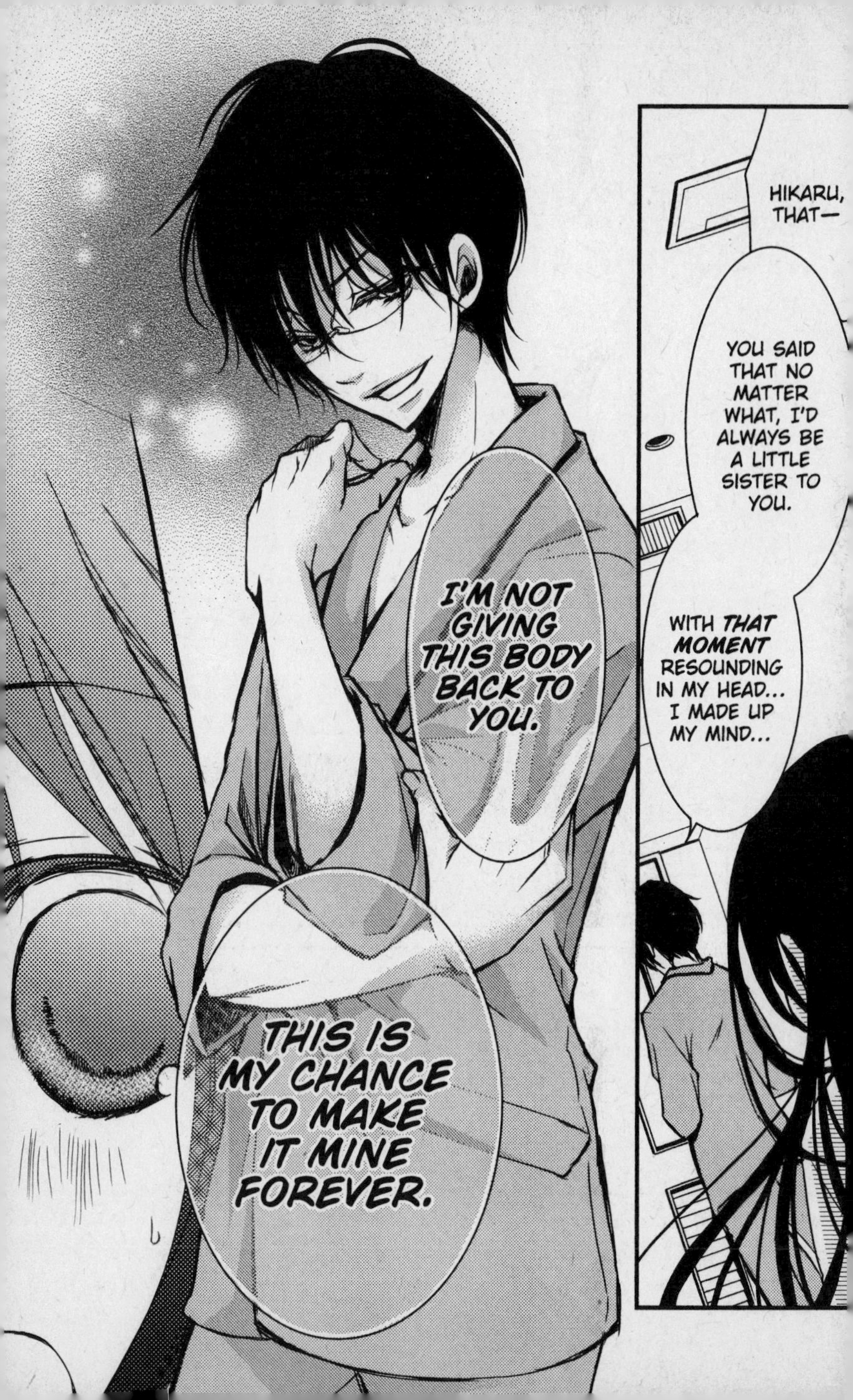
HIKARU, THAT—
YOU SAID THAT NO MATTER WHAT, I'D ALWAYS BE A LITTLE SISTER TO YOU.
WITH *THAT MOMENT* RESOUNDING IN MY HEAD... I MADE UP MY MIND...
I'M NOT GIVING THIS BODY BACK TO YOU.
THIS IS MY CHANCE TO MAKE IT MINE FOREVER.

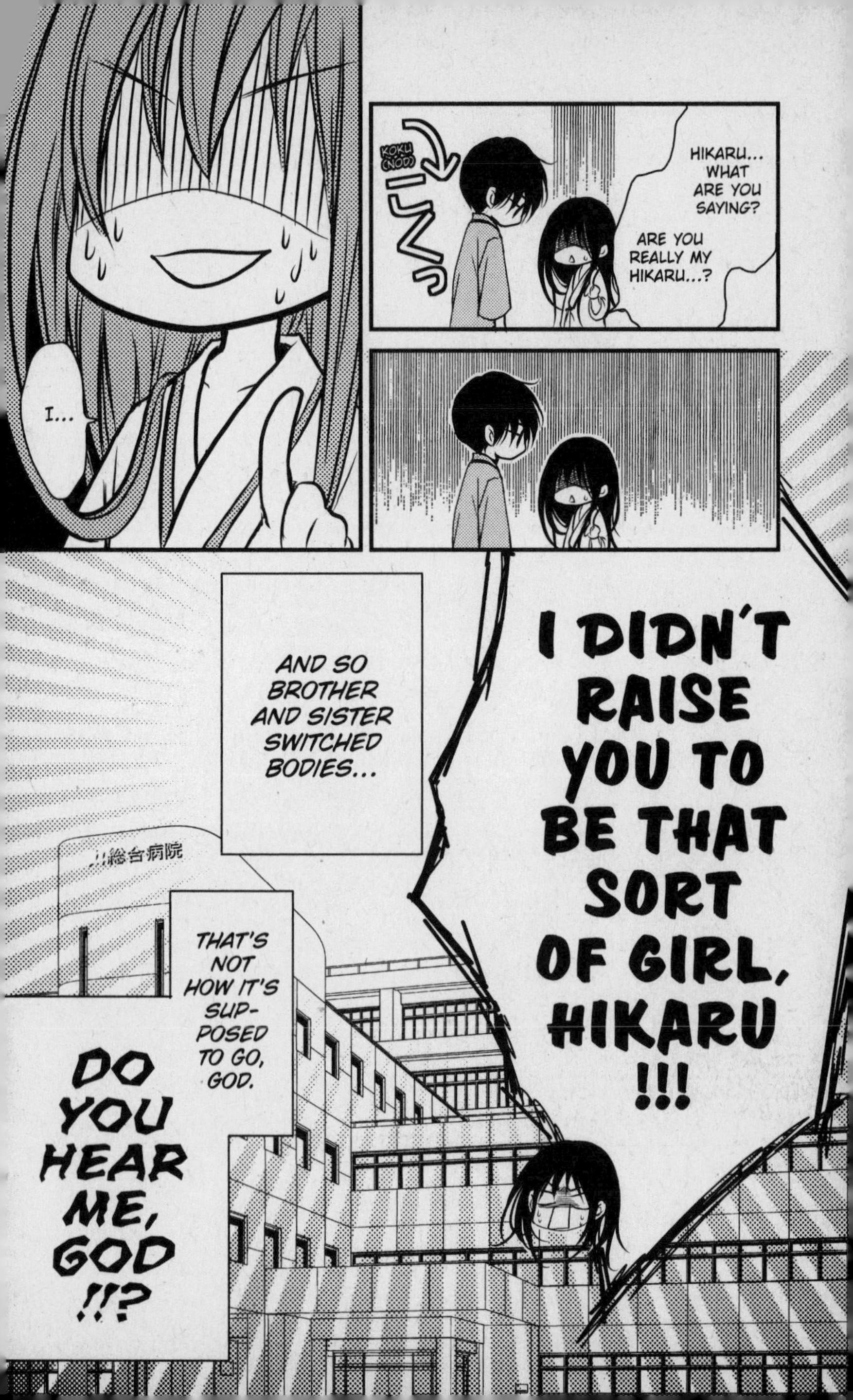
HIKARU... WHAT ARE YOU SAYING?
ARE YOU REALLY MY HIKARU...?
KOKU (NOD)
I...
I DIDN'T RAISE YOU TO BE THAT SORT OF GIRL, HIKARU!!!
AND SO BROTHER AND SISTER SWITCHED BODIES...
総合病院
THAT'S NOT HOW IT'S SUP-POSED TO GO, GOD.
DO YOU HEAR ME, GOD!!?

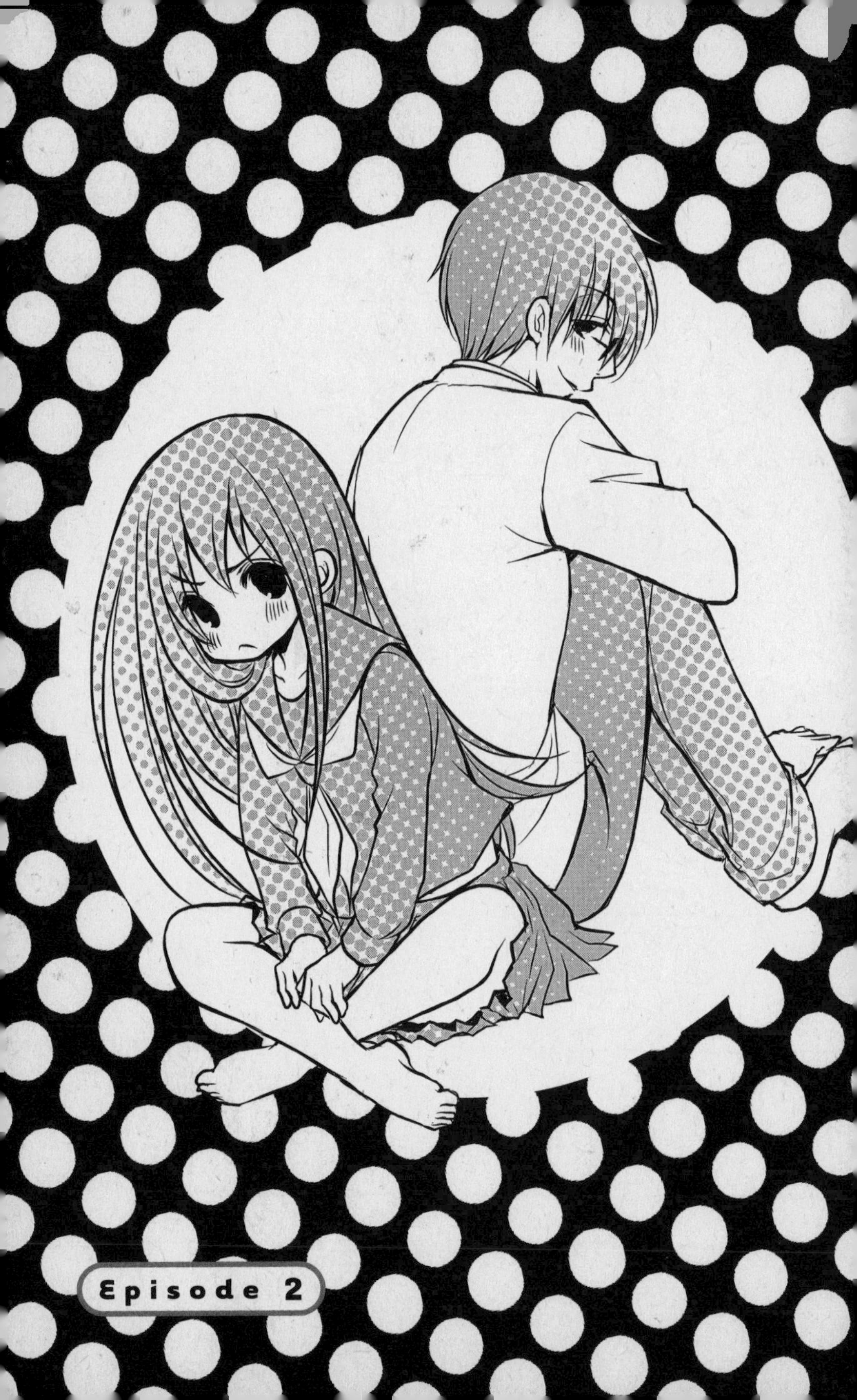
Episode 2

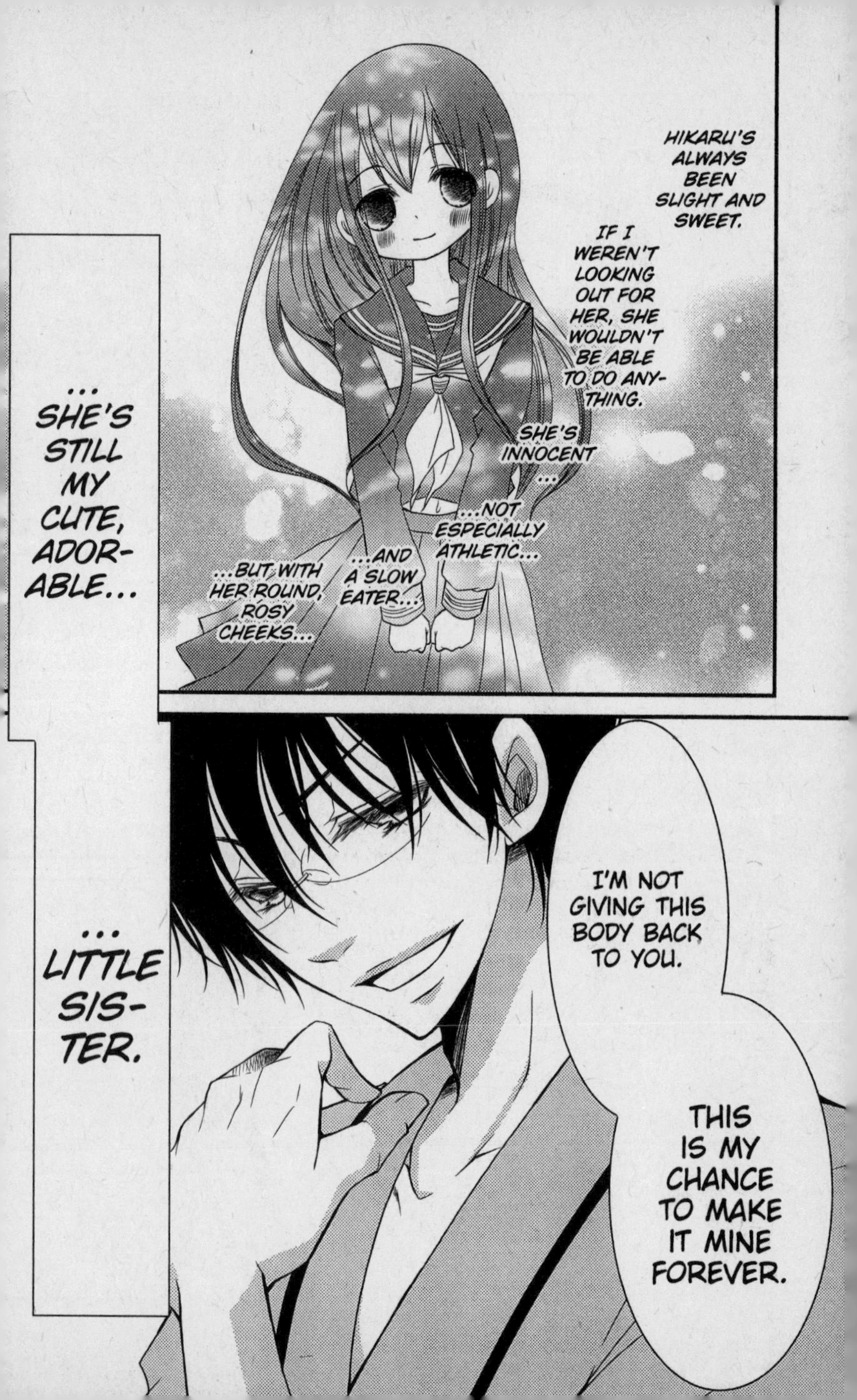
HIKARU'S ALWAYS BEEN SLIGHT AND SWEET.
IF I WEREN'T LOOKING OUT FOR HER, SHE WOULDN'T BE ABLE TO DO ANY-THING.
SHE'S INNOCENT...
...NOT ESPECIALLY ATHLETIC...
...AND A SLOW EATER...
...BUT WITH HER ROUND, ROSY CHEEKS...
...SHE'S STILL MY CUTE, ADOR-ABLE...
...LITTLE SIS-TER.
I'M NOT GIVING THIS BODY BACK TO YOU.
THIS IS MY CHANCE TO MAKE IT MINE FOREVER.

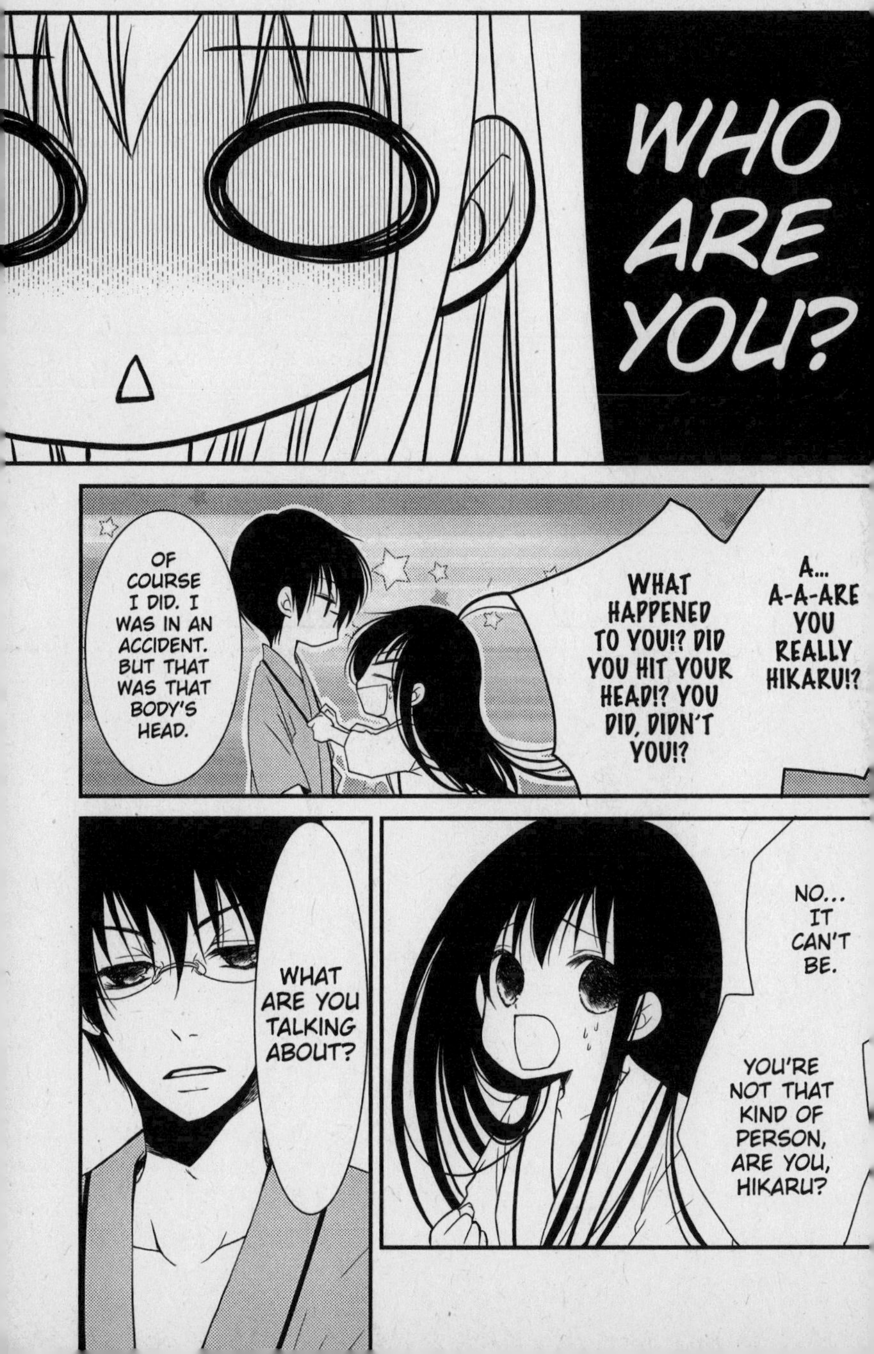
WHO ARE YOU?
A... A-A-ARE YOU REALLY HIKARU!?
WHAT HAPPENED TO YOU!? DID YOU HIT YOUR HEAD!? YOU DID, DIDN'T YOU!?
OF COURSE I DID. I WAS IN AN ACCIDENT. BUT THAT WAS THAT BODY'S HEAD.
NO... IT CAN'T BE.
YOU'RE NOT THAT KIND OF PERSON, ARE YOU, HIKARU?
WHAT ARE YOU TALKING ABOUT?

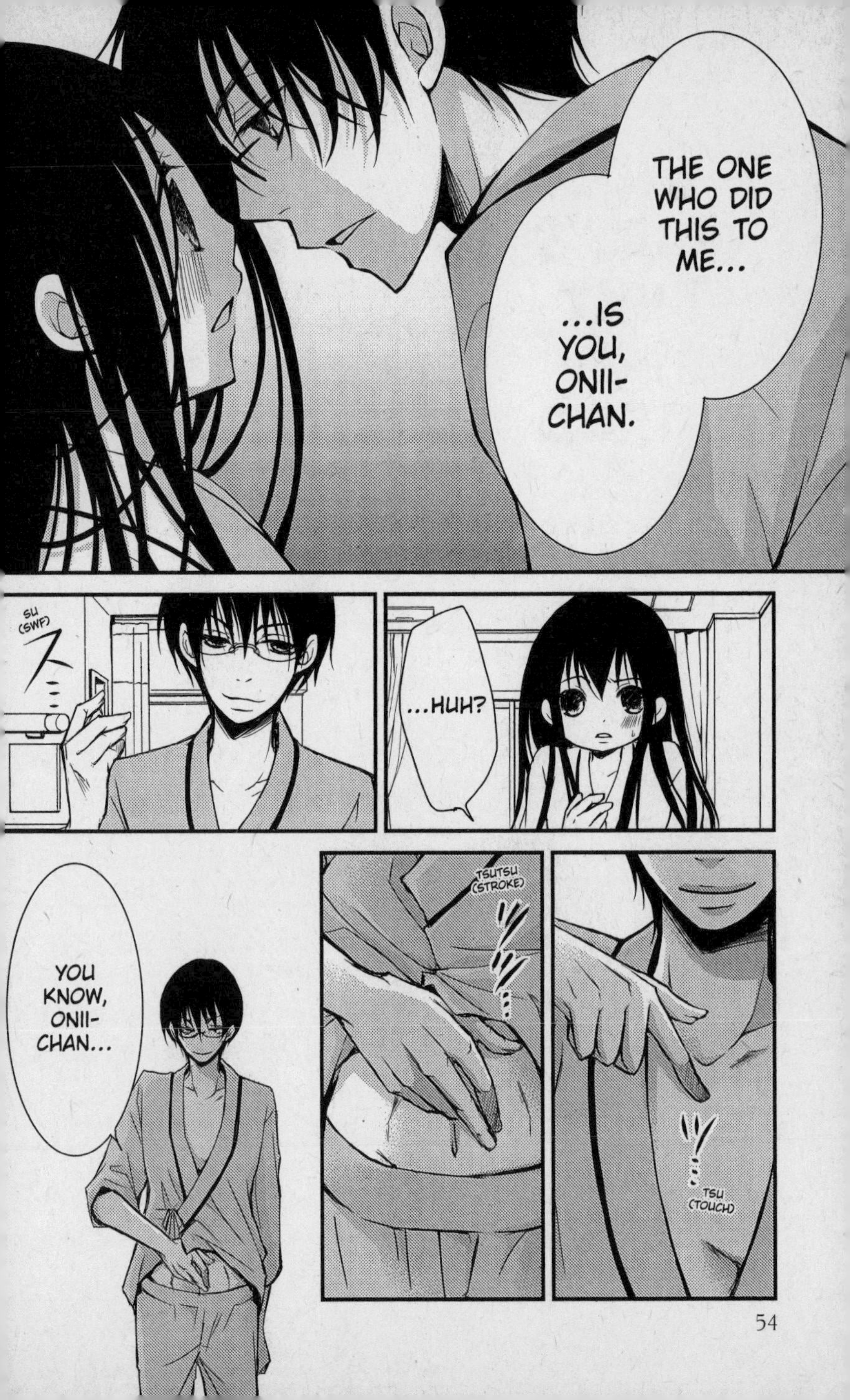
THE ONE WHO DID THIS TO ME...
...IS YOU, ONII-CHAN.
...HUH?
SU (SWF)
TSU (TOUCH)
TSUTSU (STROKE)
YOU KNOW, ONII-CHAN...

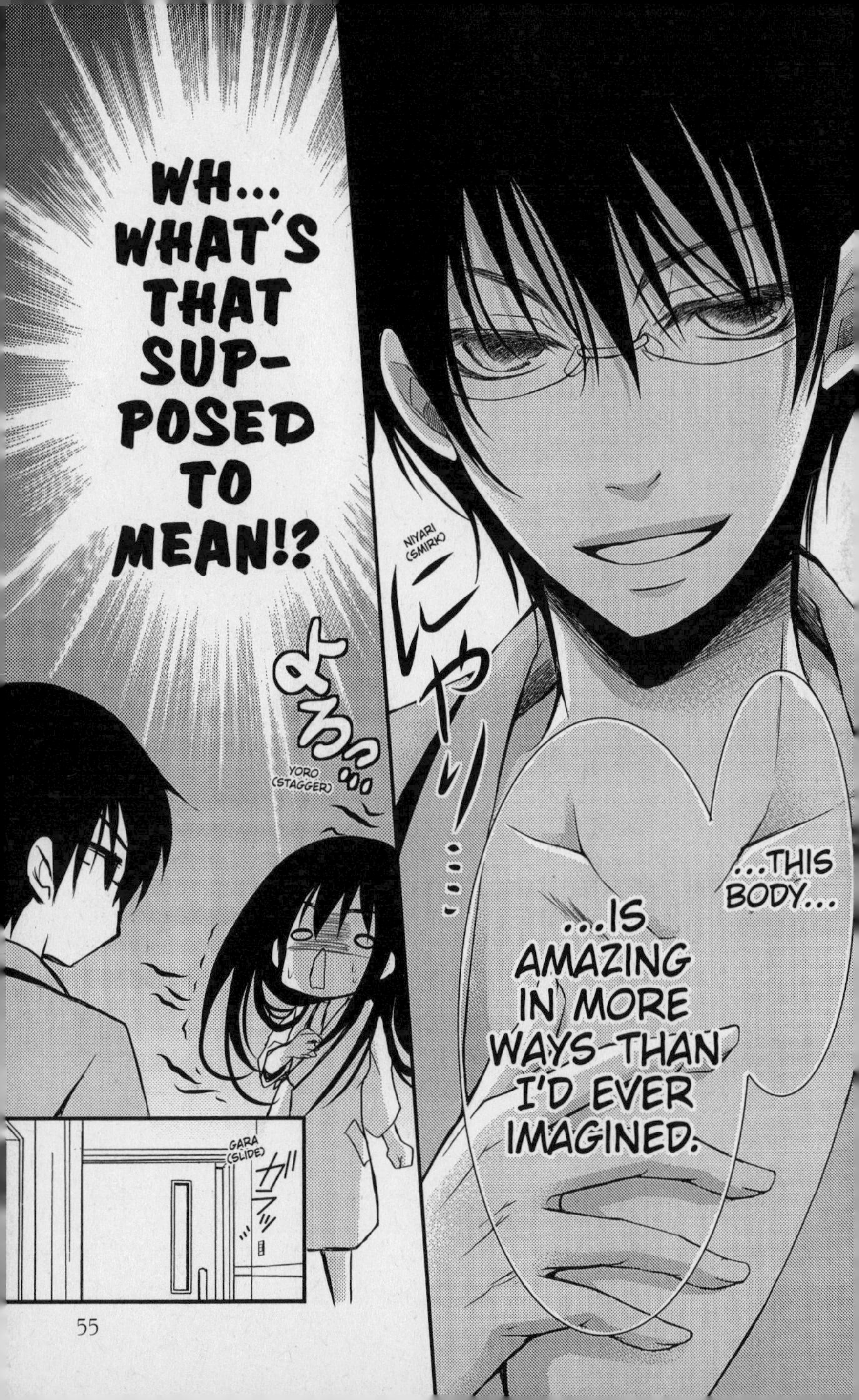

...THIS BODY...
...IS AMAZING IN MORE WAYS THAN I'D EVER IMAGINED.
NIYARI (SMIRK)
WH... WHAT'S THAT SUP-POSED TO MEAN!?
YORO (STAGGER)
GARA (SLIDE)

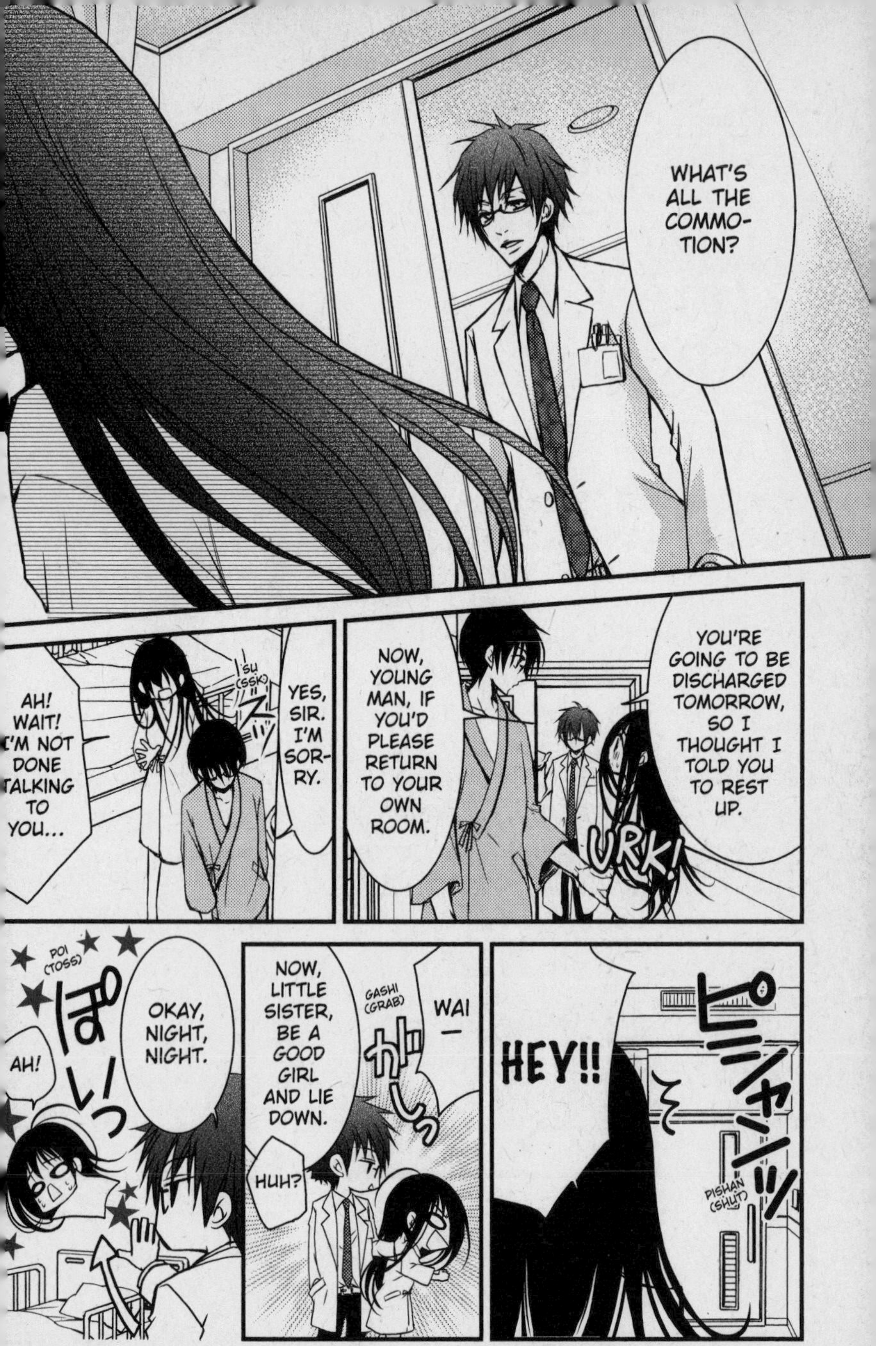
WHAT'S ALL THE COMMOTION?
YOU'RE GOING TO BE DISCHARGED TOMORROW, SO I THOUGHT I TOLD YOU TO REST UP.
URK!
NOW, YOUNG MAN, IF YOU'D PLEASE RETURN TO YOUR OWN ROOM.
YES, SIR. I'M SORRY.
SU (SSK)
AH! WAIT! I'M NOT DONE TALKING TO YOU...
HEY!!
ピシャンッ
PISHAN (SHUT)
WAI—
GASHI (GRAB)
がしっ
NOW, LITTLE SISTER, BE A GOOD GIRL AND LIE DOWN.
HUH?
OKAY, NIGHT, NIGHT.
POI (TOSS)
ぽいっ
AH!

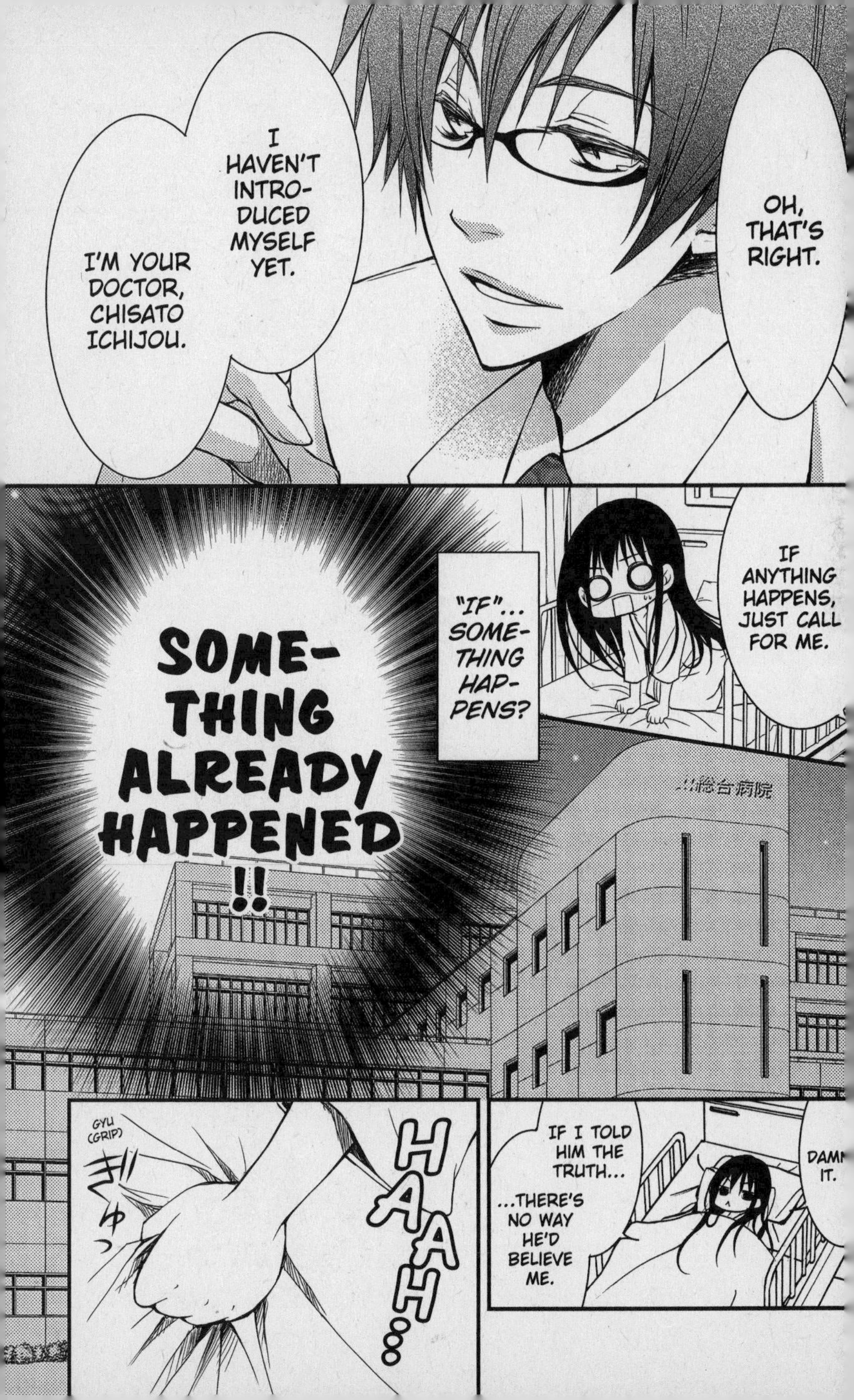
OH, THAT'S RIGHT.
I HAVEN'T INTRO-DUCED MYSELF YET.
I'M YOUR DOCTOR, CHISATO ICHIJOU.
IF ANYTHING HAPPENS, JUST CALL FOR ME.
"IF"... SOME-THING HAP-PENS?
SOME-THING ALREADY HAPPENED!!
DAMN IT.
IF I TOLD HIM THE TRUTH...
...THERE'S NO WAY HE'D BELIEVE ME.
HAAH...
GYU (GRIP)
ぎゅっ

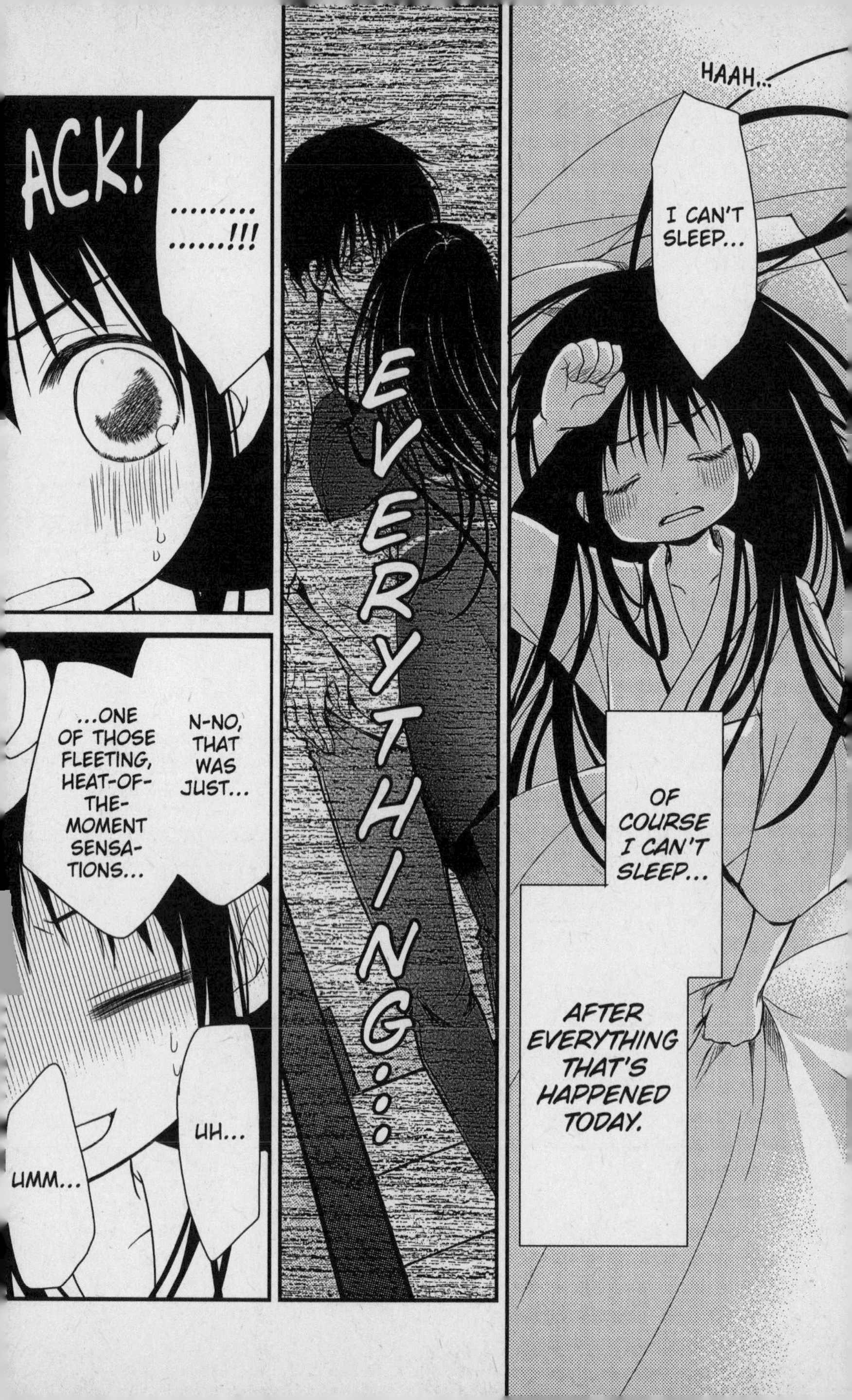
HAAH...
I CAN'T SLEEP...
OF COURSE I CAN'T SLEEP...
AFTER EVERYTHING THAT'S HAPPENED TODAY.
EVERYTHING...
....
.......!!!
ACK!
N-NO, THAT WAS JUST...
...ONE OF THOSE FLEETING, HEAT-OF-THE-MOMENT SENSATIONS...
UH...
UMM...

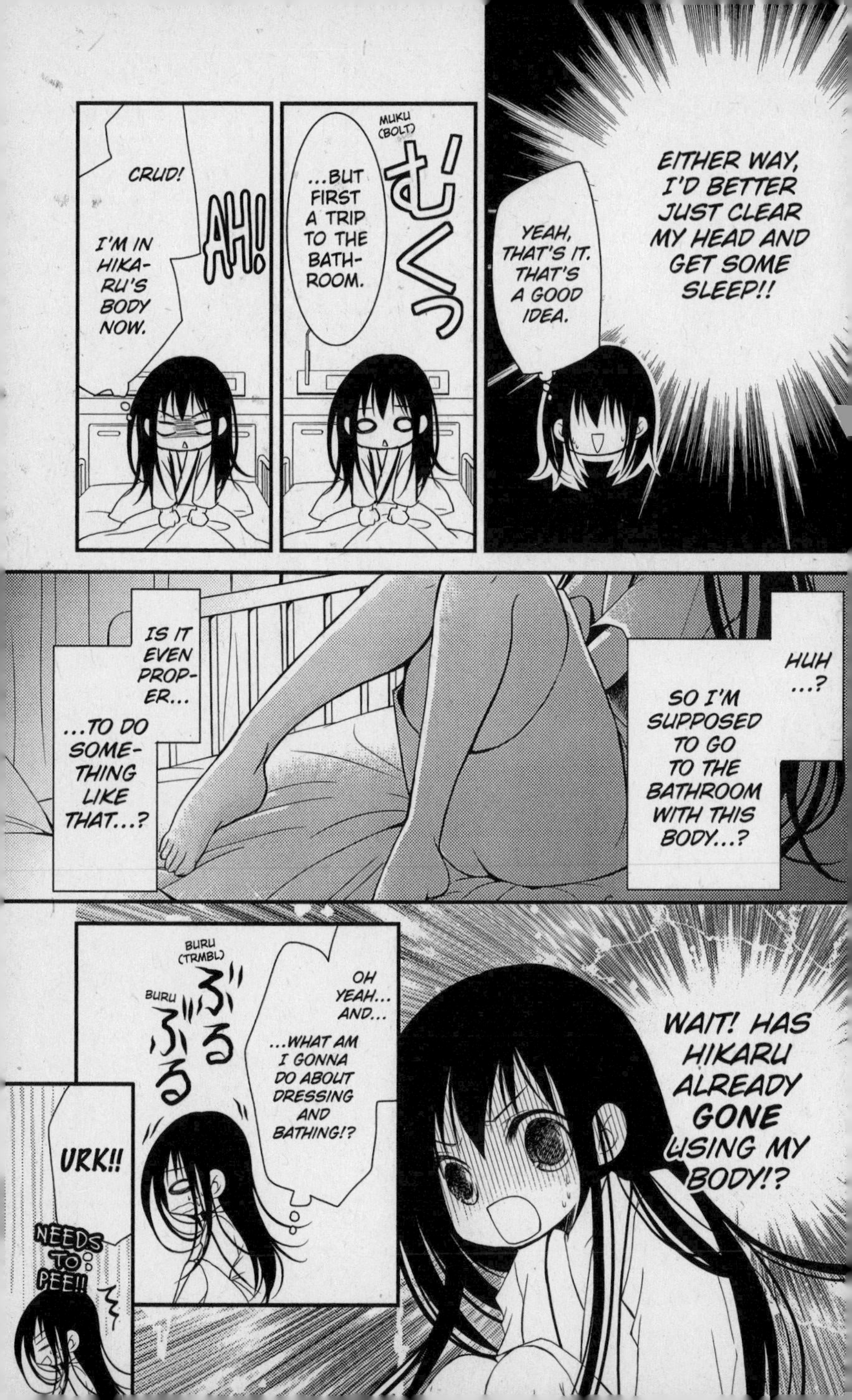
EITHER WAY, I'D BETTER JUST CLEAR MY HEAD AND GET SOME SLEEP!!
YEAH, THAT'S IT. THAT'S A GOOD IDEA.
MUKU (BOLT)
むくっ
...BUT FIRST A TRIP TO THE BATHROOM.
AH!
CRUD!
I'M IN HIKARU'S BODY NOW.
HUH ...?
SO I'M SUPPOSED TO GO TO THE BATHROOM WITH THIS BODY...?
IS IT EVEN PROPER...
...TO DO SOMETHING LIKE THAT...?
WAIT! HAS HIKARU ALREADY GONE USING MY BODY!?
OH YEAH... AND...
...WHAT AM I GONNA DO ABOUT DRESSING AND BATHING!?
BURU (TRMBL)
BURU
ぶるぶる
URK!!
NEEDS TO PEE!!

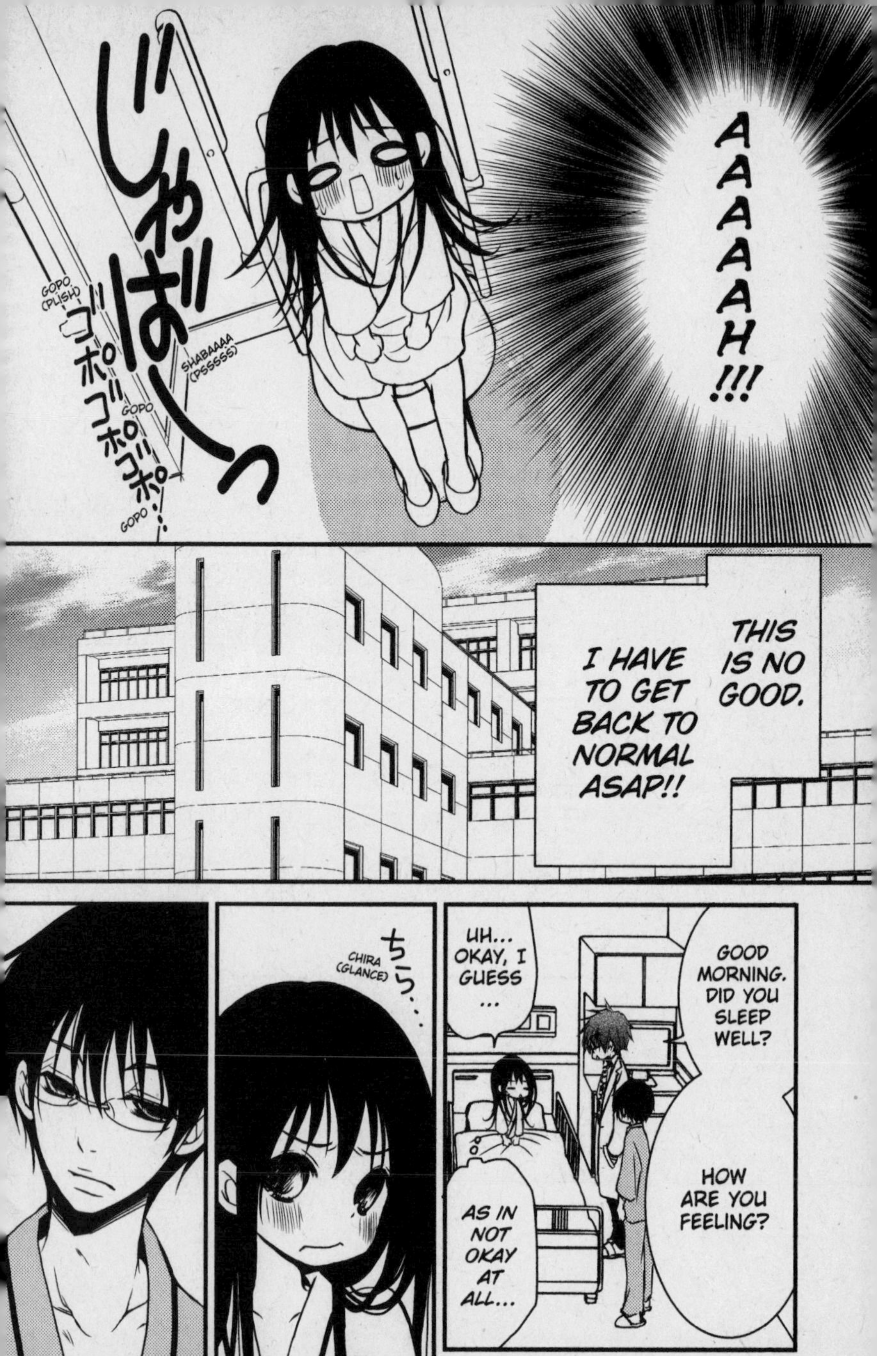
AAAAAH!!!
じゃばーっ
SHABAAAA (PSSSSS)
ゴポゴポゴポ…
GOPO (PLISH)
GOPO
GOPO
THIS IS NO GOOD.
I HAVE TO GET BACK TO NORMAL ASAP!!
GOOD MORNING. DID YOU SLEEP WELL?
HOW ARE YOU FEELING?
UH... OKAY, I GUESS ...
AS IN NOT OKAY AT ALL...
ちら…
CHIRA (GLANCE)

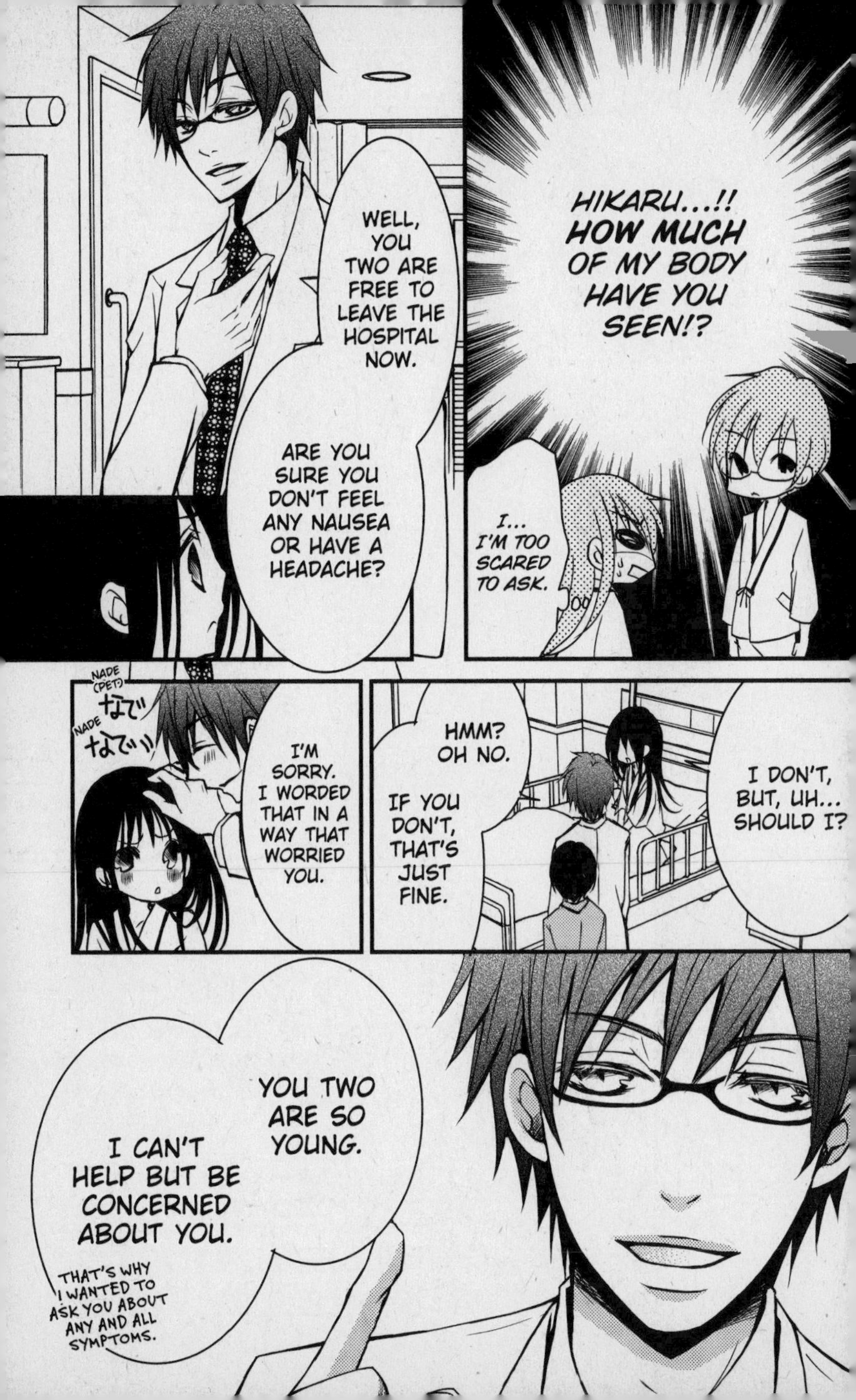

HIKARU...!! HOW MUCH OF MY BODY HAVE YOU SEEN!?
I... I'M TOO SCARED TO ASK.
WELL, YOU TWO ARE FREE TO LEAVE THE HOSPITAL NOW.
ARE YOU SURE YOU DON'T FEEL ANY NAUSEA OR HAVE A HEADACHE?
I DON'T, BUT, UH... SHOULD I?
HMM? OH NO.
IF YOU DON'T, THAT'S JUST FINE.
NADE (PET) なで
NADE なで
I'M SORRY. I WORDED THAT IN A WAY THAT WORRIED YOU.
YOU TWO ARE SO YOUNG.
I CAN'T HELP BUT BE CONCERNED ABOUT YOU.
THAT'S WHY I WANTED TO ASK YOU ABOUT ANY AND ALL SYMPTOMS.

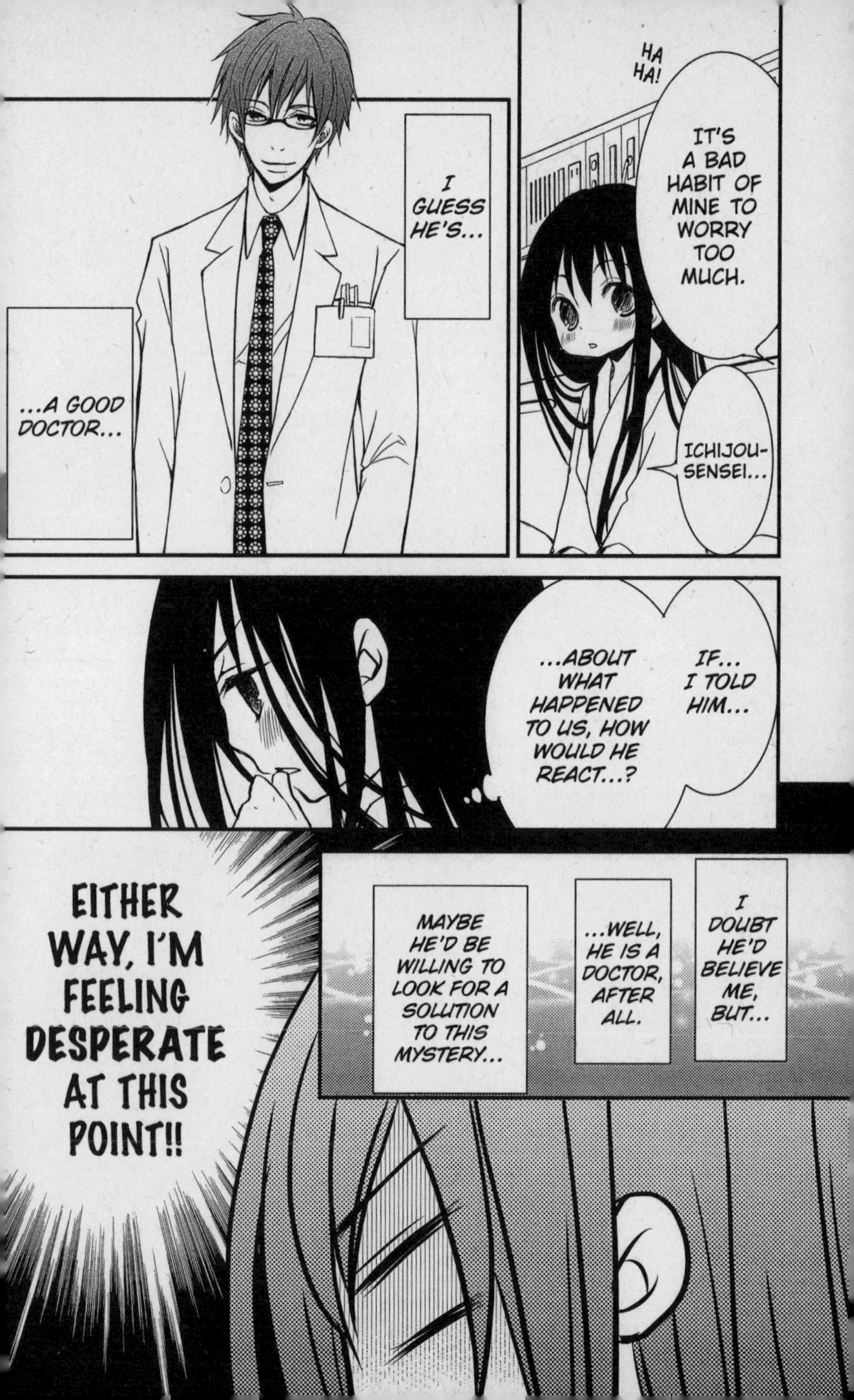

HA HA!
IT'S A BAD HABIT OF MINE TO WORRY TOO MUCH.
ICHIJOU-SENSEI...
I GUESS HE'S...
...A GOOD DOCTOR...
IF... I TOLD HIM...
...ABOUT WHAT HAPPENED TO US, HOW WOULD HE REACT...?
I DOUBT HE'D BELIEVE ME, BUT...
...WELL, HE IS A DOCTOR, AFTER ALL.
MAYBE HE'D BE WILLING TO LOOK FOR A SOLUTION TO THIS MYSTERY...
EITHER WAY, I'M FEELING DESPERATE AT THIS POINT!!

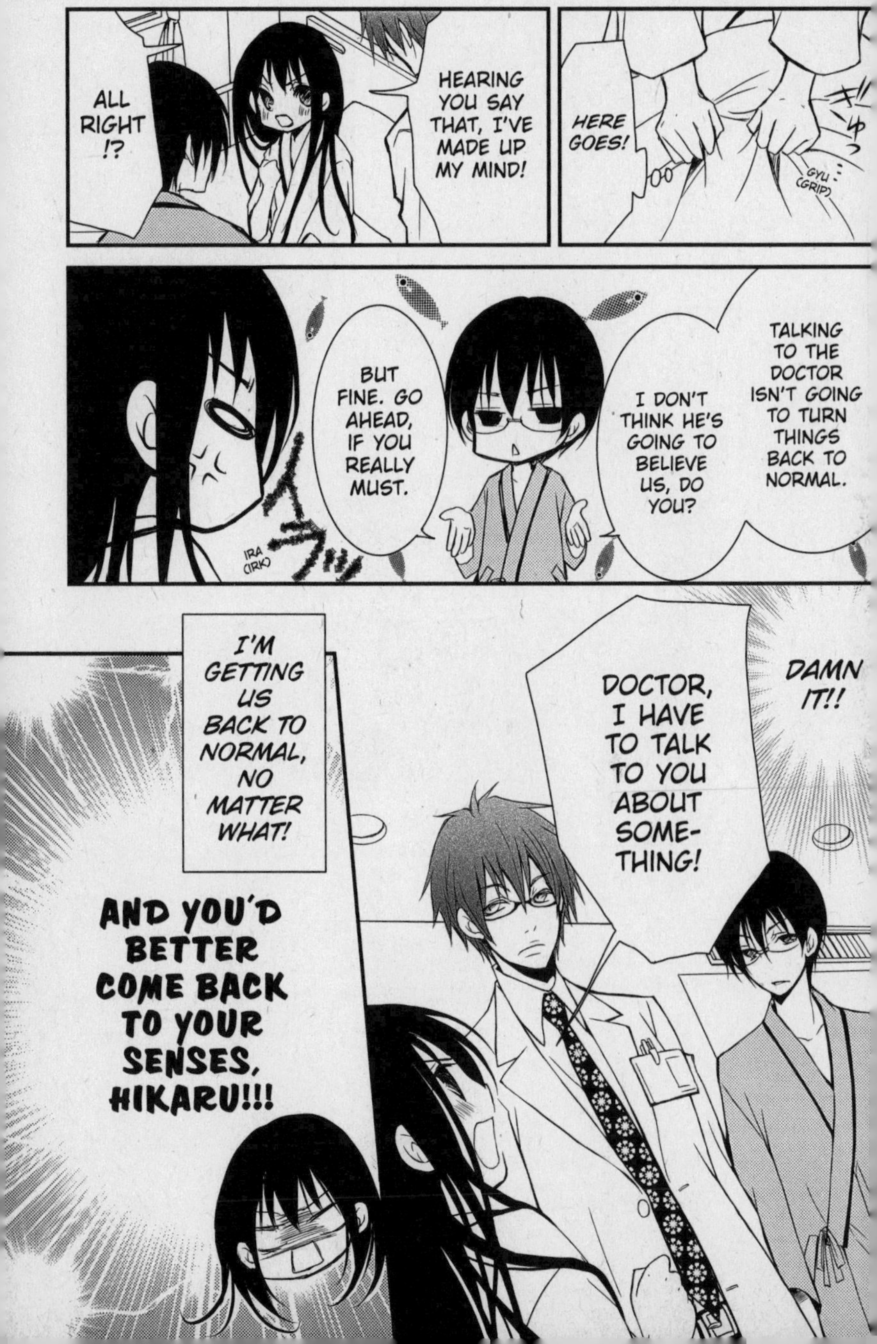
HERE GOES!
GYU (GRIP)
HEARING YOU SAY THAT, I'VE MADE UP MY MIND!
ALL RIGHT!?
TALKING TO THE DOCTOR ISN'T GOING TO TURN THINGS BACK TO NORMAL.
I DON'T THINK HE'S GOING TO BELIEVE US, DO YOU?
BUT FINE. GO AHEAD, IF YOU REALLY MUST.
IRA (IRK)
DAMN IT!!
DOCTOR, I HAVE TO TALK TO YOU ABOUT SOMETHING!
I'M GETTING US BACK TO NORMAL, NO MATTER WHAT!
AND YOU'D BETTER COME BACK TO YOUR SENSES, HIKARU!!!

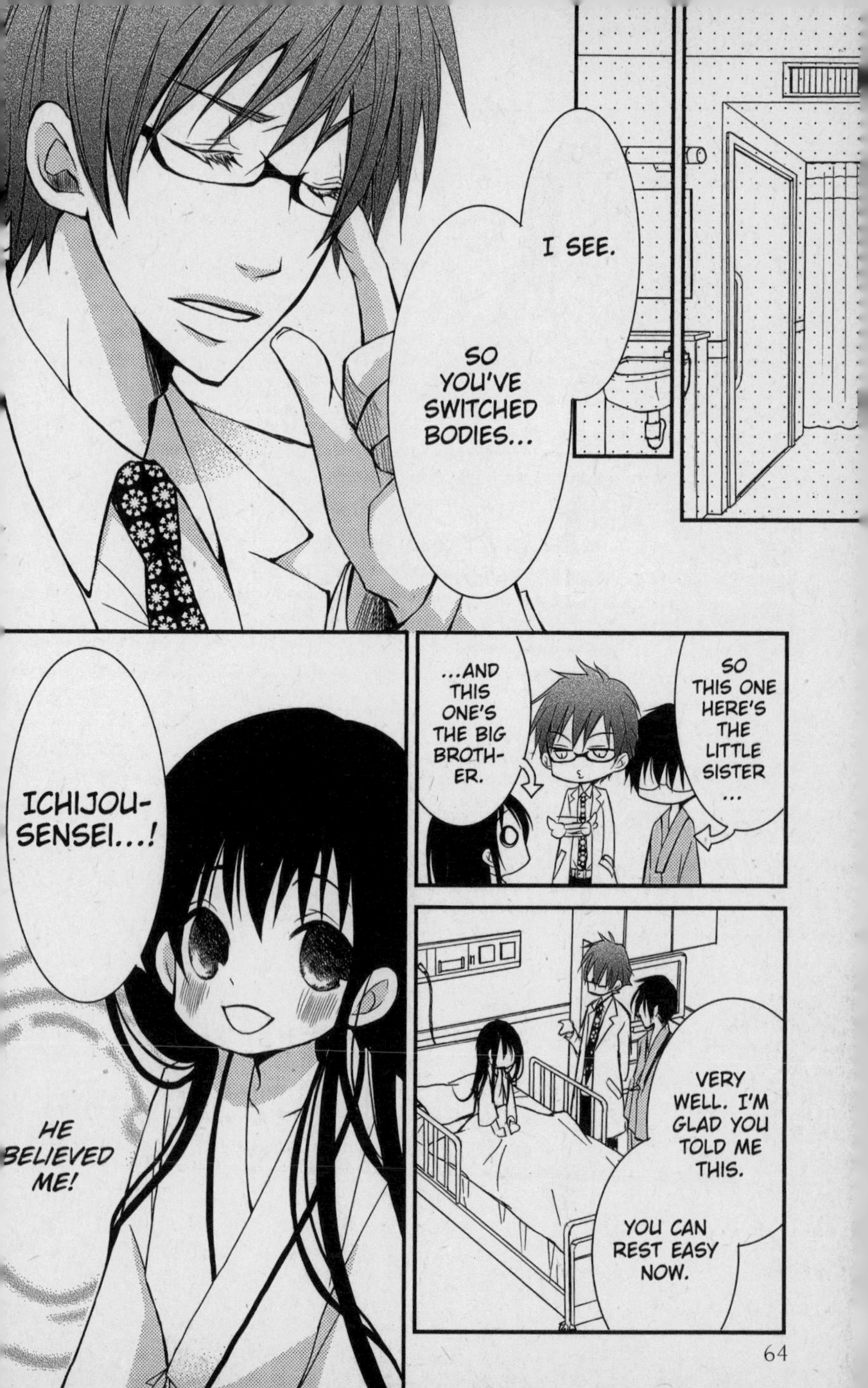
I SEE.
SO YOU'VE SWITCHED BODIES...
SO THIS ONE HERE'S THE LITTLE SISTER...
...AND THIS ONE'S THE BIG BROTHER.
VERY WELL. I'M GLAD YOU TOLD ME THIS.
YOU CAN REST EASY NOW.
ICHIJOU-SENSEI...!
HE BELIEVED ME!

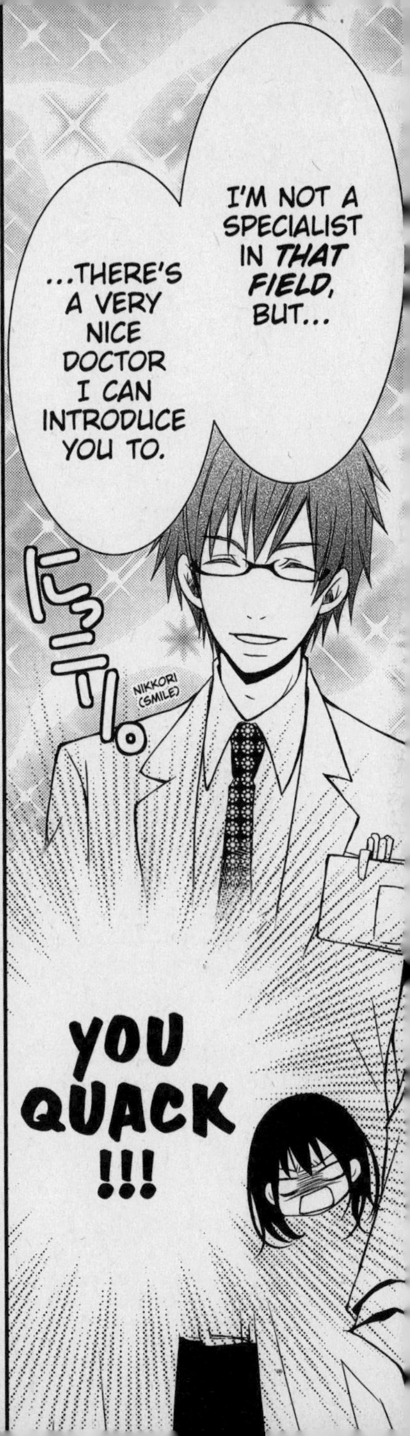
I'M NOT A SPECIALIST IN *THAT FIELD*, BUT...
...THERE'S A VERY NICE DOCTOR I CAN INTRODUCE YOU TO.
NIKKORI (SMILE)
YOU QUACK!!!

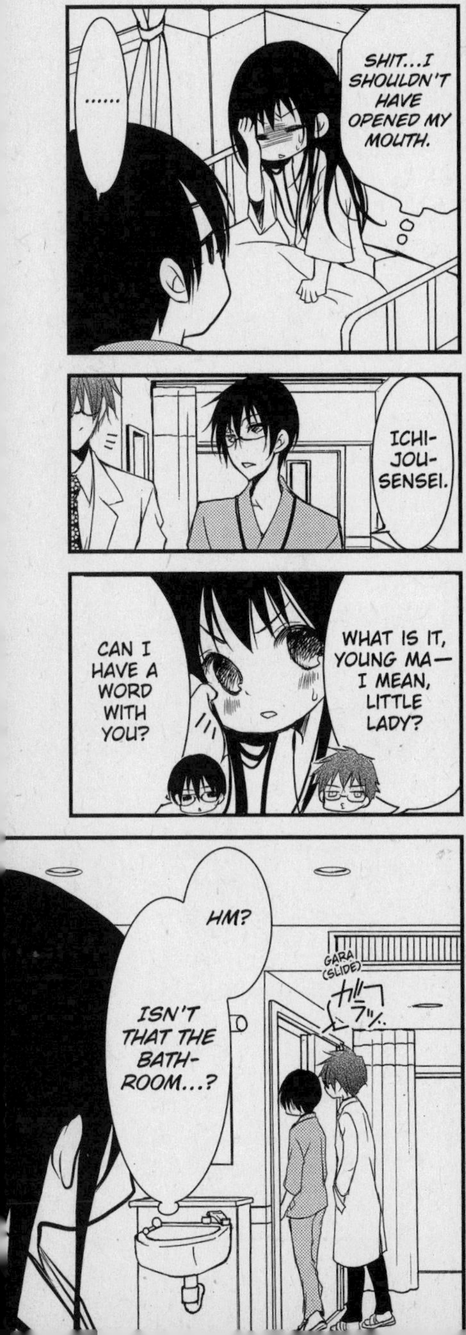
SHIT...I SHOULDN'T HAVE OPENED MY MOUTH.
......
ICHIJOU-SENSEI.
WHAT IS IT, YOUNG MA— I MEAN, LITTLE LADY?
CAN I HAVE A WORD WITH YOU?
GARA (SLIDE)
HM?
ISN'T THAT THE BATHROOM...?

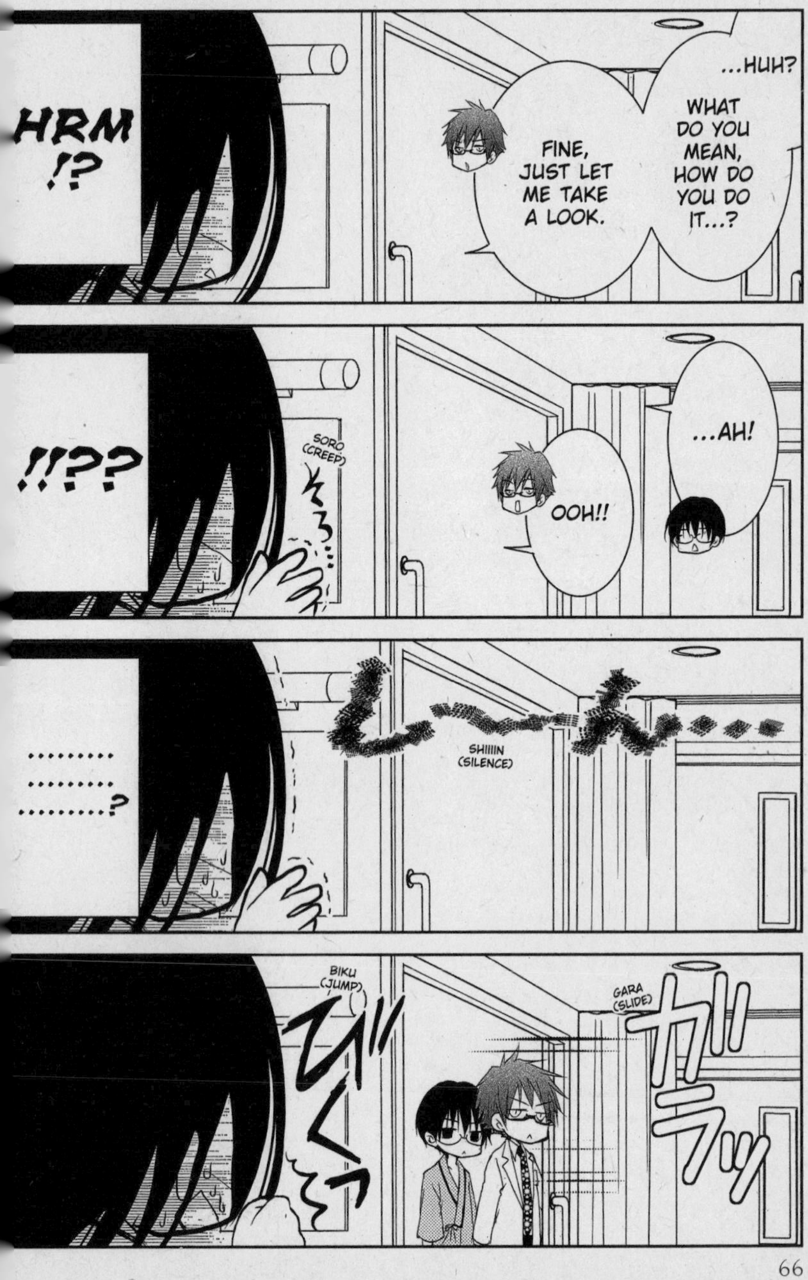
...HUH?
WHAT DO YOU MEAN, HOW DO YOU DO IT...?
FINE, JUST LET ME TAKE A LOOK.
HRM !?
...AH!
OOH!!
SORO (CREEP)
!!??
SHIIIIN (SILENCE)
....
....
.........?
GARA (SLIDE)
BIKU (JUMP)

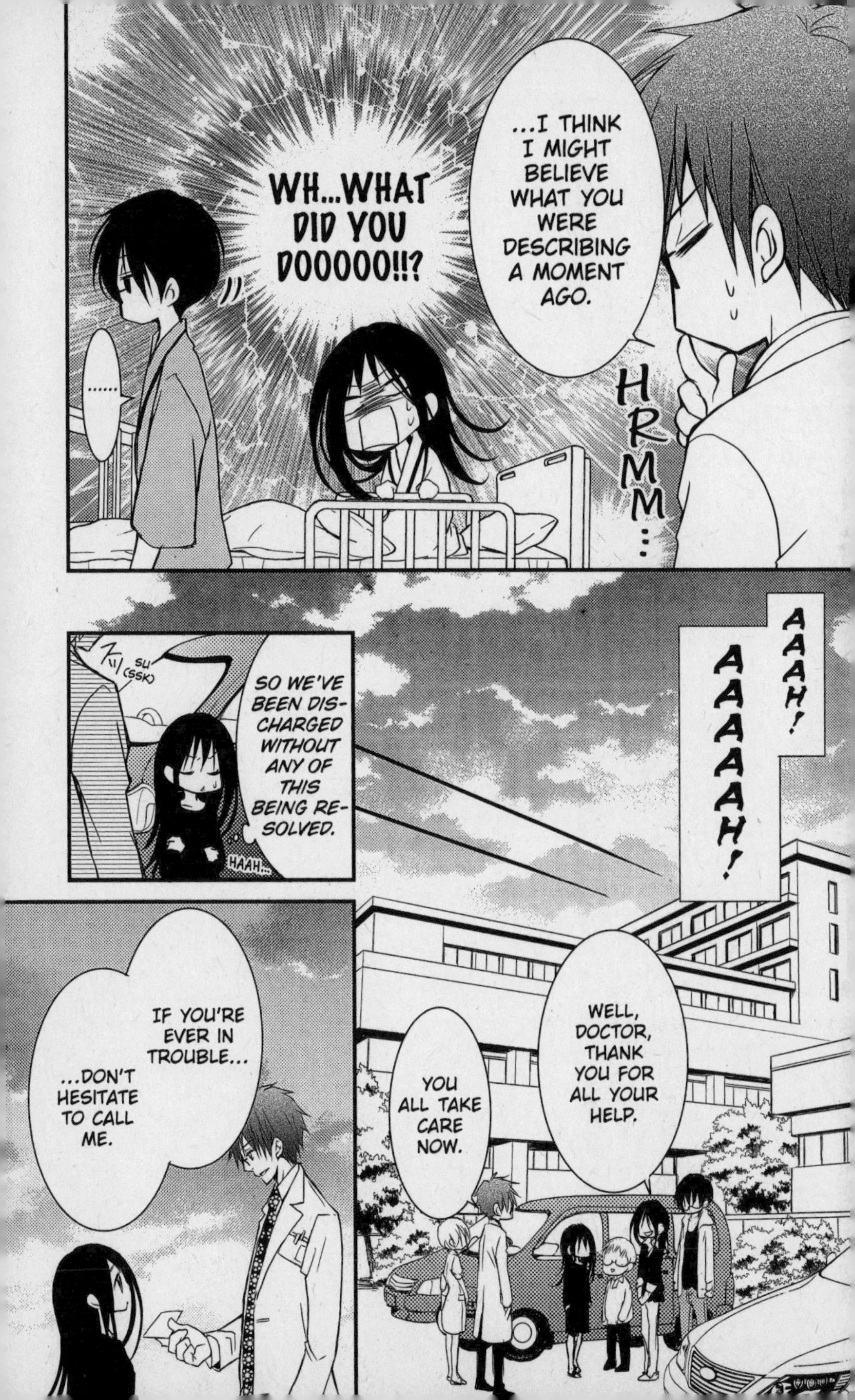
...I THINK I MIGHT BELIEVE WHAT YOU WERE DESCRIBING A MOMENT AGO.
WH...WHAT DID YOU DOOOOO!!?
HRMM...
......
AAAH! AAAAAAH!
SO WE'VE BEEN DIS-CHARGED WITHOUT ANY OF THIS BEING RE-SOLVED.
SU (SSK)
HAAH...
WELL, DOCTOR, THANK YOU FOR ALL YOUR HELP.
YOU ALL TAKE CARE NOW.
IF YOU'RE EVER IN TROUBLE...
...DON'T HESITATE TO CALL ME.

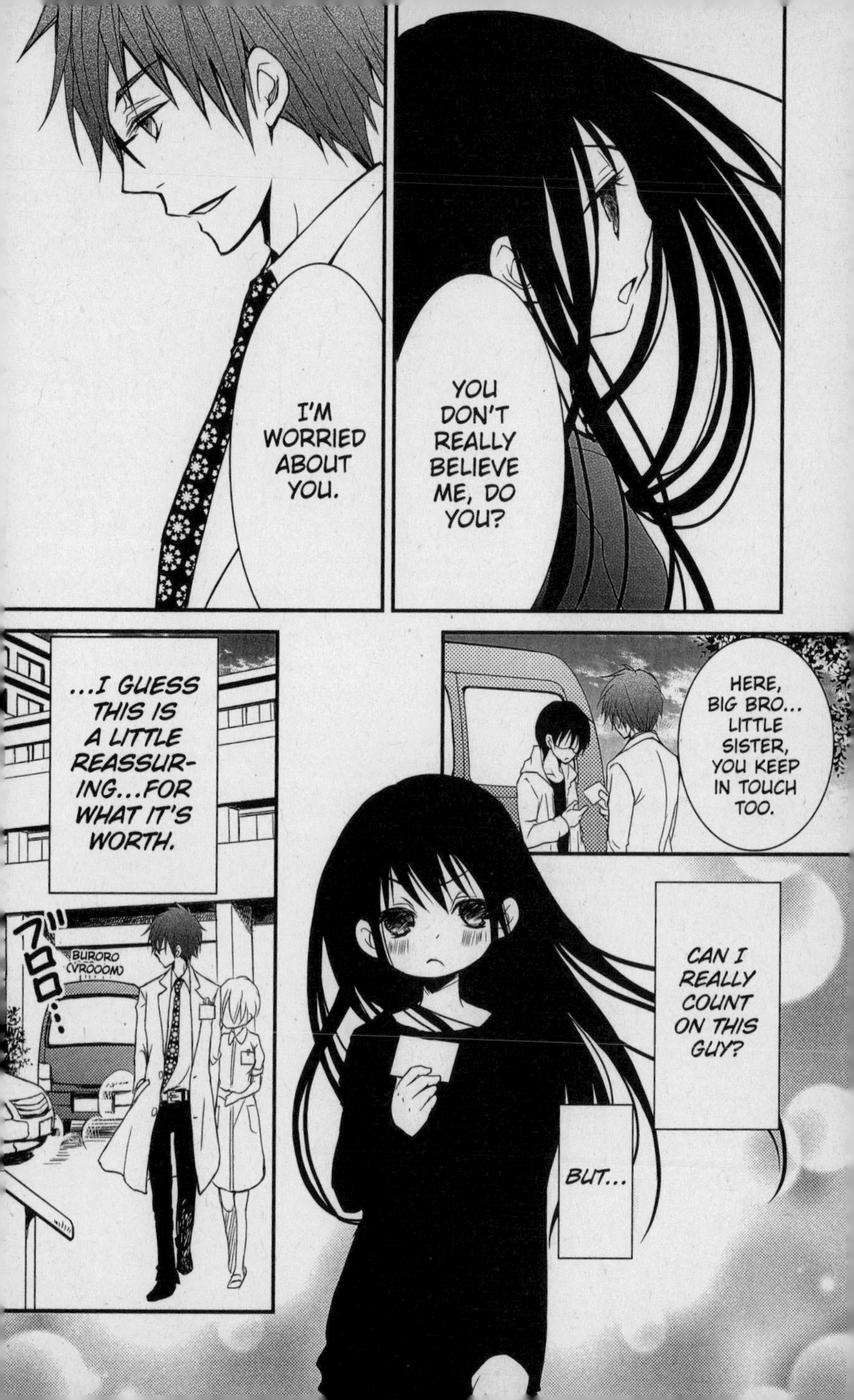
YOU DON'T REALLY BELIEVE ME, DO YOU?
I'M WORRIED ABOUT YOU.
HERE, BIG BRO... LITTLE SISTER, YOU KEEP IN TOUCH TOO.
...I GUESS THIS IS A LITTLE REASSURING...FOR WHAT IT'S WORTH.
CAN I REALLY COUNT ON THIS GUY?
BUT...
ブロロ…
BURORO (VROOOM)

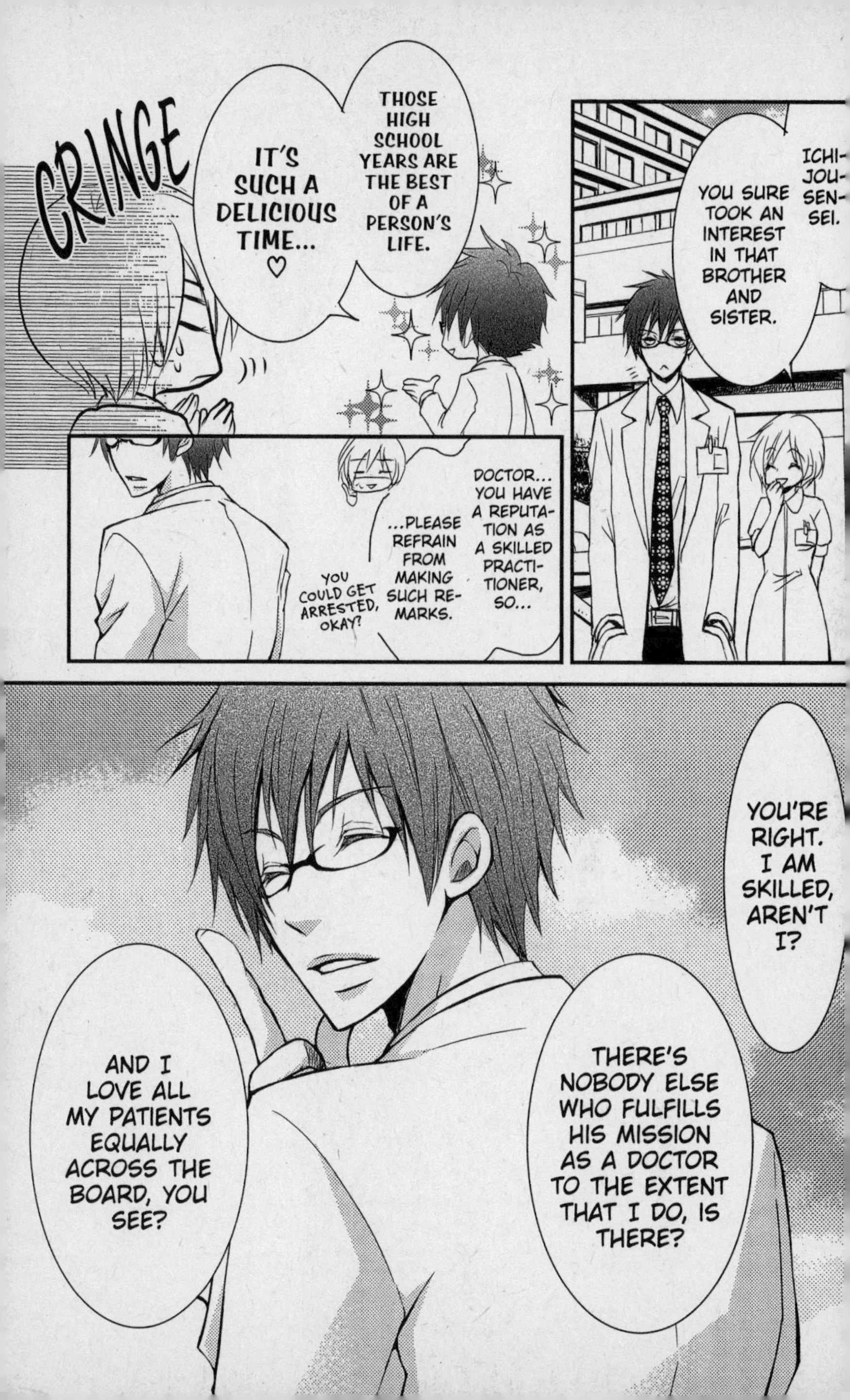

ICHIJOU-SENSEI.
YOU SURE TOOK AN INTEREST IN THAT BROTHER AND SISTER.
THOSE HIGH SCHOOL YEARS ARE THE BEST OF A PERSON'S LIFE.
IT'S SUCH A DELICIOUS TIME... ♡
CRINGE
DOCTOR... YOU HAVE A REPUTATION AS A SKILLED PRACTITIONER, SO...
...PLEASE REFRAIN FROM MAKING SUCH REMARKS.
YOU COULD GET ARRESTED, OKAY?
YOU'RE RIGHT. I AM SKILLED, AREN'T I?
THERE'S NOBODY ELSE WHO FULFILLS HIS MISSION AS A DOCTOR TO THE EXTENT THAT I DO, IS THERE?
AND I LOVE ALL MY PATIENTS EQUALLY ACROSS THE BOARD, YOU SEE?

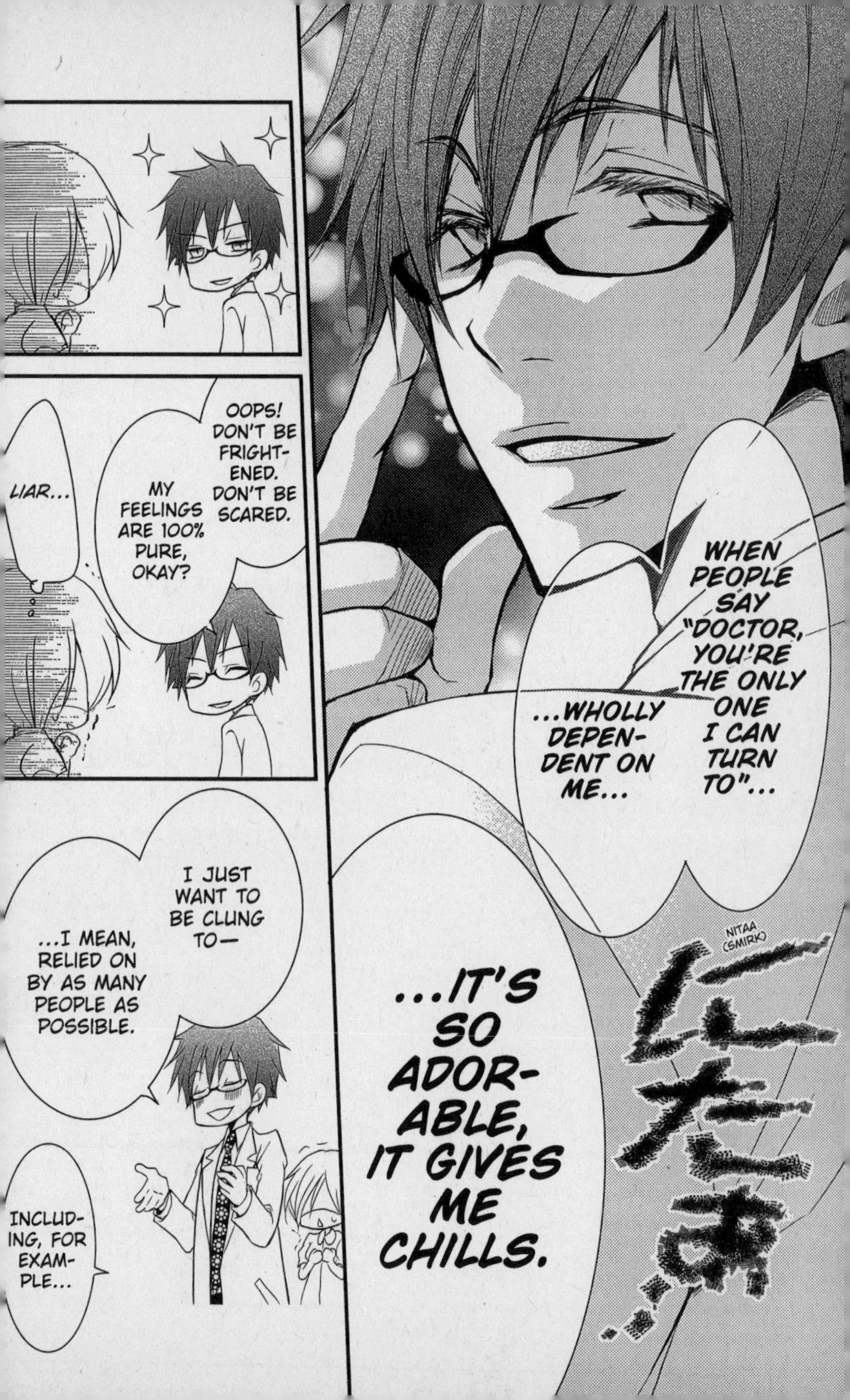
WHEN PEOPLE SAY "DOCTOR, YOU'RE THE ONLY ONE I CAN TURN TO"...
...WHOLLY DEPEN-DENT ON ME...
...IT'S SO ADOR-ABLE, IT GIVES ME CHILLS.
NITAA (SMIRK)
OOPS! DON'T BE FRIGHT-ENED. DON'T BE SCARED.
MY FEELINGS ARE 100% PURE, OKAY?
LIAR...
I JUST WANT TO BE CLUNG TO—
...I MEAN, RELIED ON BY AS MANY PEOPLE AS POSSIBLE.
INCLUD-ING, FOR EXAM-PLE...

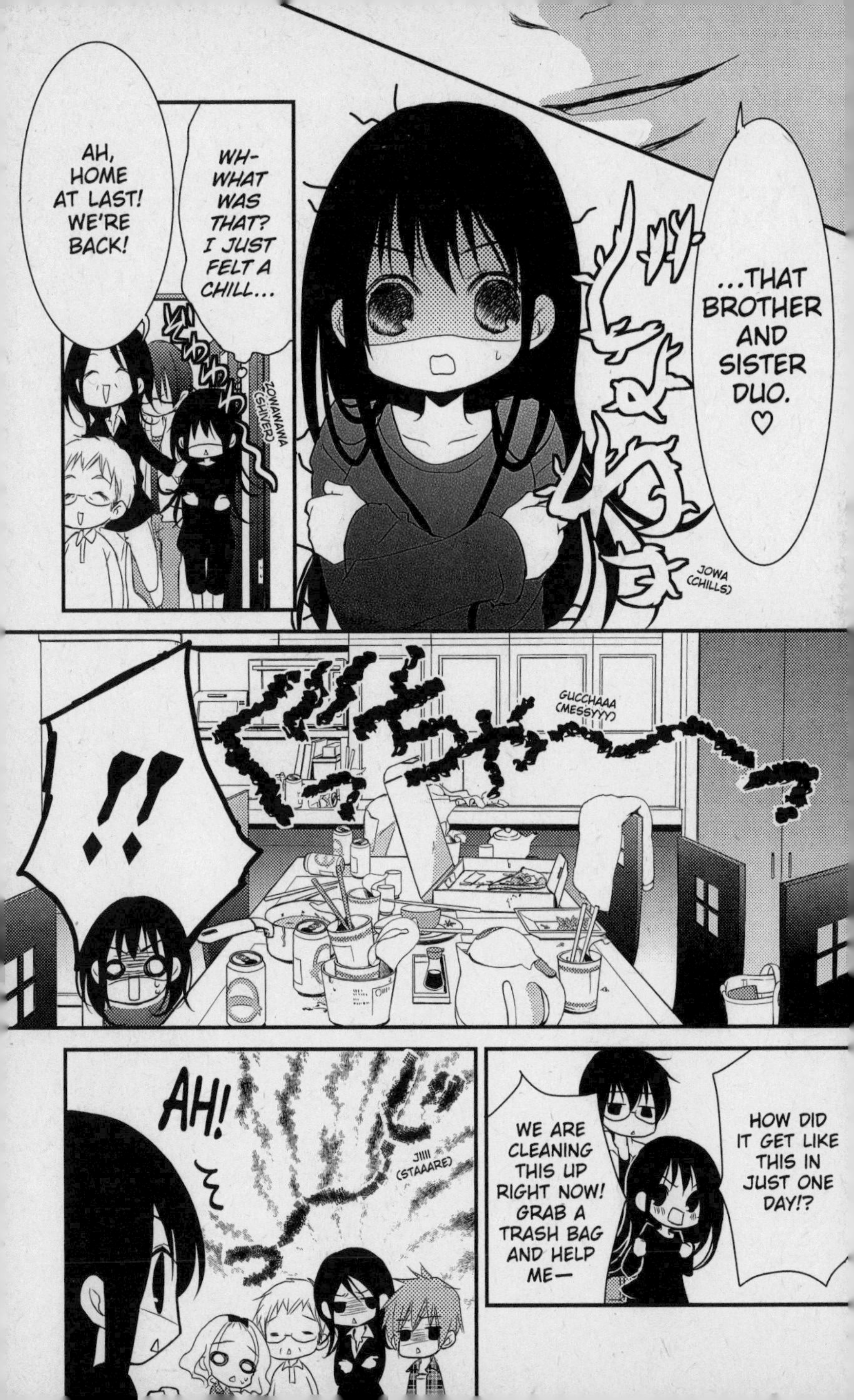
...THAT BROTHER AND SISTER DUO. ♡
JOWA (CHILLS)
WH- WHAT WAS THAT? I JUST FELT A CHILL...
ZOWAWAWA (SHIVER)
AH, HOME AT LAST! WE'RE BACK!
GUCCHAAA (MESSYYY)
!!
HOW DID IT GET LIKE THIS IN JUST ONE DAY!?
WE ARE CLEANING THIS UP RIGHT NOW! GRAB A TRASH BAG AND HELP ME—
JIIII (STAAARE)
AH!

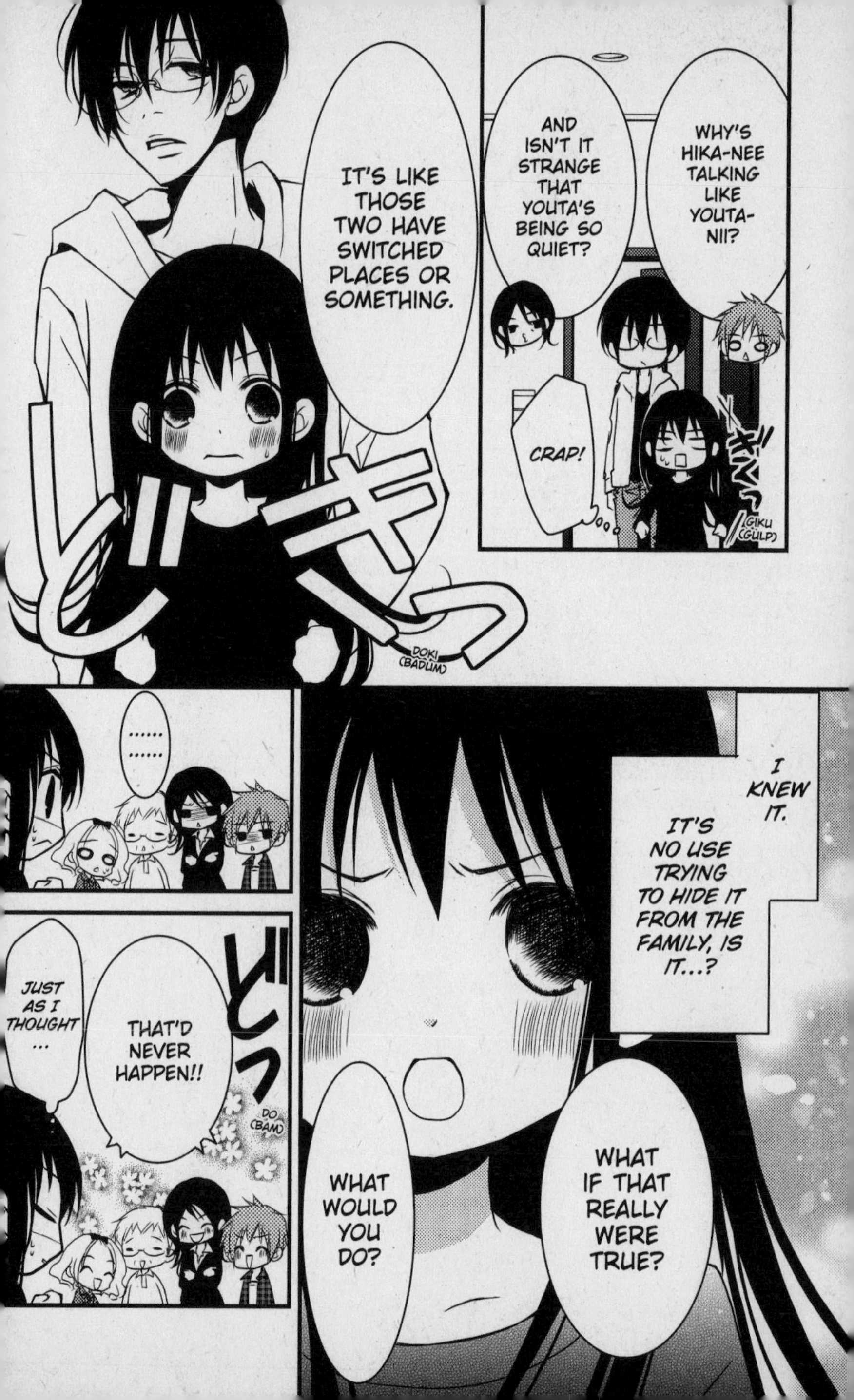
WHY'S HIKA-NEE TALKING LIKE YOUTA-NII?
AND ISN'T IT STRANGE THAT YOUTA'S BEING SO QUIET?
GIKU (GULP)
CRAP!
IT'S LIKE THOSE TWO HAVE SWITCHED PLACES OR SOMETHING.
DOKI (BADUM)
I KNEW IT.
IT'S NO USE TRYING TO HIDE IT FROM THE FAMILY, IS IT...?
WHAT IF THAT REALLY WERE TRUE?
WHAT WOULD YOU DO?
....
THAT'D NEVER HAPPEN!!
DO (BAM)
JUST AS I THOUGHT...

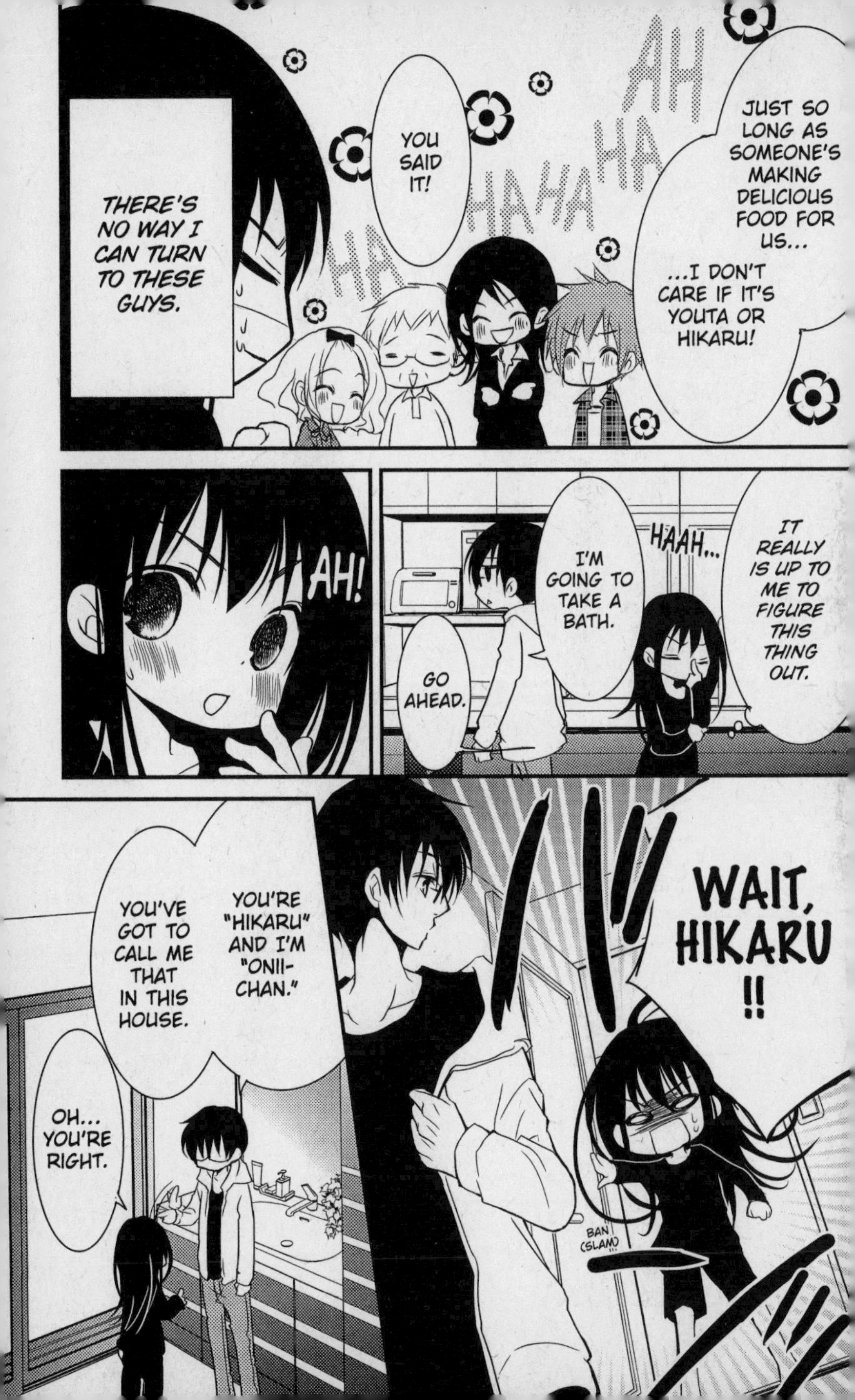

JUST SO LONG AS SOMEONE'S MAKING DELICIOUS FOOD FOR US...
...I DON'T CARE IF IT'S YOUTA OR HIKARU!
AH HA HA HA HA HA
YOU SAID IT!
THERE'S NO WAY I CAN TURN TO THESE GUYS.
IT REALLY IS UP TO ME TO FIGURE THIS THING OUT.
HAAH...
I'M GOING TO TAKE A BATH.
GO AHEAD.
AH!
WAIT, HIKARU!!
BAN (SLAM)!!
YOU'RE "HIKARU" AND I'M "ONII-CHAN."
YOU'VE GOT TO CALL ME THAT IN THIS HOUSE.
OH... YOU'RE RIGHT.

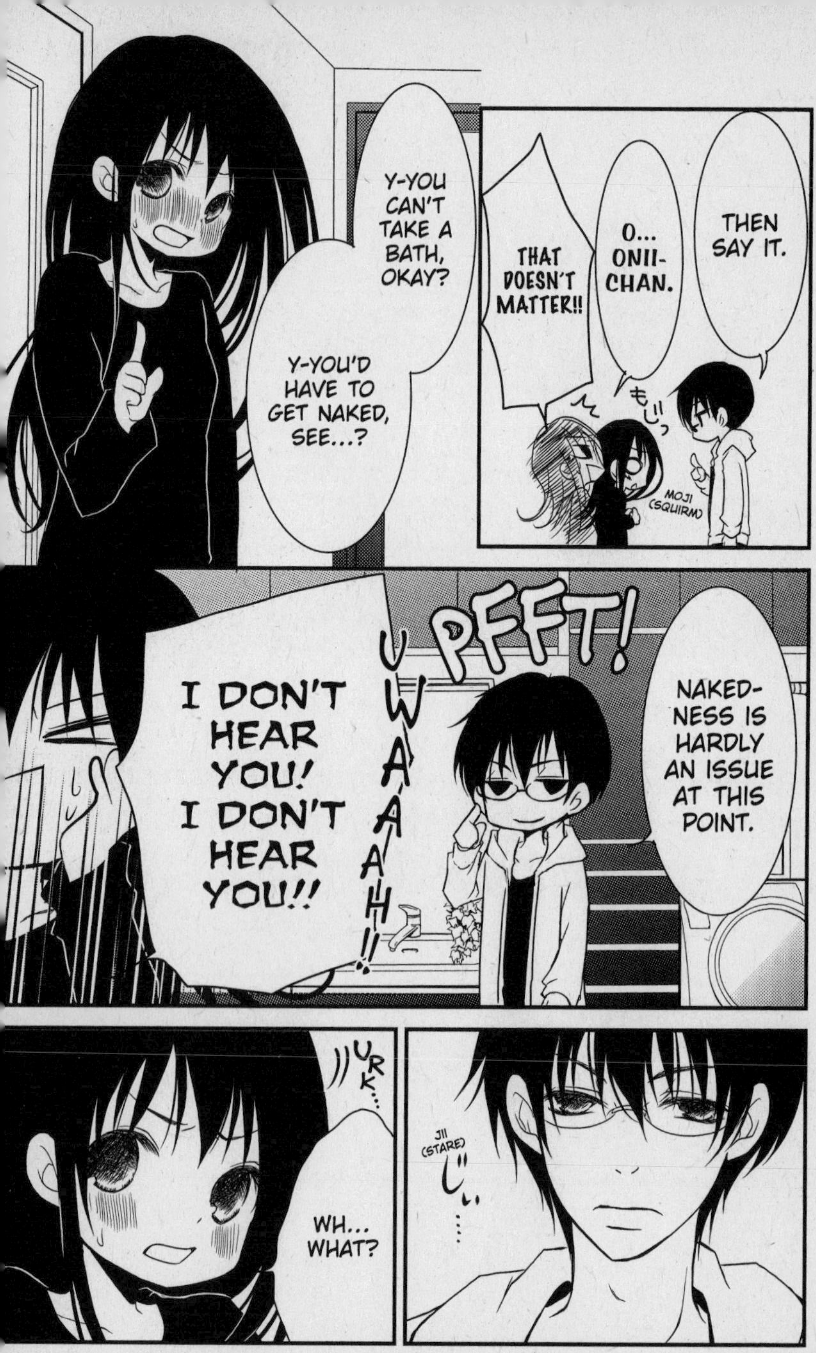
THEN SAY IT.
O... ONII-CHAN.
THAT DOESN'T MATTER!!
MOJI (SQUIRM)
Y-YOU CAN'T TAKE A BATH, OKAY?
Y-YOU'D HAVE TO GET NAKED, SEE...?
NAKED-NESS IS HARDLY AN ISSUE AT THIS POINT.
PFFT!
UWAAAAH!!
I DON'T HEAR YOU! I DON'T HEAR YOU!!
JII (STARE)
URK...
WH... WHAT?

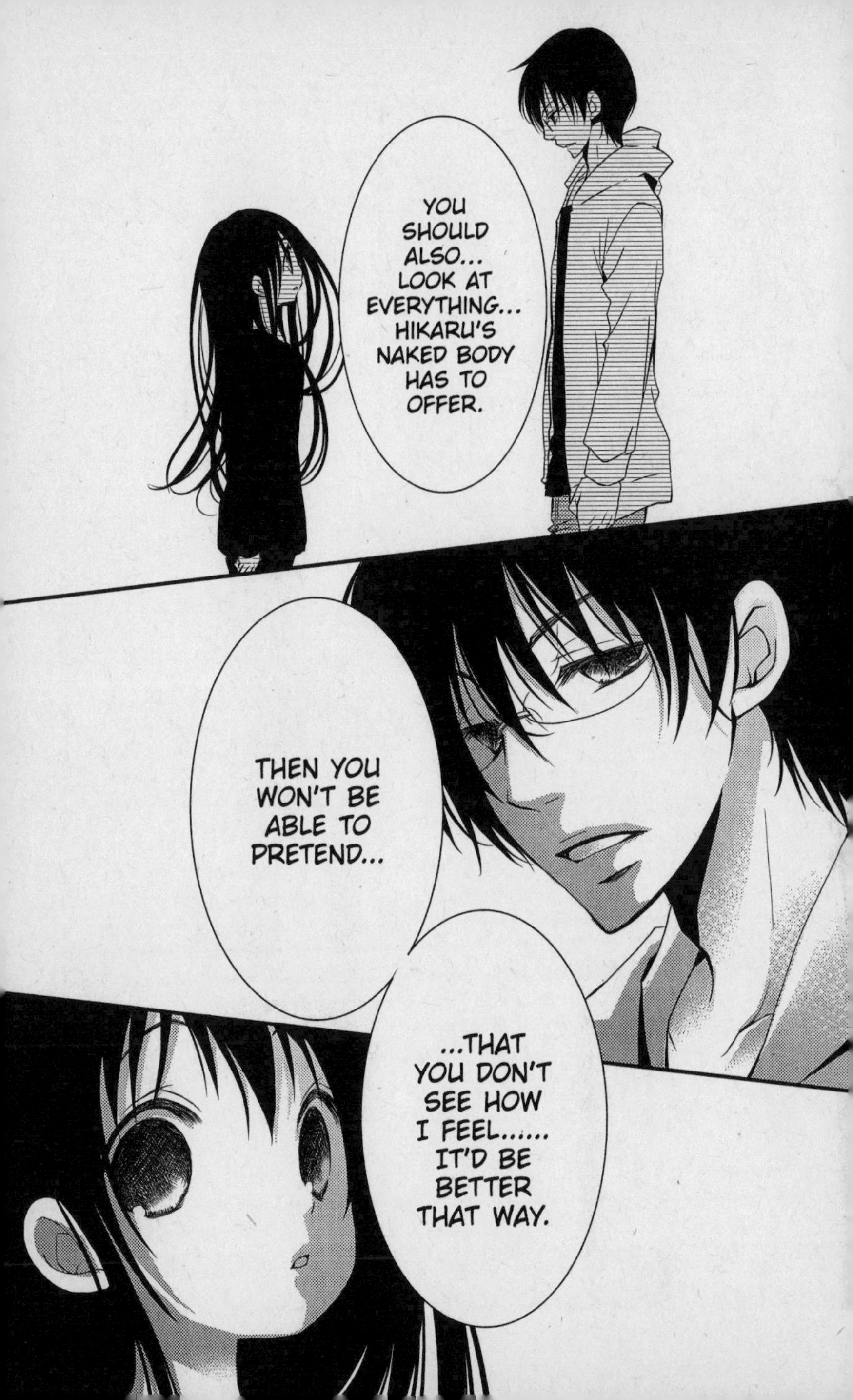
YOU SHOULD ALSO... LOOK AT EVERYTHING... HIKARU'S NAKED BODY HAS TO OFFER.
THEN YOU WON'T BE ABLE TO PRETEND...
...THAT YOU DON'T SEE HOW I FEEL...... IT'D BE BETTER THAT WAY.

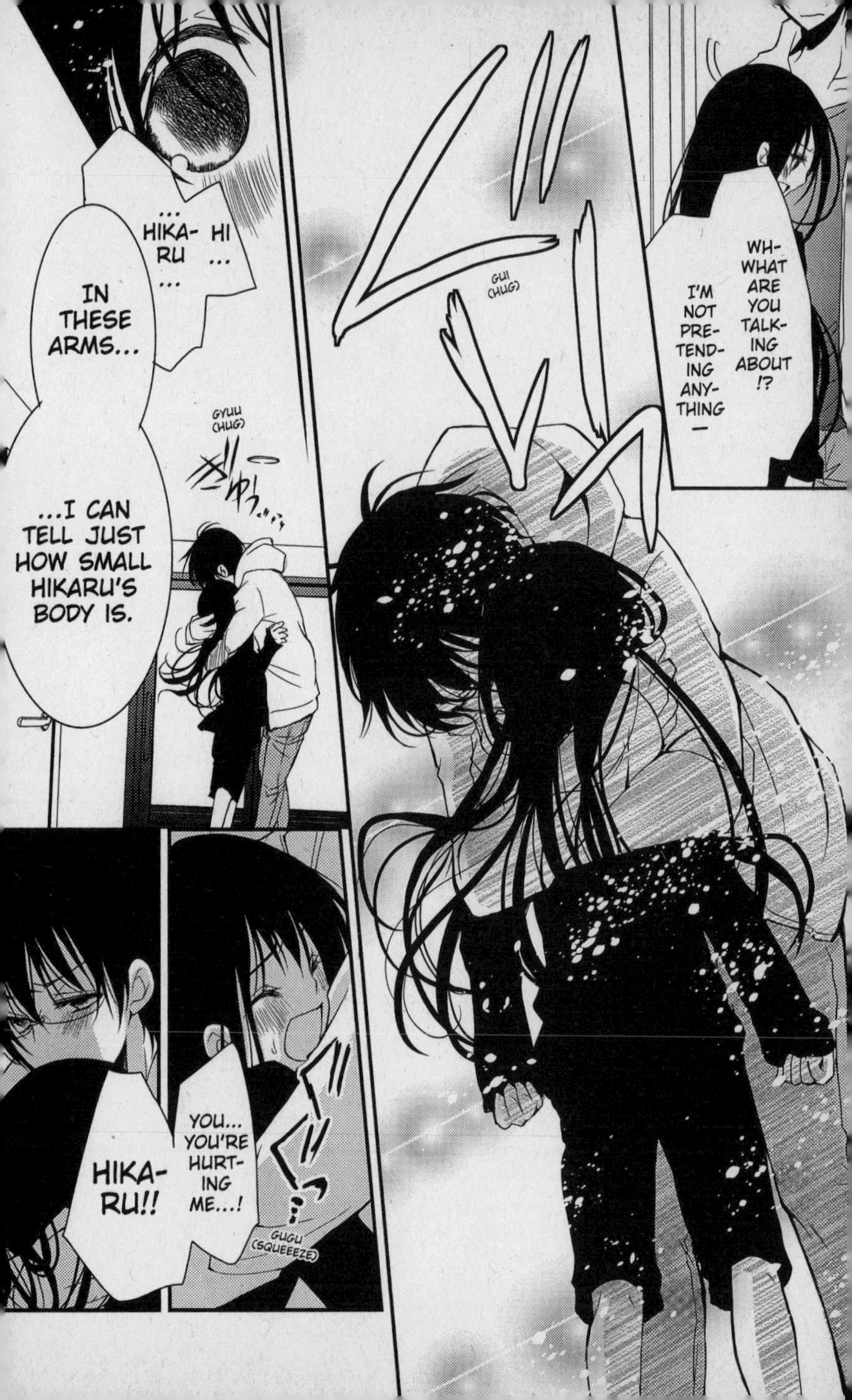
WH-WHAT ARE YOU TALKING ABOUT!?
I'M NOT PRETENDING ANYTHING—
GUI (HUG)
HI...
...HIKARU...
IN THESE ARMS...
GYUU (HUG)
...I CAN TELL JUST HOW SMALL HIKARU'S BODY IS.
YOU... YOU'RE HURTING ME...!
GUGU (SQUEEEZE)
HIKARU!!

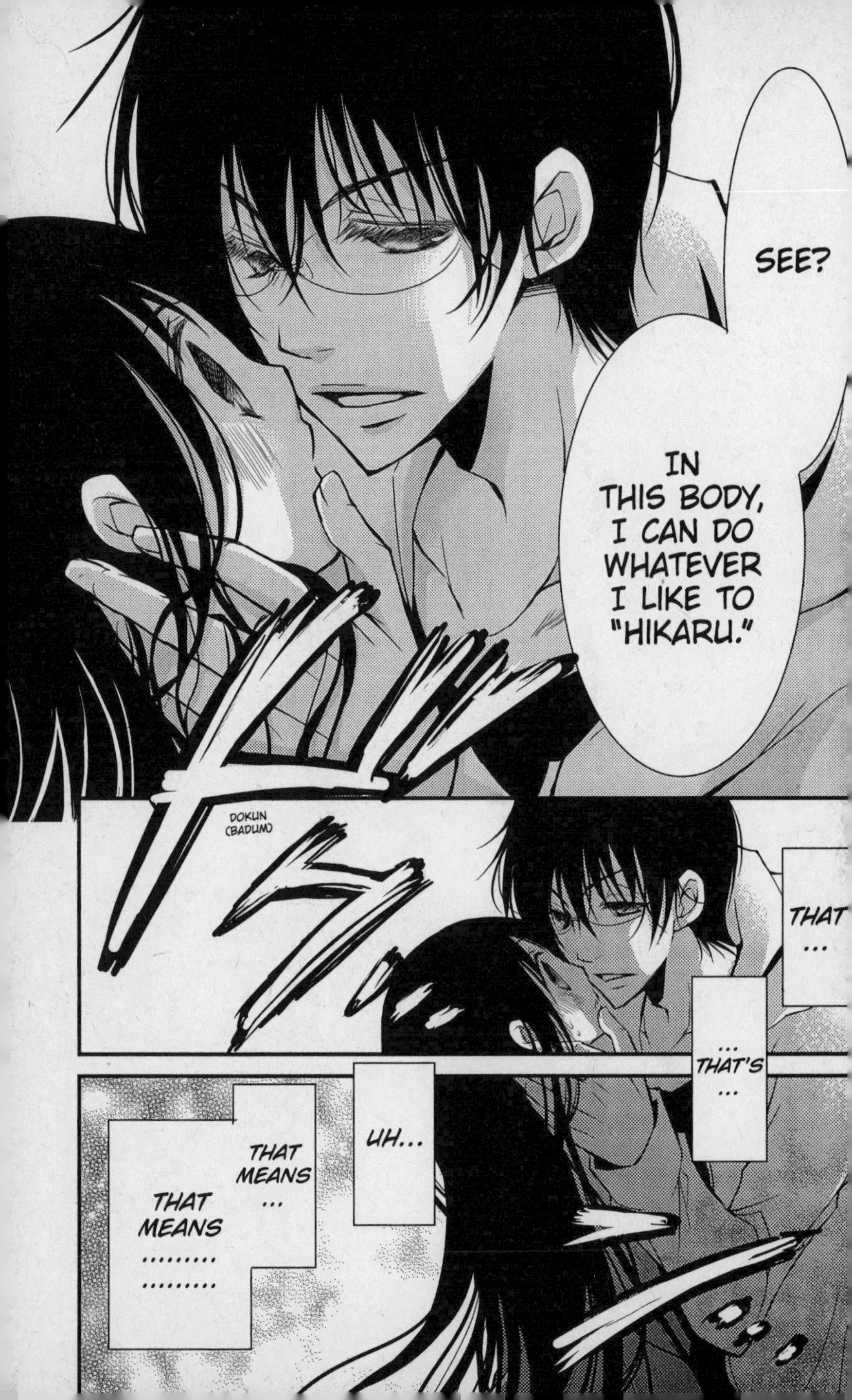
SEE?
IN THIS BODY, I CAN DO WHATEVER I LIKE TO "HIKARU."
DOKUN (BADUM)
THAT ...
... THAT'S ...
UH...
THAT MEANS ...
THAT MEANS ....
....

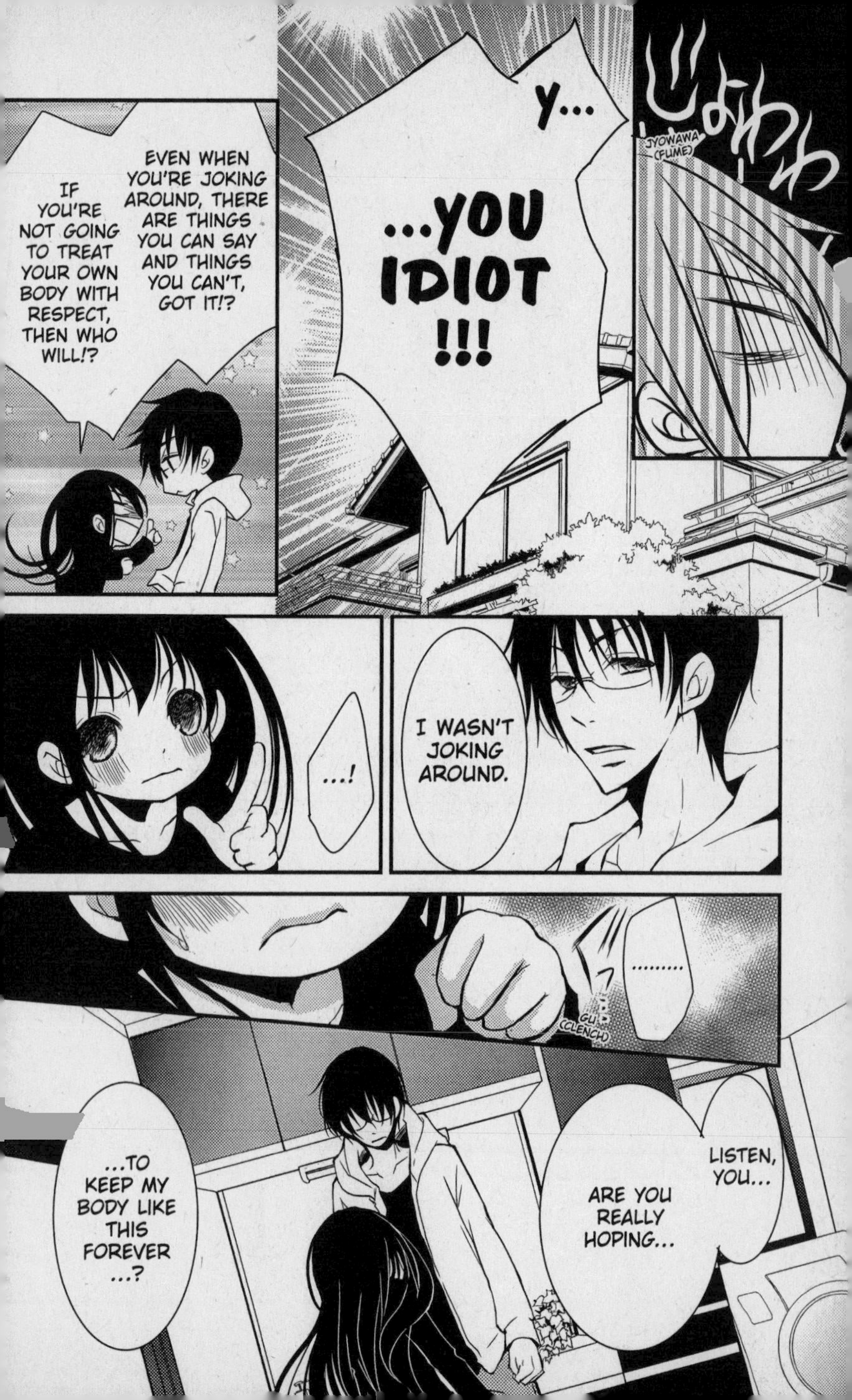
じょわわ
JYOWAWA (FUME)
Y...
...YOU IDIOT!!!
EVEN WHEN YOU'RE JOKING AROUND, THERE ARE THINGS YOU CAN SAY AND THINGS YOU CAN'T, GOT IT!?
IF YOU'RE NOT GOING TO TREAT YOUR OWN BODY WITH RESPECT, THEN WHO WILL!?
I WASN'T JOKING AROUND.
...!
....
GU (CLENCH)
LISTEN, YOU...
ARE YOU REALLY HOPING...
...TO KEEP MY BODY LIKE THIS FOREVER...?

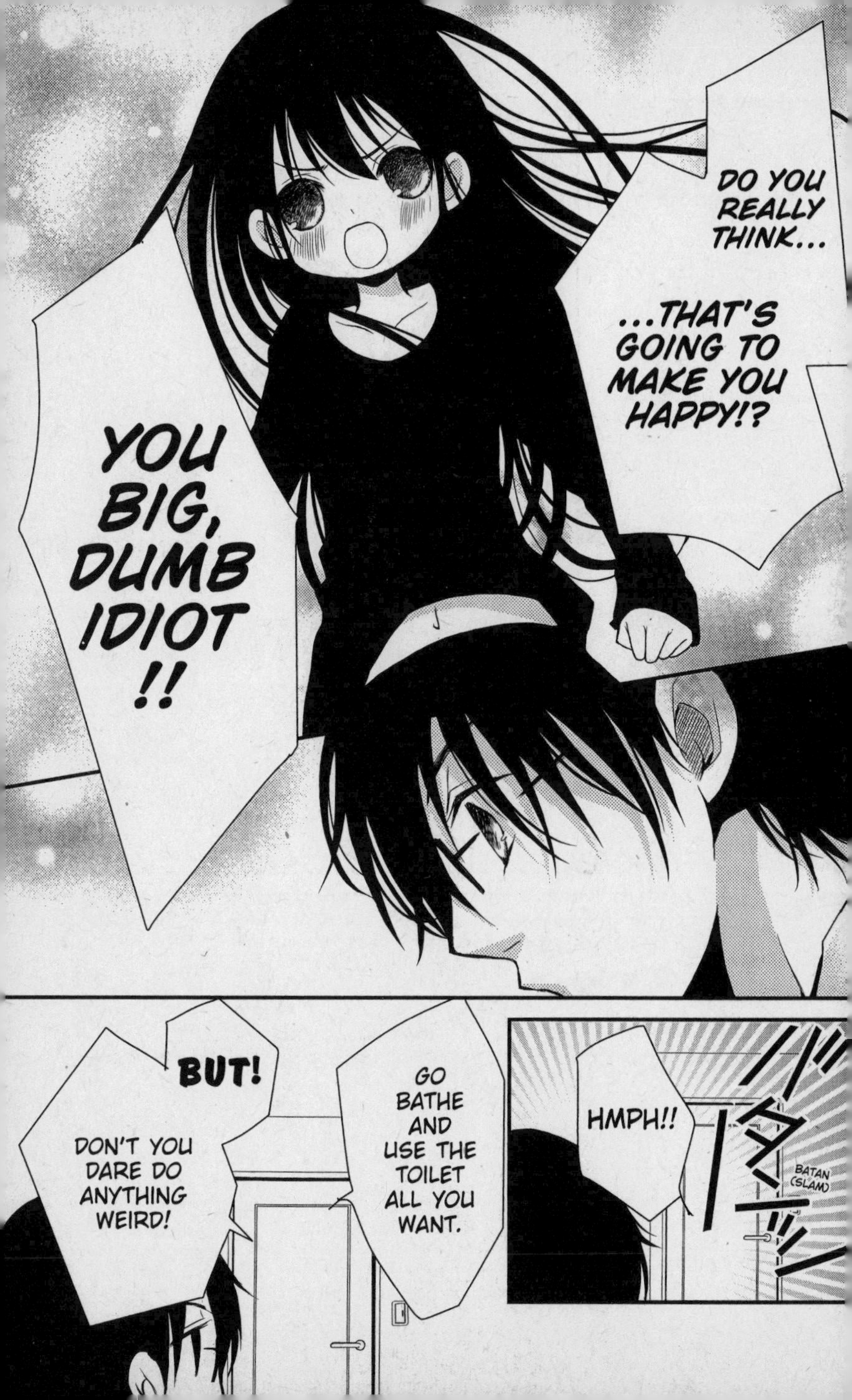
DO YOU REALLY THINK...
...THAT'S GOING TO MAKE YOU HAPPY!?
YOU BIG, DUMB IDIOT!!
HMPH!!
BATAN (SLAM)
GO BATHE AND USE THE TOILET ALL YOU WANT.
BUT! DON'T YOU DARE DO ANYTHING WEIRD!

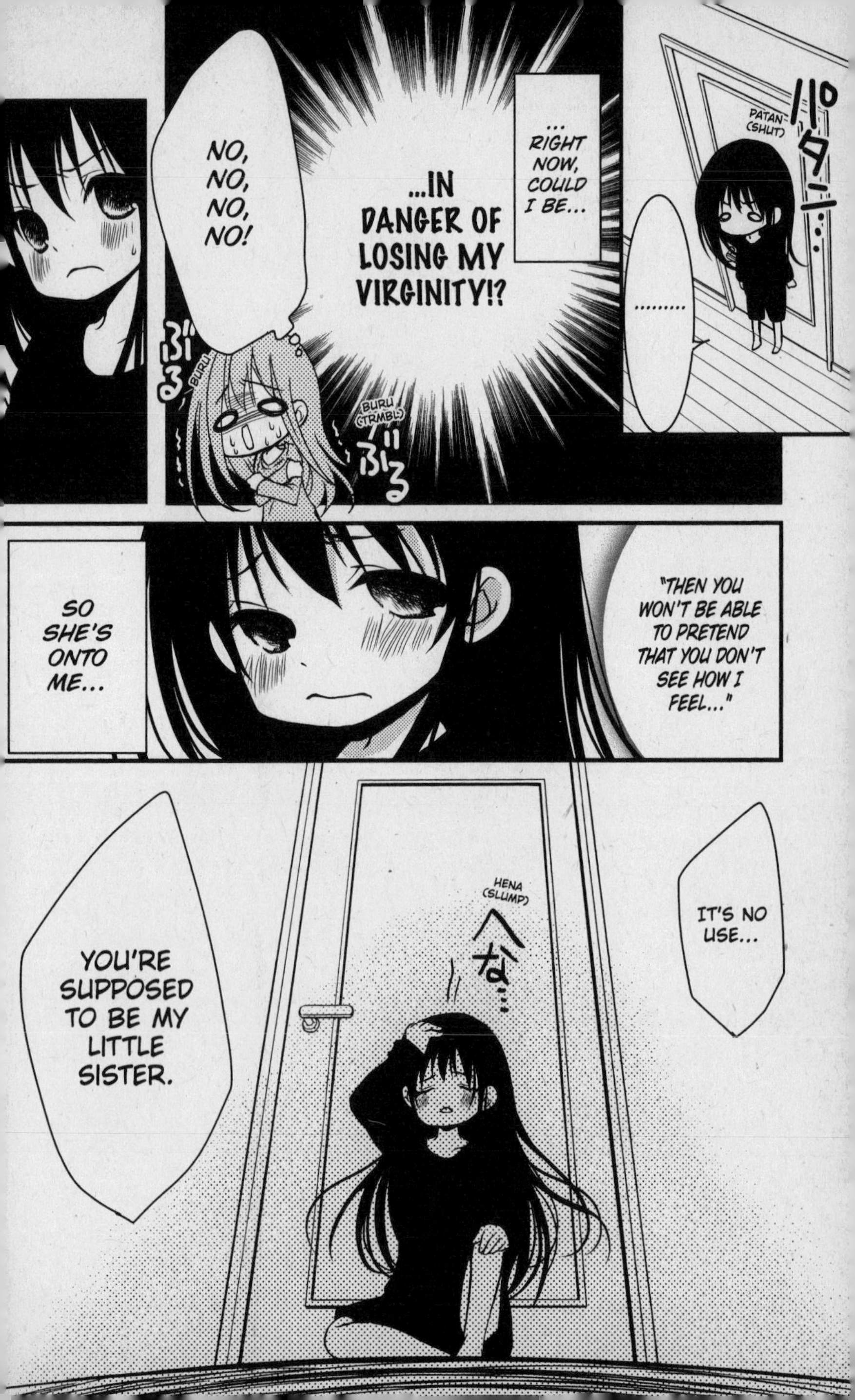

PATAN (SHUT)
パタン…
....
...RIGHT NOW, COULD I BE...
...IN DANGER OF LOSING MY VIRGINITY!?
BURU (TRMBL)
ぶる
NO, NO, NO, NO!
BURU
ぶる
"THEN YOU WON'T BE ABLE TO PRETEND THAT YOU DON'T SEE HOW I FEEL..."
SO SHE'S ONTO ME...
IT'S NO USE...
HENA (SLUMP)
へな…
YOU'RE SUPPOSED TO BE MY LITTLE SISTER.

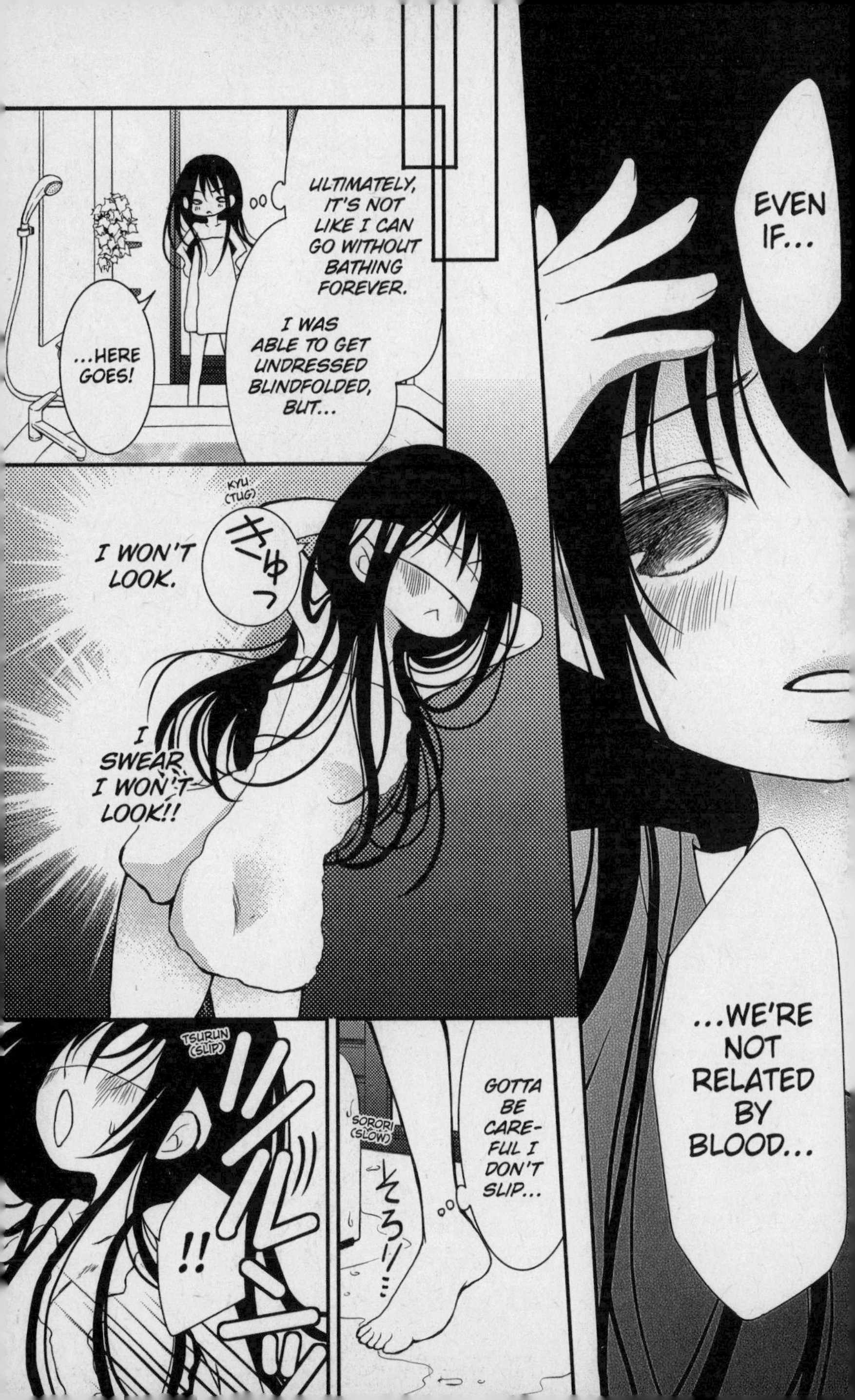
EVEN IF...
...WE'RE NOT RELATED BY BLOOD...
ULTIMATELY, IT'S NOT LIKE I CAN GO WITHOUT BATHING FOREVER.
I WAS ABLE TO GET UNDRESSED BLINDFOLDED, BUT...
...HERE GOES!
KYU (TUG)
きゅっ
I WON'T LOOK.
I SWEAR I WON'T LOOK!!
SORORI (SLOW)
GOTTA BE CARE-FUL I DON'T SLIP...
TSURUN (SLIP)
!!

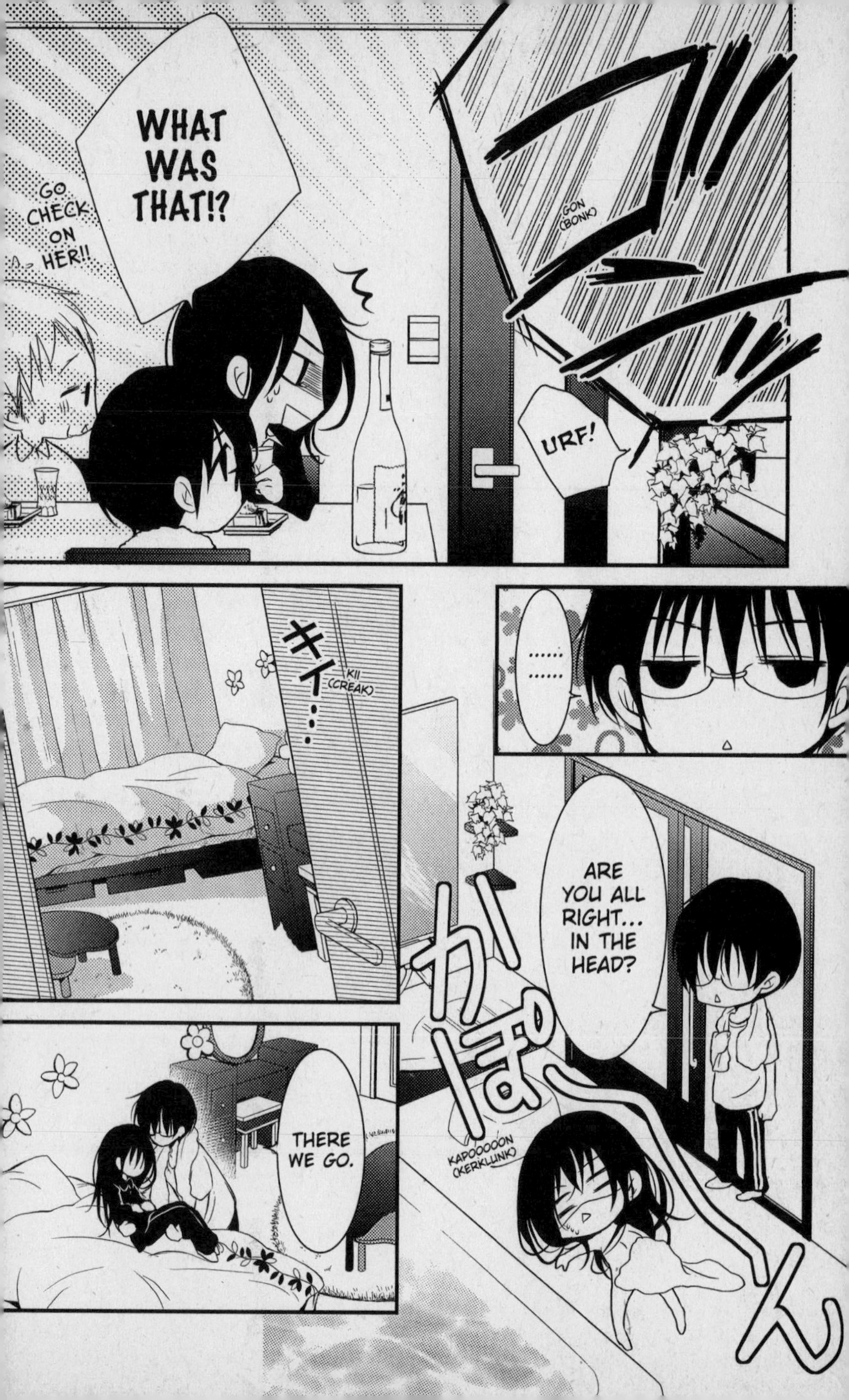
GON (BONK)
URF!
WHAT WAS THAT!?
GO CHECK ON HER!!
......
......
ARE YOU ALL RIGHT... IN THE HEAD?
かぽーん
KAPOOOOON (KERKLUNK)
キイ…
KII (CREAK)
THERE WE GO.

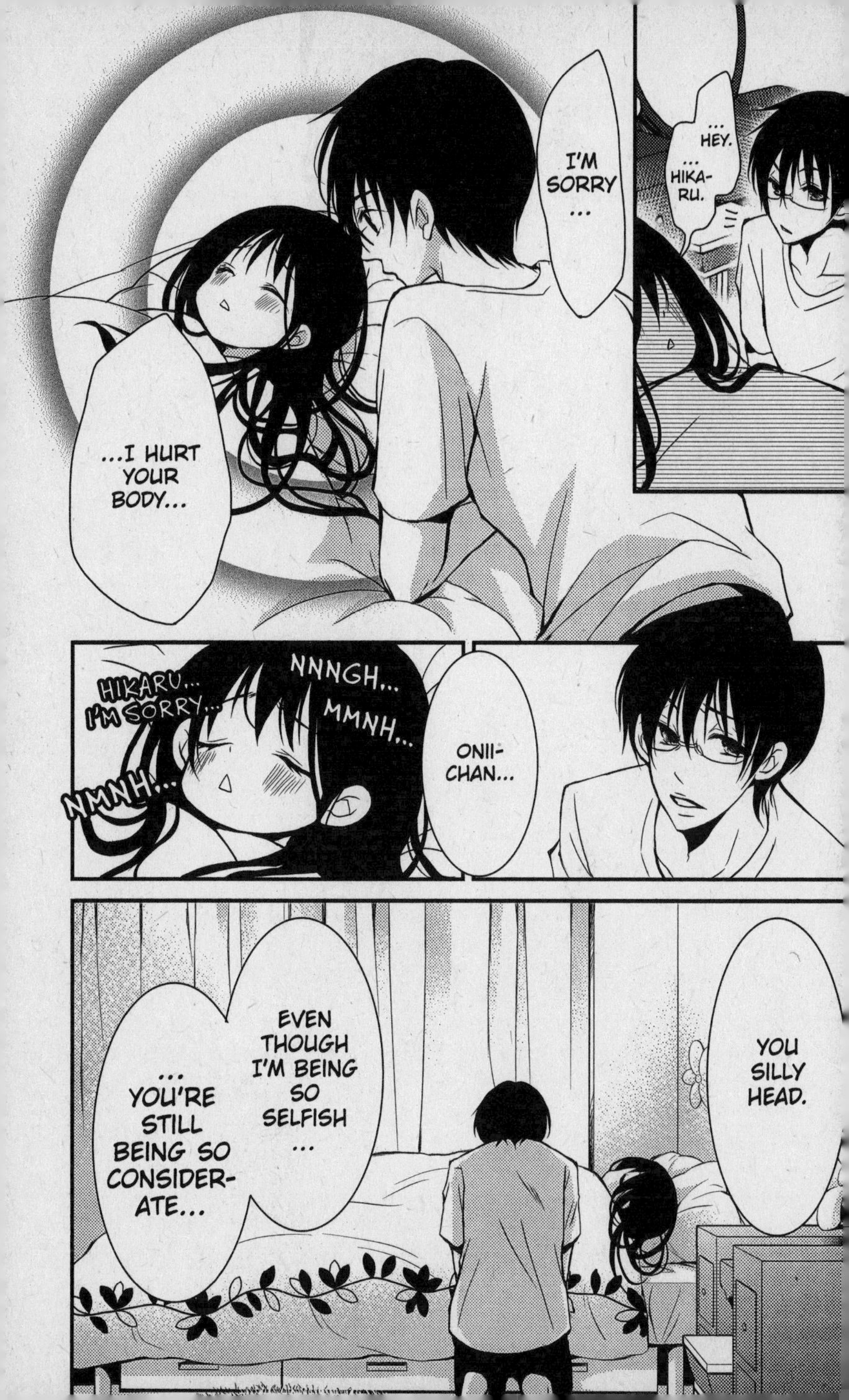
... HEY. ... HIKARU.
I'M SORRY ...
...I HURT YOUR BODY...
ONII-CHAN...
NNNGH... MMNH...
HIKARU... I'M SORRY...
NMNH...
YOU SILLY HEAD.
EVEN THOUGH I'M BEING SO SELFISH ...
... YOU'RE STILL BEING SO CONSIDER-ATE...

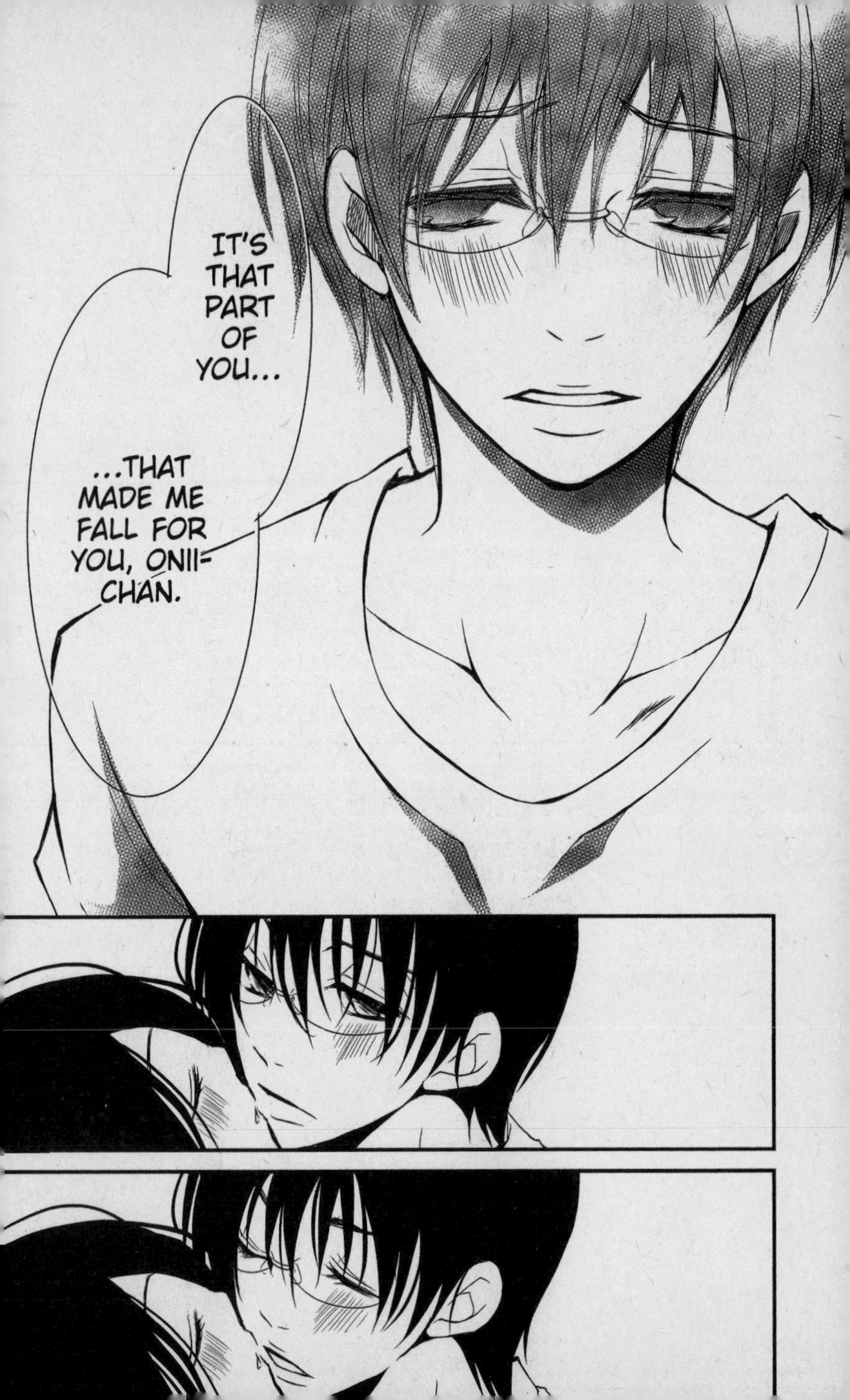
IT'S THAT PART OF YOU...
...THAT MADE ME FALL FOR YOU, ONII-CHAN.

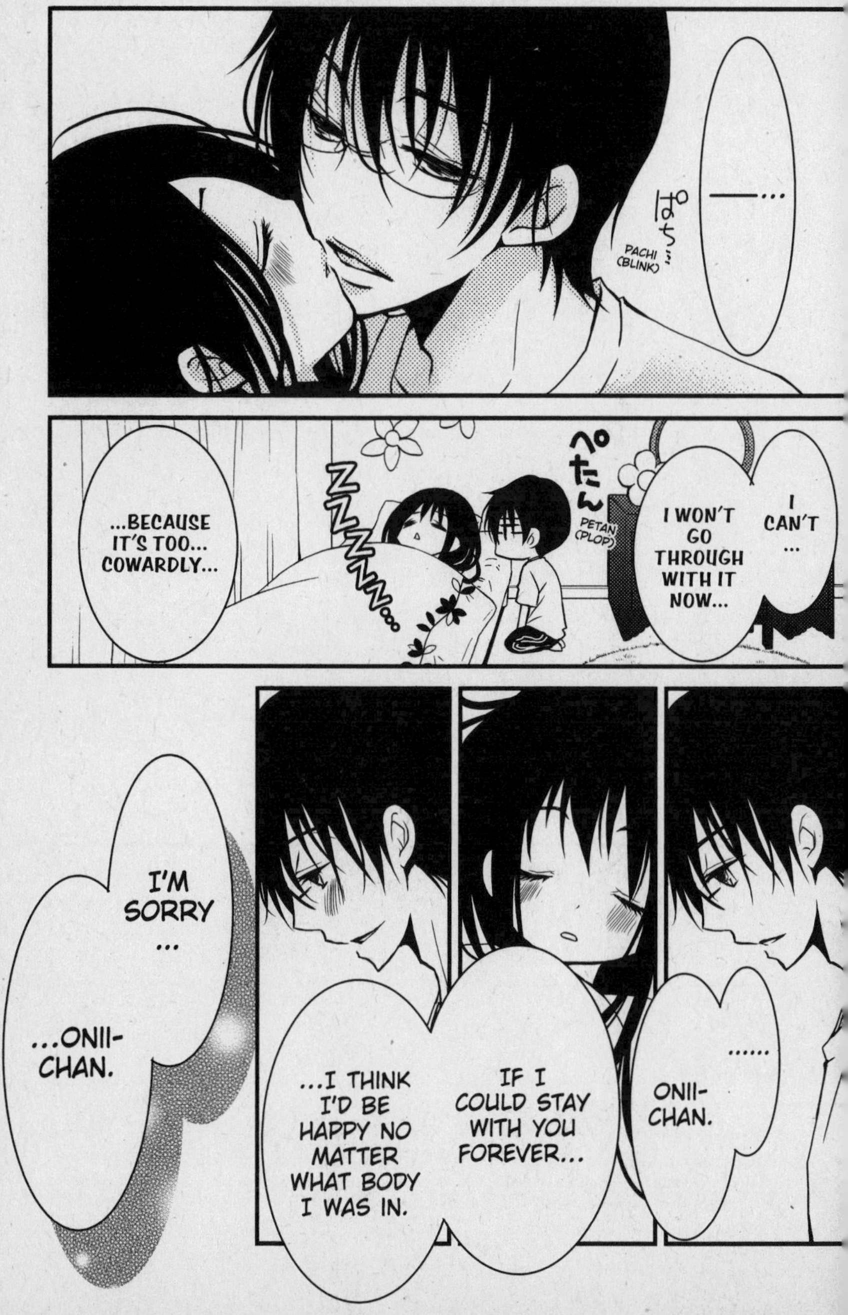
—...
ぱち…
PACHI (BLINK)
I CAN'T ...
I WON'T GO THROUGH WITH IT NOW...
ぺたん
PETAN (PLOP)
ZZZZZZ...
...BECAUSE IT'S TOO... COWARDLY...
......
ONII-CHAN.
IF I COULD STAY WITH YOU FOREVER...
...I THINK I'D BE HAPPY NO MATTER WHAT BODY I WAS IN.
I'M SORRY ...
...ONII-CHAN.

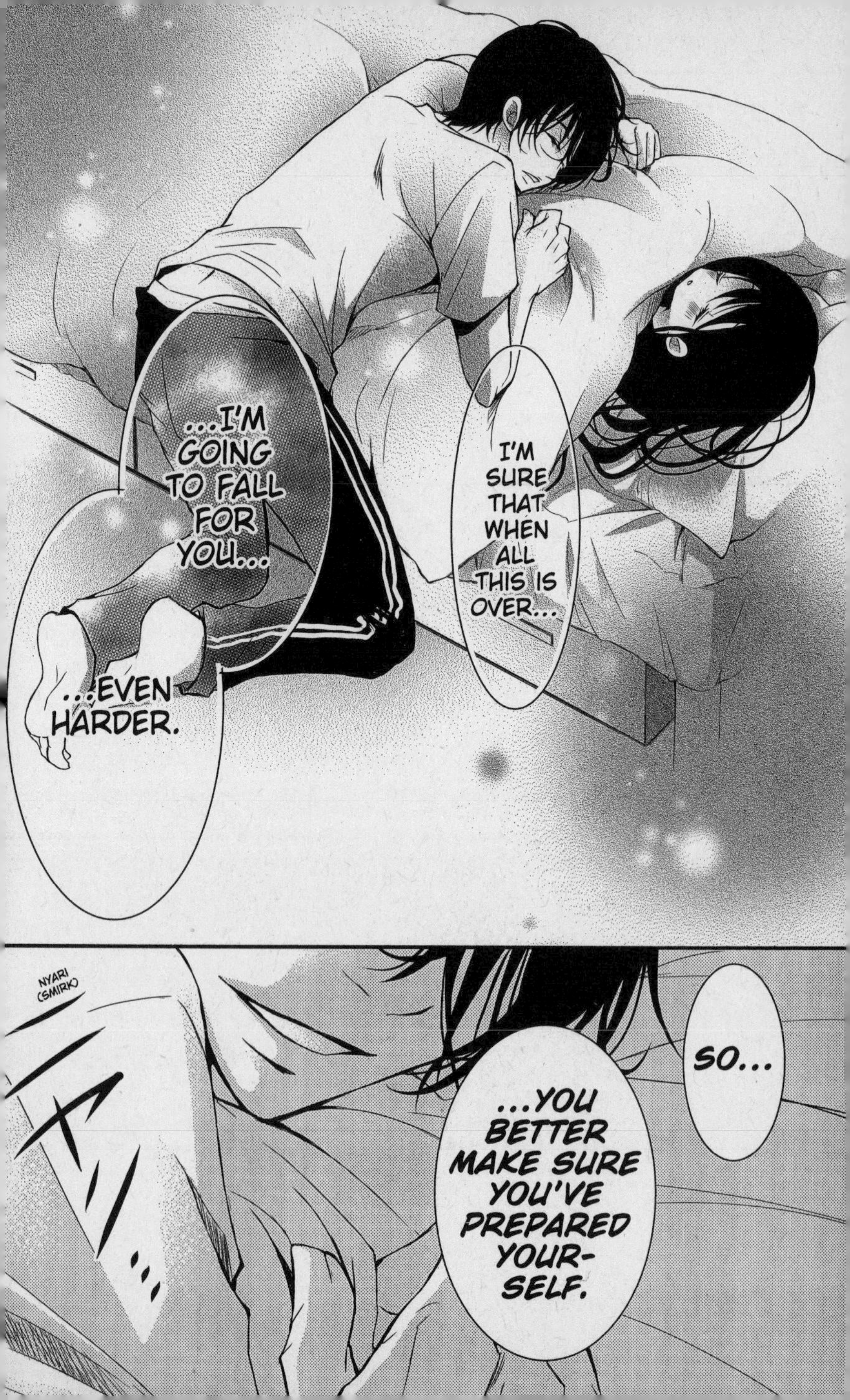
I'M SURE THAT WHEN ALL THIS IS OVER...
...I'M GOING TO FALL FOR YOU...
...EVEN HARDER.
SO...
...YOU BETTER MAKE SURE YOU'VE PREPARED YOUR-SELF.
NYARI (SMIRK)

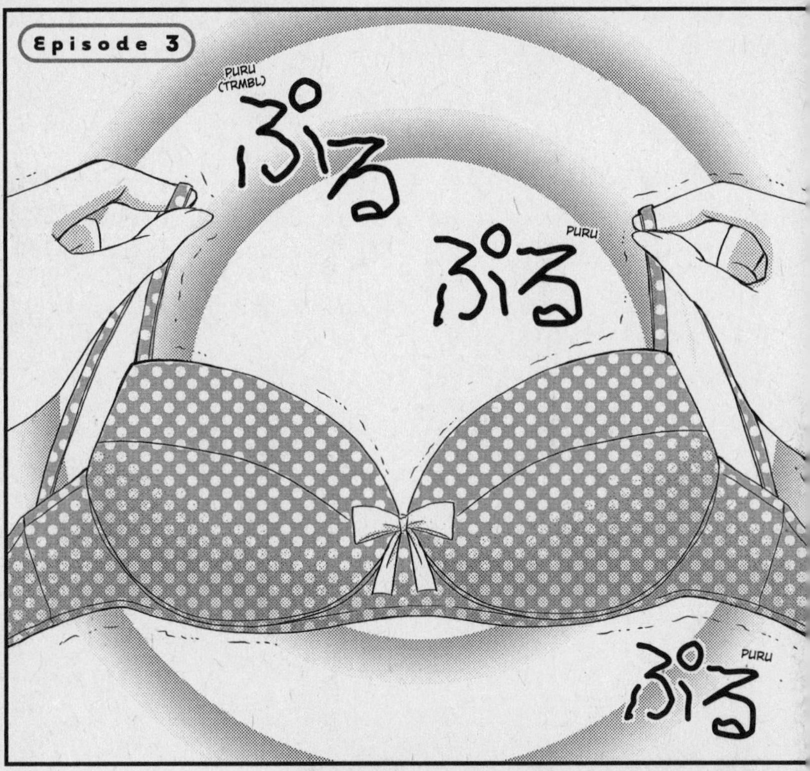
Episode 3
PURU (TRMBL)
ぷる
PURU
ぷる
PURU
ぷる

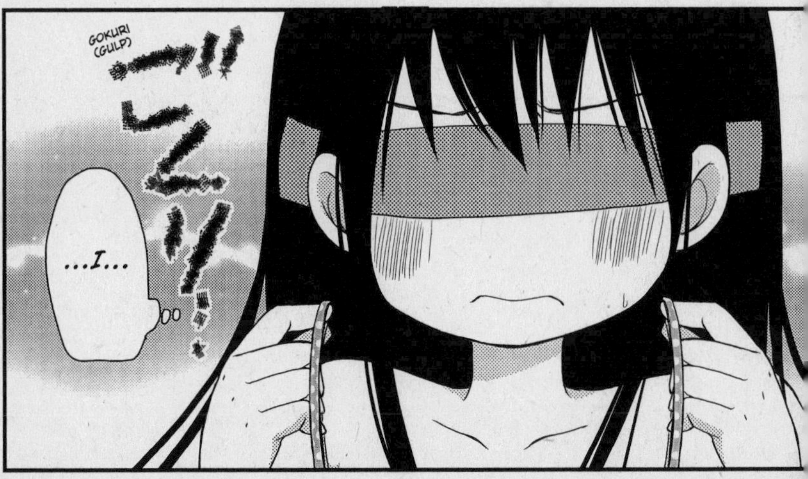
GOKURI (GULP)
...I...

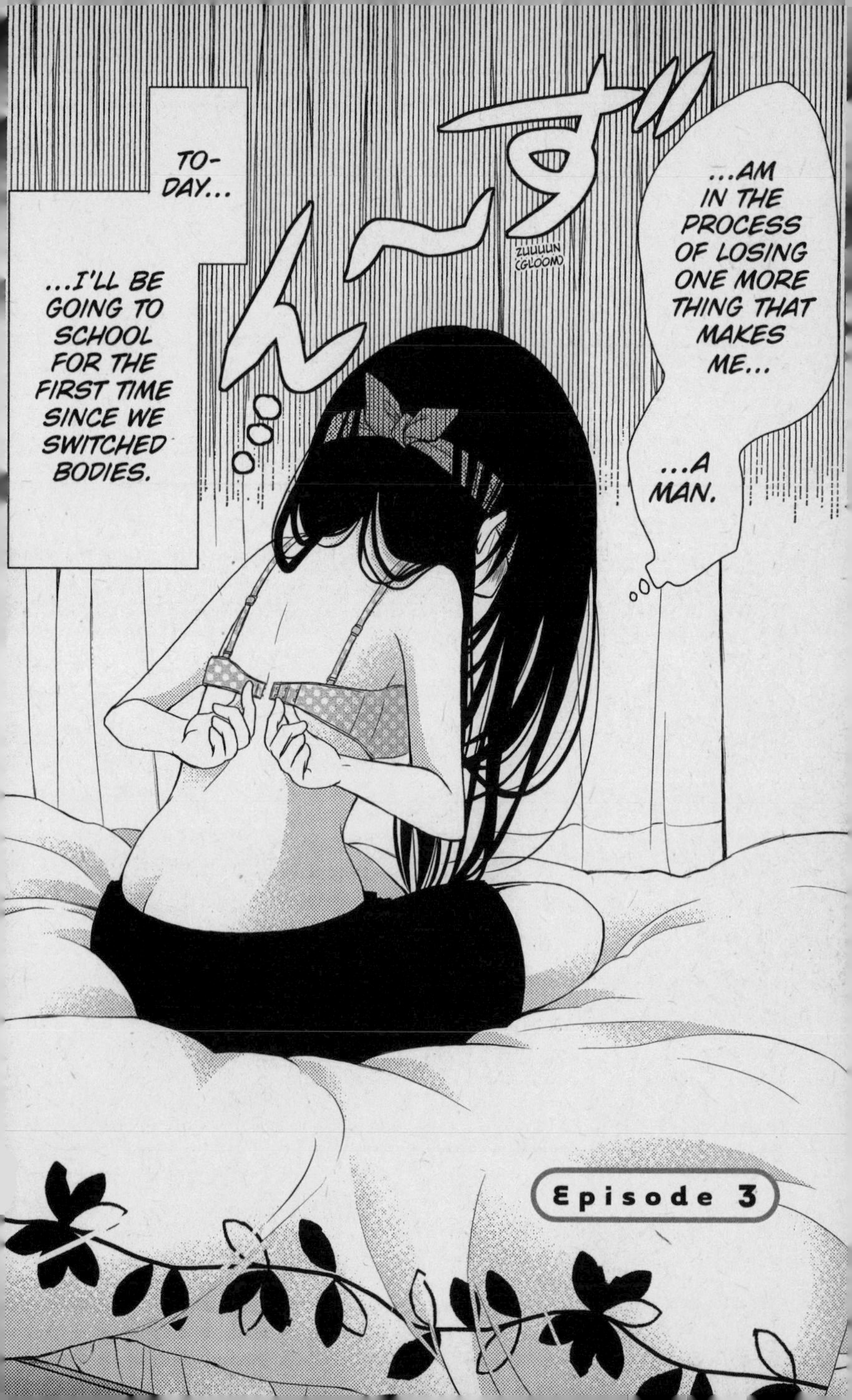
TO-DAY...
...I'LL BE GOING TO SCHOOL FOR THE FIRST TIME SINCE WE SWITCHED BODIES.
ZUUUUN (GLOOM)
...AM IN THE PROCESS OF LOSING ONE MORE THING THAT MAKES ME...
...A MAN.
Episode 3

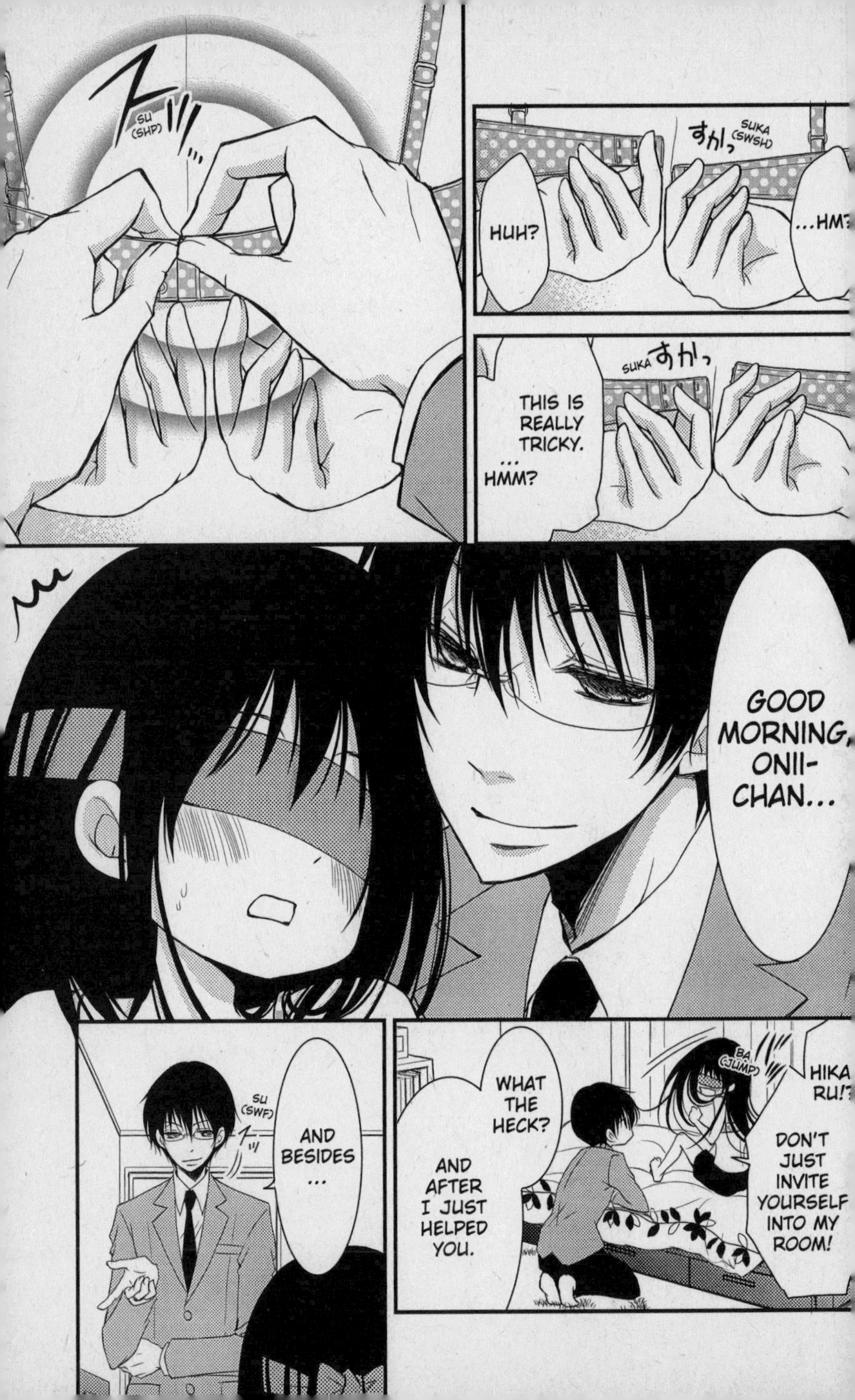
すかっ SUKA (SWSH)
...HM?
HUH?
SUKA すかっ
THIS IS REALLY TRICKY.
... HMM?
SU (SHP)
GOOD MORNING, ONII-CHAN...
HIKARU!?
BA (JUMP)
DON'T JUST INVITE YOURSELF INTO MY ROOM!
WHAT THE HECK?
AND AFTER I JUST HELPED YOU.
SU (SWF)
AND BESIDES ...

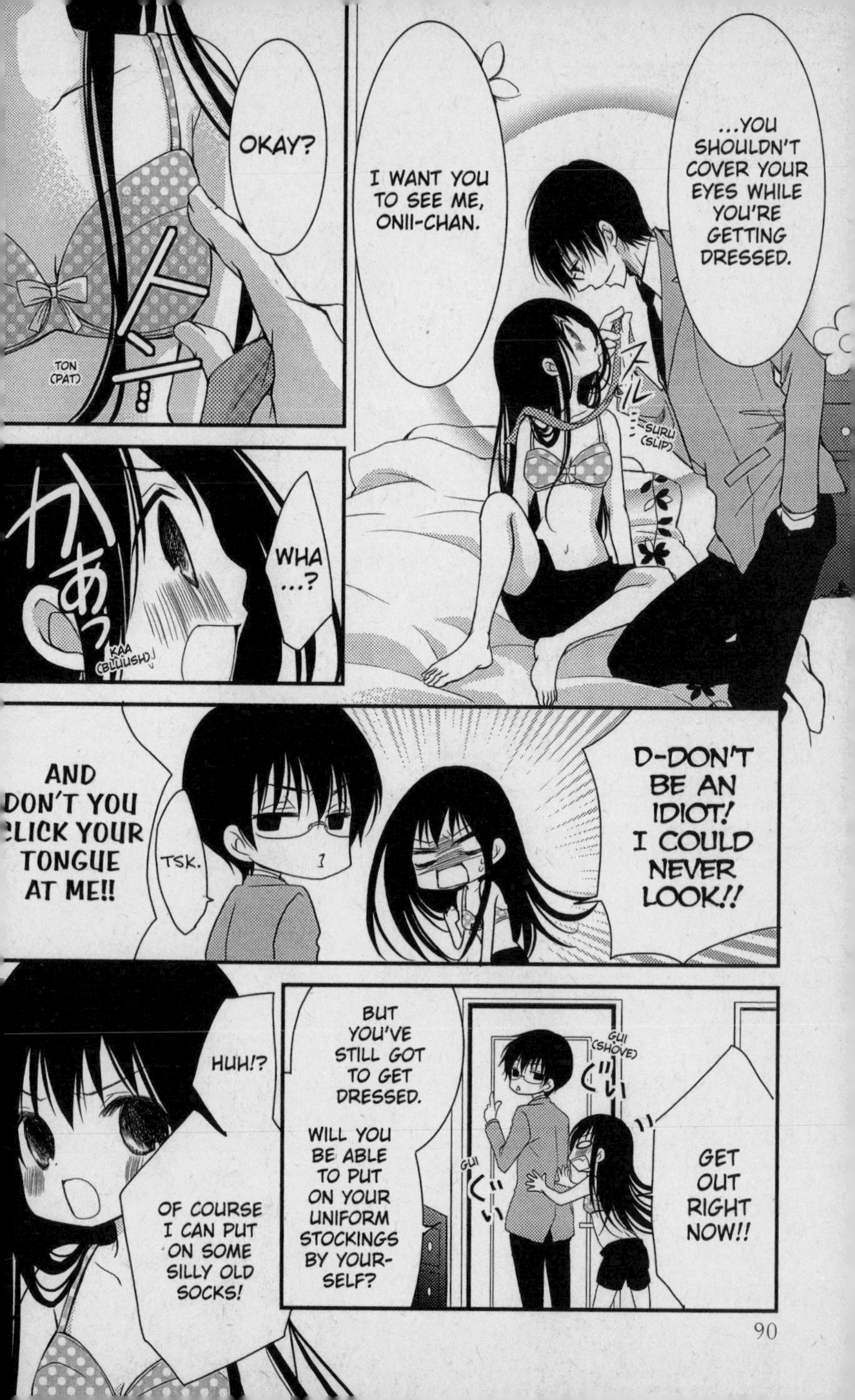
...YOU SHOULDN'T COVER YOUR EYES WHILE YOU'RE GETTING DRESSED.
I WANT YOU TO SEE ME, ONII-CHAN.
SURU (SLIP)
OKAY?
TON (PAT)
WHA...?
KAA (BLUUSH)
D-DON'T BE AN IDIOT! I COULD NEVER LOOK!!
TSK.
AND DON'T YOU CLICK YOUR TONGUE AT ME!!
GET OUT RIGHT NOW!!
GUI (SHOVE)
GUI
BUT YOU'VE STILL GOT TO GET DRESSED.
WILL YOU BE ABLE TO PUT ON YOUR UNIFORM STOCKINGS BY YOUR-SELF?
HUH!?
OF COURSE I CAN PUT ON SOME SILLY OLD SOCKS!

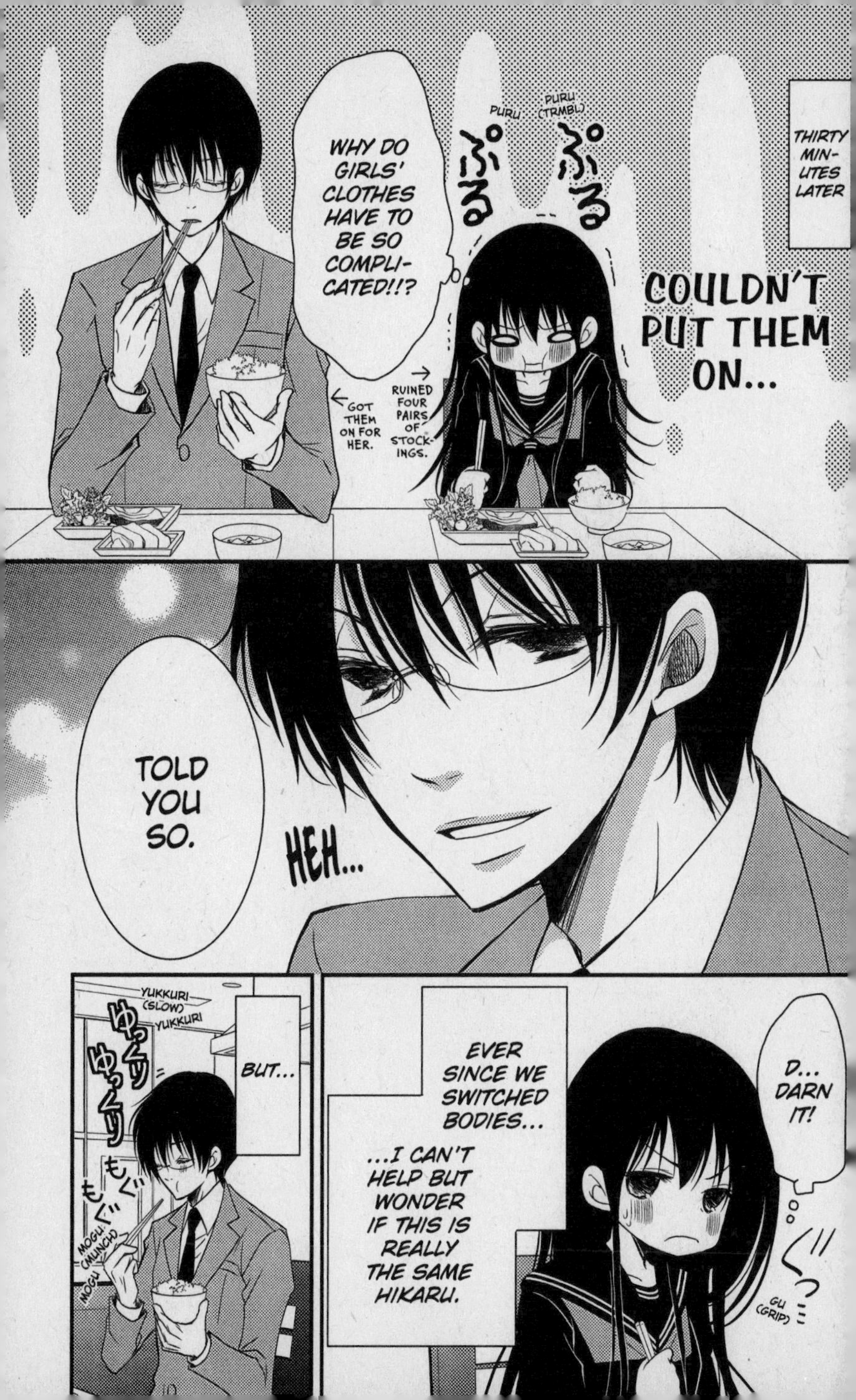
THIRTY MIN-UTES LATER
COULDN'T PUT THEM ON...
ぷる ぷる
PURU PURU (TRMBL)
WHY DO GIRLS' CLOTHES HAVE TO BE SO COMPLI-CATED!!?
RUINED FOUR PAIRS OF STOCK-INGS.
GOT THEM ON FOR HER.
HEH...
TOLD YOU SO.
D... DARN IT!
ぐっ
GU (GRIP)
EVER SINCE WE SWITCHED BODIES...
...I CAN'T HELP BUT WONDER IF THIS IS REALLY THE SAME HIKARU.
BUT...
ゆっくり ゆっくり
YUKKURI (SLOW) YUKKURI
もぐ もぐ
MOGU (MUNCH) MOGU

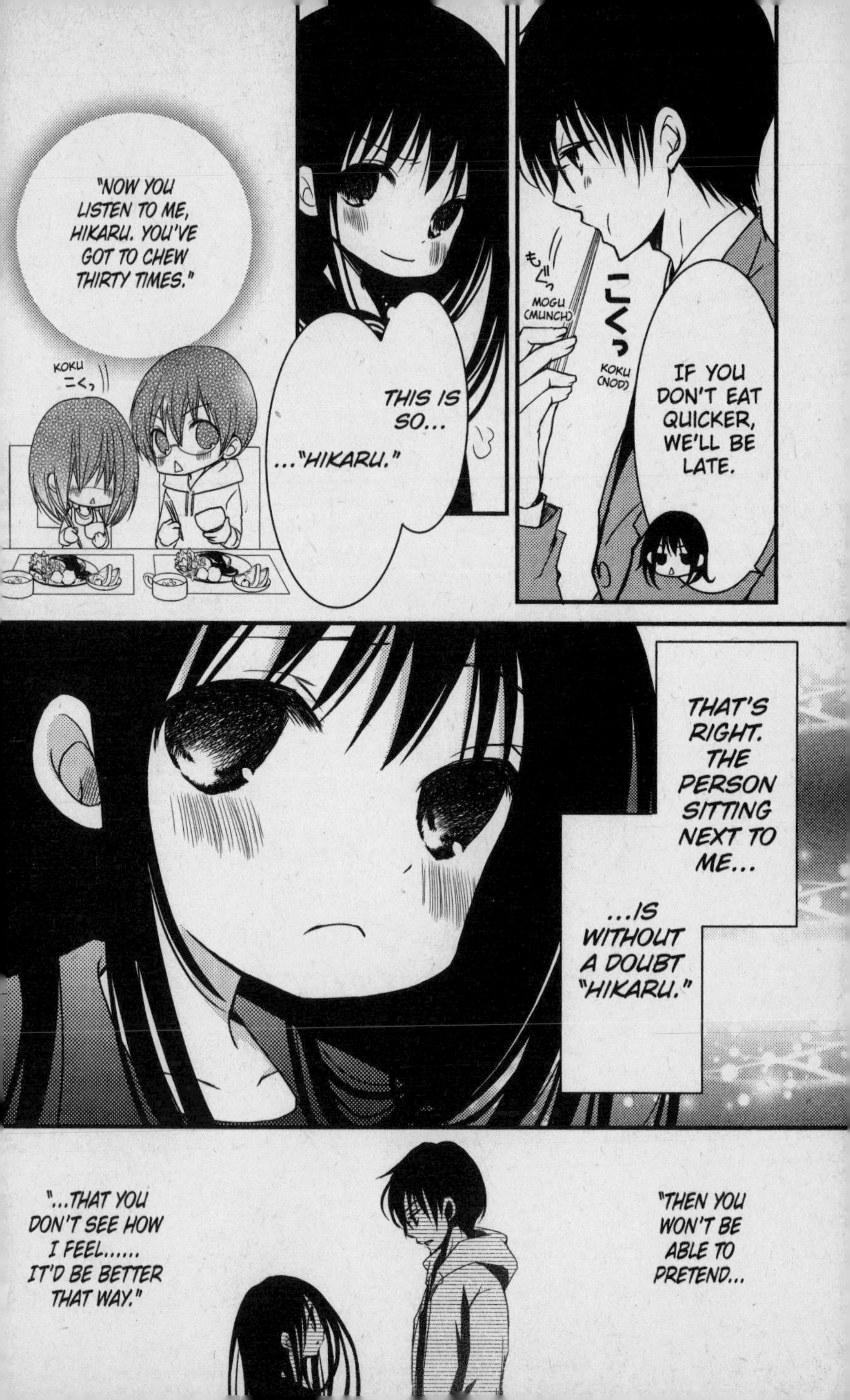
IF YOU DON'T EAT QUICKER, WE'LL BE LATE.
こくっ KOKU (NOD)
もぐっ MOGU (MUNCH)
THIS IS SO...
..."HIKARU."
"NOW YOU LISTEN TO ME, HIKARU. YOU'VE GOT TO CHEW THIRTY TIMES."
KOKU こくっ
THAT'S RIGHT. THE PERSON SITTING NEXT TO ME...
...IS WITHOUT A DOUBT "HIKARU."
"THEN YOU WON'T BE ABLE TO PRETEND...
"...THAT YOU DON'T SEE HOW I FEEL...... IT'D BE BETTER THAT WAY."

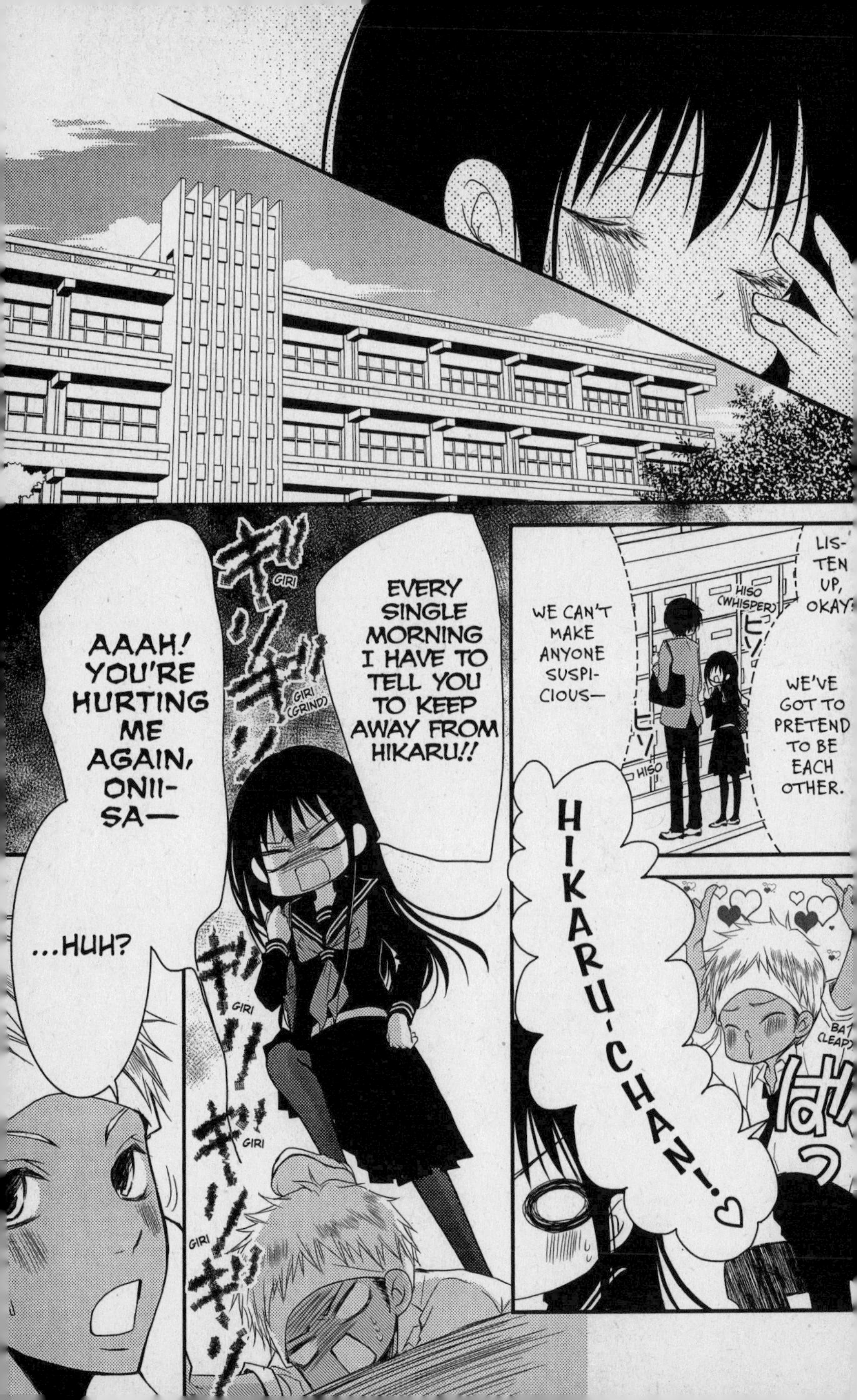

LISTEN UP, OKAY?
WE'VE GOT TO PRETEND TO BE EACH OTHER.
HISO (WHISPER)
WE CAN'T MAKE ANYONE SUSPICIOUS—
HISO
HIKARU-CHAN!!♡
(LEAP)
EVERY SINGLE MORNING I HAVE TO TELL YOU TO KEEP AWAY FROM HIKARU!!
GIRI
GIRI (GRIND)
AAAH! YOU'RE HURTING ME AGAIN, ONII-SA—
GIRI
GIRI
GIRI
...HUH?

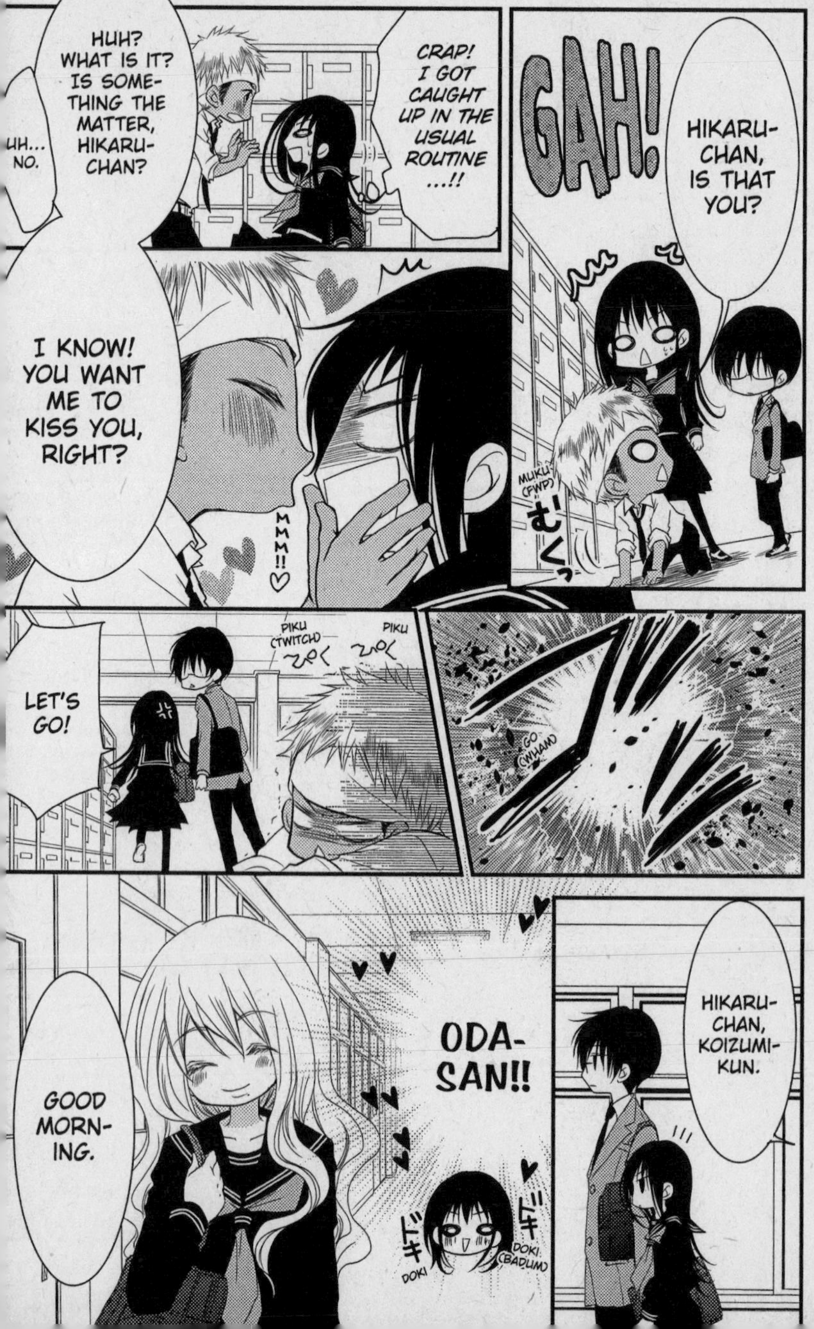
GAH!
HIKARU-CHAN, IS THAT YOU?
MUKU (FWP)
むくっ
CRAP! I GOT CAUGHT UP IN THE USUAL ROUTINE ...!!
HUH? WHAT IS IT? IS SOMETHING THE MATTER, HIKARU-CHAN?
UH... NO.
I KNOW! YOU WANT ME TO KISS YOU, RIGHT?
MMM!!♡
GO (WHAM)
PIKU (TWITCH)
ぴく
PIKU
ぴく
LET'S GO!
HIKARU-CHAN, KOIZUMI-KUN.
ODA-SAN!!
ドキ
DOKI (BADUMP)
ドキ
DOKI
GOOD MORNING.

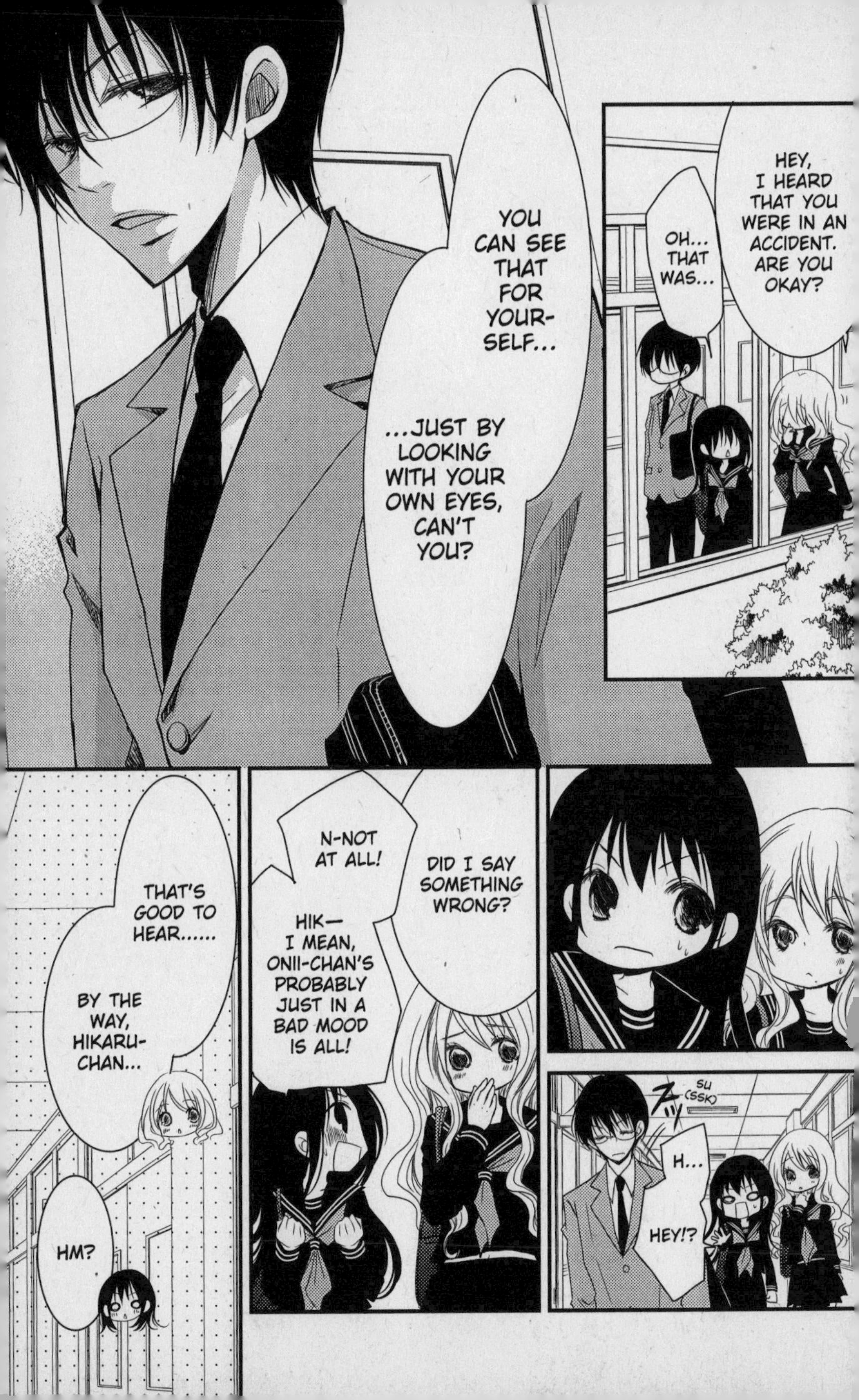
HEY, I HEARD THAT YOU WERE IN AN ACCIDENT. ARE YOU OKAY?
OH... THAT WAS...
YOU CAN SEE THAT FOR YOUR-SELF...
...JUST BY LOOKING WITH YOUR OWN EYES, CAN'T YOU?
SU (SSK)
H...
HEY!?
DID I SAY SOMETHING WRONG?
N-NOT AT ALL!
HIK— I MEAN, ONII-CHAN'S PROBABLY JUST IN A BAD MOOD IS ALL!
THAT'S GOOD TO HEAR......
BY THE WAY, HIKARU-CHAN...
HM?

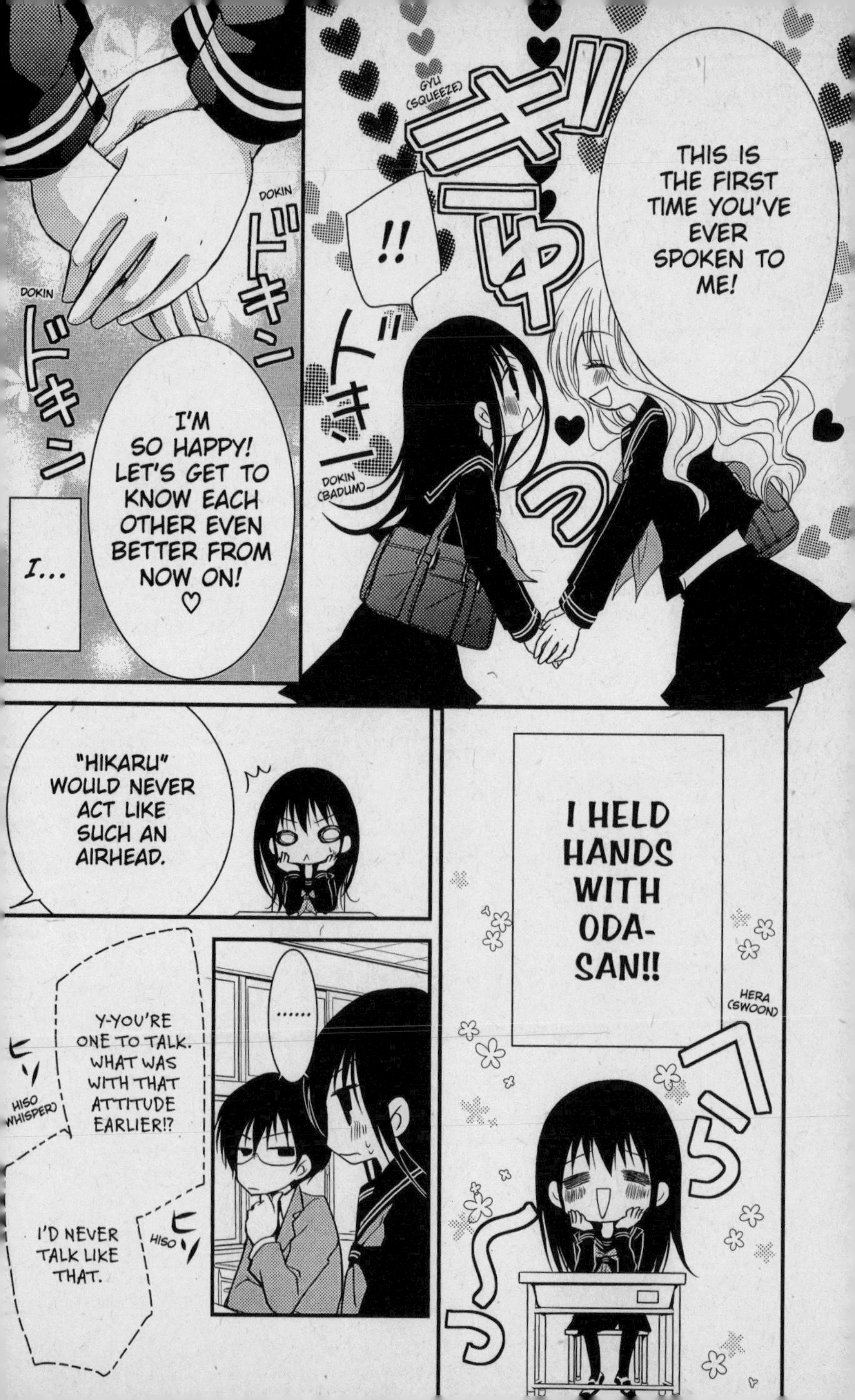
GYU (SQUEEZE)
THIS IS THE FIRST TIME YOU'VE EVER SPOKEN TO ME!
!!
DOKIN (BADUM)
DOKIN
DOKIN
I'M SO HAPPY! LET'S GET TO KNOW EACH OTHER EVEN BETTER FROM NOW ON! ♡
I...
I HELD HANDS WITH ODA-SAN!!
HERA (SWOON)
"HIKARU" WOULD NEVER ACT LIKE SUCH AN AIRHEAD.
......
Y-YOU'RE ONE TO TALK. WHAT WAS WITH THAT ATTITUDE EARLIER!?
HISO WHISPER
HISO
I'D NEVER TALK LIKE THAT.

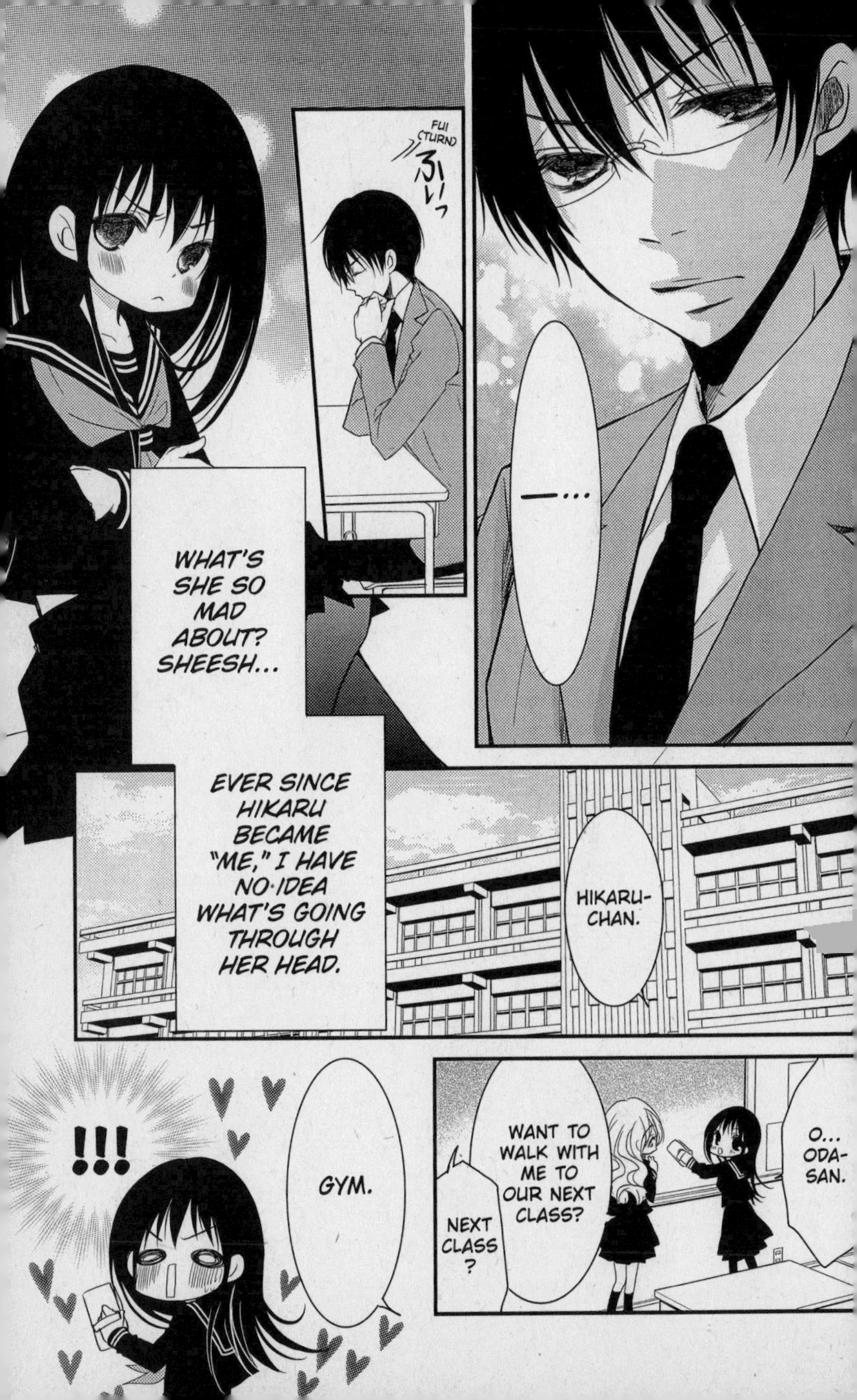
—...
FUI (TURN)
ふいっ
WHAT'S SHE SO MAD ABOUT? SHEESH...
EVER SINCE HIKARU BECAME "ME," I HAVE NO IDEA WHAT'S GOING THROUGH HER HEAD.
HIKARU-CHAN.
O... ODA-SAN.
WANT TO WALK WITH ME TO OUR NEXT CLASS?
NEXT CLASS ?
GYM.
!!!

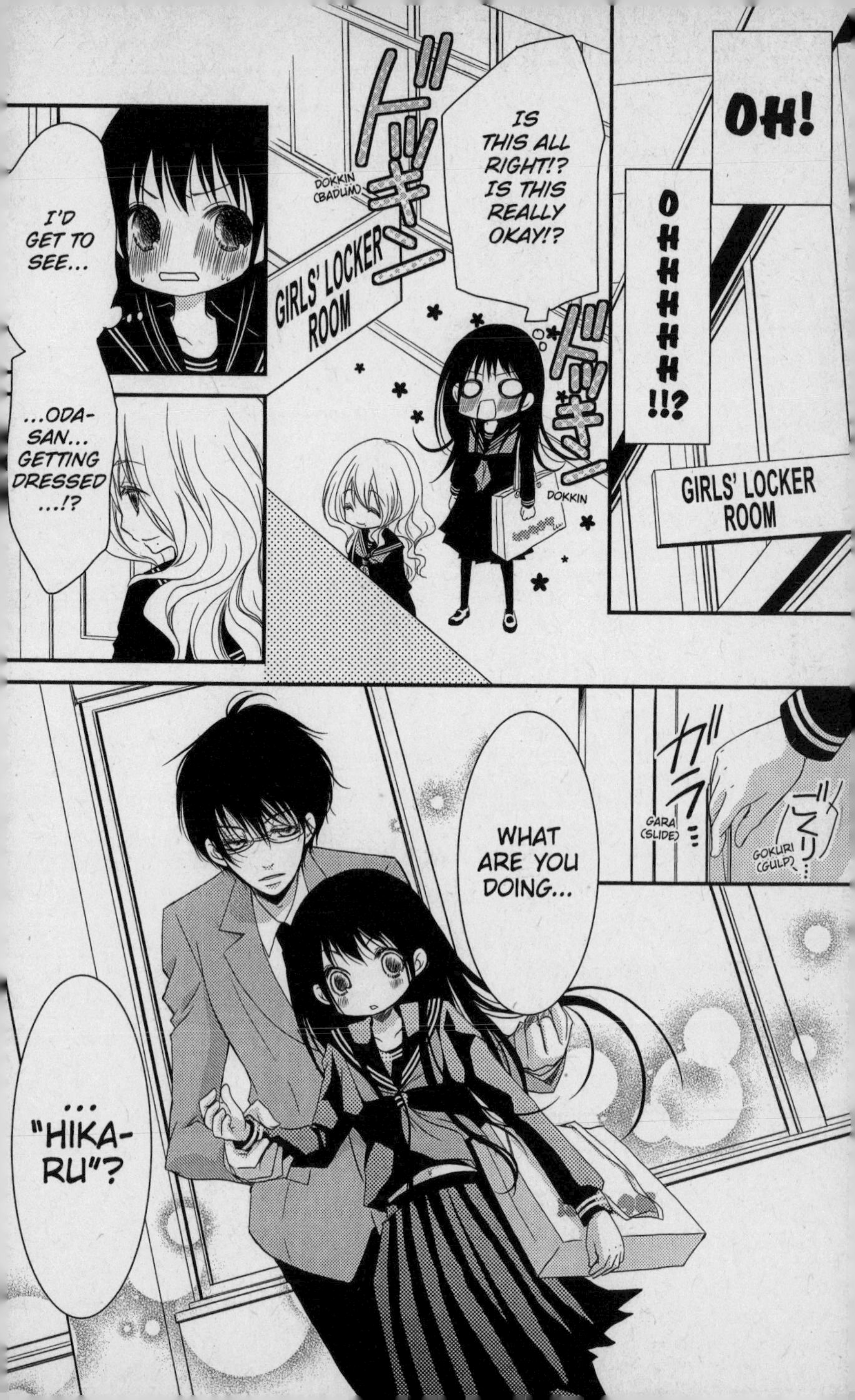
OH!
OHHHHHH!!?
GIRLS' LOCKER ROOM
DOKKIN (BADUM)
IS THIS ALL RIGHT!? IS THIS REALLY OKAY!?
GIRLS' LOCKER ROOM
DOKKIN
I'D GET TO SEE...
...ODA-SAN... GETTING DRESSED...!?
GARA (SLIDE)
GOKURI (GULP)...
WHAT ARE YOU DOING...
..."HIKARU"?

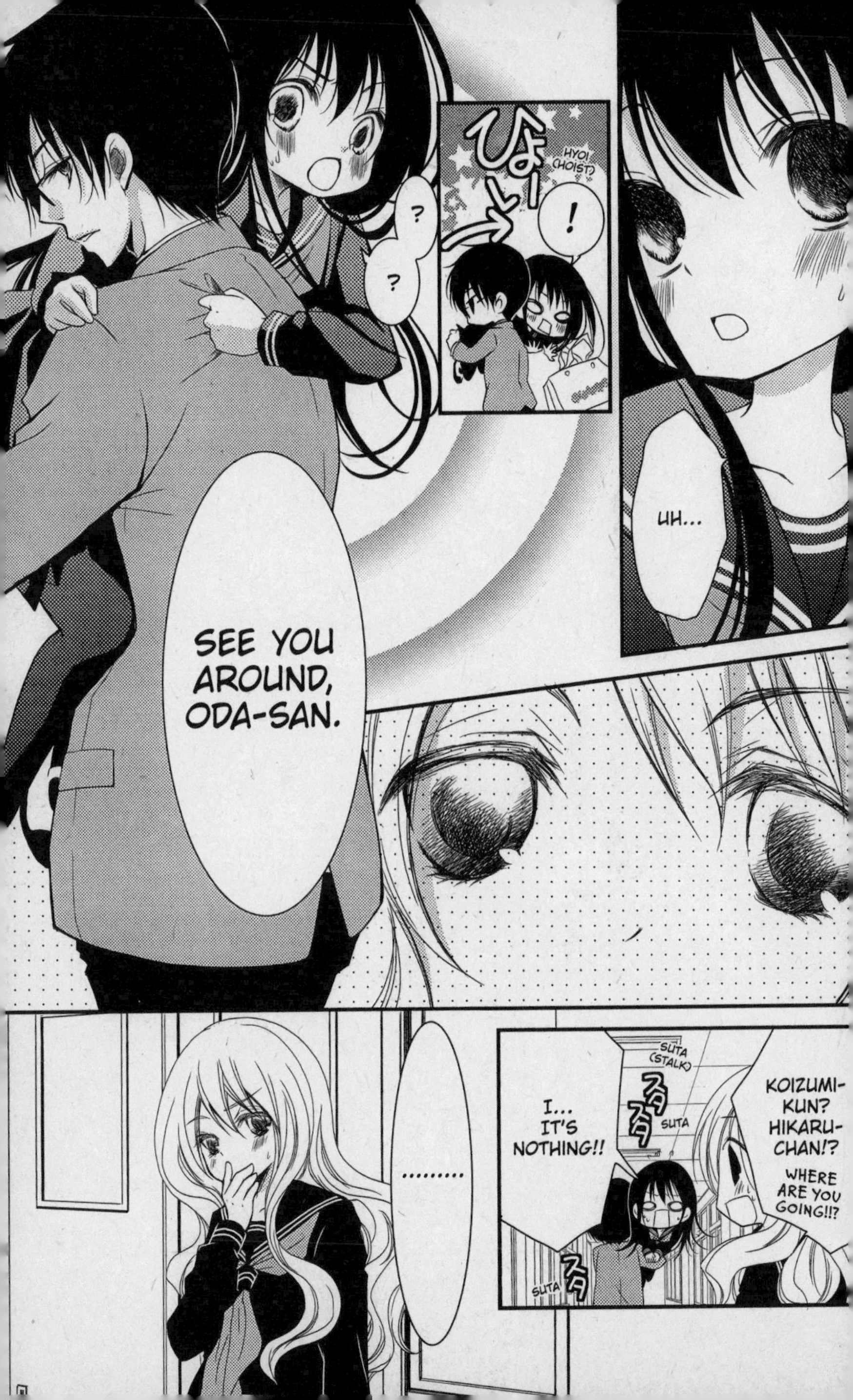
ひょーい
HYOI (HOIST)
!
?
?
SEE YOU AROUND, ODA-SAN.
UH...
KOIZUMI-KUN? HIKARU-CHAN!?
WHERE ARE YOU GOING!!?
I... IT'S NOTHING!!
スタ
SUTA (STALK)
スタ
SUTA
スタ
SUTA
....

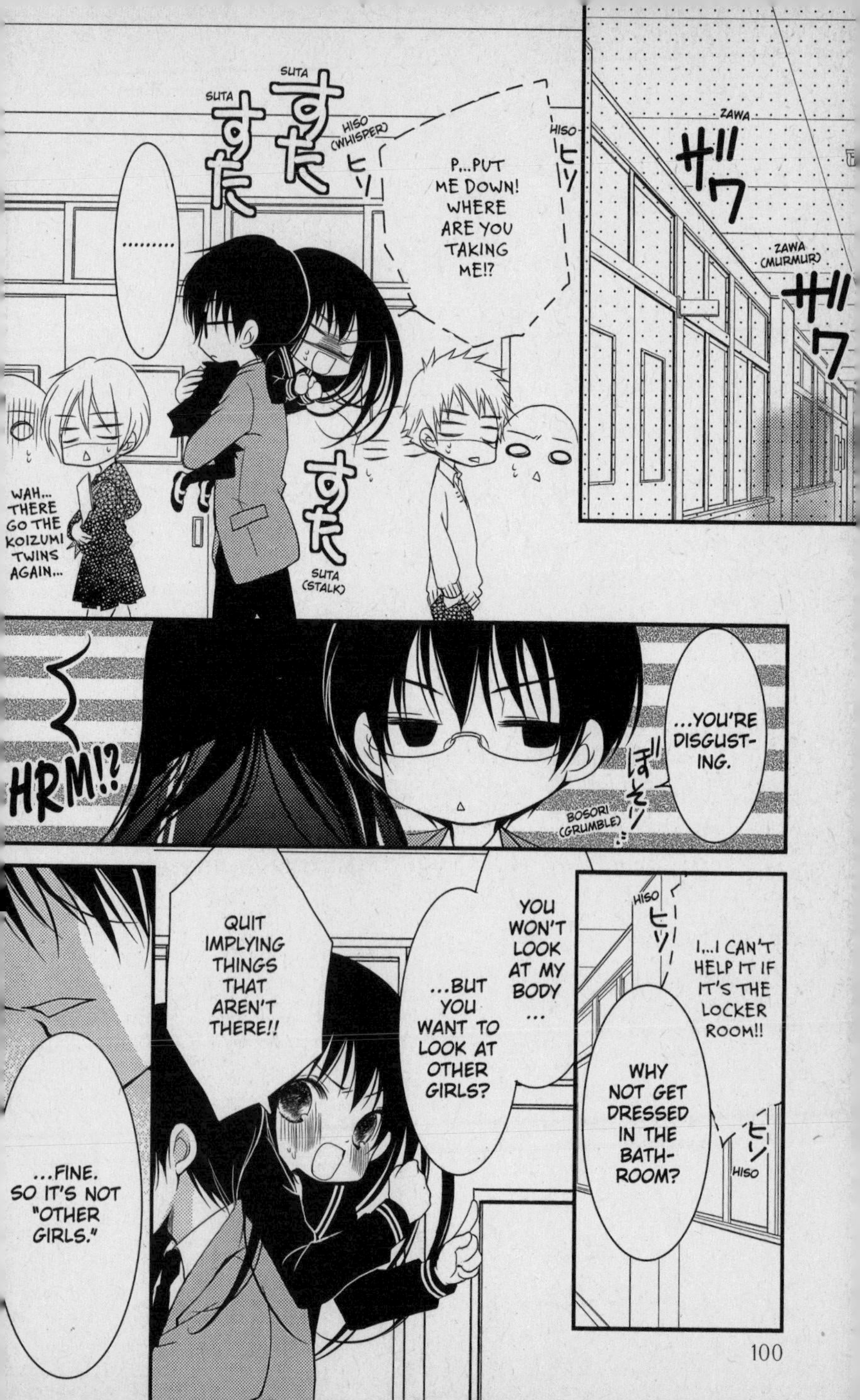
ZAWA
ザワ
ZAWA (MURMUR)
ザワ
HISO
ヒソ
P...PUT ME DOWN! WHERE ARE YOU TAKING ME!?
HISO (WHISPER)
ヒソ
SUTA
すた
SUTA
すた
....
すた
SUTA (STALK)
WAH... THERE GO THE KOIZUMI TWINS AGAIN...
...YOU'RE DISGUST-ING.
ぼそっ
BOSORI (GRUMBLE)
HRM!?
I...I CAN'T HELP IT IF IT'S THE LOCKER ROOM!!
HISO
ヒソ
WHY NOT GET DRESSED IN THE BATH-ROOM?
ヒソ
HISO
YOU WON'T LOOK AT MY BODY ...
...BUT YOU WANT TO LOOK AT OTHER GIRLS?
QUIT IMPLYING THINGS THAT AREN'T THERE!!
...FINE. SO IT'S NOT "OTHER GIRLS."

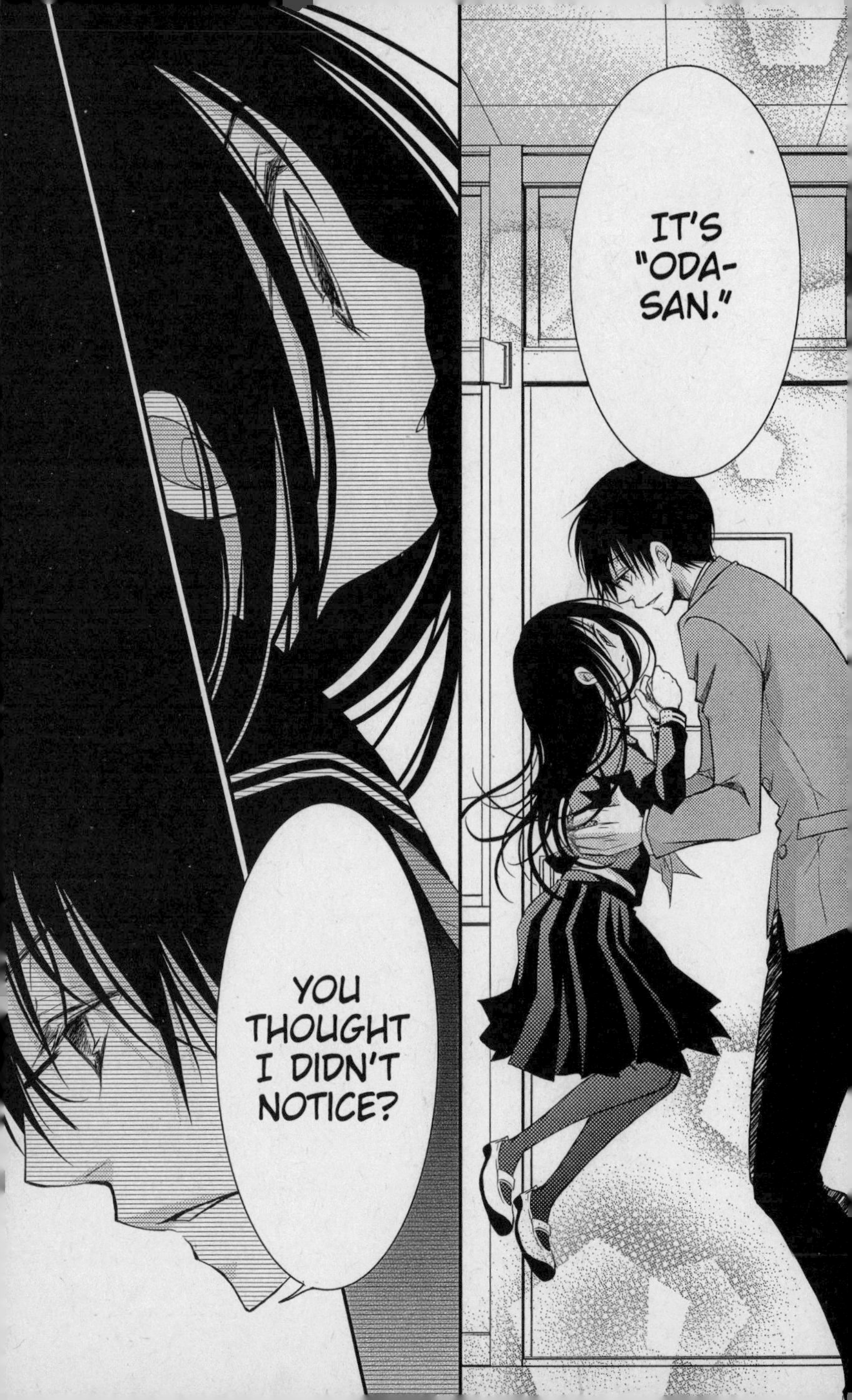
IT'S "ODA-SAN."
YOU THOUGHT I DIDN'T NOTICE?

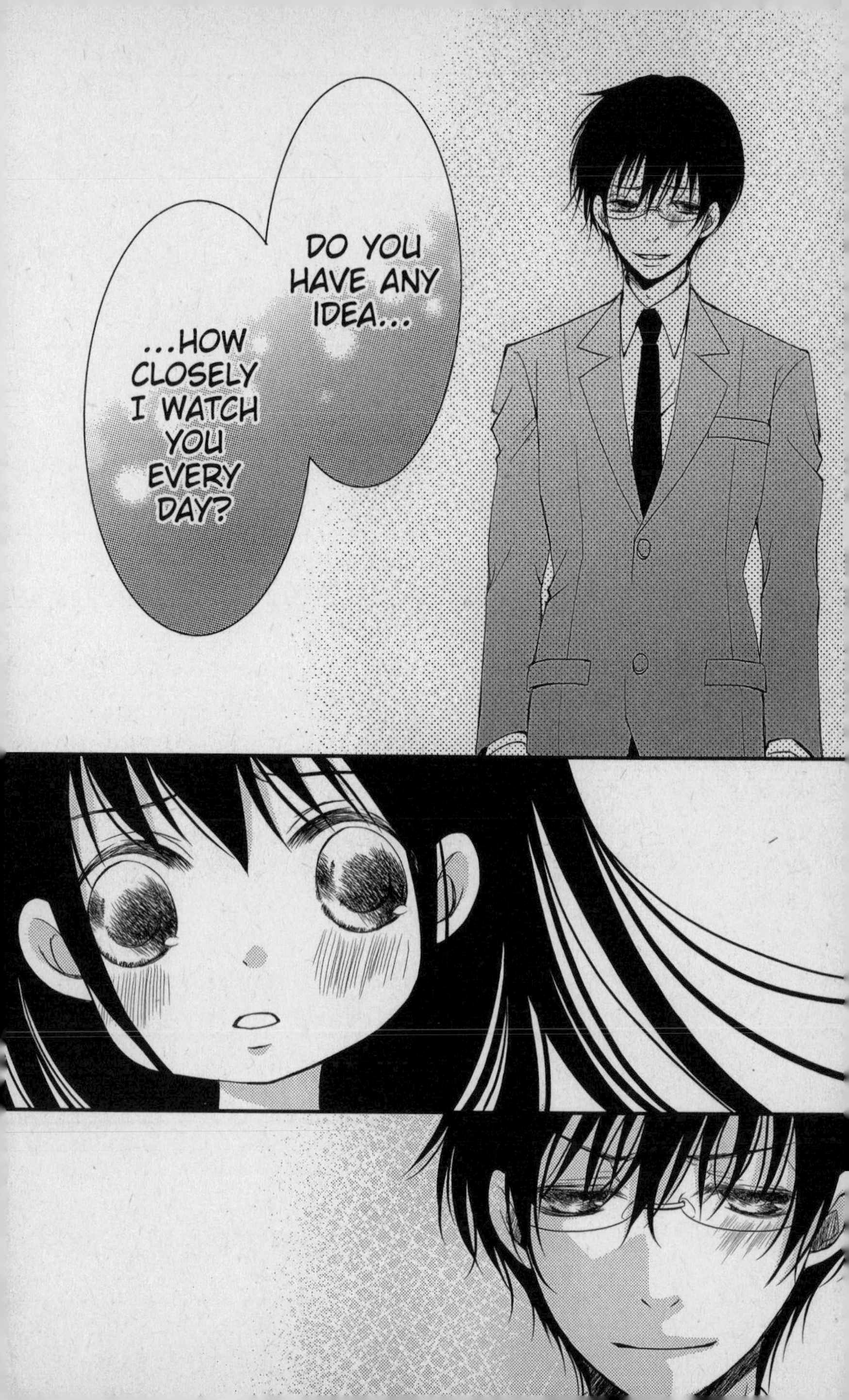
DO YOU HAVE ANY IDEA...
...HOW CLOSELY I WATCH YOU EVERY DAY?

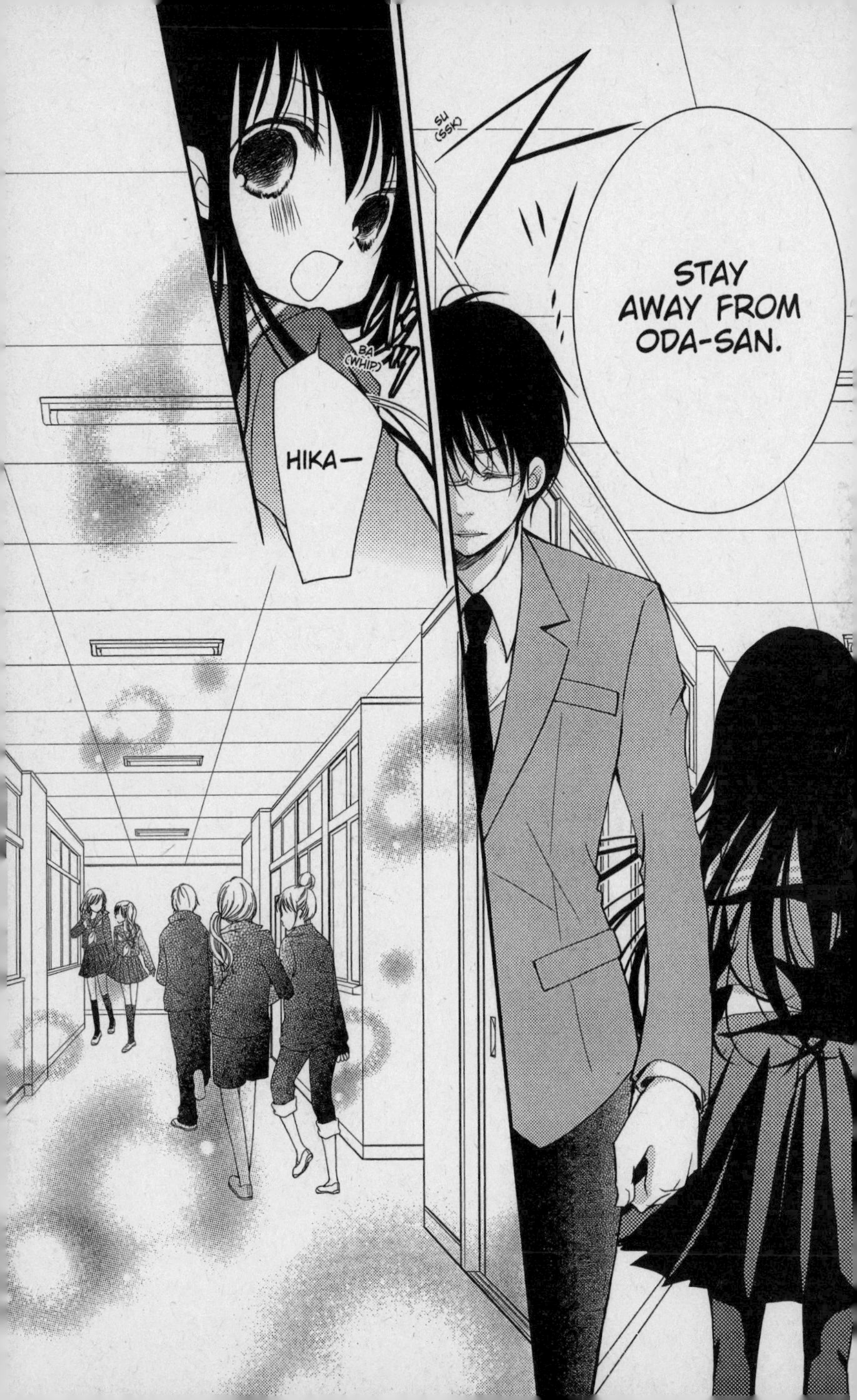
STAY AWAY FROM ODA-SAN.
SU (SSK)
BA (WHIP)
HIKA—

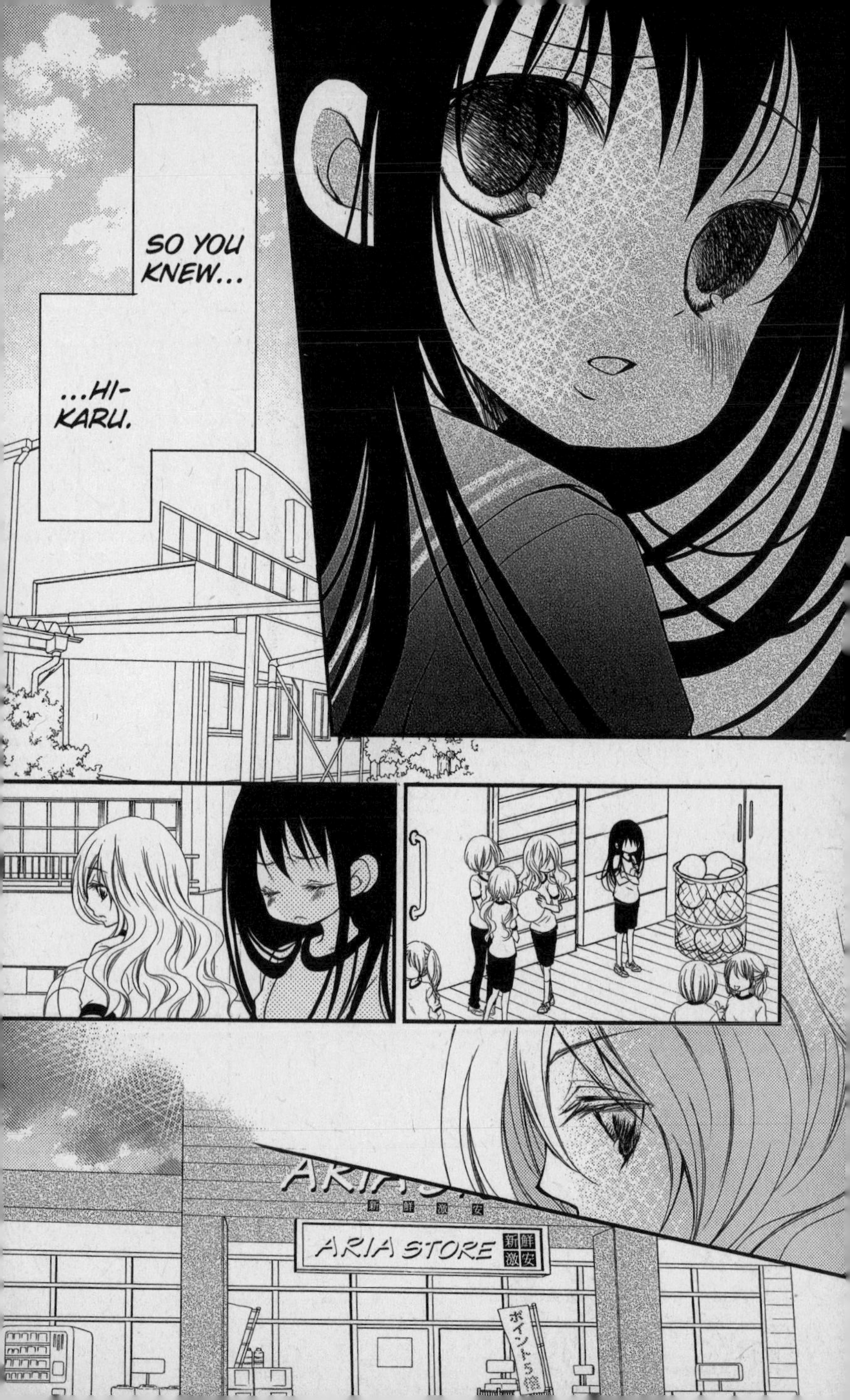
SO YOU KNEW...
...HI-KARU.
ARIA STORE
新鮮
激安

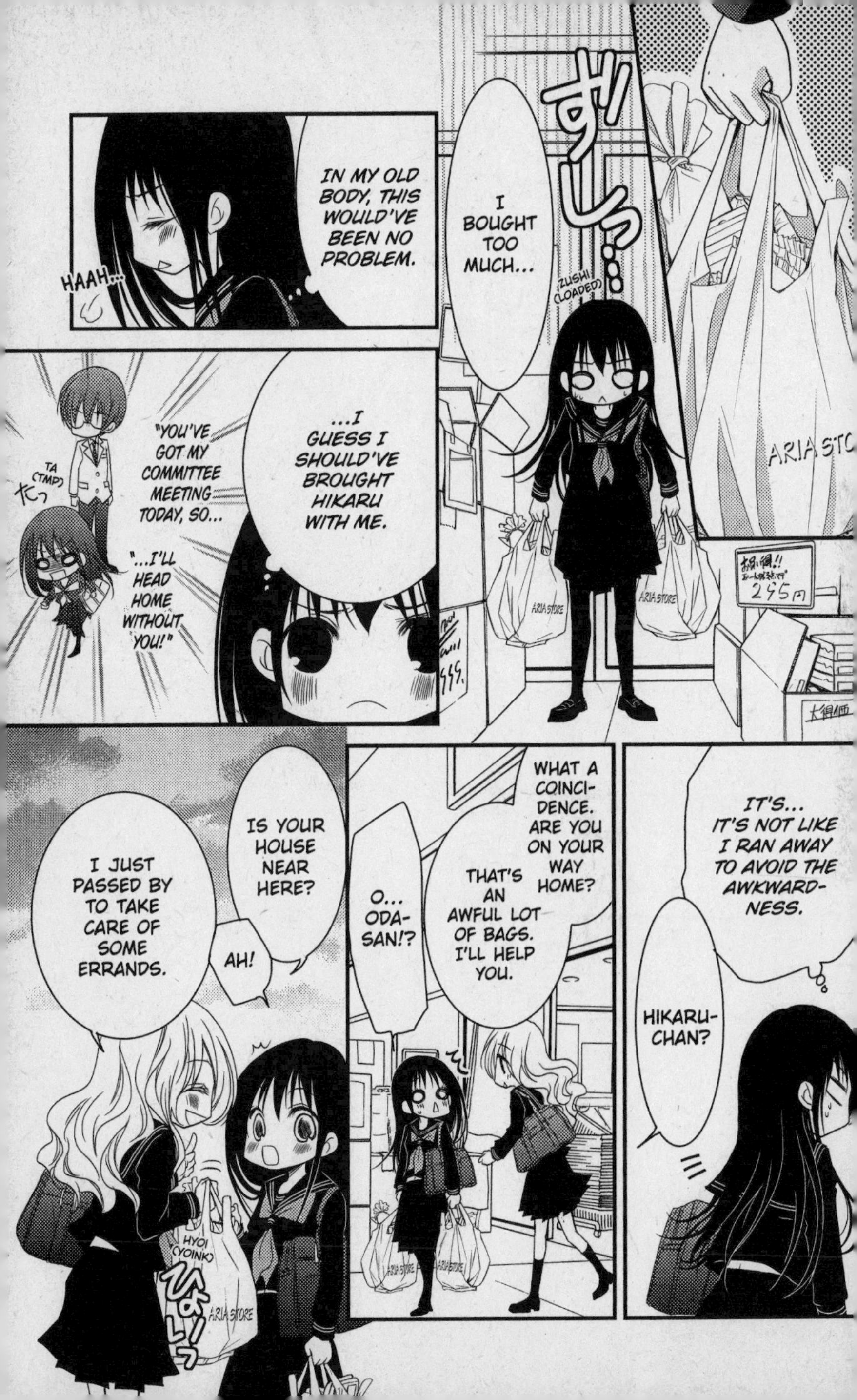

ずしっ…
ZUSHI (LOADED)
I BOUGHT TOO MUCH...
ARIA STORE
お買い得!!
295円
大得価
IN MY OLD BODY, THIS WOULD'VE BEEN NO PROBLEM.
HAAH...
...I GUESS I SHOULD'VE BROUGHT HIKARU WITH ME.
"YOU'VE GOT MY COMMITTEE MEETING TODAY, SO...
"...I'LL HEAD HOME WITHOUT YOU!"
TA (TMP)
たっ
IT'S... IT'S NOT LIKE I RAN AWAY TO AVOID THE AWKWARDNESS.
HIKARU-CHAN?
WHAT A COINCIDENCE. ARE YOU ON YOUR WAY HOME?
THAT'S AN AWFUL LOT OF BAGS. I'LL HELP YOU.
O... ODA-SAN!?
IS YOUR HOUSE NEAR HERE?
AH!
I JUST PASSED BY TO TAKE CARE OF SOME ERRANDS.
HYOI (YOINK)
ひょいっ
ARIA STORE

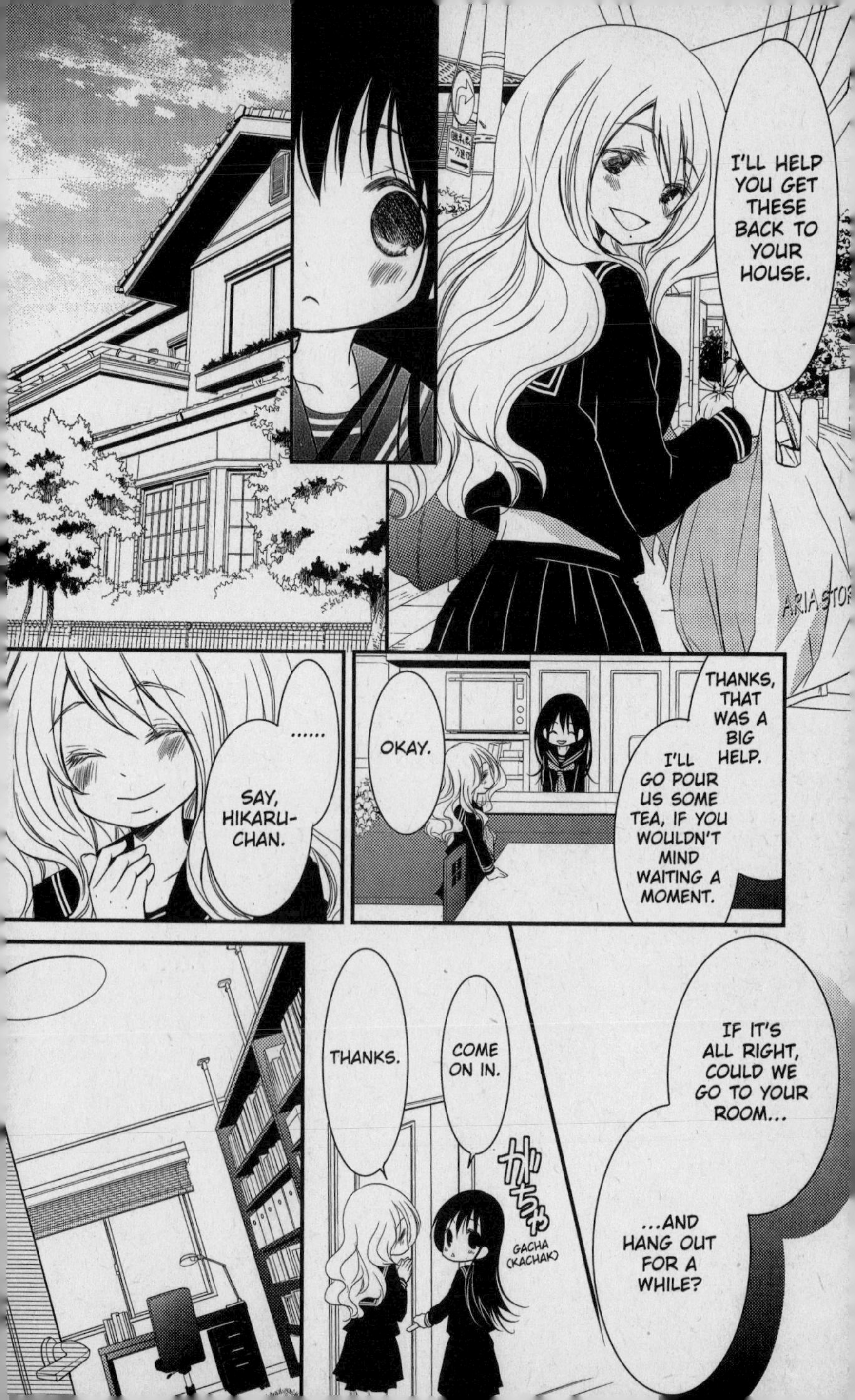
I'LL HELP YOU GET THESE BACK TO YOUR HOUSE.
THANKS, THAT WAS A BIG HELP.
I'LL GO POUR US SOME TEA, IF YOU WOULDN'T MIND WAITING A MOMENT.
OKAY.
......
SAY, HIKARU-CHAN.
IF IT'S ALL RIGHT, COULD WE GO TO YOUR ROOM...
...AND HANG OUT FOR A WHILE?
COME ON IN.
THANKS.
がちゃ
GACHA (KACHAK)

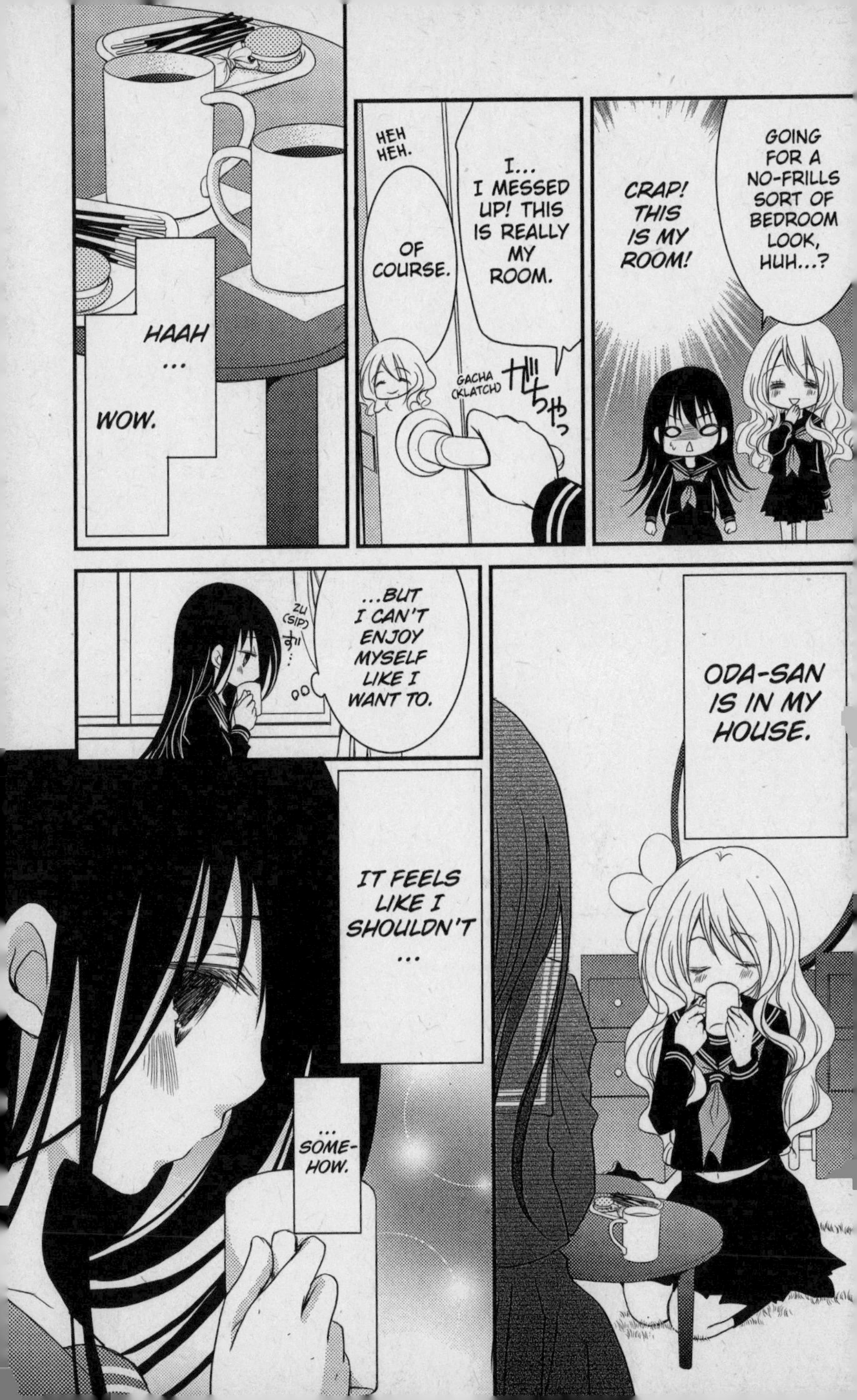
GOING FOR A NO-FRILLS SORT OF BEDROOM LOOK, HUH...?
CRAP! THIS IS MY ROOM!
I... I MESSED UP! THIS IS REALLY MY ROOM.
HEH HEH.
OF COURSE.
GACHA (KLATCH)
HAAH ... WOW.
ODA-SAN IS IN MY HOUSE.
ZU (SIP)
...BUT I CAN'T ENJOY MYSELF LIKE I WANT TO.
IT FEELS LIKE I SHOULDN'T ...
... SOME-HOW.

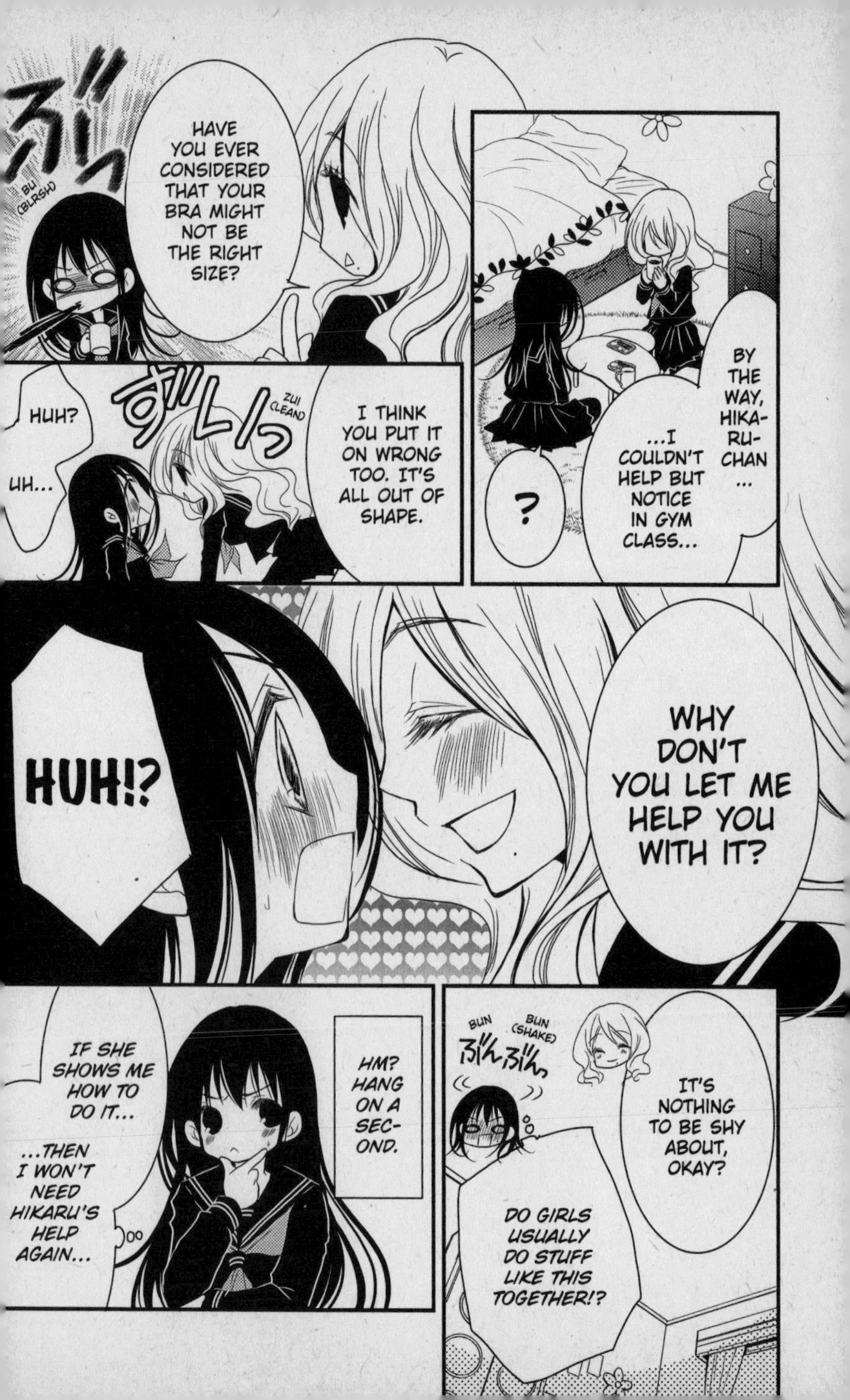
BY THE WAY, HIKARU-CHAN...
...I COULDN'T HELP BUT NOTICE IN GYM CLASS...
?
HAVE YOU EVER CONSIDERED THAT YOUR BRA MIGHT NOT BE THE RIGHT SIZE?
ぶっ
BU (BLRSH)
I THINK YOU PUT IT ON WRONG TOO. IT'S ALL OUT OF SHAPE.
ずいっ
ZUI (CLEAN)
HUH?
UH...
WHY DON'T YOU LET ME HELP YOU WITH IT?
HUH!?
IT'S NOTHING TO BE SHY ABOUT, OKAY?
ぶんぶん
BUN BUN (SHAKE)
DO GIRLS USUALLY DO STUFF LIKE THIS TOGETHER!?
HM? HANG ON A SEC-OND.
IF SHE SHOWS ME HOW TO DO IT...
...THEN I WON'T NEED HIKARU'S HELP AGAIN...

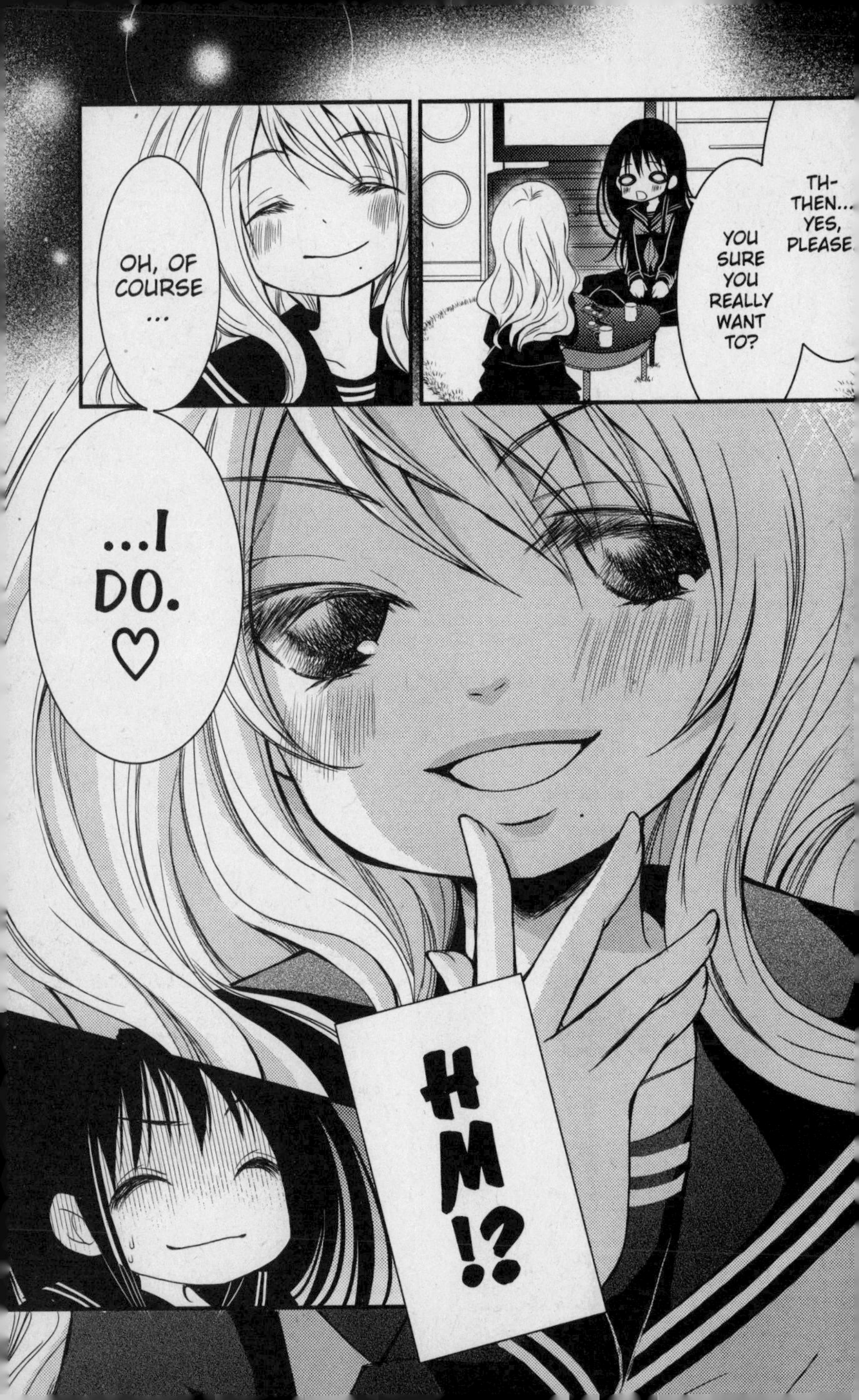
TH-THEN... YES, PLEASE
YOU SURE YOU REALLY WANT TO?
OH, OF COURSE ...
...I DO. ♡
HM!?

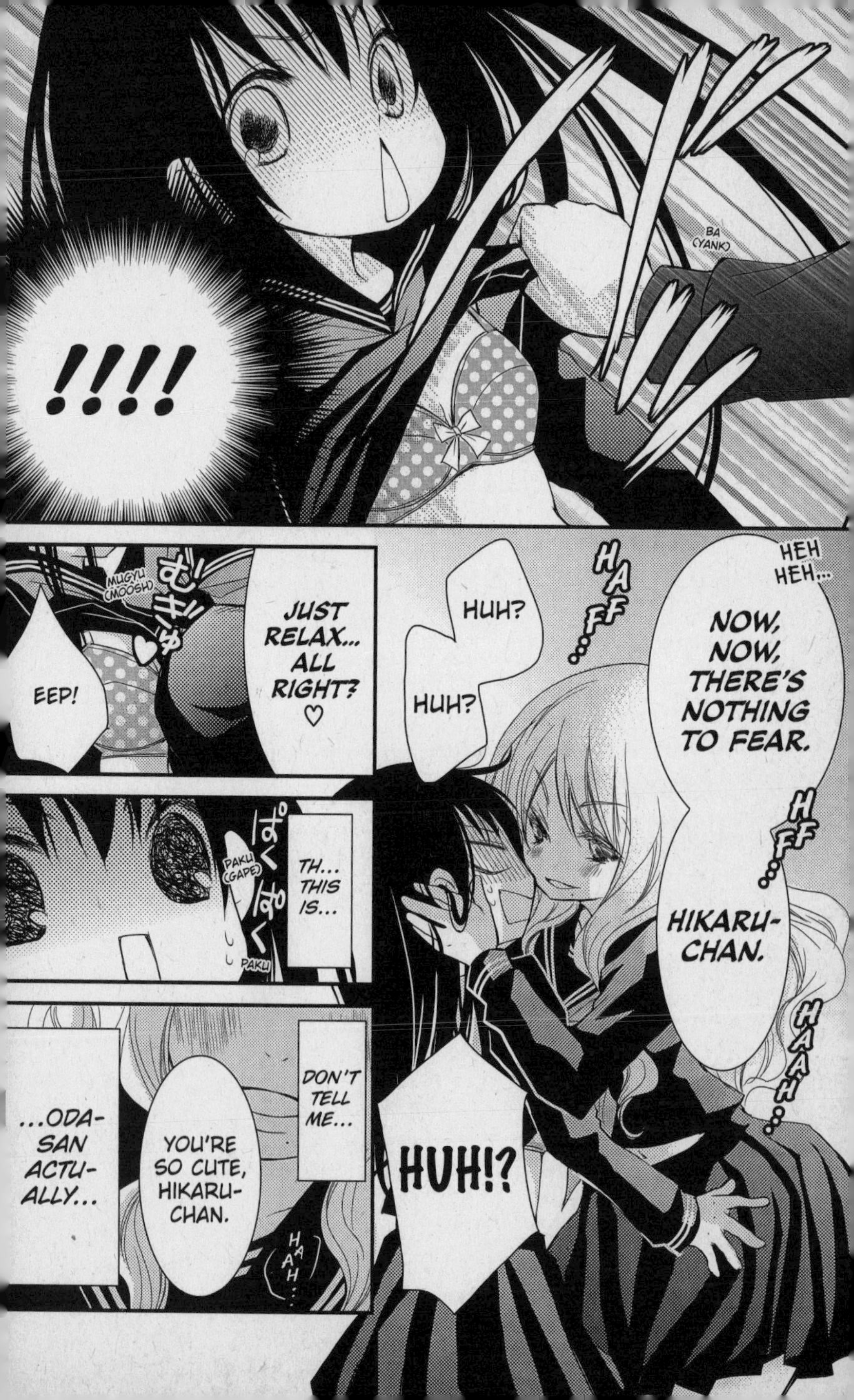
BA
(YANK)
!!!!
HEH HEH...
NOW, NOW, THERE'S NOTHING TO FEAR.
HAFF...
HUH?
HUH?
HFF...
HIKARU-CHAN.
HAAAH...
HUH!?
JUST RELAX... ALL RIGHT? ♡
むぎゅ
MUGYU
(MOOSH)
EEP!
TH... THIS IS...
ぱくぱく
PAKU
(GAPE)
PAKU
DON'T TELL ME...
YOU'RE SO CUTE, HIKARU-CHAN.
...ODA-SAN ACTU-ALLY...
HAH...

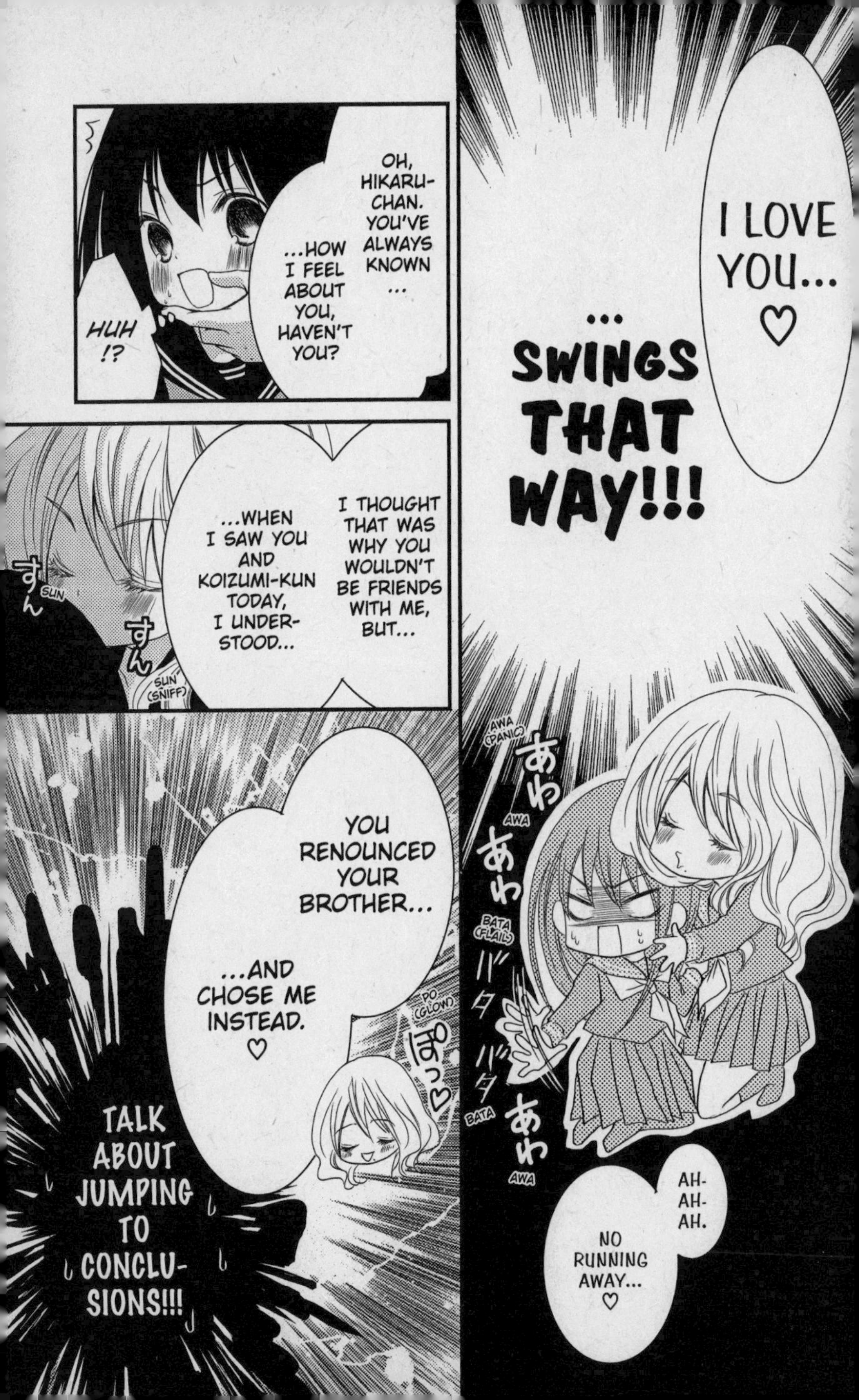
I LOVE YOU... ♡
...SWINGS THAT WAY!!!
AWA (PANIC)
あわ
AWA
あわ
BATA (FLAIL)
バタ
バタ
BATA
あわ
AWA
AH-AH-AH.
NO RUNNING AWAY... ♡
OH, HIKARU-CHAN. YOU'VE ALWAYS KNOWN...
...HOW I FEEL ABOUT YOU, HAVEN'T YOU?
HUH!?
I THOUGHT THAT WAS WHY YOU WOULDN'T BE FRIENDS WITH ME, BUT...
...WHEN I SAW YOU AND KOIZUMI-KUN TODAY, I UNDERSTOOD...
すん
SUN
すん
SUN (SNIFF)
YOU RENOUNCED YOUR BROTHER...
...AND CHOSE ME INSTEAD. ♡
PO (GLOW)
ぽっ♡
TALK ABOUT JUMPING TO CONCLUSIONS!!!

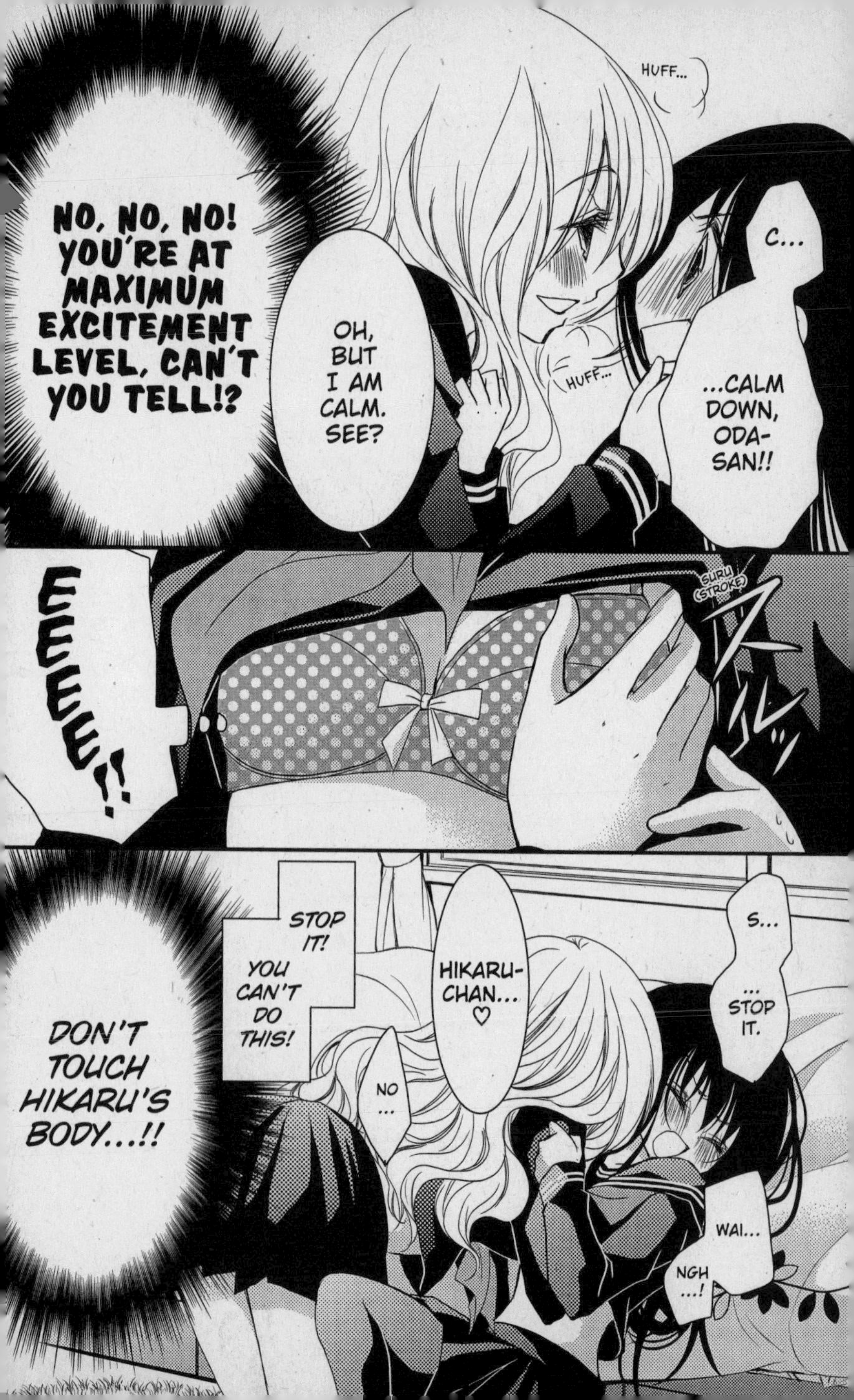
HUFF...
C...
...CALM DOWN, ODA-SAN!!
HUFF...
OH, BUT I AM CALM. SEE?
NO, NO, NO! YOU'RE AT MAXIMUM EXCITEMENT LEVEL, CAN'T YOU TELL!?
SURU (STROKE)
EEEEE!!
S... ...STOP IT.
HIKARU-CHAN... ♡
STOP IT! YOU CAN'T DO THIS!
NO...
DON'T TOUCH HIKARU'S BODY...!!
WAI...
NGH...!

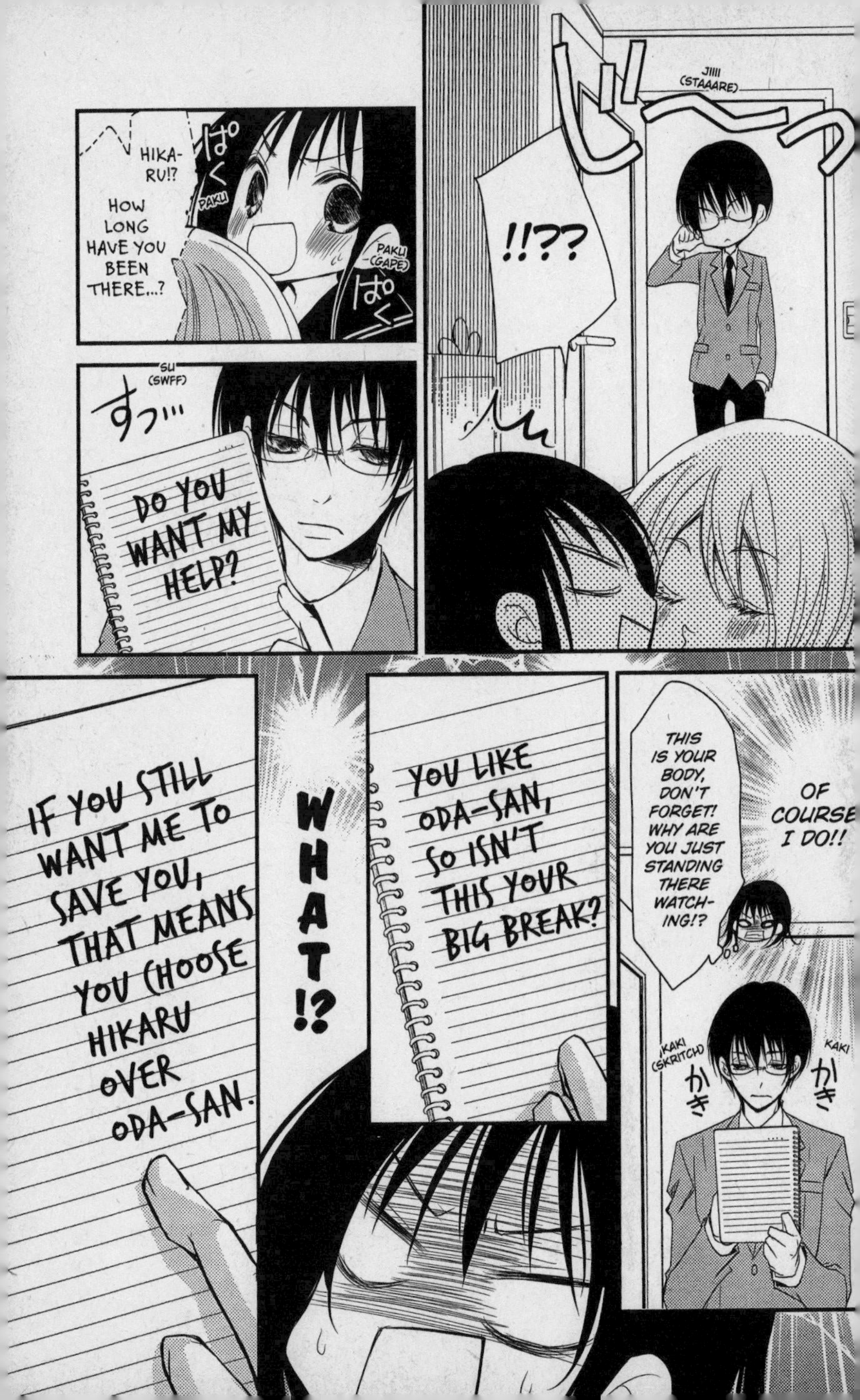
じ～っ
JIIII (STAAARE)
!!??
ぱく
PAKU
HIKA-RU!?
HOW LONG HAVE YOU BEEN THERE...?
ぱく
PAKU (GAPE)
すっ
SU (SWFF)
DO YOU WANT MY HELP?
OF COURSE I DO!!
THIS IS YOUR BODY, DON'T FORGET! WHY ARE YOU JUST STANDING THERE WATCH-ING!?
かき
KAKI
かき
KAKI (SKRITCH)
YOU LIKE ODA-SAN, SO ISN'T THIS YOUR BIG BREAK?
WHAT!?
IF YOU STILL WANT ME TO SAVE YOU, THAT MEANS YOU CHOOSE HIKARU OVER ODA-SAN.

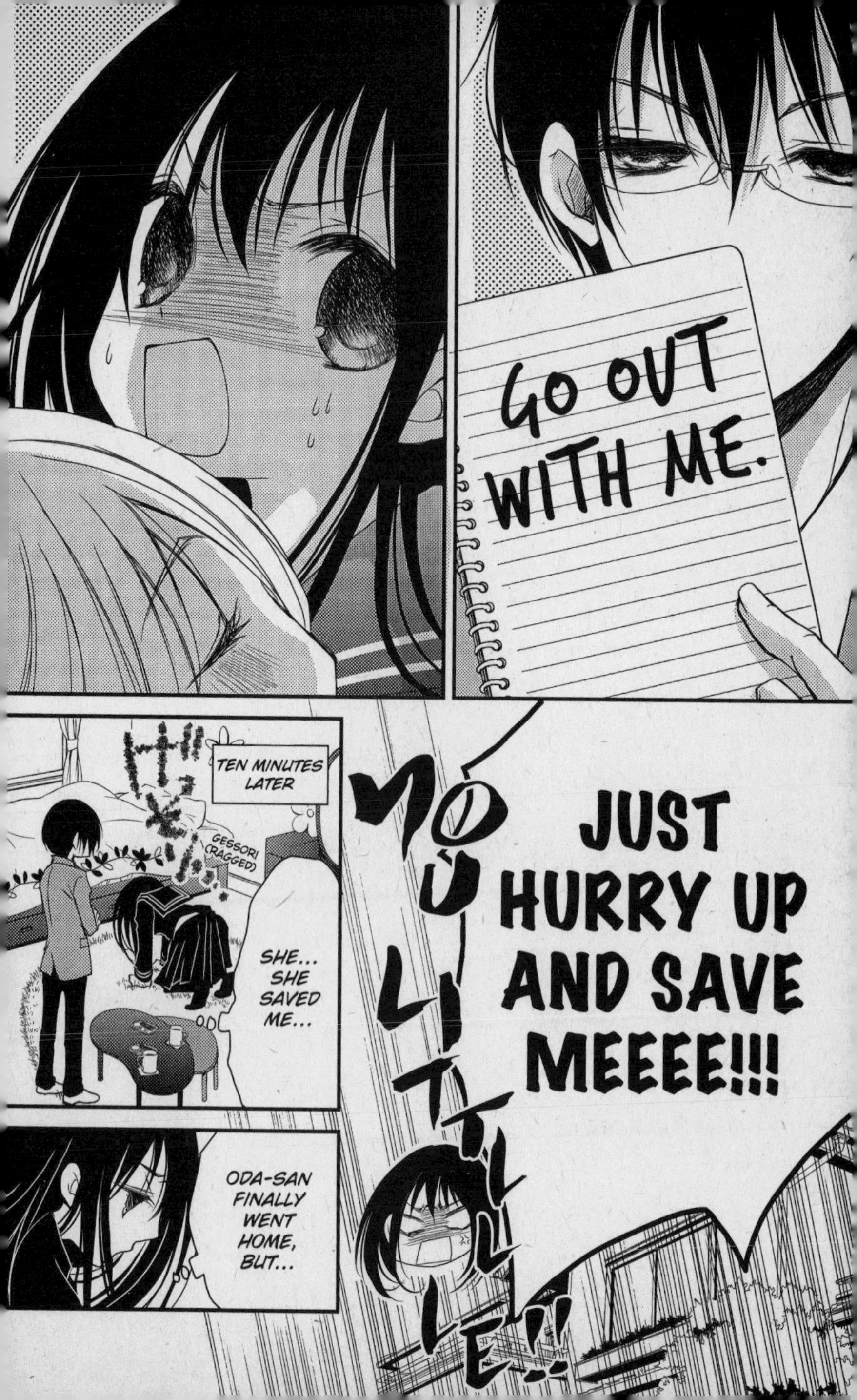
GO OUT WITH ME.
JUST HURRY UP AND SAVE MEEEE!!!
YOU LITTLE!!
TEN MINUTES LATER
GESSORI (RAGGED)
SHE... SHE SAVED ME...
ODA-SAN FINALLY WENT HOME, BUT...

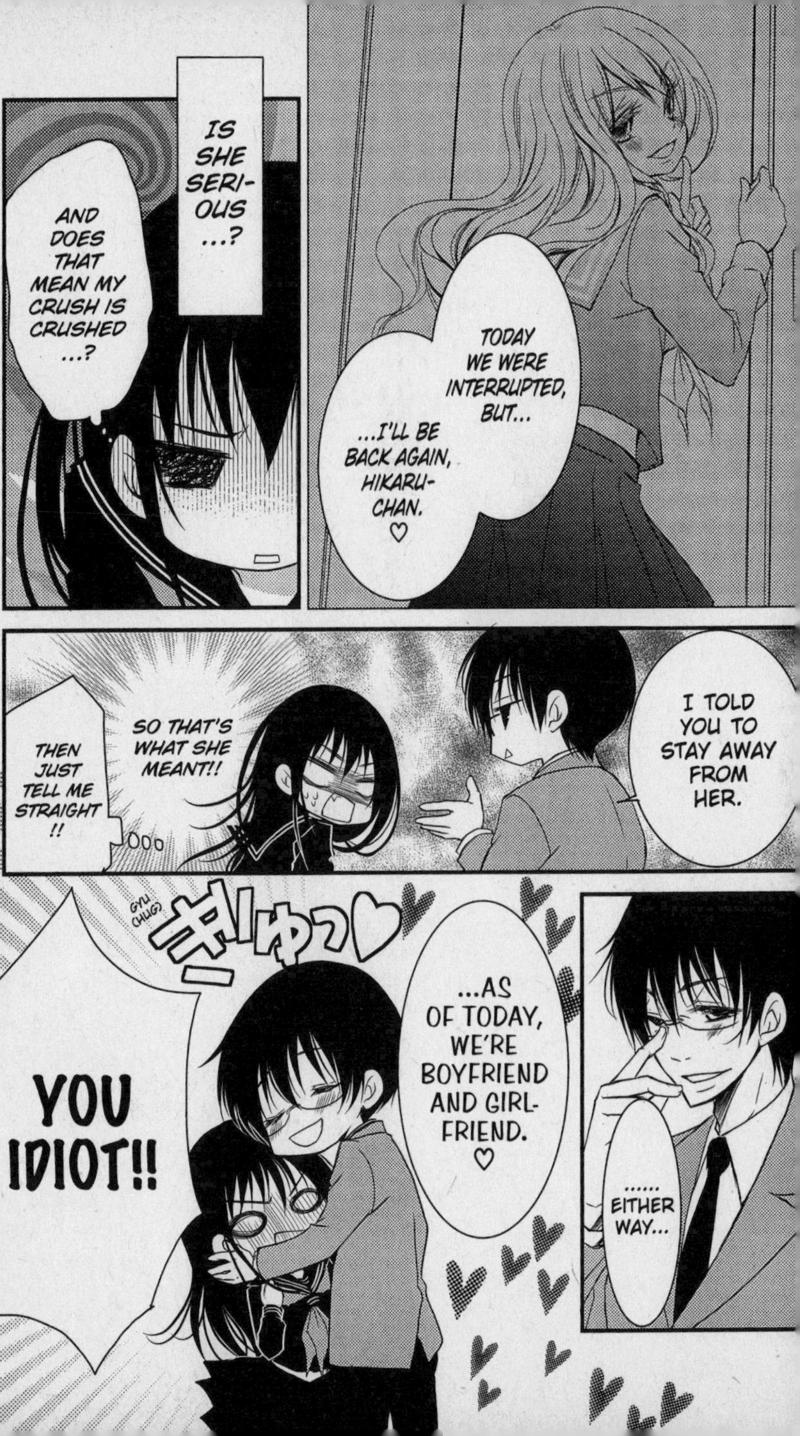
TODAY WE WERE INTERRUPTED, BUT...
...I'LL BE BACK AGAIN, HIKARU-CHAN. ♡
IS SHE SERIOUS...?
AND DOES THAT MEAN MY CRUSH IS CRUSHED...?
I TOLD YOU TO STAY AWAY FROM HER.
SO THAT'S WHAT SHE MEANT!!
THEN JUST TELL ME STRAIGHT!!
......EITHER WAY...
...AS OF TODAY, WE'RE BOYFRIEND AND GIRLFRIEND. ♡
ぎゅっ♡
GYU (HUG)
YOU IDIOT!!

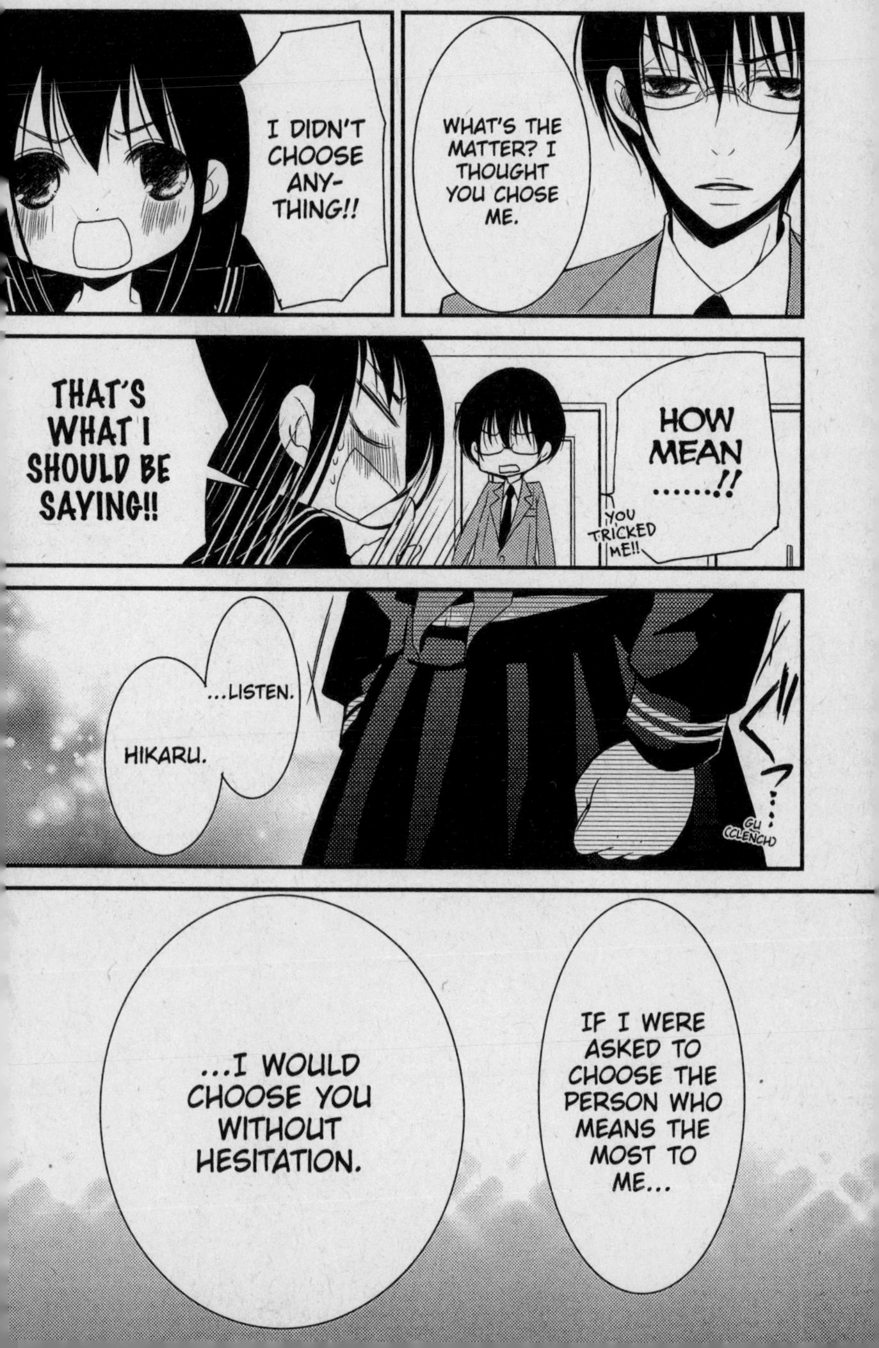
WHAT'S THE MATTER? I THOUGHT YOU CHOSE ME.
I DIDN'T CHOOSE ANY-THING!!
HOW MEAN......!!
YOU TRICKED ME!!
THAT'S WHAT I SHOULD BE SAYING!!
GU (CLENCH)
...LISTEN.
HIKARU.
IF I WERE ASKED TO CHOOSE THE PERSON WHO MEANS THE MOST TO ME...
...I WOULD CHOOSE YOU WITHOUT HESITATION.

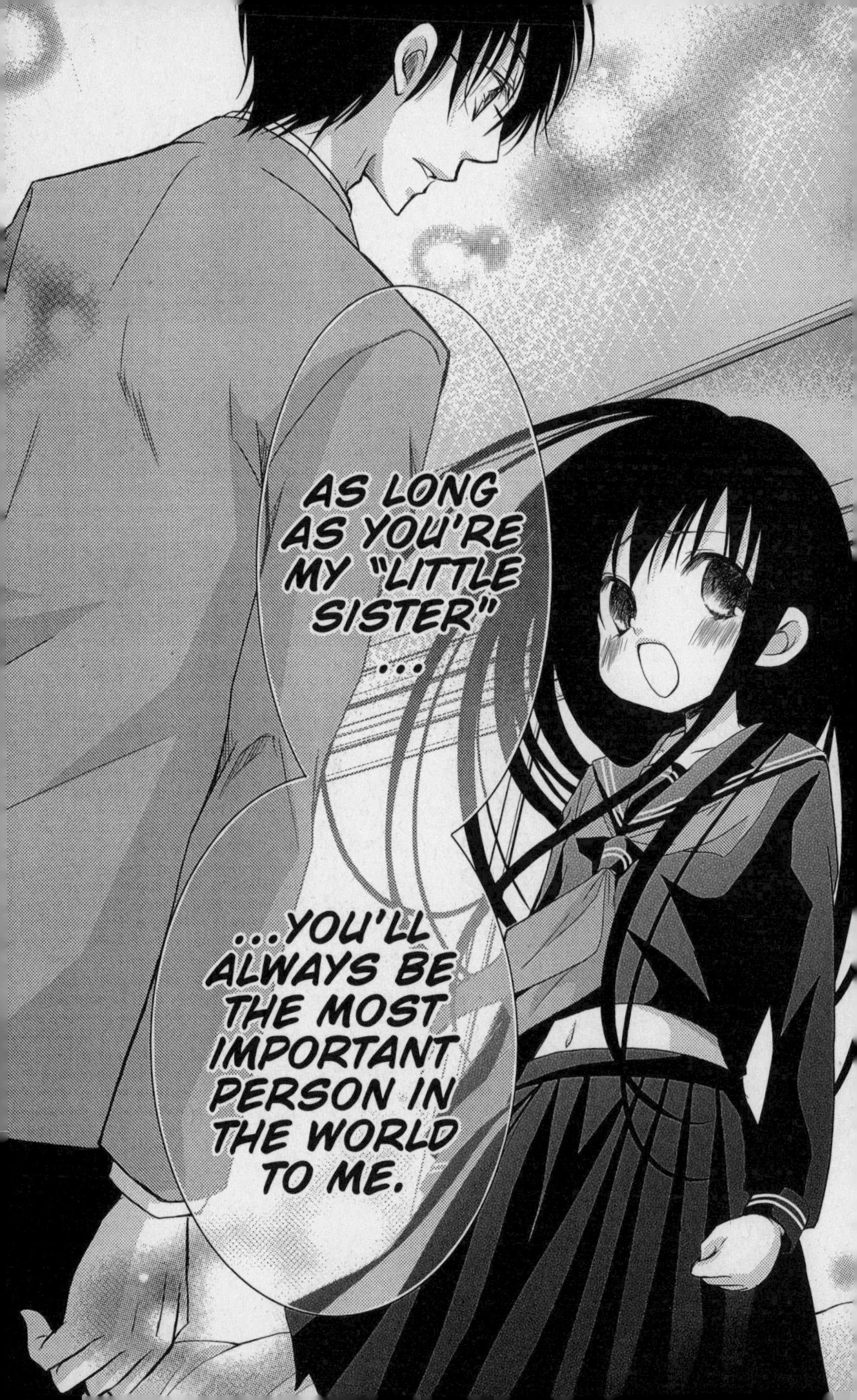
AS LONG AS YOU'RE MY "LITTLE SISTER"...
...YOU'LL ALWAYS BE THE MOST IMPORTANT PERSON IN THE WORLD TO ME.

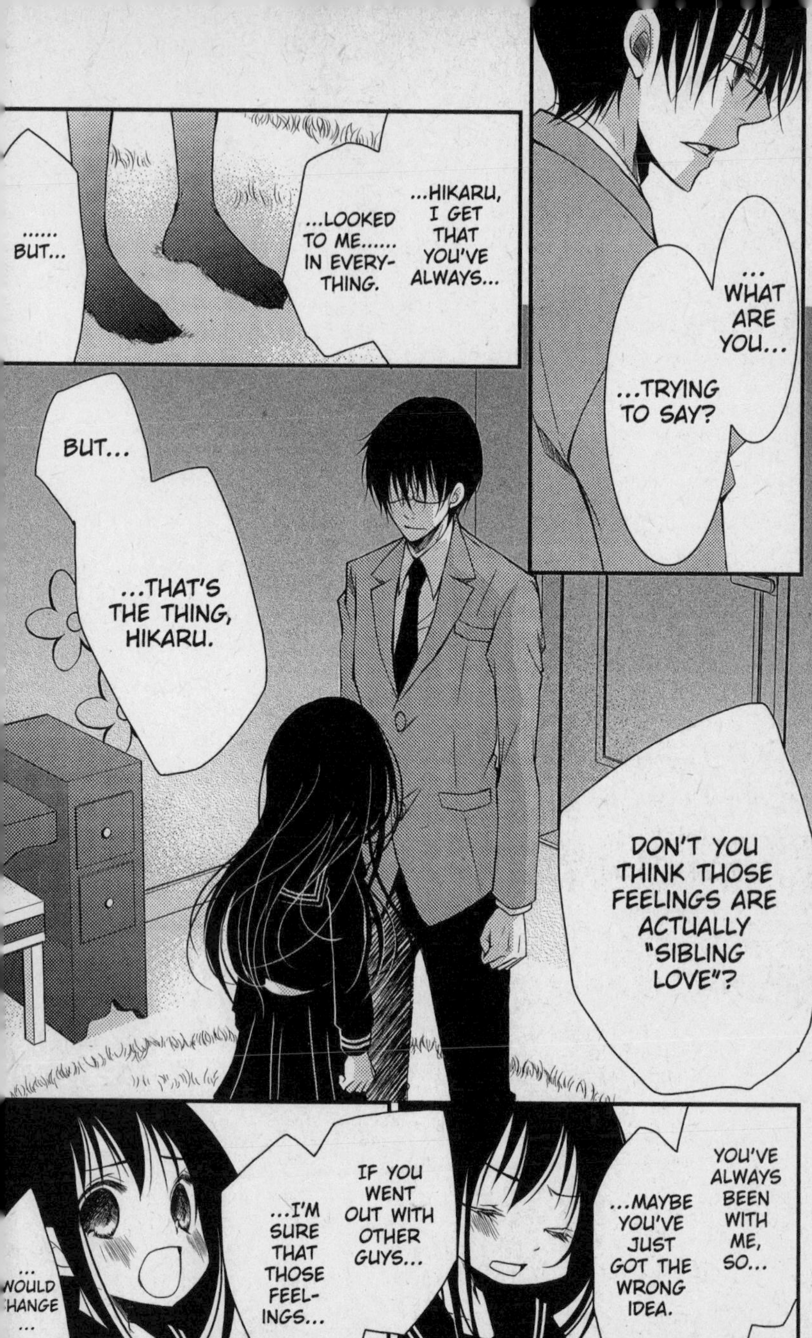
...WHAT ARE YOU...
...TRYING TO SAY?
...HIKARU, I GET THAT YOU'VE ALWAYS...
...LOOKED TO ME...... IN EVERY-THING.
...... BUT...
BUT...
...THAT'S THE THING, HIKARU.
DON'T YOU THINK THOSE FEELINGS ARE ACTUALLY "SIBLING LOVE"?
YOU'VE ALWAYS BEEN WITH ME, SO...
...MAYBE YOU'VE JUST GOT THE WRONG IDEA.
IF YOU WENT OUT WITH OTHER GUYS...
...I'M SURE THAT THOSE FEEL-INGS...
...WOULD HANGE...

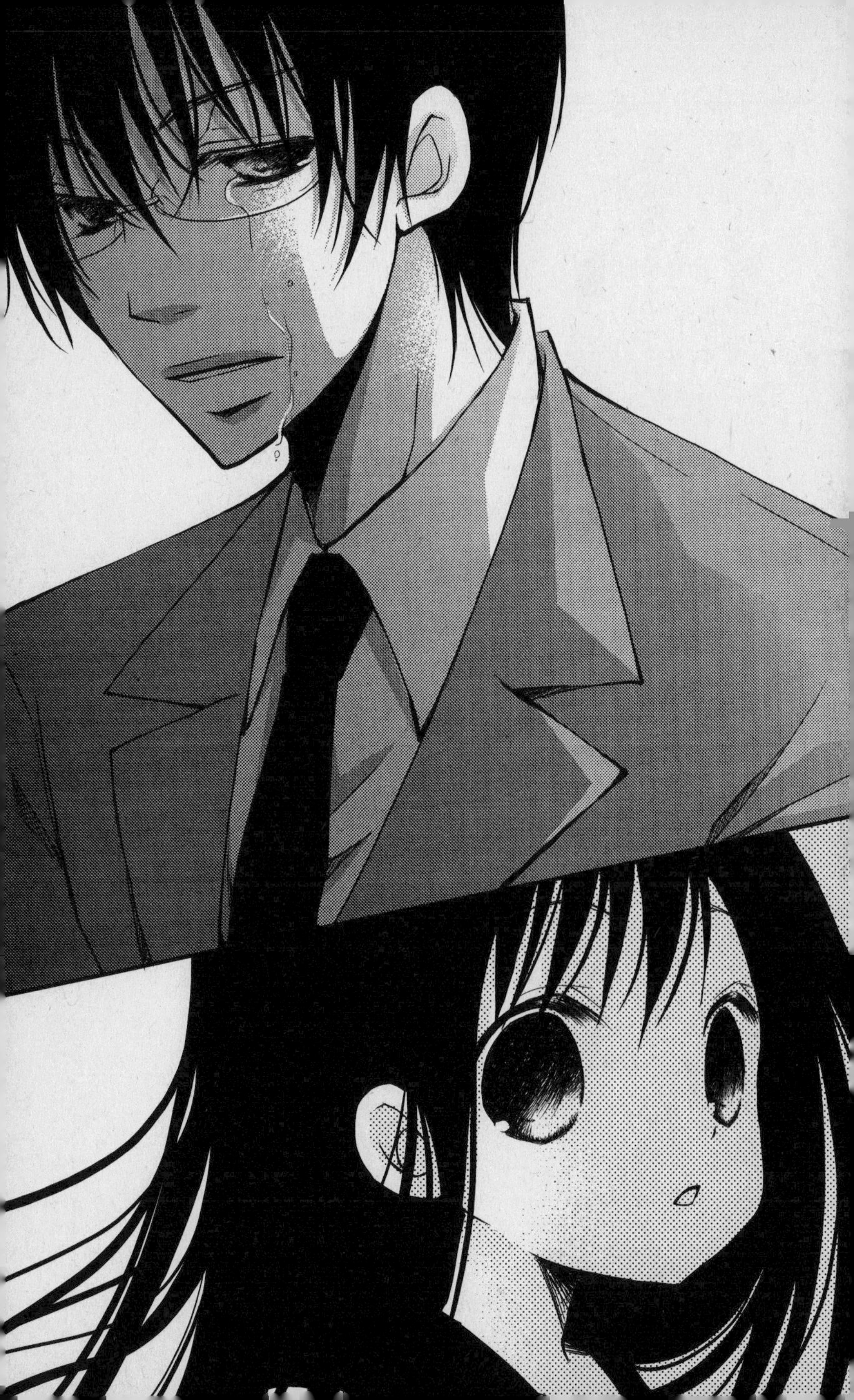

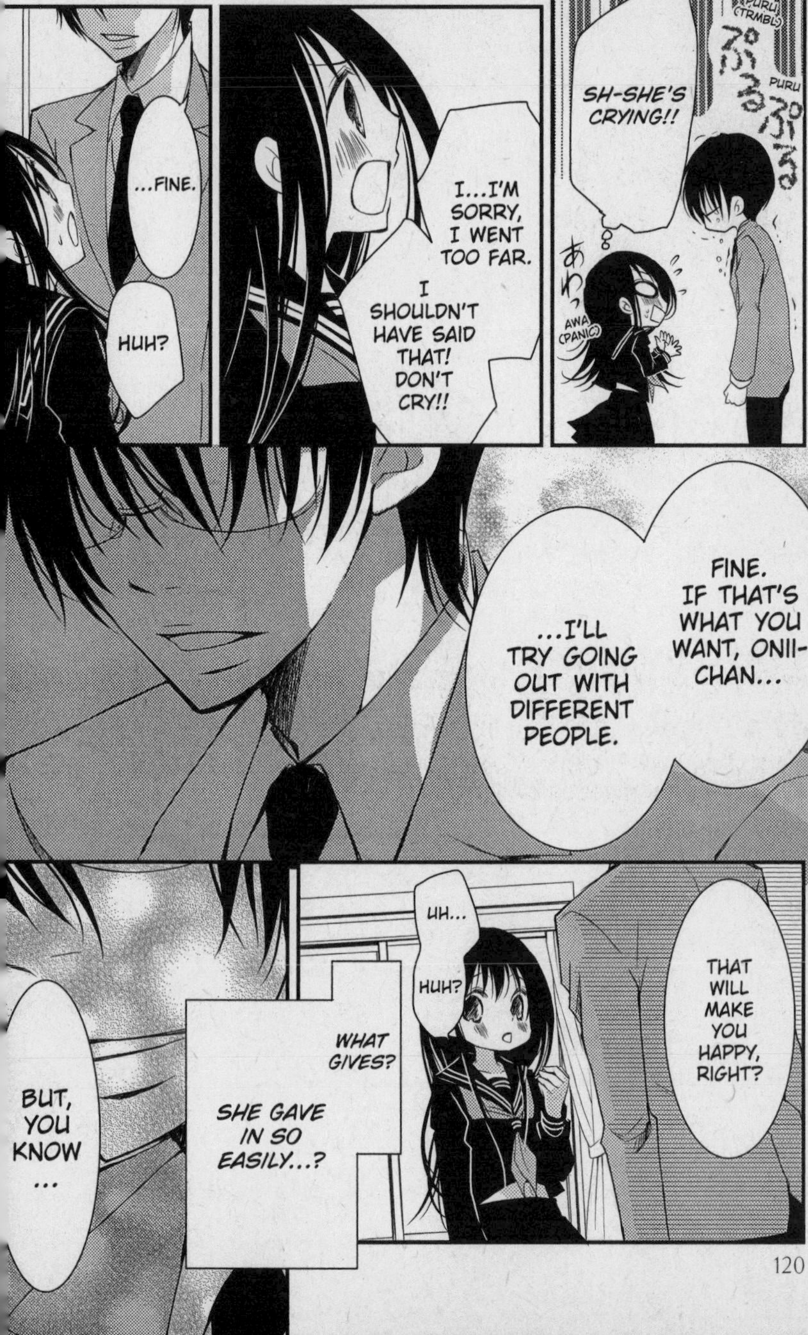
PURU (TRMBL)
ぷる
PURU
ぷる
SH-SHE'S CRYING!!
あわ
AWA (PANIC)
I...I'M SORRY, I WENT TOO FAR.
I SHOULDN'T HAVE SAID THAT! DON'T CRY!!
...FINE.
HUH?
FINE. IF THAT'S WHAT YOU WANT, ONII-CHAN...
...I'LL TRY GOING OUT WITH DIFFERENT PEOPLE.
THAT WILL MAKE YOU HAPPY, RIGHT?
UH...
HUH?
WHAT GIVES?
SHE GAVE IN SO EASILY...?
BUT, YOU KNOW...

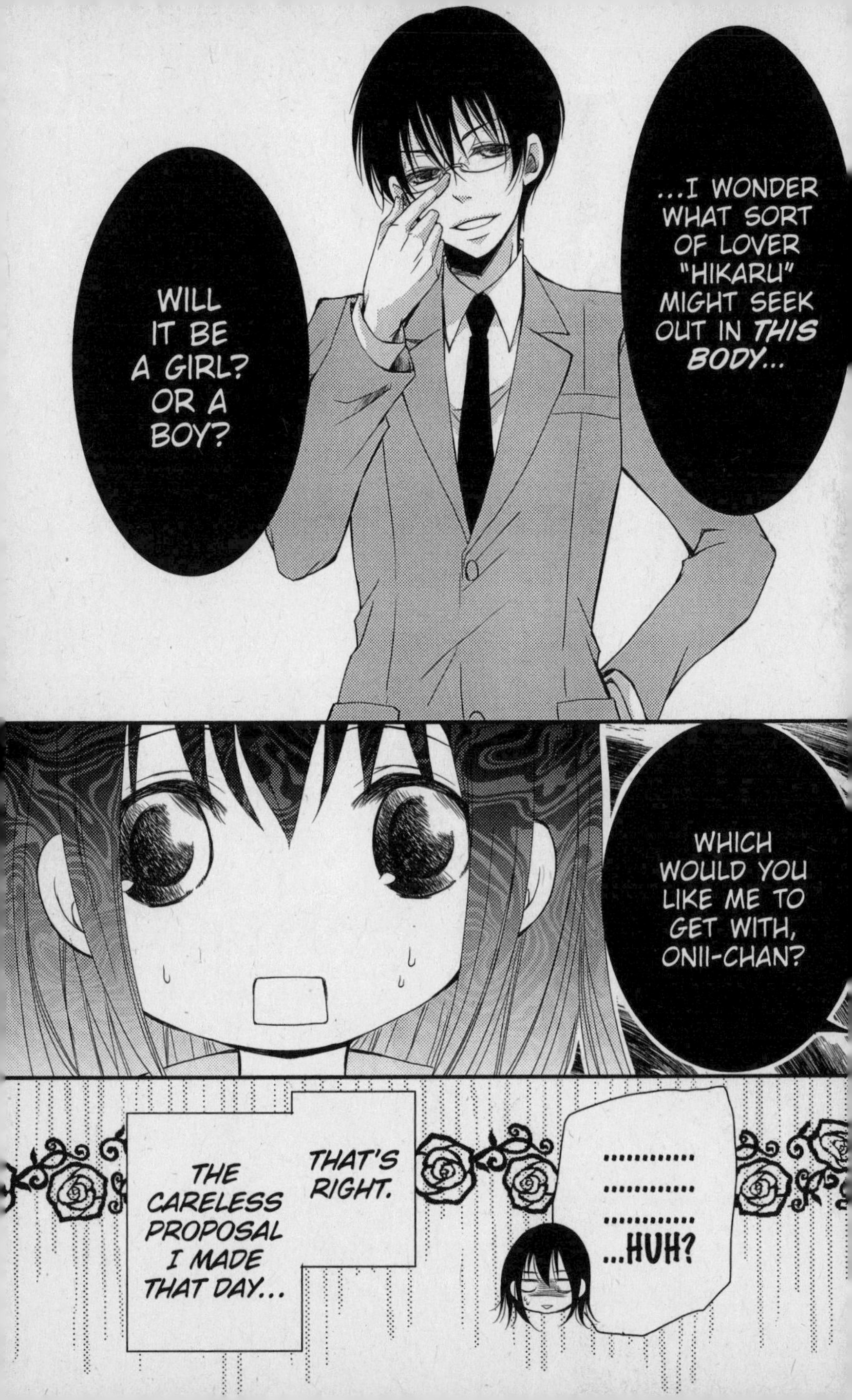
...I WONDER WHAT SORT OF LOVER "HIKARU" MIGHT SEEK OUT IN *THIS BODY*...
WILL IT BE A GIRL? OR A BOY?
WHICH WOULD YOU LIKE ME TO GET WITH, ONII-CHAN?
....HUH?
THAT'S RIGHT.
THE CARELESS PROPOSAL I MADE THAT DAY...

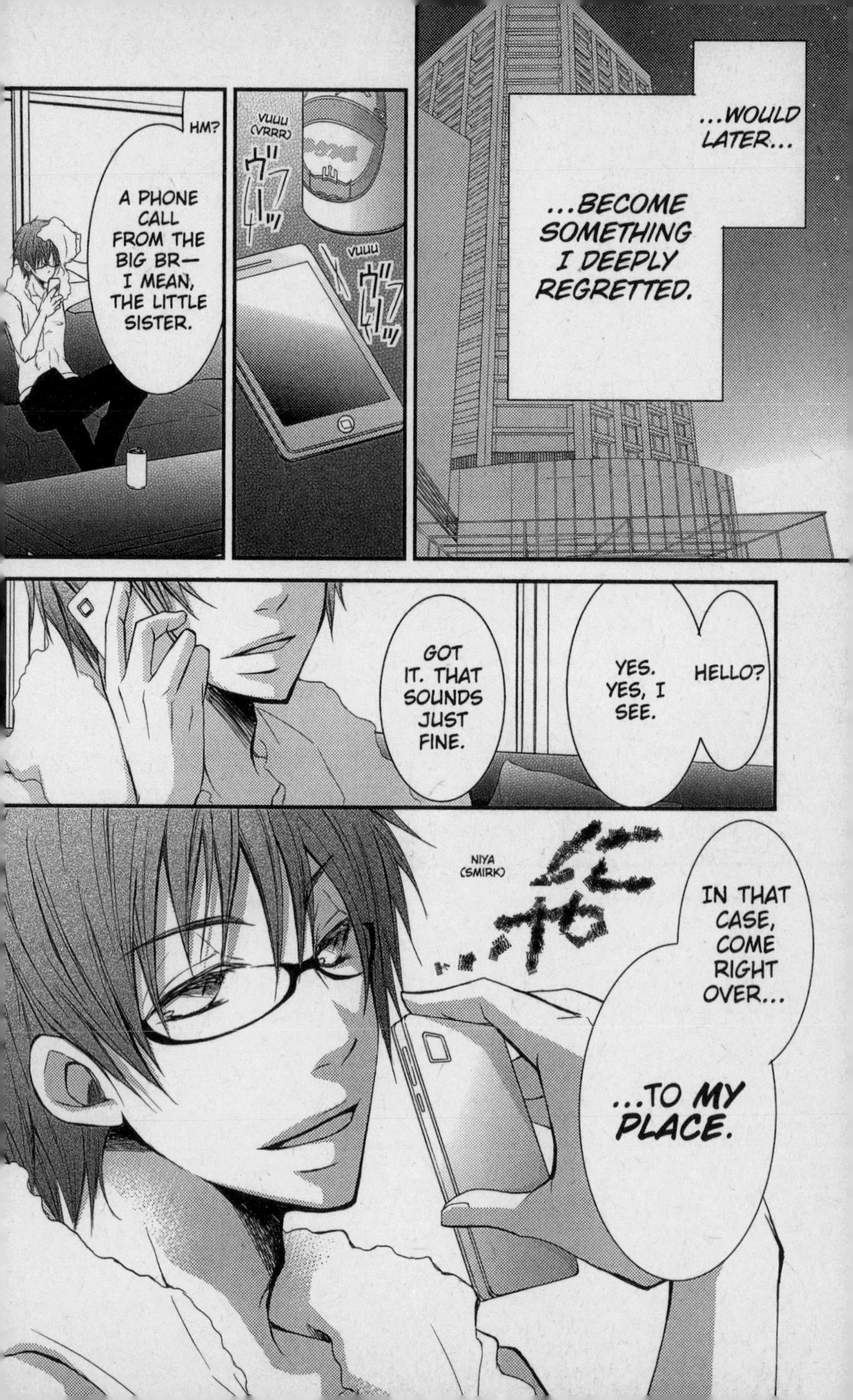
...WOULD LATER...
...BECOME SOMETHING I DEEPLY REGRETTED.
VUUU (VRRR)
VUUU
HM?
A PHONE CALL FROM THE BIG BR— I MEAN, THE LITTLE SISTER.
HELLO?
YES. YES, I SEE.
GOT IT. THAT SOUNDS JUST FINE.
IN THAT CASE, COME RIGHT OVER...
...TO *MY* *PLACE*.
NIYA (SMIRK)

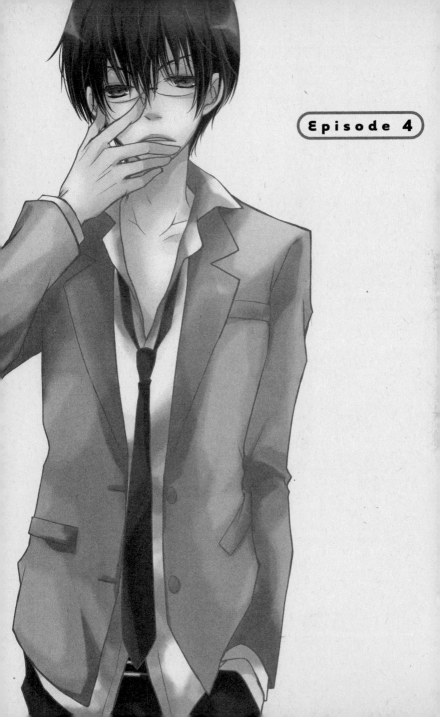

Episode 4

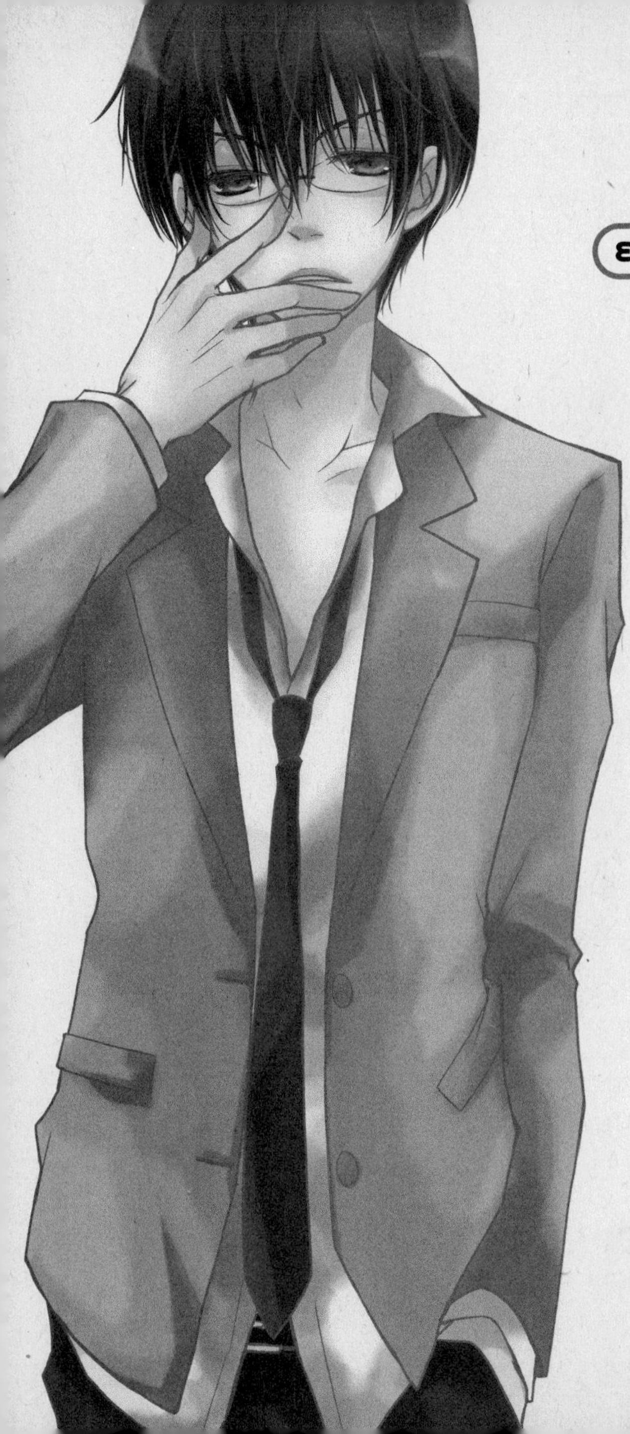

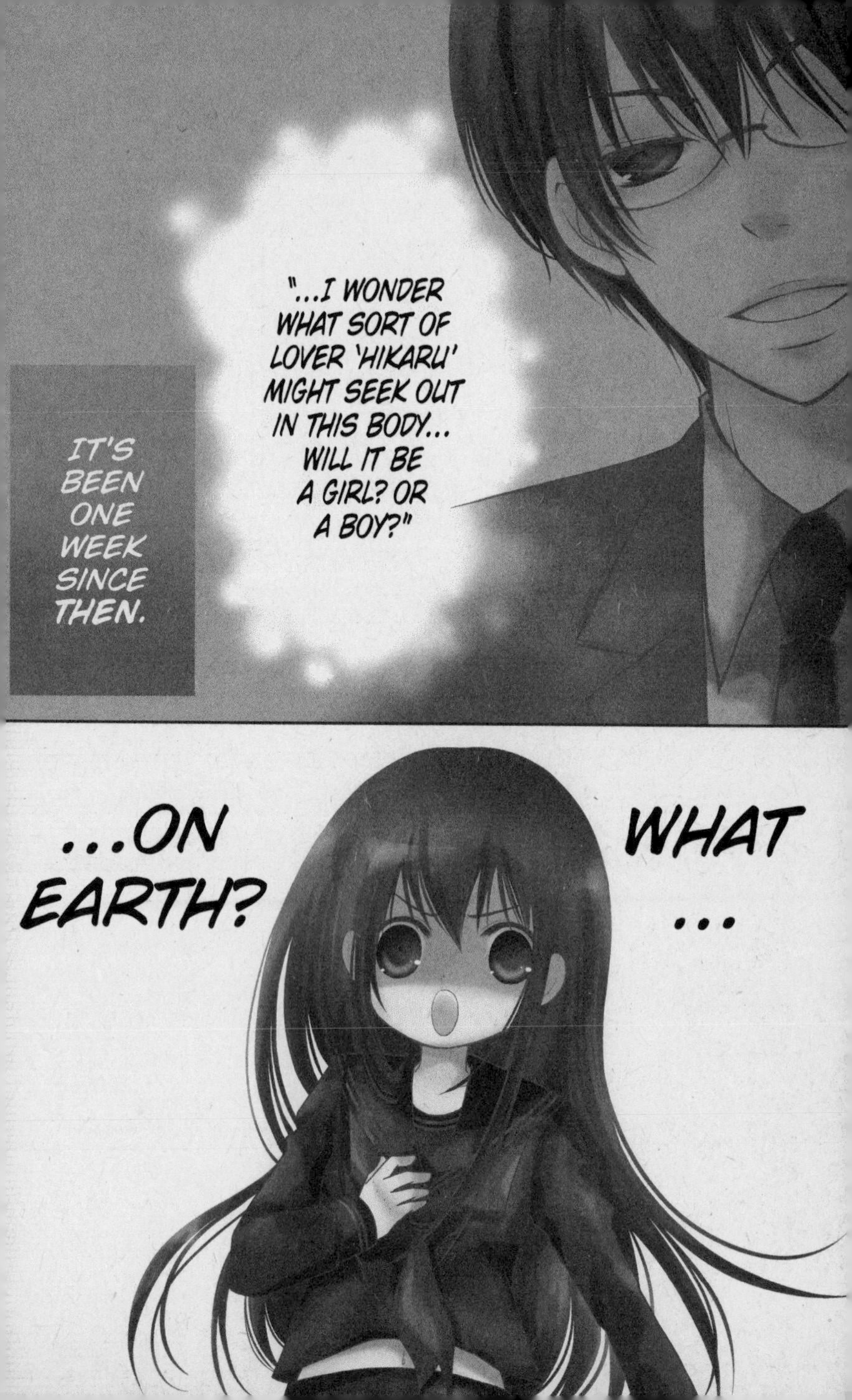
"...I WONDER WHAT SORT OF LOVER 'HIKARU' MIGHT SEEK OUT IN THIS BODY... WILL IT BE A GIRL? OR A BOY?"
IT'S BEEN ONE WEEK SINCE THEN.
WHAT ...
...ON EARTH?

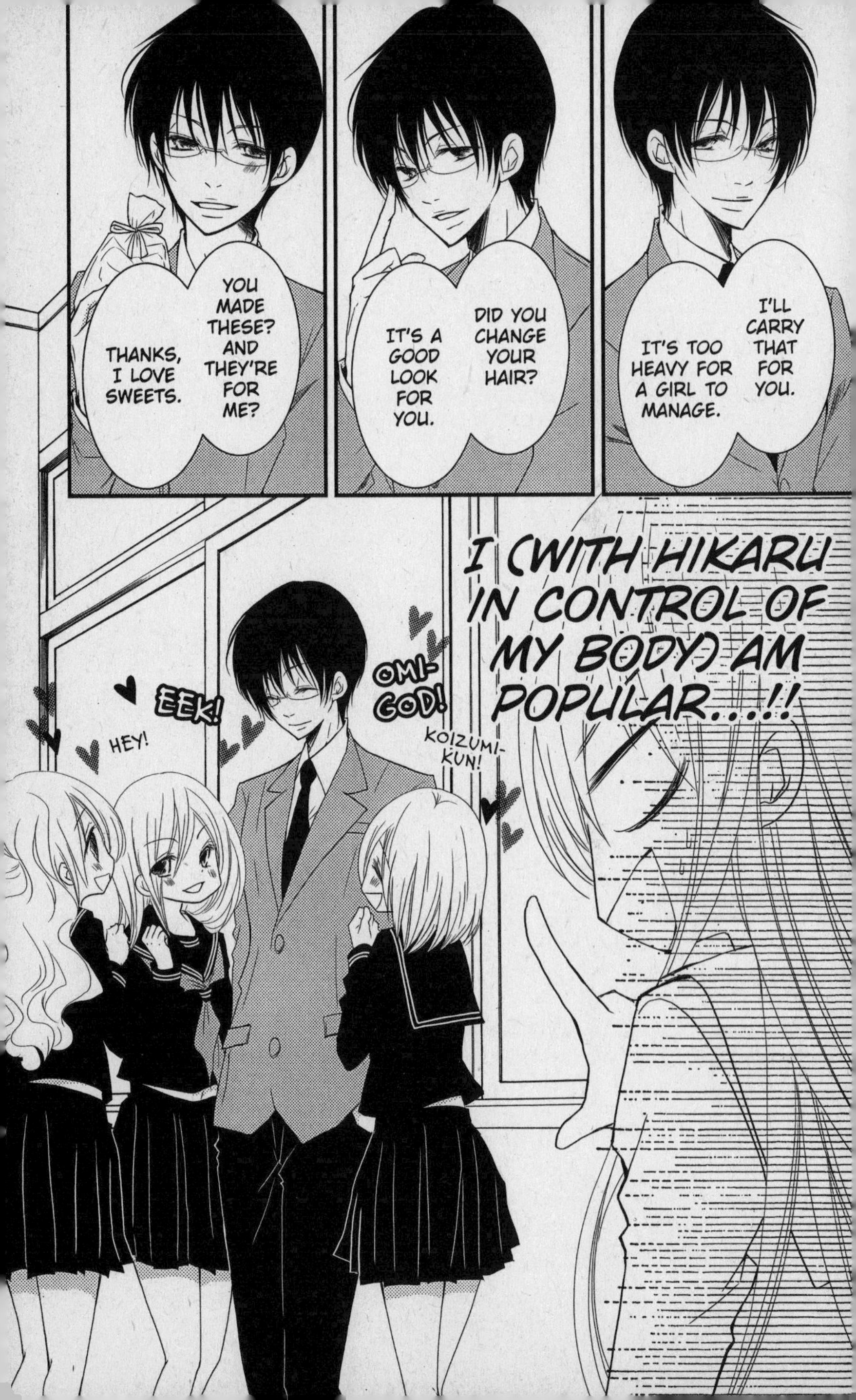
I'LL CARRY THAT FOR YOU.
IT'S TOO HEAVY FOR A GIRL TO MANAGE.
DID YOU CHANGE YOUR HAIR?
IT'S A GOOD LOOK FOR YOU.
YOU MADE THESE? AND THEY'RE FOR ME?
THANKS, I LOVE SWEETS.
I (WITH HIKARU IN CONTROL OF MY BODY) AM POPULAR...!!
KOIZUMI-KUN!
OMI-GOD!
EEK!
HEY!

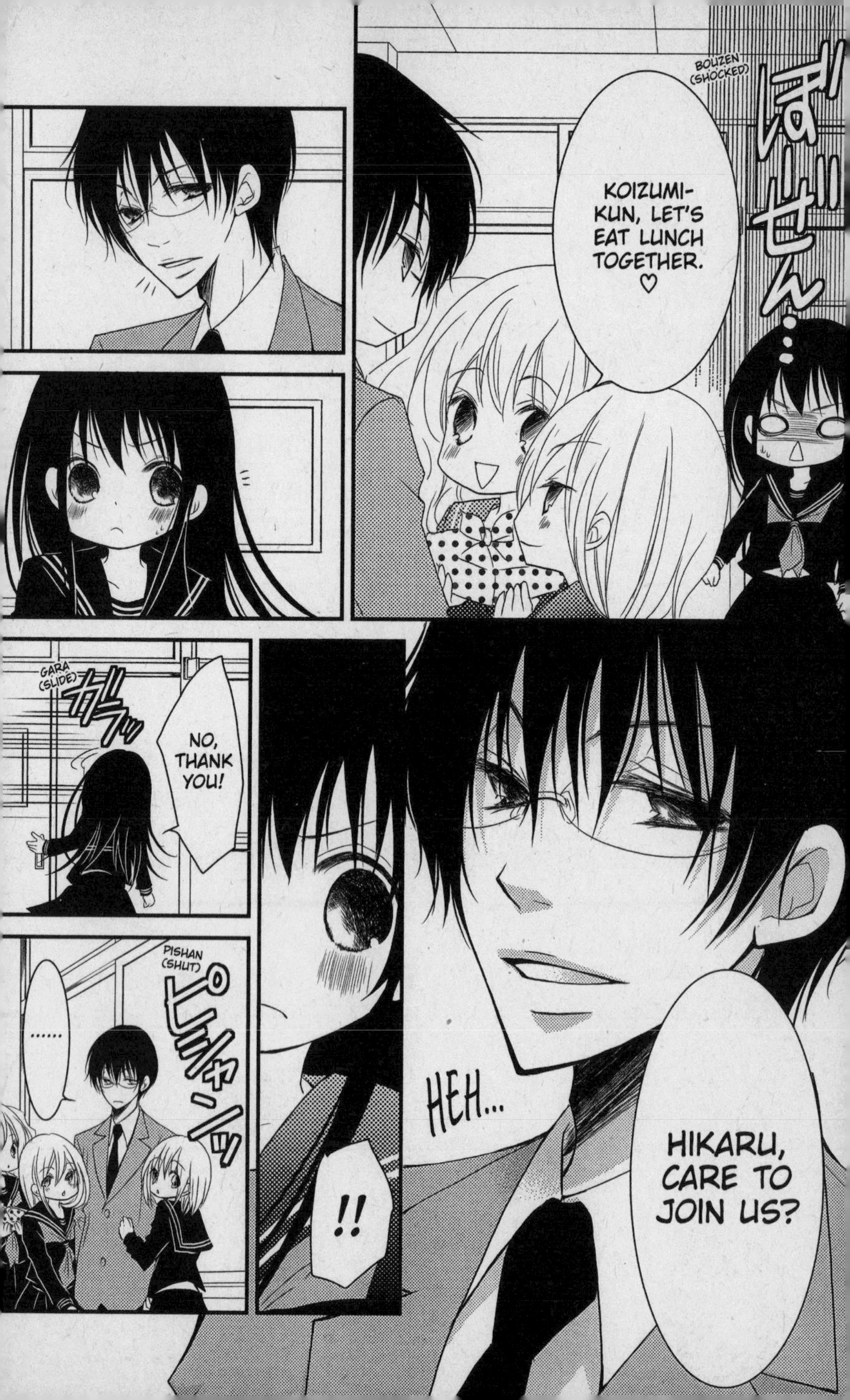

BOUZEN (SHOCKED)
ぼうぜん
KOIZUMI-KUN, LET'S EAT LUNCH TOGETHER. ♡
HIKARU, CARE TO JOIN US?
HEH...
!!
GARA (SLIDE)
ガラッ
NO, THANK YOU!
PISHAN (SHUT)
ピシャーンッ
......

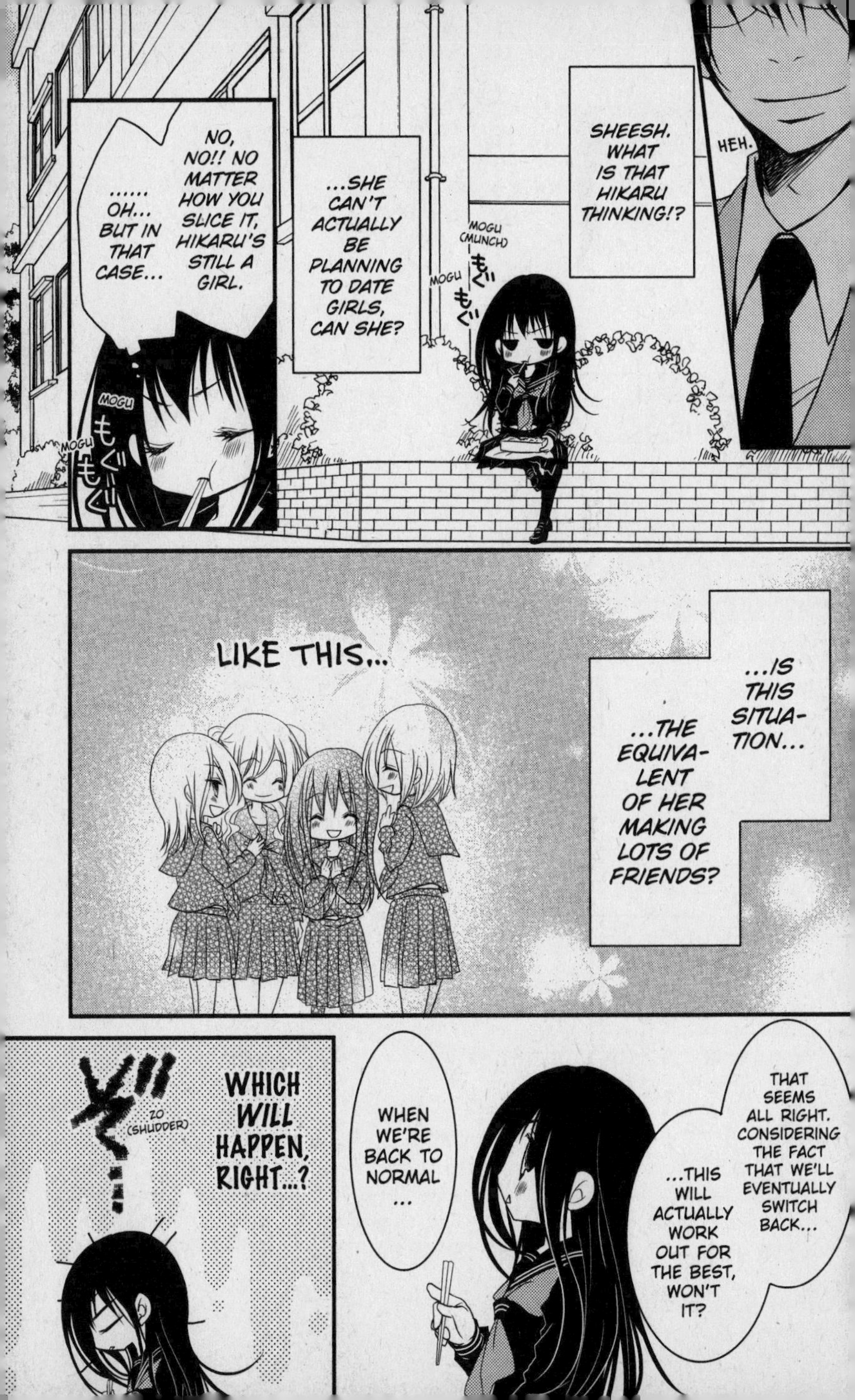
HEH.
SHEESH. WHAT IS THAT HIKARU THINKING!?
MOGU (MUNCH) もぐ
MOGU もぐ
...SHE CAN'T ACTUALLY BE PLANNING TO DATE GIRLS, CAN SHE?
NO, NO!! NO MATTER HOW YOU SLICE IT, HIKARU'S STILL A GIRL.
......OH... BUT IN THAT CASE...
MOGU もぐ
MOGU もぐ
...IS THIS SITUATION...
...THE EQUIVALENT OF HER MAKING LOTS OF FRIENDS?
LIKE THIS...
THAT SEEMS ALL RIGHT. CONSIDERING THE FACT THAT WE'LL EVENTUALLY SWITCH BACK...
...THIS WILL ACTUALLY WORK OUT FOR THE BEST, WON'T IT?
WHEN WE'RE BACK TO NORMAL...
WHICH WILL HAPPEN, RIGHT...?
ZO (SHUDDER)

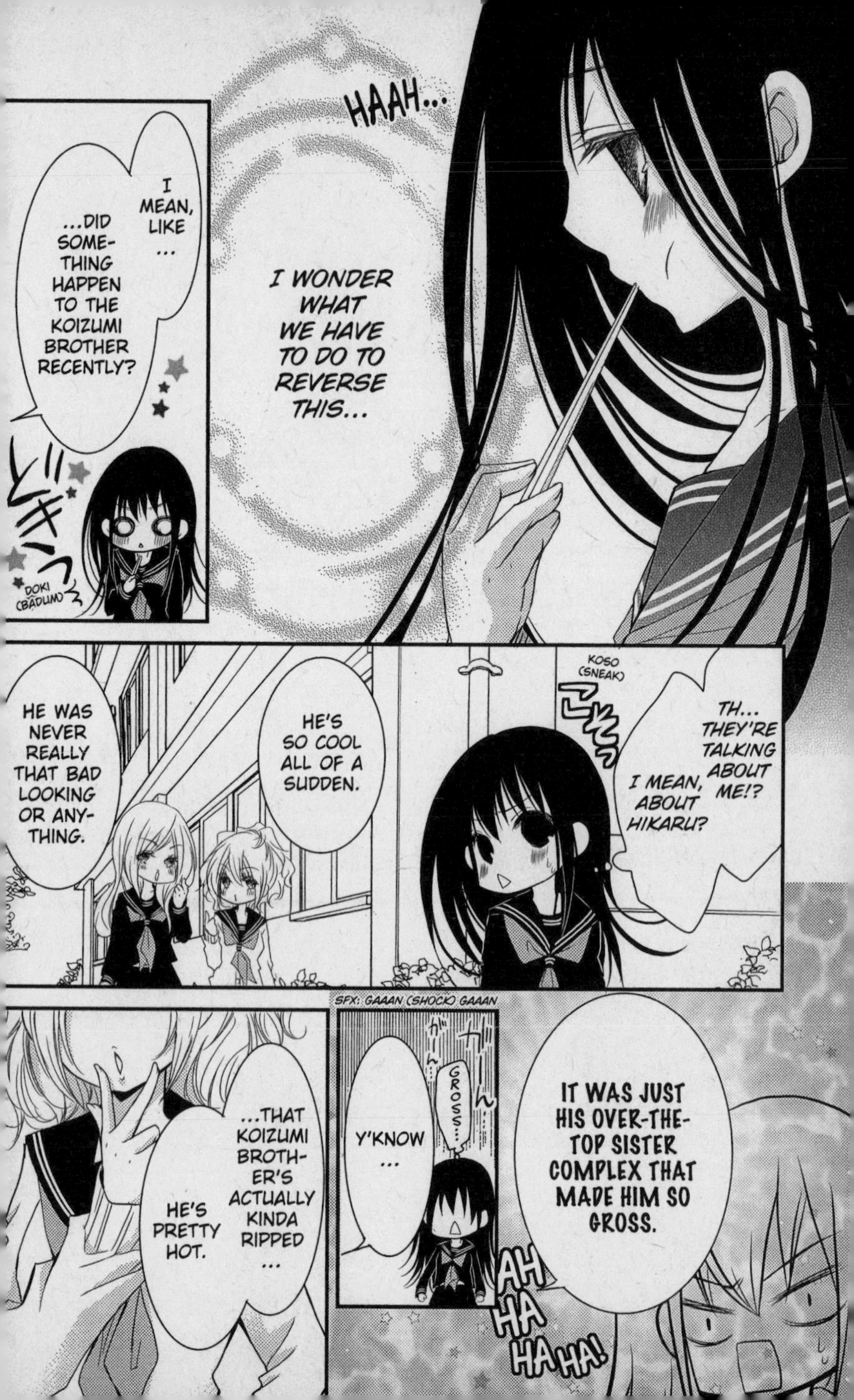
HAAH...
I WONDER WHAT WE HAVE TO DO TO REVERSE THIS...
I MEAN, LIKE...
...DID SOMETHING HAPPEN TO THE KOIZUMI BROTHER RECENTLY?
DOKI (BADUM)
KOSO (SNEAK)
TH... THEY'RE TALKING ABOUT ME!?
I MEAN, ABOUT HIKARU?
HE'S SO COOL ALL OF A SUDDEN.
HE WAS NEVER REALLY THAT BAD LOOKING OR ANY-THING.
IT WAS JUST HIS OVER-THE-TOP SISTER COMPLEX THAT MADE HIM SO GROSS.
AH HA HA HA HA!
SFX: GAAAN (SHOCK) GAAAN
GROSS...
Y'KNOW...
...THAT KOIZUMI BROTH-ER'S ACTUALLY KINDA RIPPED...
HE'S PRETTY HOT.

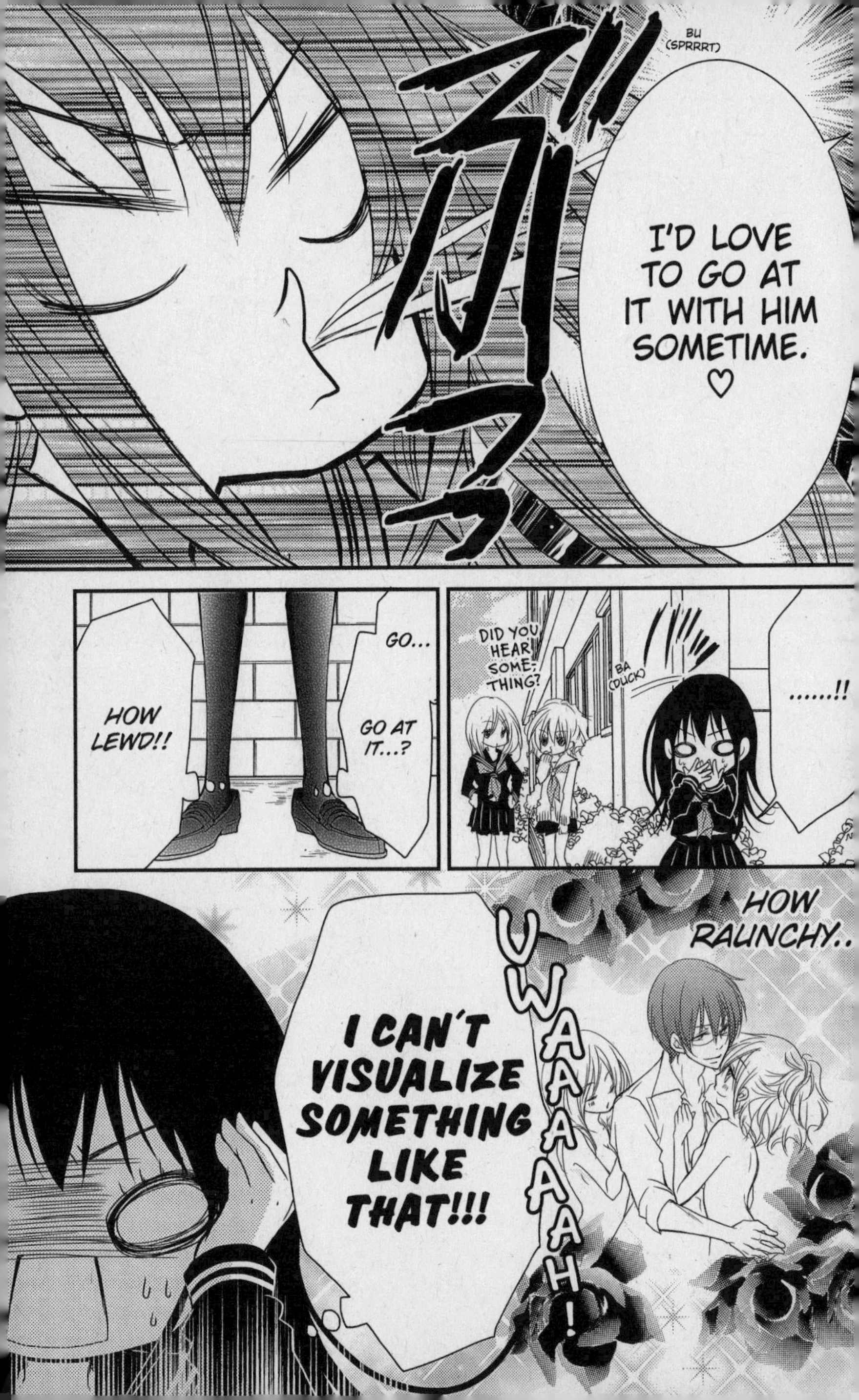
BU
(SPRRRT)
I'D LOVE TO GO AT IT WITH HIM SOMETIME. ♡
......!!
BA
(DUCK)
DID YOU HEAR SOMETHING?
GO...
GO AT IT...?
HOW LEWD!!
HOW RAUNCHY..
UWAAAAAAH!
I CAN'T VISUALIZE SOMETHING LIKE THAT!!!

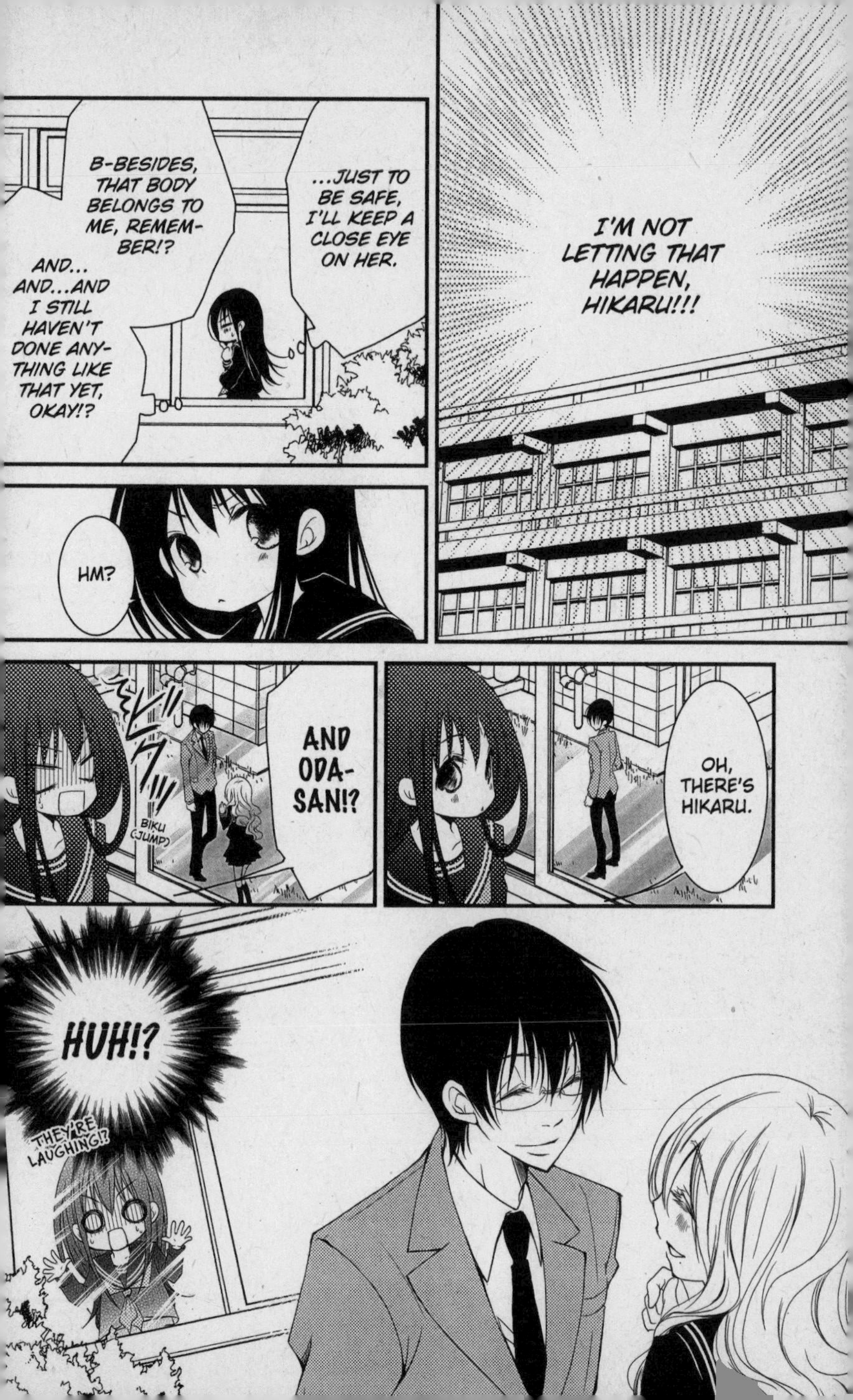
I'M NOT LETTING THAT HAPPEN, HIKARU!!!
...JUST TO BE SAFE, I'LL KEEP A CLOSE EYE ON HER.
B-BESIDES, THAT BODY BELONGS TO ME, REMEM-BER!?
AND... AND...AND I STILL HAVEN'T DONE ANY-THING LIKE THAT YET, OKAY!?
HM?
OH, THERE'S HIKARU.
AND ODA-SAN!?
BIKU (JUMP)
HUH!?
THEY'RE LAUGHING!?

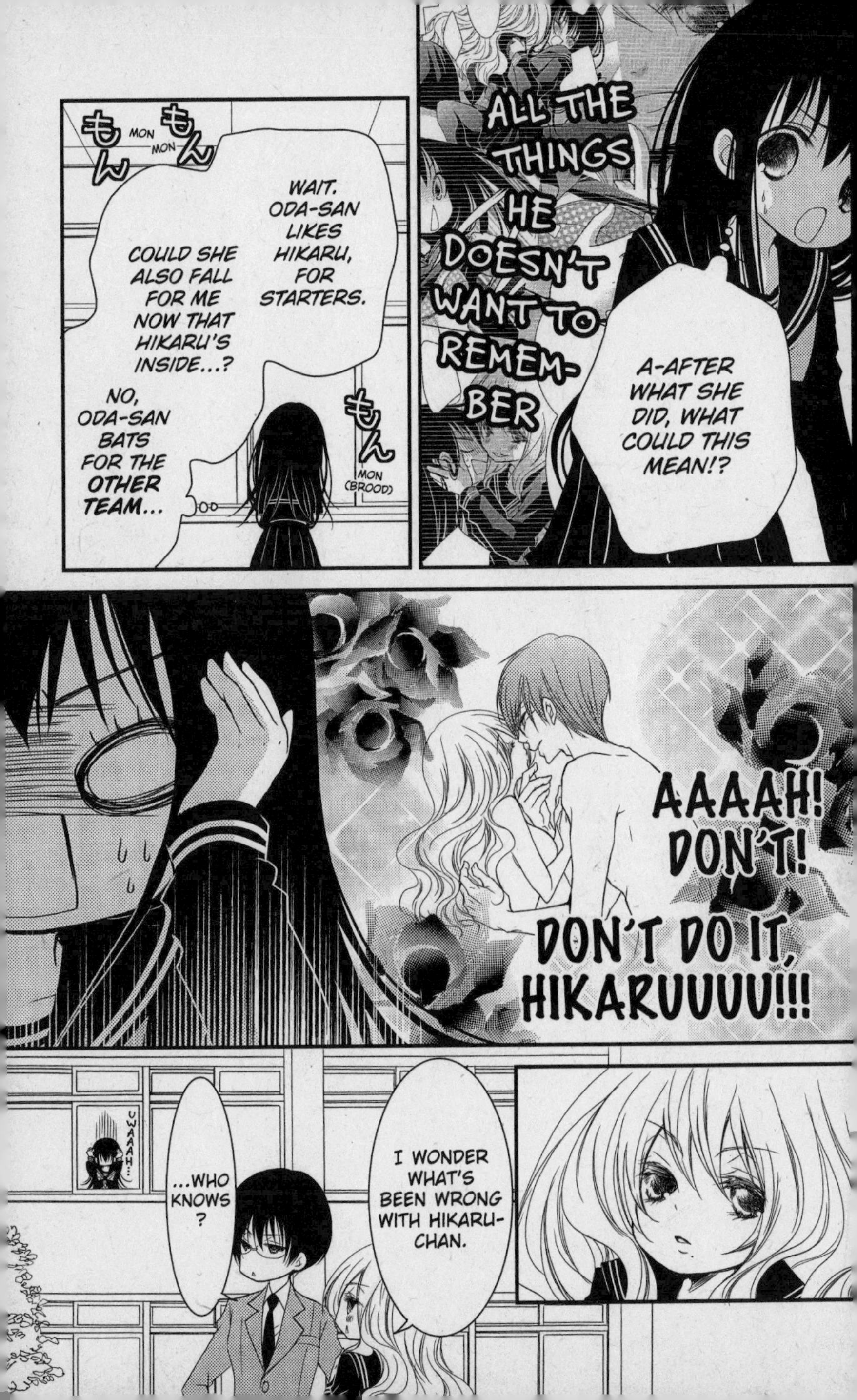
ALL THE THINGS HE DOESN'T WANT TO REMEMBER
A-AFTER WHAT SHE DID, WHAT COULD THIS MEAN!?
もん もん
MON MON
WAIT. ODA-SAN LIKES HIKARU, FOR STARTERS.
COULD SHE ALSO FALL FOR ME NOW THAT HIKARU'S INSIDE...?
NO, ODA-SAN BATS FOR THE OTHER TEAM...
もん
MON (BROOD)
AAAAH! DON'T!
DON'T DO IT, HIKARUUUU!!!
I WONDER WHAT'S BEEN WRONG WITH HIKARU-CHAN.
...WHO KNOWS?
UWAAAH...

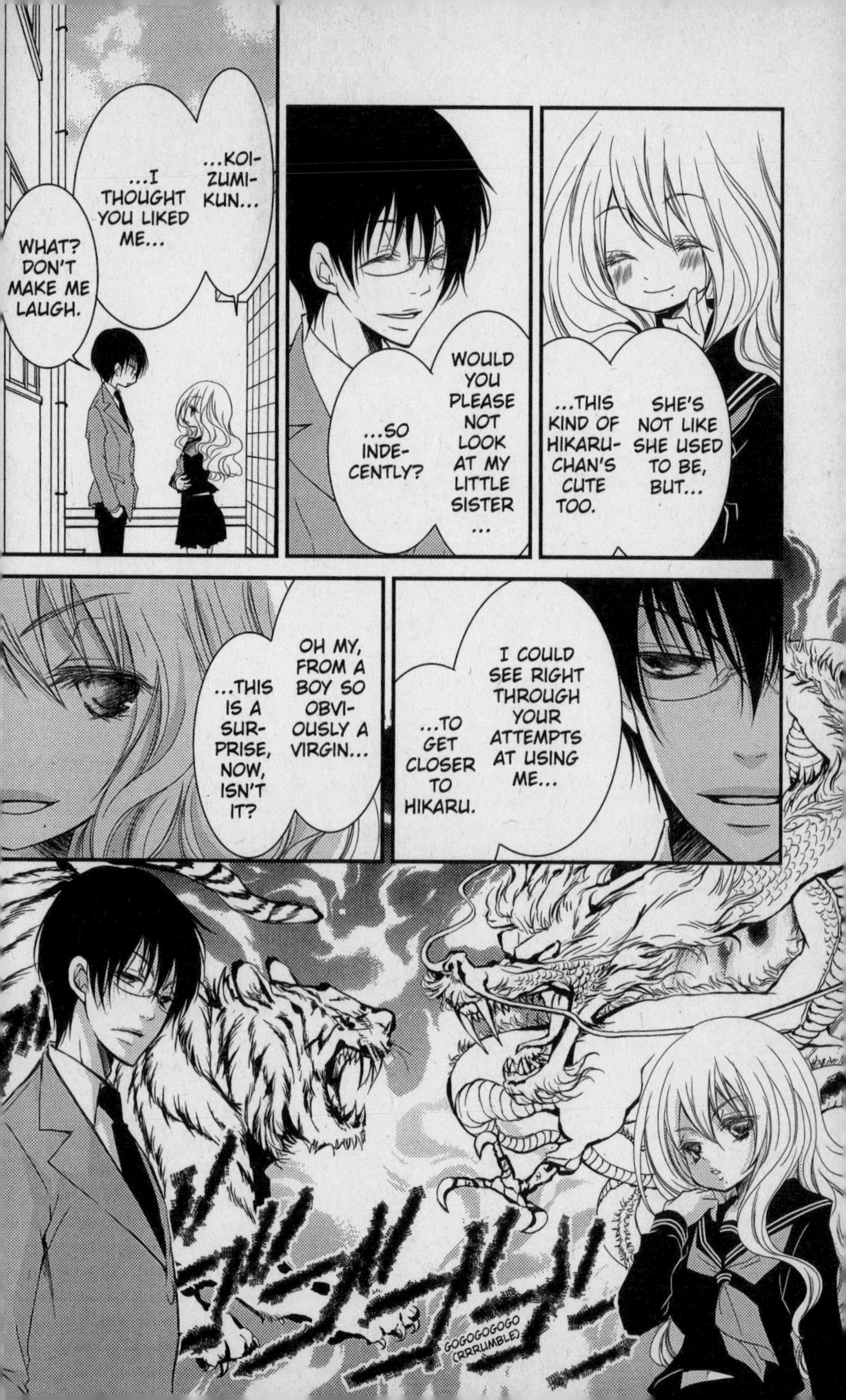
SHE'S NOT LIKE SHE USED TO BE, BUT...
...THIS KIND OF HIKARU-CHAN'S CUTE TOO.
WOULD YOU PLEASE NOT LOOK AT MY LITTLE SISTER ...
...SO INDE-CENTLY?
...KOI-ZUMI-KUN...
...I THOUGHT YOU LIKED ME...
WHAT? DON'T MAKE ME LAUGH.
I COULD SEE RIGHT THROUGH YOUR ATTEMPTS AT USING ME...
...TO GET CLOSER TO HIKARU.
OH MY, FROM A BOY SO OBVI-OUSLY A VIRGIN...
...THIS IS A SUR-PRISE, NOW, ISN'T IT?
GOGOGOGOGO (RRRUMBLE)

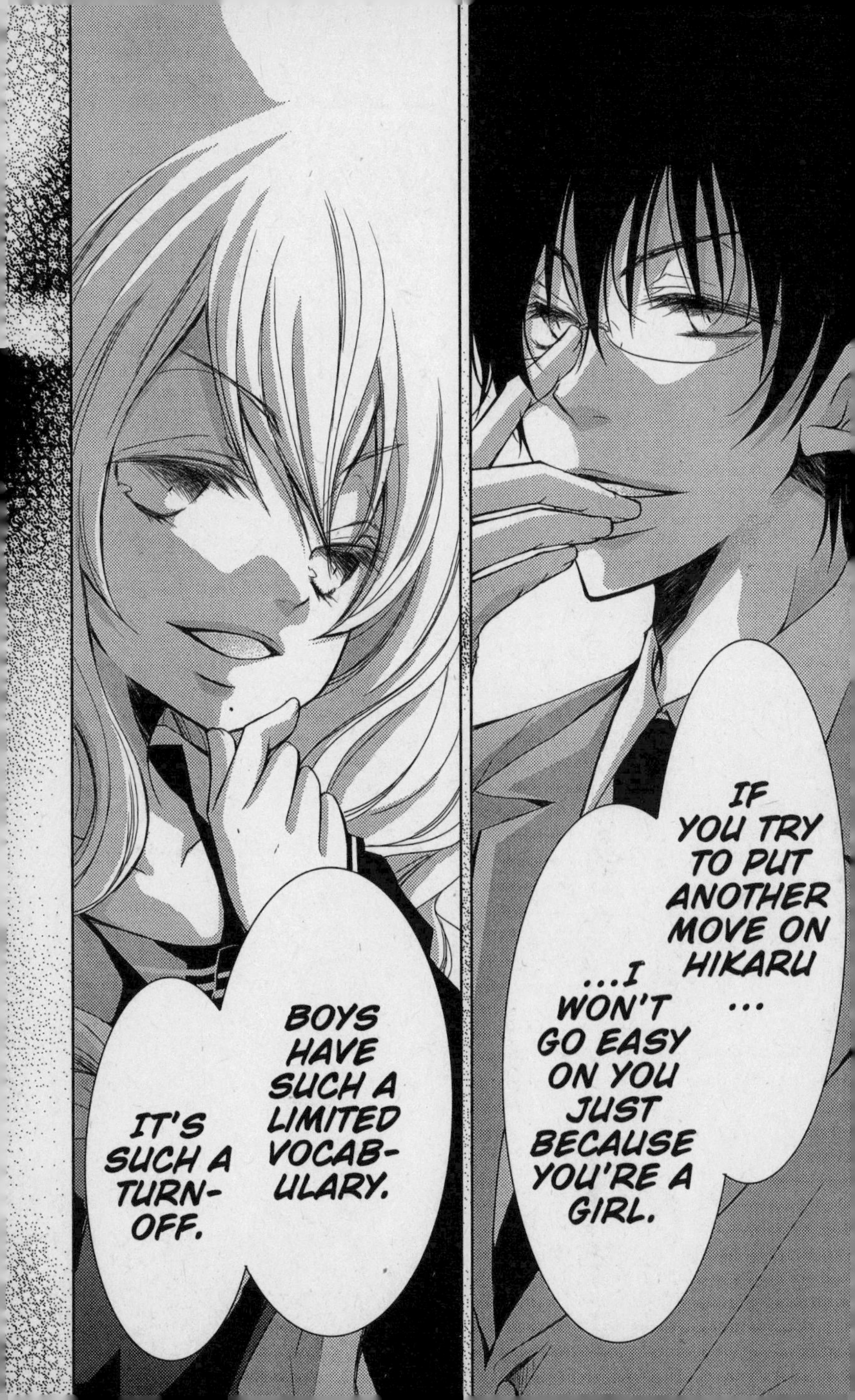
IF YOU TRY TO PUT ANOTHER MOVE ON HIKARU ...
...I WON'T GO EASY ON YOU JUST BECAUSE YOU'RE A GIRL.
BOYS HAVE SUCH A LIMITED VOCAB-ULARY.
IT'S SUCH A TURN-OFF.

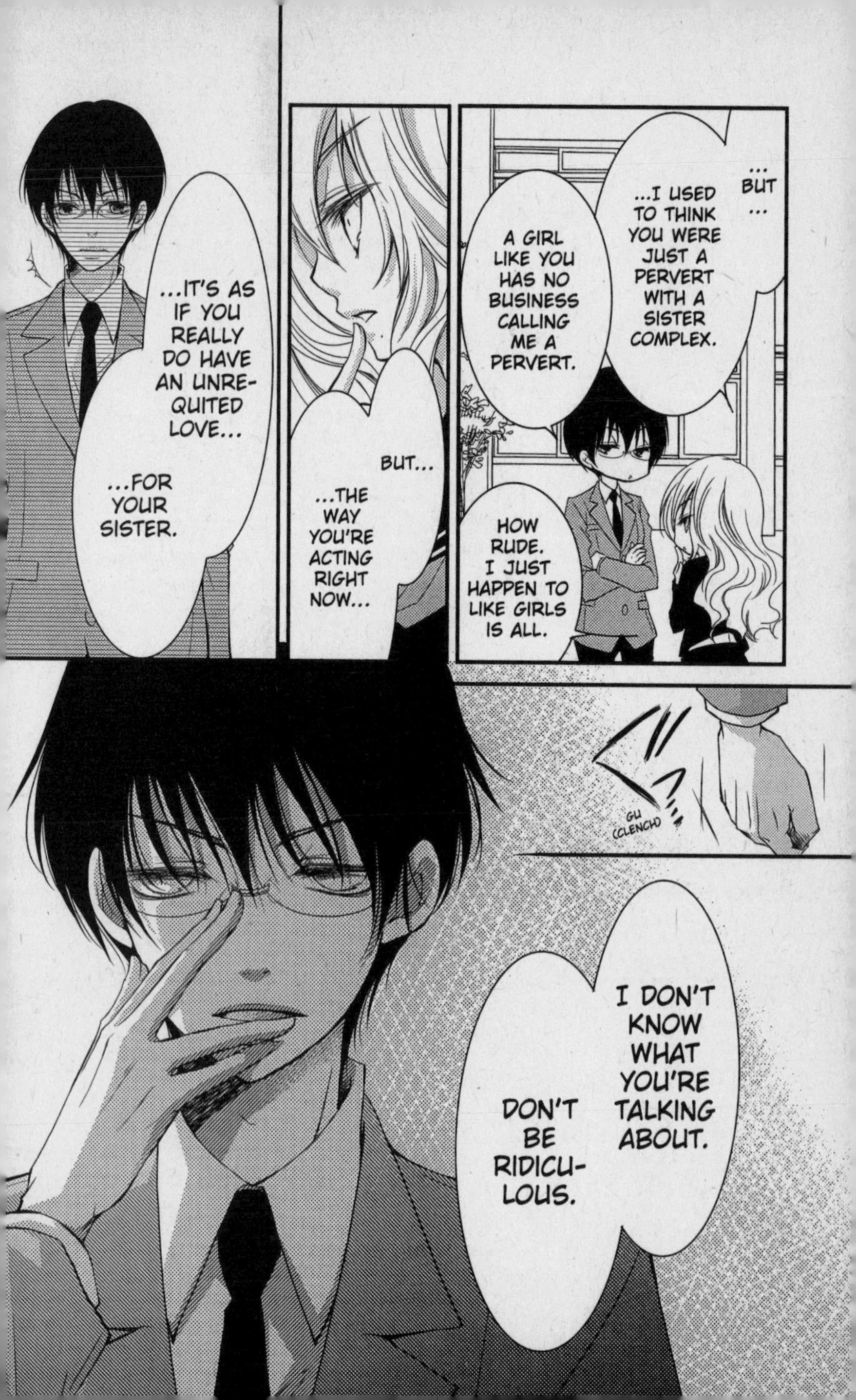
...BUT...
...I USED TO THINK YOU WERE JUST A PERVERT WITH A SISTER COMPLEX.
A GIRL LIKE YOU HAS NO BUSINESS CALLING ME A PERVERT.
HOW RUDE. I JUST HAPPEN TO LIKE GIRLS IS ALL.
BUT...
...THE WAY YOU'RE ACTING RIGHT NOW...
...IT'S AS IF YOU REALLY DO HAVE AN UNREQUITED LOVE...
...FOR YOUR SISTER.
GU (CLENCH)
I DON'T KNOW WHAT YOU'RE TALKING ABOUT.
DON'T BE RIDICULOUS.

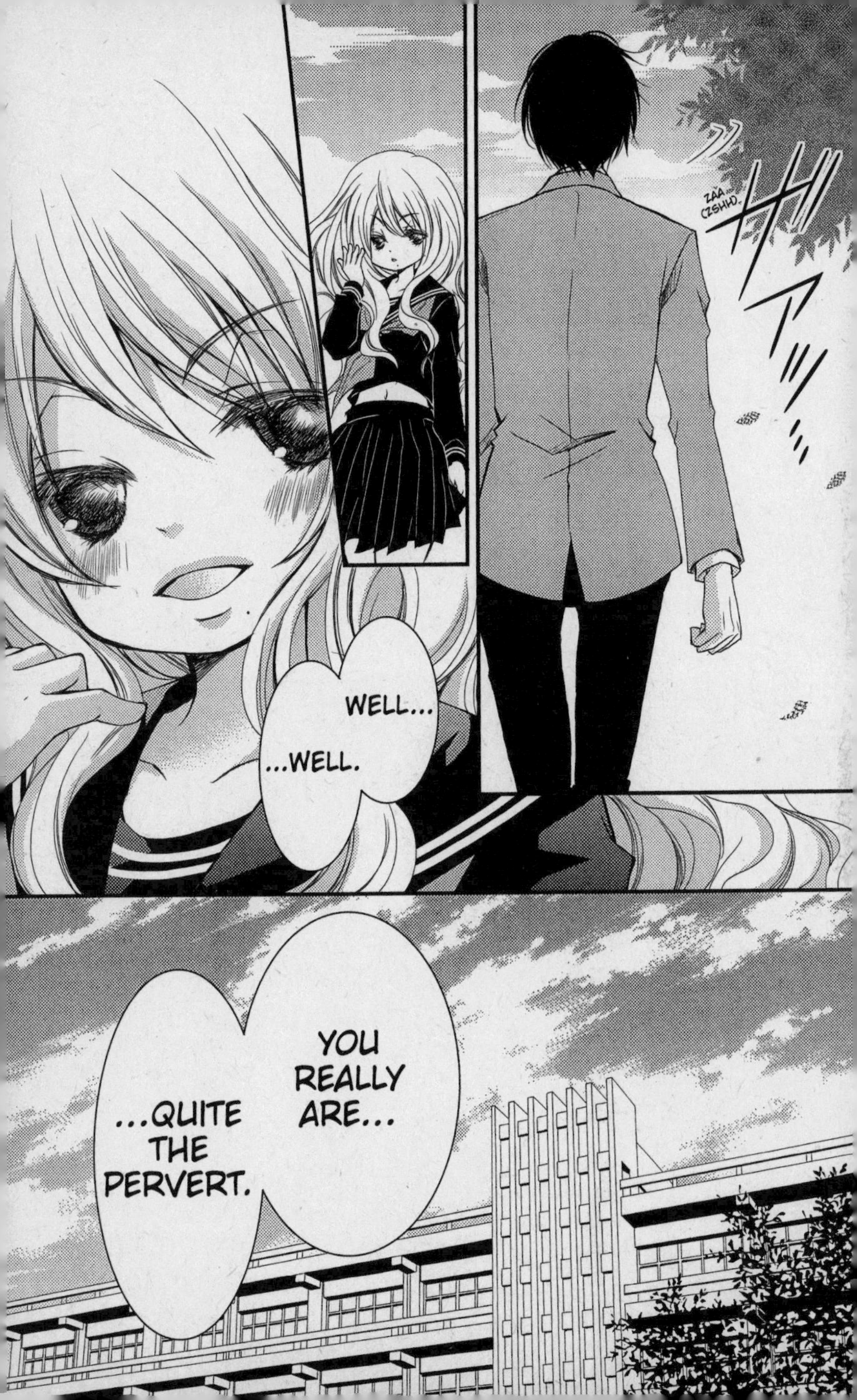
ZAA... (ZSHH)
WELL...
...WELL.
YOU REALLY ARE...
...QUITE THE PERVERT.

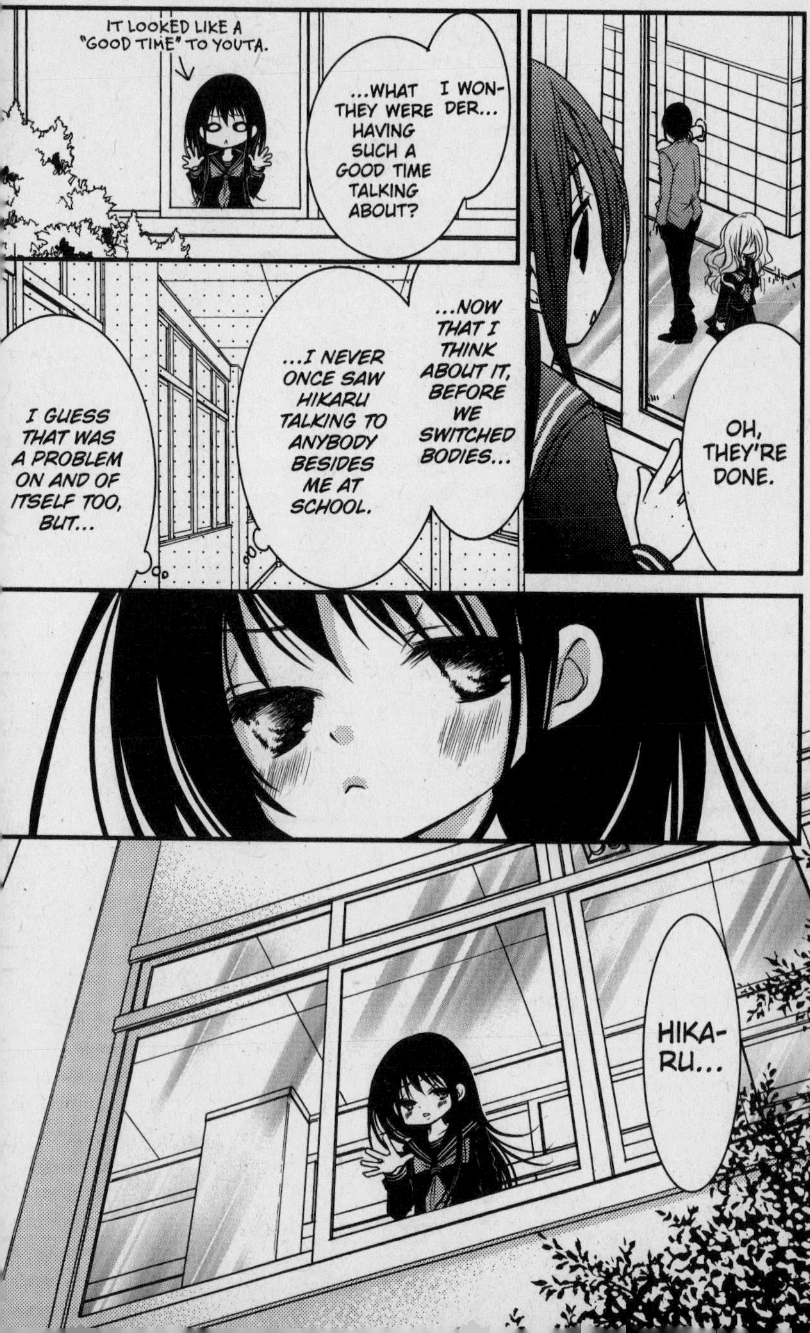
OH, THEY'RE DONE.
I WONDER... ...WHAT THEY WERE HAVING SUCH A GOOD TIME TALKING ABOUT?
IT LOOKED LIKE A "GOOD TIME" TO YOUTA.
...NOW THAT I THINK ABOUT IT, BEFORE WE SWITCHED BODIES...
...I NEVER ONCE SAW HIKARU TALKING TO ANYBODY BESIDES ME AT SCHOOL.
I GUESS THAT WAS A PROBLEM ON AND OF ITSELF TOO, BUT...
HIKA-RU...

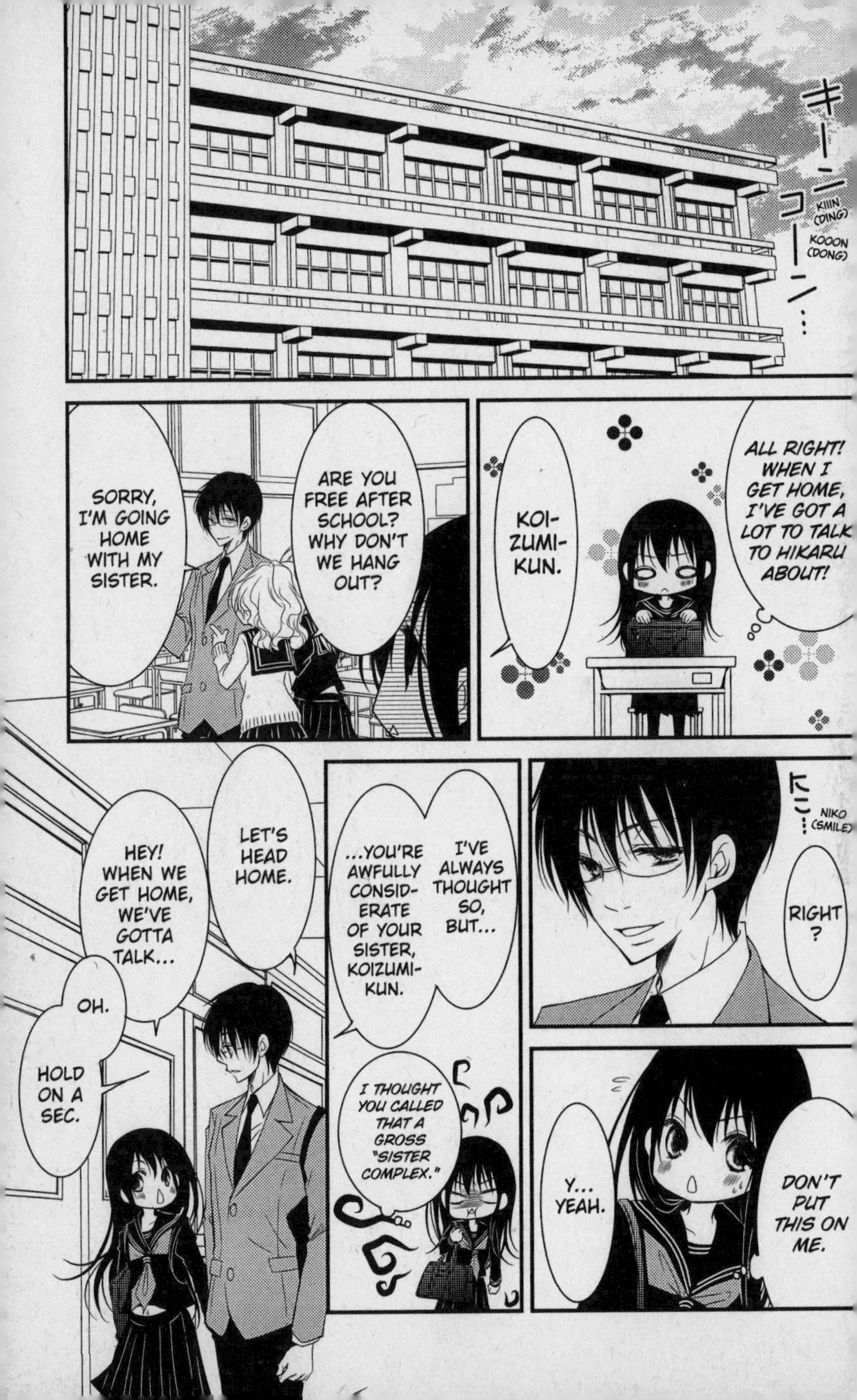
キーンコーン…
KIIN (DING)
KOOON (DONG)
ALL RIGHT! WHEN I GET HOME, I'VE GOT A LOT TO TALK TO HIKARU ABOUT!
KOI-ZUMI-KUN.
ARE YOU FREE AFTER SCHOOL? WHY DON'T WE HANG OUT?
SORRY, I'M GOING HOME WITH MY SISTER.
ニコ…
NIKO (SMILE)
RIGHT?
DON'T PUT THIS ON ME.
Y... YEAH.
I'VE ALWAYS THOUGHT SO, BUT...
...YOU'RE AWFULLY CONSID-ERATE OF YOUR SISTER, KOIZUMI-KUN.
I THOUGHT YOU CALLED THAT A GROSS "SISTER COMPLEX."
LET'S HEAD HOME.
HEY! WHEN WE GET HOME, WE'VE GOTTA TALK...
OH.
HOLD ON A SEC.

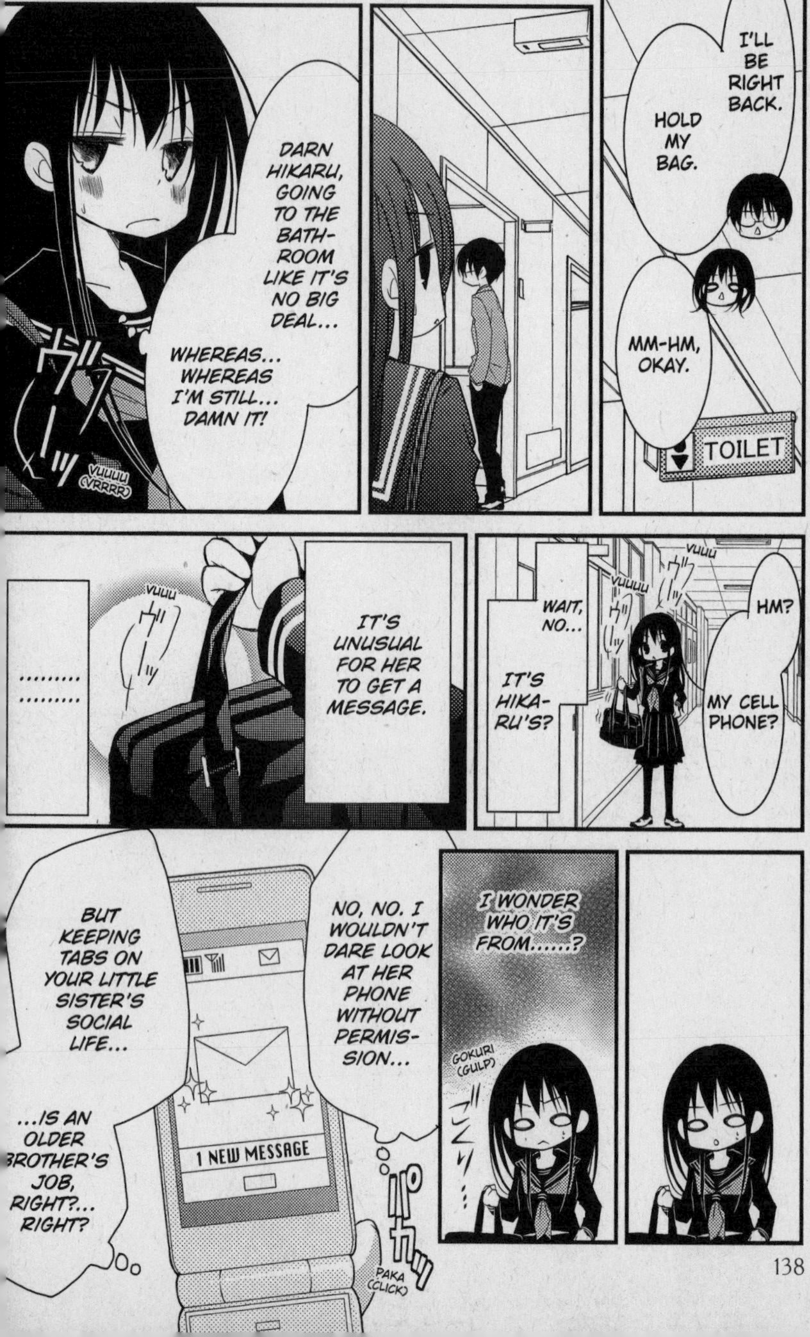

I'LL BE RIGHT BACK.
HOLD MY BAG.
MM-HM, OKAY.
TOILET
DARN HIKARU, GOING TO THE BATH-ROOM LIKE IT'S NO BIG DEAL...
WHEREAS... WHEREAS I'M STILL... DAMN IT!
VUUUU (VRRRR)
VUUU
VUUUU
HM?
MY CELL PHONE?
WAIT, NO...
IT'S HIKA-RU'S?
VUUU
IT'S UNUSUAL FOR HER TO GET A MESSAGE.
....
....
I WONDER WHO IT'S FROM......?
GOKURI (GULP)
NO, NO. I WOULDN'T DARE LOOK AT HER PHONE WITHOUT PERMIS-SION...
BUT KEEPING TABS ON YOUR LITTLE SISTER'S SOCIAL LIFE...
...IS AN OLDER BROTHER'S JOB, RIGHT?... RIGHT?
1 NEW MESSAGE
PAKA (CLICK)

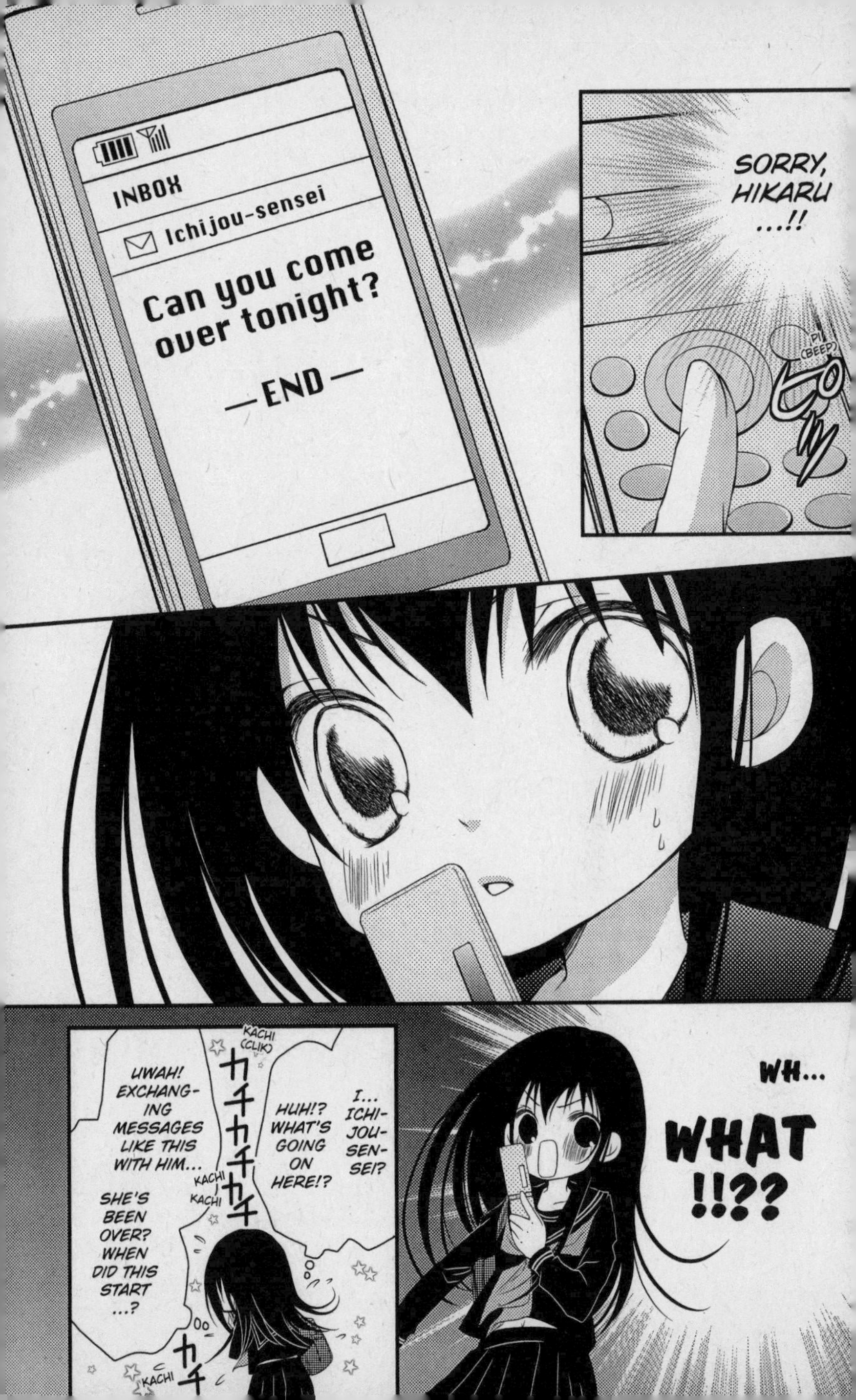
SORRY, HIKARU ...!!
PI (BEEP)
ピッ
INBOX
Ichijou-sensei
Can you come over tonight?
—END—
WH...
WHAT !!??
I... ICHI-JOU-SEN-SEI?
HUH!? WHAT'S GOING ON HERE!?
KACHI (CLIK)
カチカチカチ
KACHI KACHI
UWAH! EXCHANG-ING MESSAGES LIKE THIS WITH HIM...
SHE'S BEEN OVER? WHEN DID THIS START ...?
カチ
KACHI

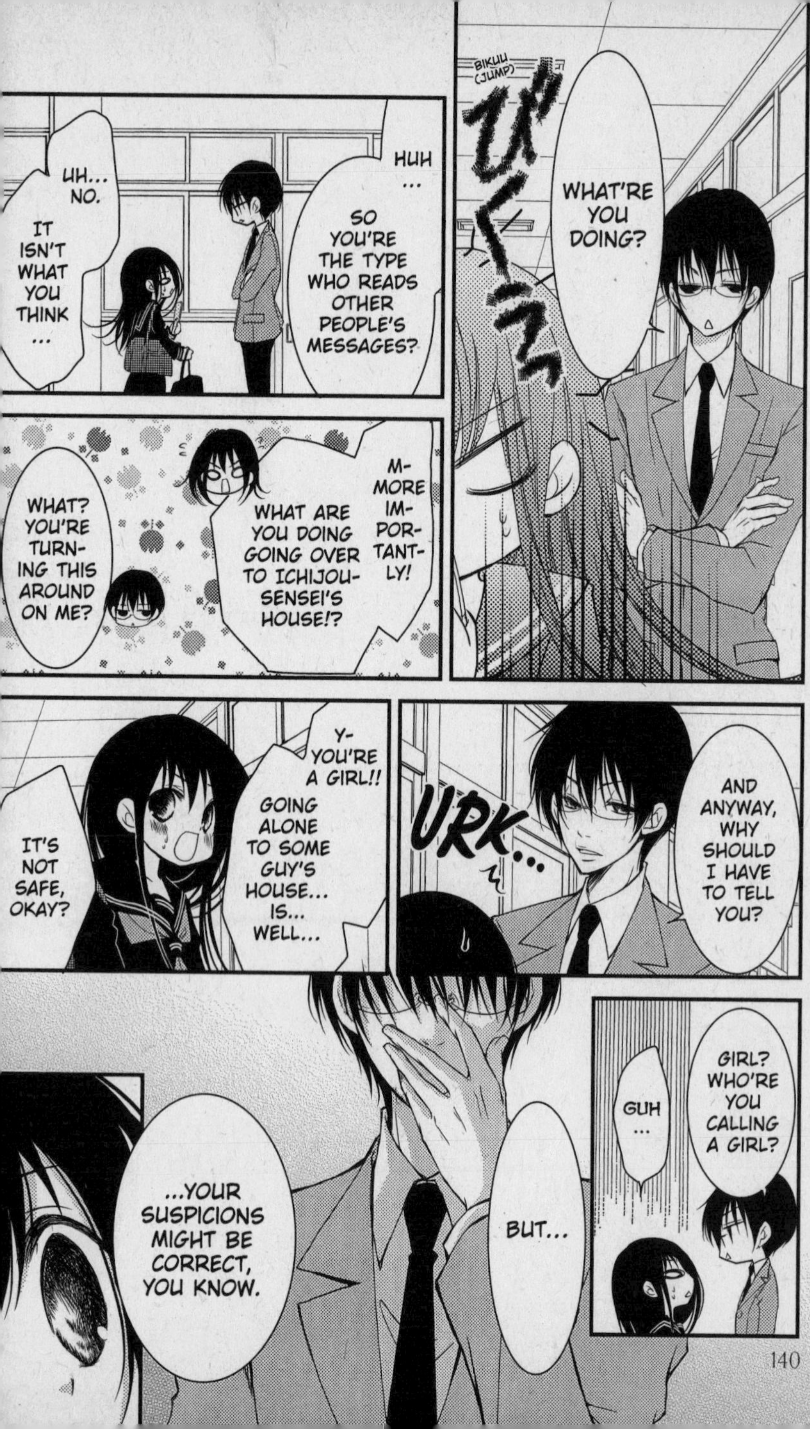
BIKUU (JUMP)
WHAT'RE YOU DOING?
HUH ...
SO YOU'RE THE TYPE WHO READS OTHER PEOPLE'S MESSAGES?
UH... NO.
IT ISN'T WHAT YOU THINK ...
M-MORE IM-POR-TANT-LY!
WHAT ARE YOU DOING GOING OVER TO ICHIJOU-SENSEI'S HOUSE!?
WHAT? YOU'RE TURN-ING THIS AROUND ON ME?
AND ANYWAY, WHY SHOULD I HAVE TO TELL YOU?
URK...
Y-YOU'RE A GIRL!!
GOING ALONE TO SOME GUY'S HOUSE... IS... WELL...
IT'S NOT SAFE, OKAY?
GIRL? WHO'RE YOU CALLING A GIRL?
GUH ...
BUT...
...YOUR SUSPICIONS MIGHT BE CORRECT, YOU KNOW.

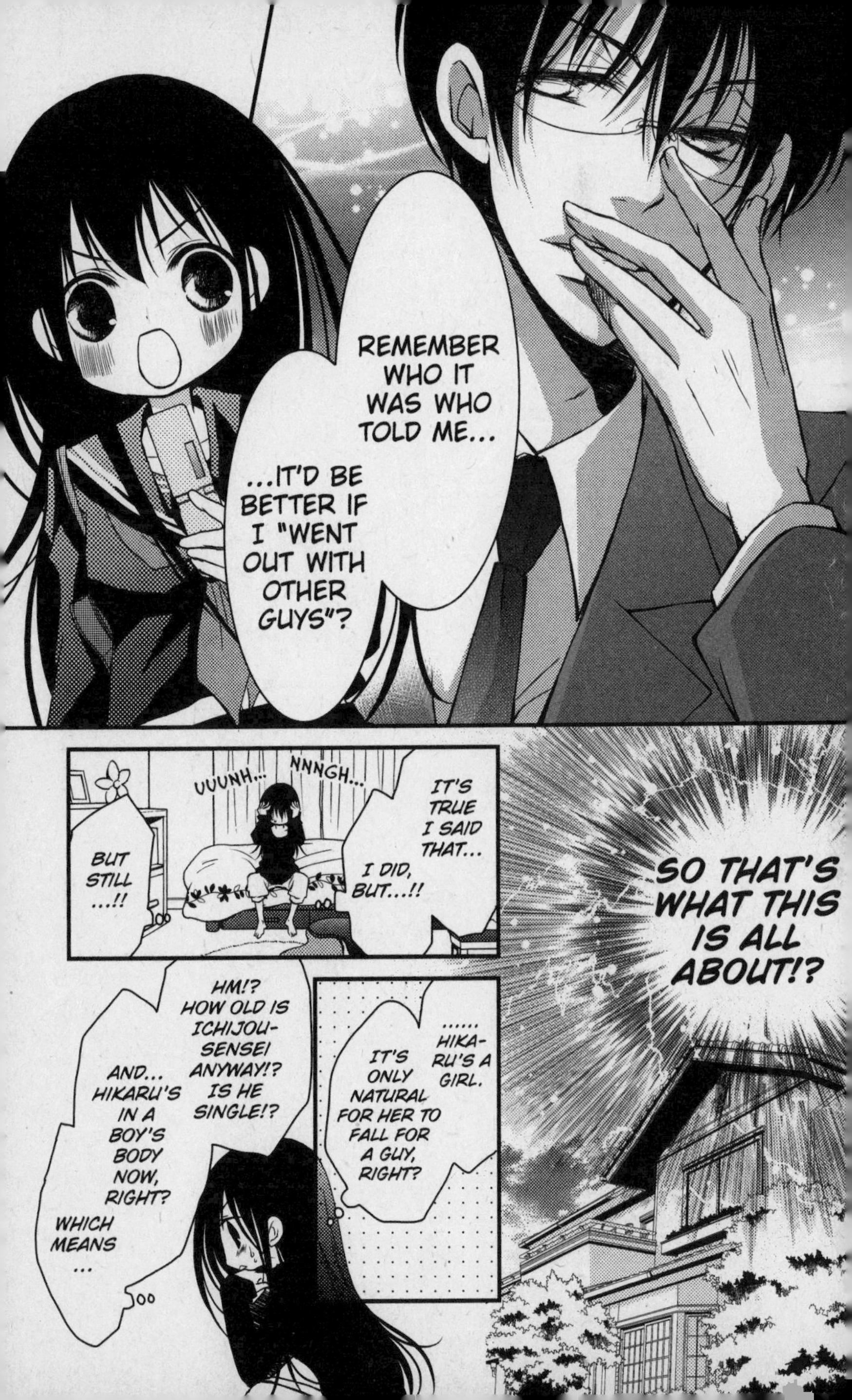
REMEMBER WHO IT WAS WHO TOLD ME...
...IT'D BE BETTER IF I "WENT OUT WITH OTHER GUYS"?
SO THAT'S WHAT THIS IS ALL ABOUT!?
NNNGH...
UUUNH...
IT'S TRUE I SAID THAT...
I DID, BUT...!!
BUT STILL ...!!
...... HIKA-RU'S A GIRL.
IT'S ONLY NATURAL FOR HER TO FALL FOR A GUY, RIGHT?
HM!? HOW OLD IS ICHIJOU-SENSEI ANYWAY!? IS HE SINGLE!?
AND... HIKARU'S IN A BOY'S BODY NOW, RIGHT?
WHICH MEANS ...

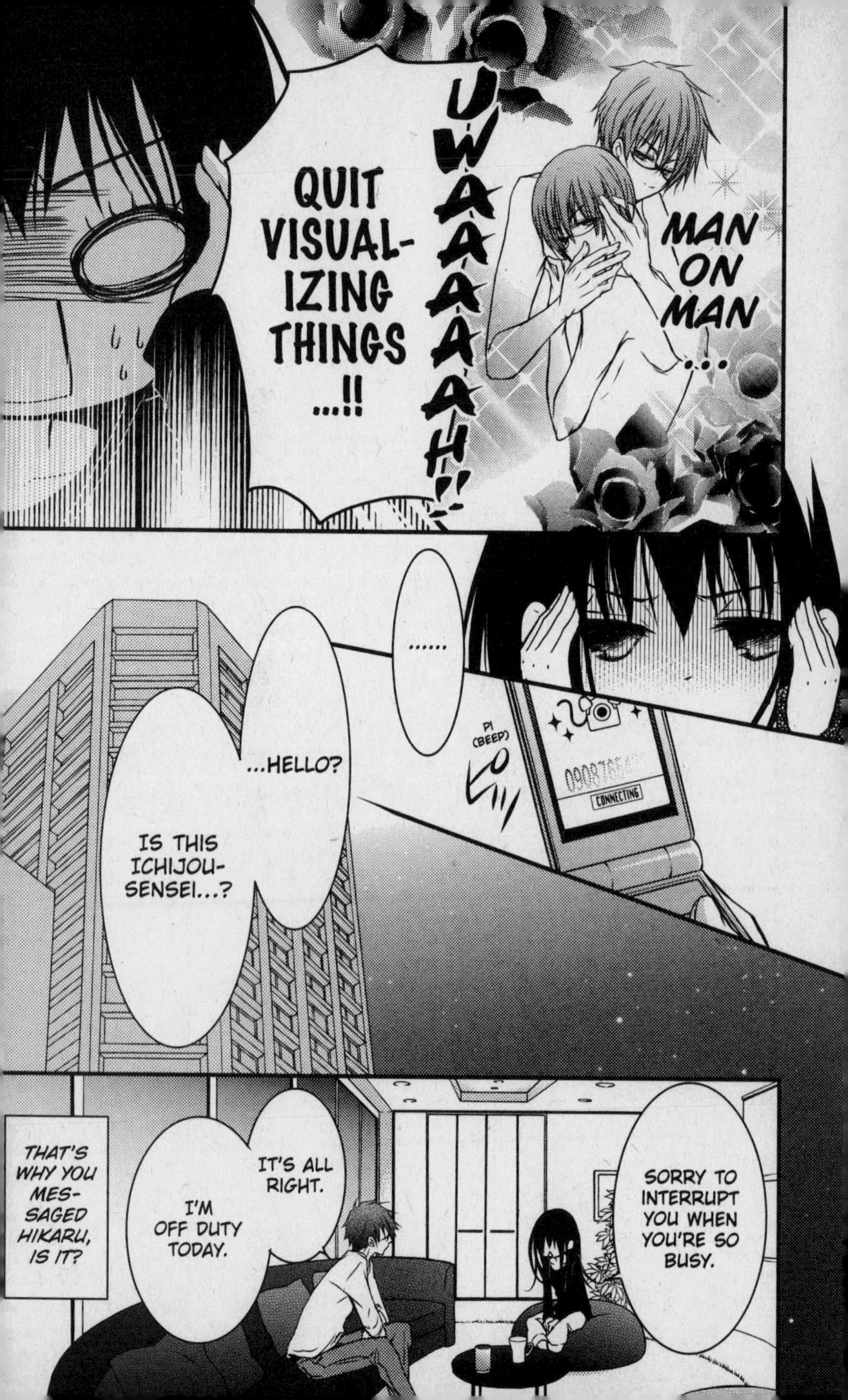
MAN ON MAN...
UWAAAAAAH!!
QUIT VISUAL-IZING THINGS...!!
......
PI (BEEP)
CONNECTING
...HELLO?
IS THIS ICHIJOU-SENSEI...?
SORRY TO INTERRUPT YOU WHEN YOU'RE SO BUSY.
IT'S ALL RIGHT.
I'M OFF DUTY TODAY.
THAT'S WHY YOU MES-SAGED HIKARU, IS IT?

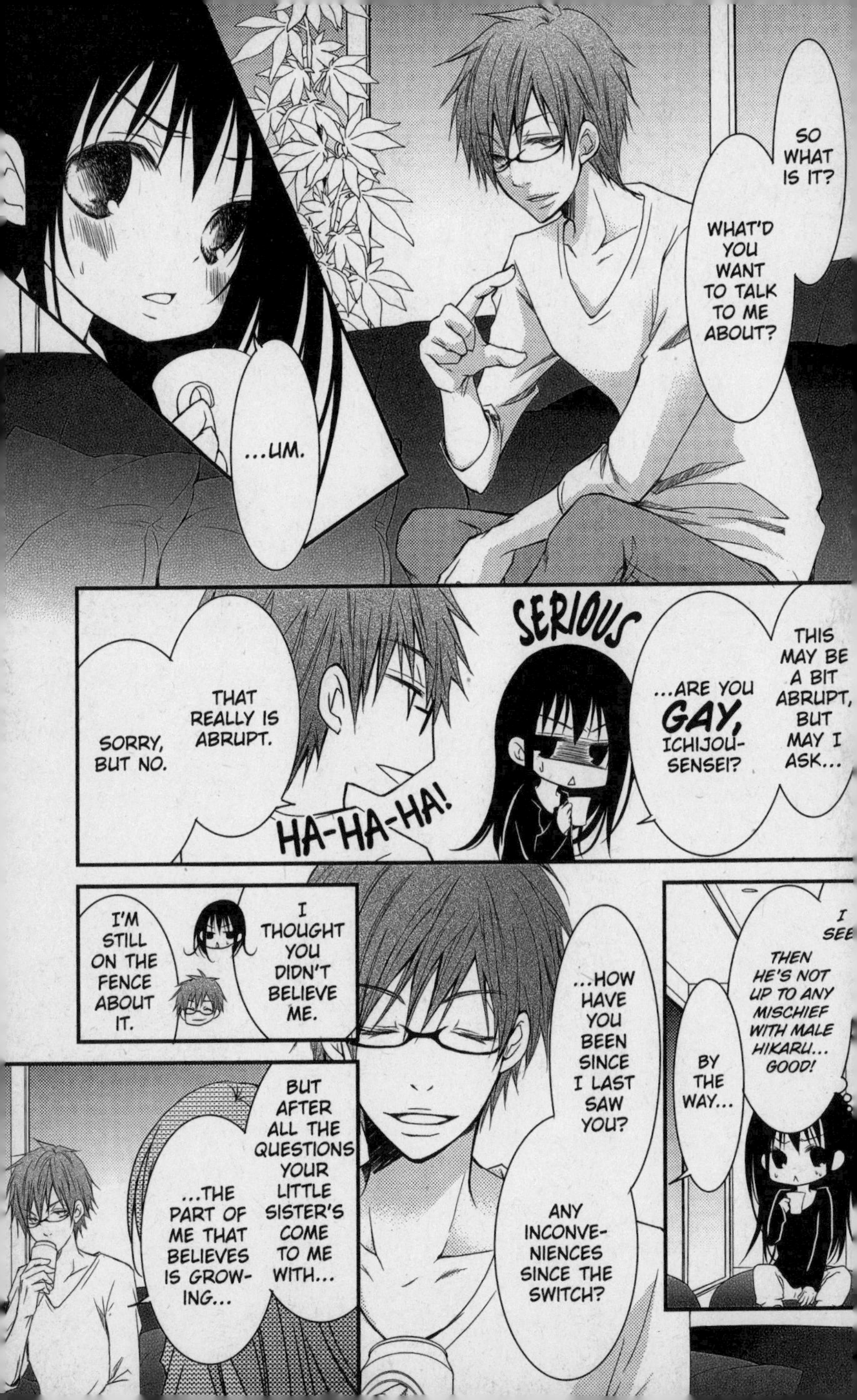
SO WHAT IS IT?
WHAT'D YOU WANT TO TALK TO ME ABOUT?
...UM.
THIS MAY BE A BIT ABRUPT, BUT MAY I ASK...
...ARE YOU GAY, ICHIJOU-SENSEI?
SERIOUS
THAT REALLY IS ABRUPT.
HA-HA-HA!
SORRY, BUT NO.
I SEE
THEN HE'S NOT UP TO ANY MISCHIEF WITH MALE HIKARU... GOOD!
BY THE WAY...
...HOW HAVE YOU BEEN SINCE I LAST SAW YOU?
ANY INCONVE-NIENCES SINCE THE SWITCH?
I THOUGHT YOU DIDN'T BELIEVE ME.
I'M STILL ON THE FENCE ABOUT IT.
BUT AFTER ALL THE QUESTIONS YOUR LITTLE SISTER'S COME TO ME WITH...
...THE PART OF ME THAT BELIEVES IS GROW-ING...

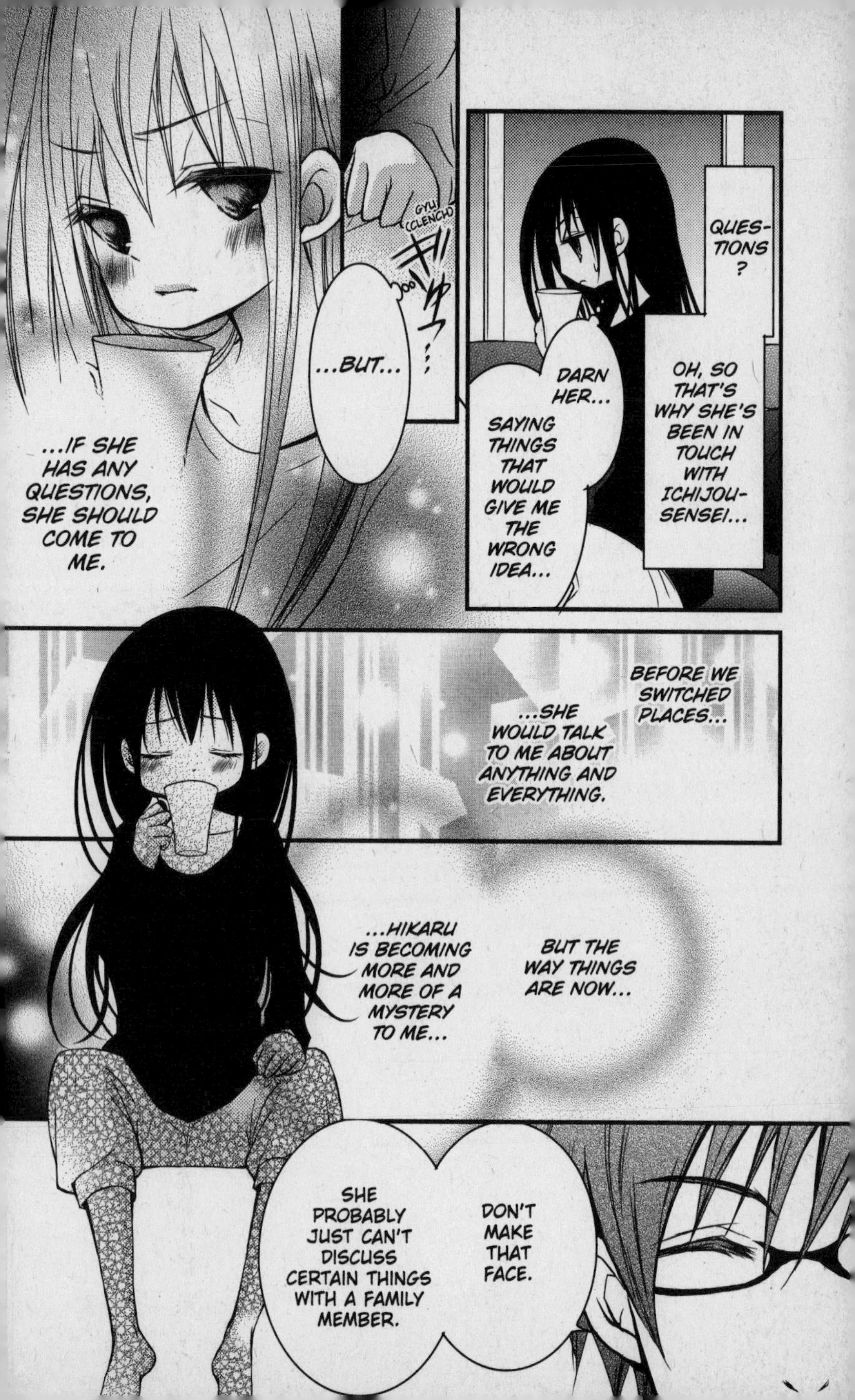
QUESTIONS?
OH, SO THAT'S WHY SHE'S BEEN IN TOUCH WITH ICHIJOU-SENSEI...
DARN HER...
SAYING THINGS THAT WOULD GIVE ME THE WRONG IDEA...
GYU (CLENCH)
...BUT...
...IF SHE HAS ANY QUESTIONS, SHE SHOULD COME TO ME.
BEFORE WE SWITCHED PLACES...
...SHE WOULD TALK TO ME ABOUT ANYTHING AND EVERYTHING.
BUT THE WAY THINGS ARE NOW...
...HIKARU IS BECOMING MORE AND MORE OF A MYSTERY TO ME...
DON'T MAKE THAT FACE.
SHE PROBABLY JUST CAN'T DISCUSS CERTAIN THINGS WITH A FAMILY MEMBER.

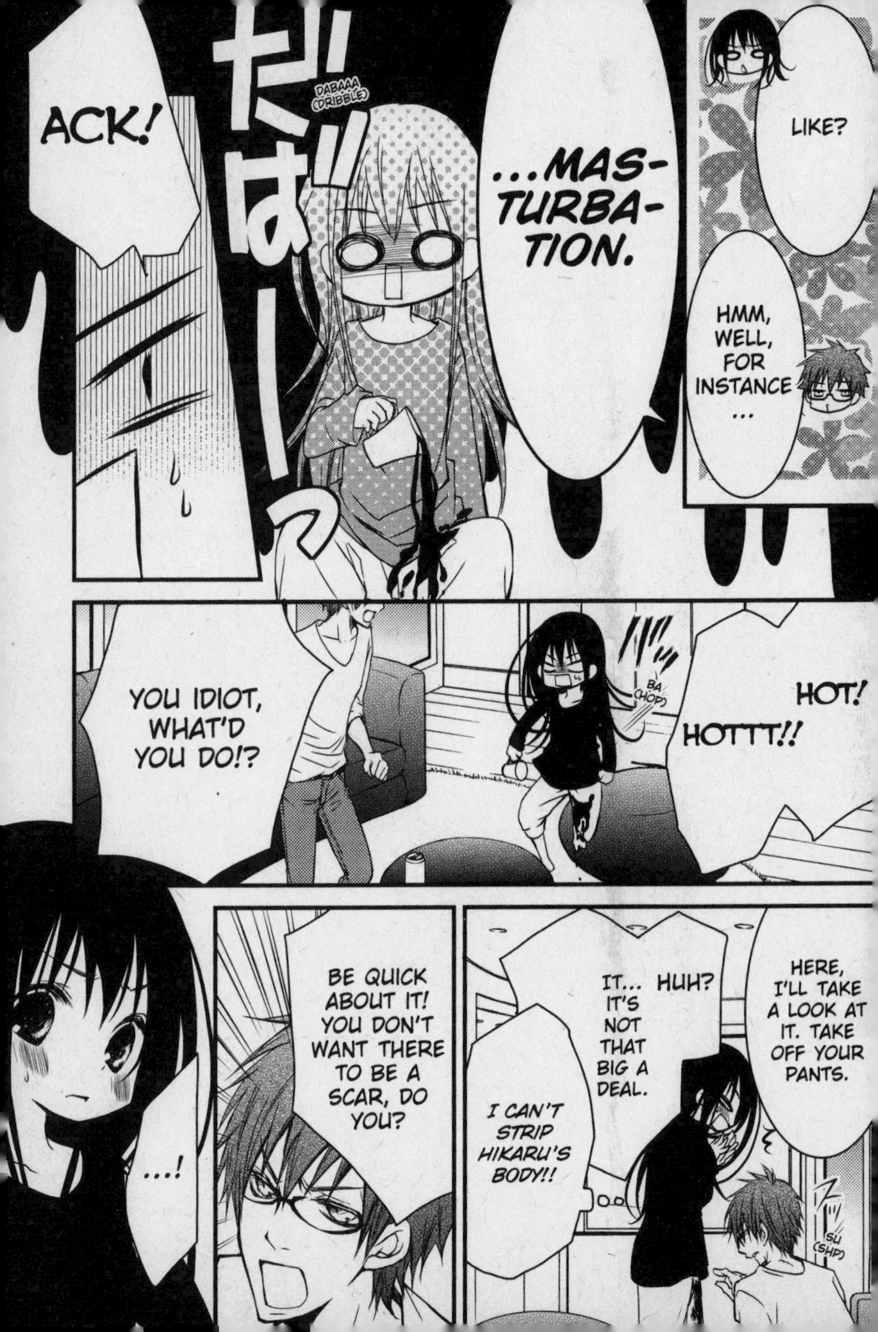
LIKE?
HMM, WELL, FOR INSTANCE...
...MAS-TURBA-TION.
だばーっ
DABAAA (DRIBBLE)
ACK!
HOT!
HOTTT!!
BA (CHOP)
YOU IDIOT, WHAT'D YOU DO!?
HERE, I'LL TAKE A LOOK AT IT. TAKE OFF YOUR PANTS.
SU (SHP)
HUH?
IT... IT'S NOT THAT BIG A DEAL.
I CAN'T STRIP HIKARU'S BODY!!
BE QUICK ABOUT IT! YOU DON'T WANT THERE TO BE A SCAR, DO YOU?
...!

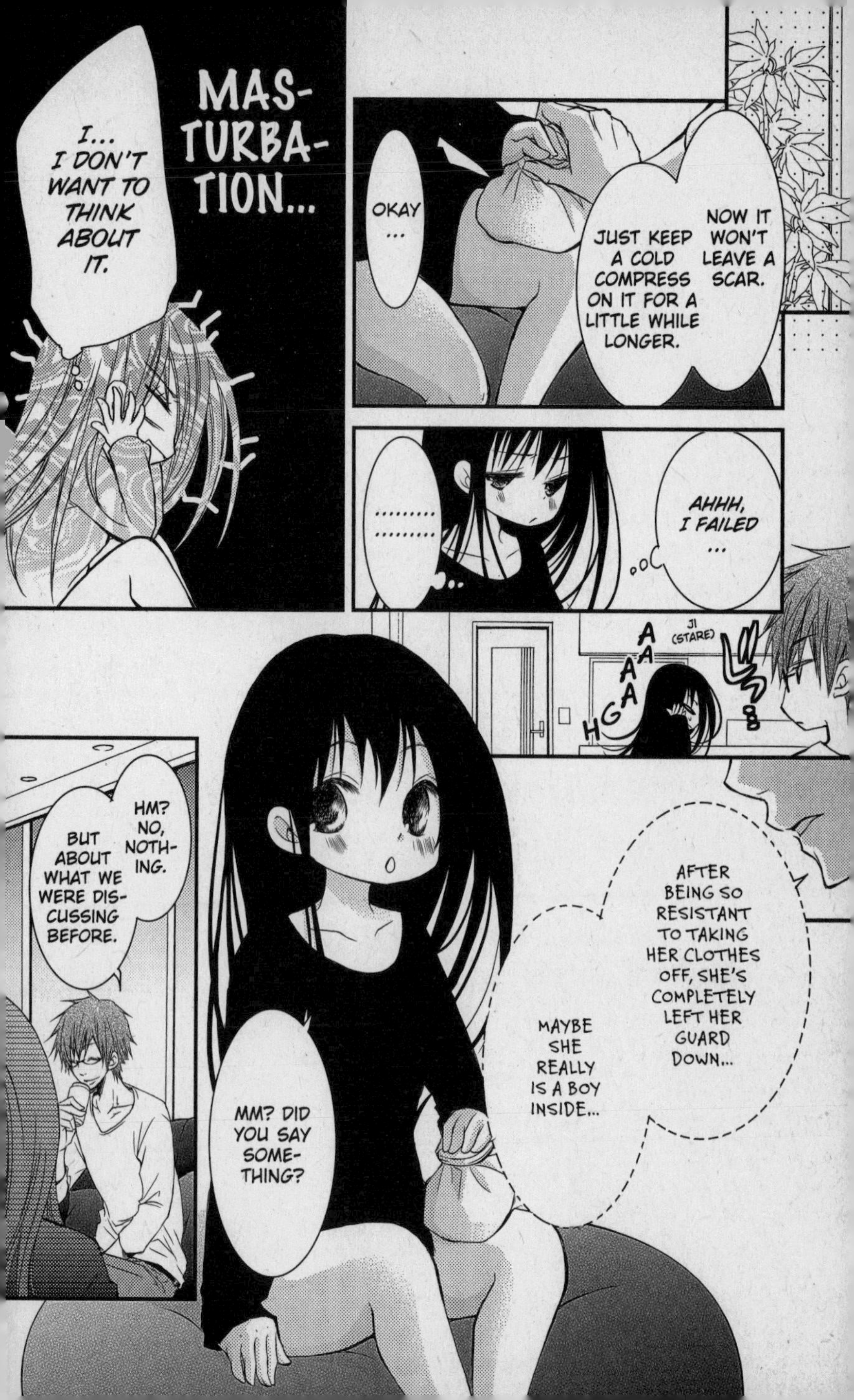
NOW IT WON'T LEAVE A SCAR.
JUST KEEP A COLD COMPRESS ON IT FOR A LITTLE WHILE LONGER.
OKAY...
AHHH, I FAILED...
....
MAS-TURBA-TION...
I... I DON'T WANT TO THINK ABOUT IT.
JI (STARE)
HGAAAA
AFTER BEING SO RESISTANT TO TAKING HER CLOTHES OFF, SHE'S COMPLETELY LEFT HER GUARD DOWN...
MAYBE SHE REALLY IS A BOY INSIDE...
MM? DID YOU SAY SOME-THING?
HM? NO, NOTH-ING.
BUT ABOUT WHAT WE WERE DIS-CUSSING BEFORE.

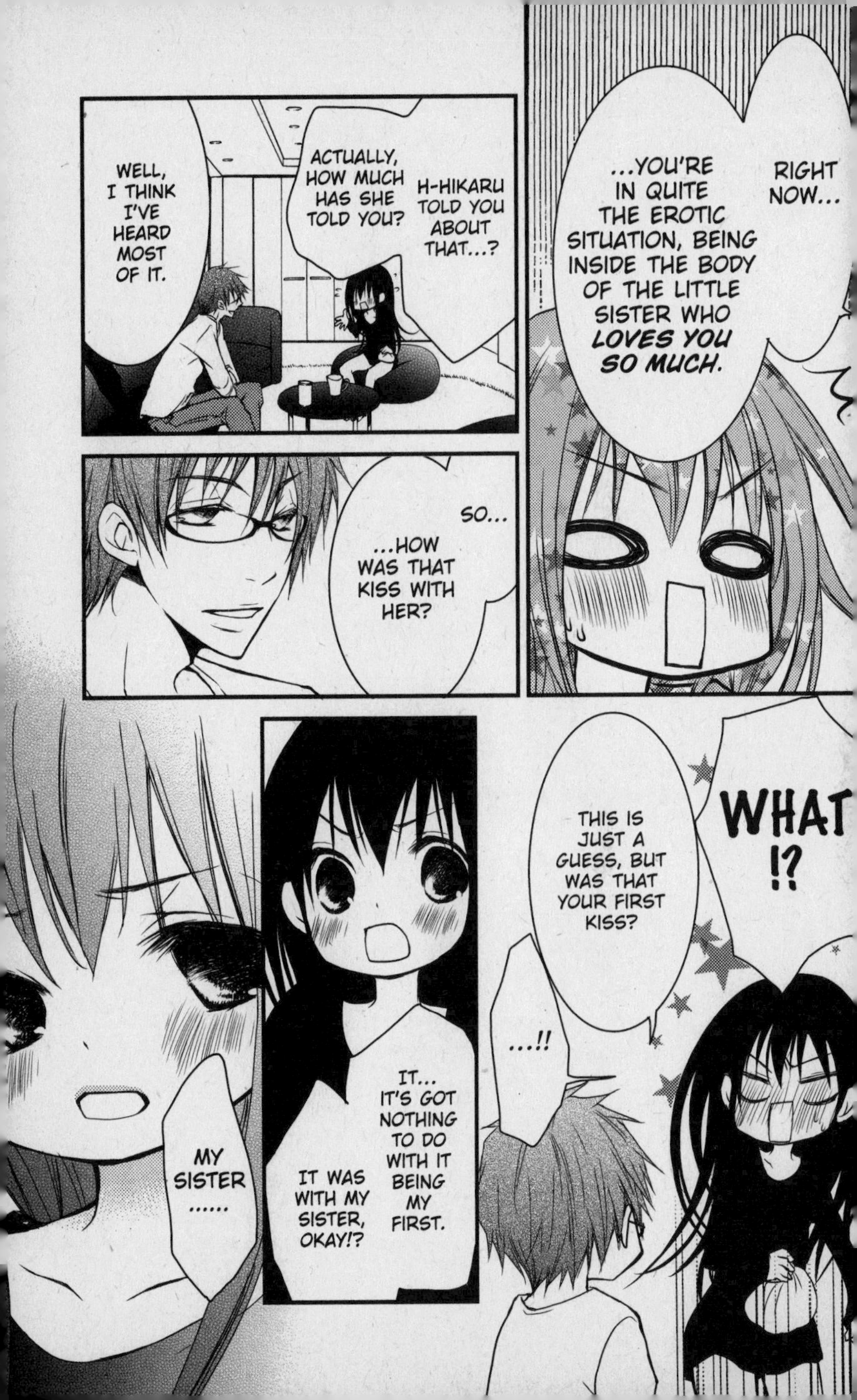
RIGHT NOW...
...YOU'RE IN QUITE THE EROTIC SITUATION, BEING INSIDE THE BODY OF THE LITTLE SISTER WHO *LOVES YOU SO MUCH.*
H-HIKARU TOLD YOU ABOUT THAT...?
ACTUALLY, HOW MUCH HAS SHE TOLD YOU?
WELL, I THINK I'VE HEARD MOST OF IT.
SO...
...HOW WAS THAT KISS WITH HER?
WHAT!?
THIS IS JUST A GUESS, BUT WAS THAT YOUR FIRST KISS?
...!!
IT... IT'S GOT NOTHING TO DO WITH IT BEING MY FIRST.
IT WAS WITH MY SISTER, OKAY!?
MY SISTER ......

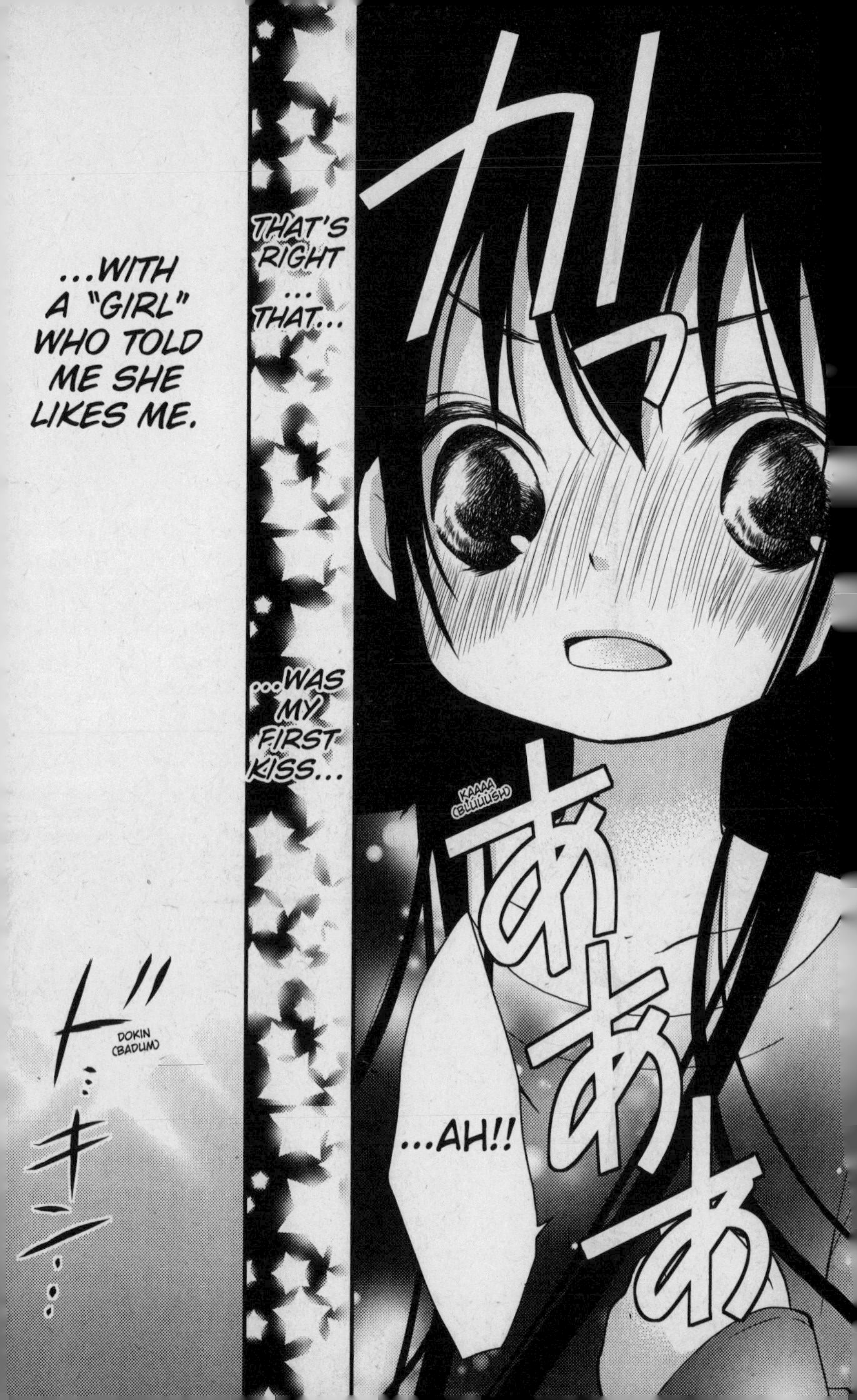
KAAAA (BLUUUSH)
...AH!!
THAT'S RIGHT ... THAT...
...WAS MY FIRST KISS...
...WITH A "GIRL" WHO TOLD ME SHE LIKES ME.
DOKIN (BADUM)

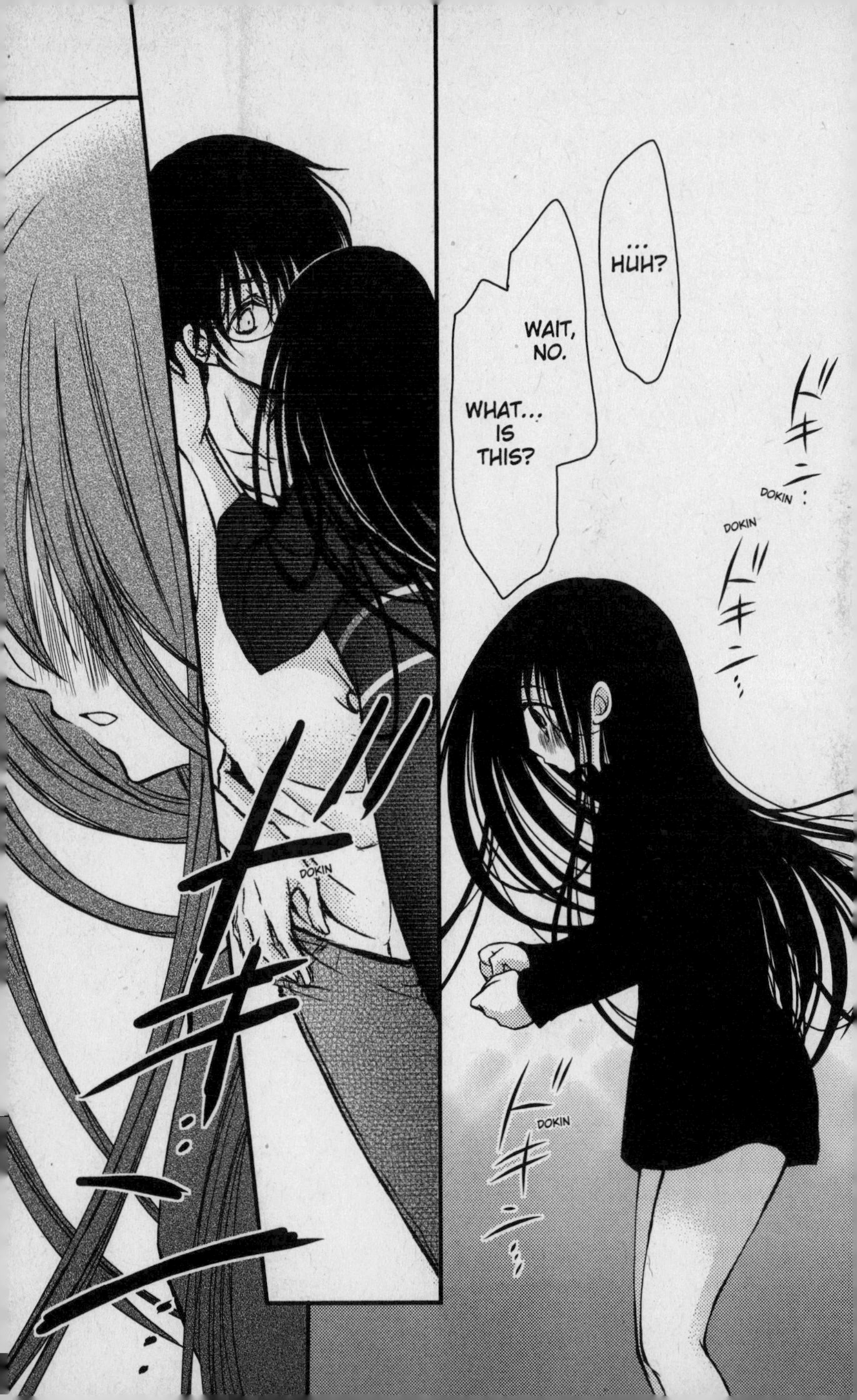

...HUH?
WAIT, NO.
WHAT... IS THIS?
DOKIN
DOKIN
DOKIN
DOKIN

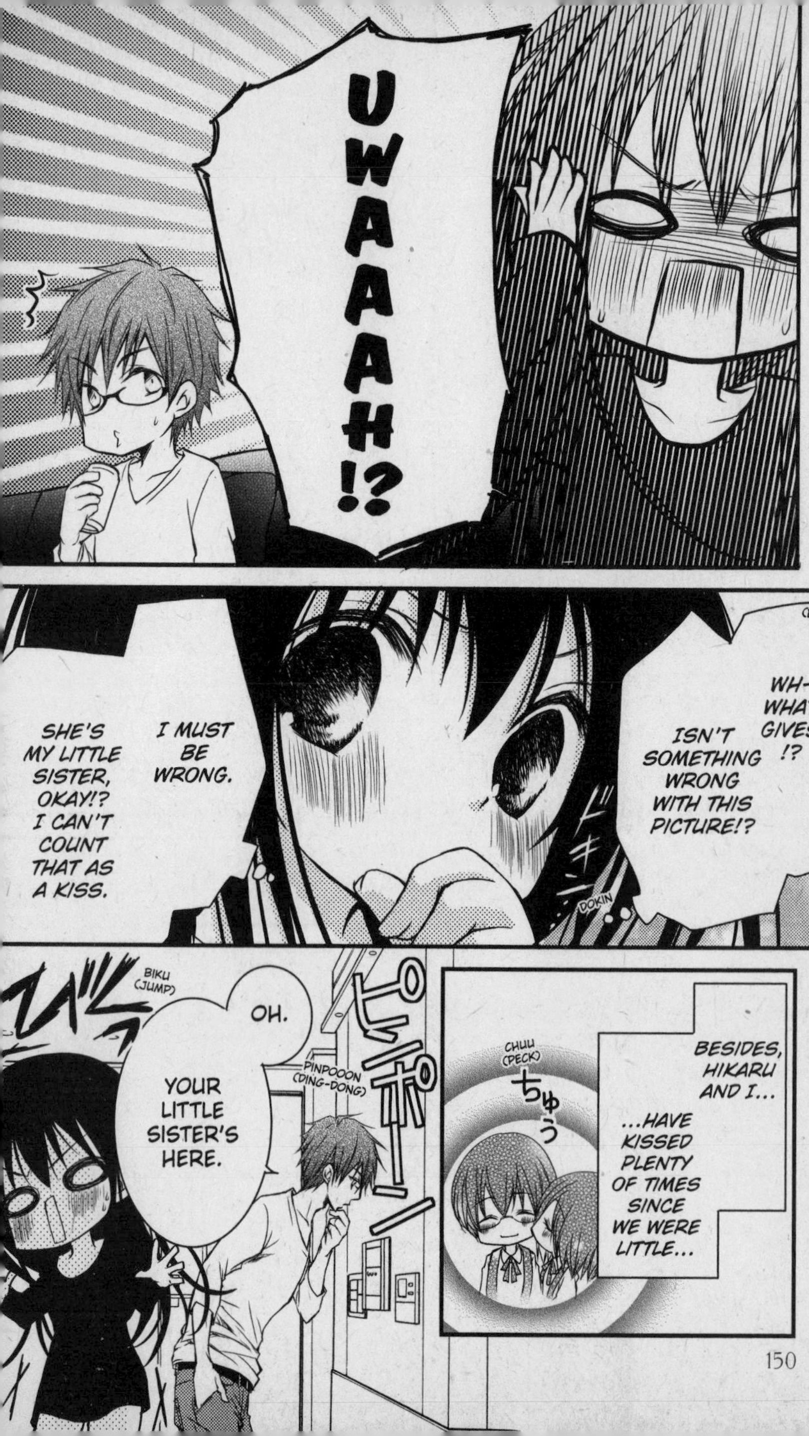
UWAAAH!?
DOKIN (BADUM)
WH-WHAT GIVES!?
ISN'T SOMETHING WRONG WITH THIS PICTURE!?
DOKIN
I MUST BE WRONG.
SHE'S MY LITTLE SISTER, OKAY!? I CAN'T COUNT THAT AS A KISS.
BESIDES, HIKARU AND I...
...HAVE KISSED PLENTY OF TIMES SINCE WE WERE LITTLE...
CHUU (PECK)
ちゅう
ピンポーン
PINPOOON (DING-DONG)
OH.
YOUR LITTLE SISTER'S HERE.
BIKU (JUMP)

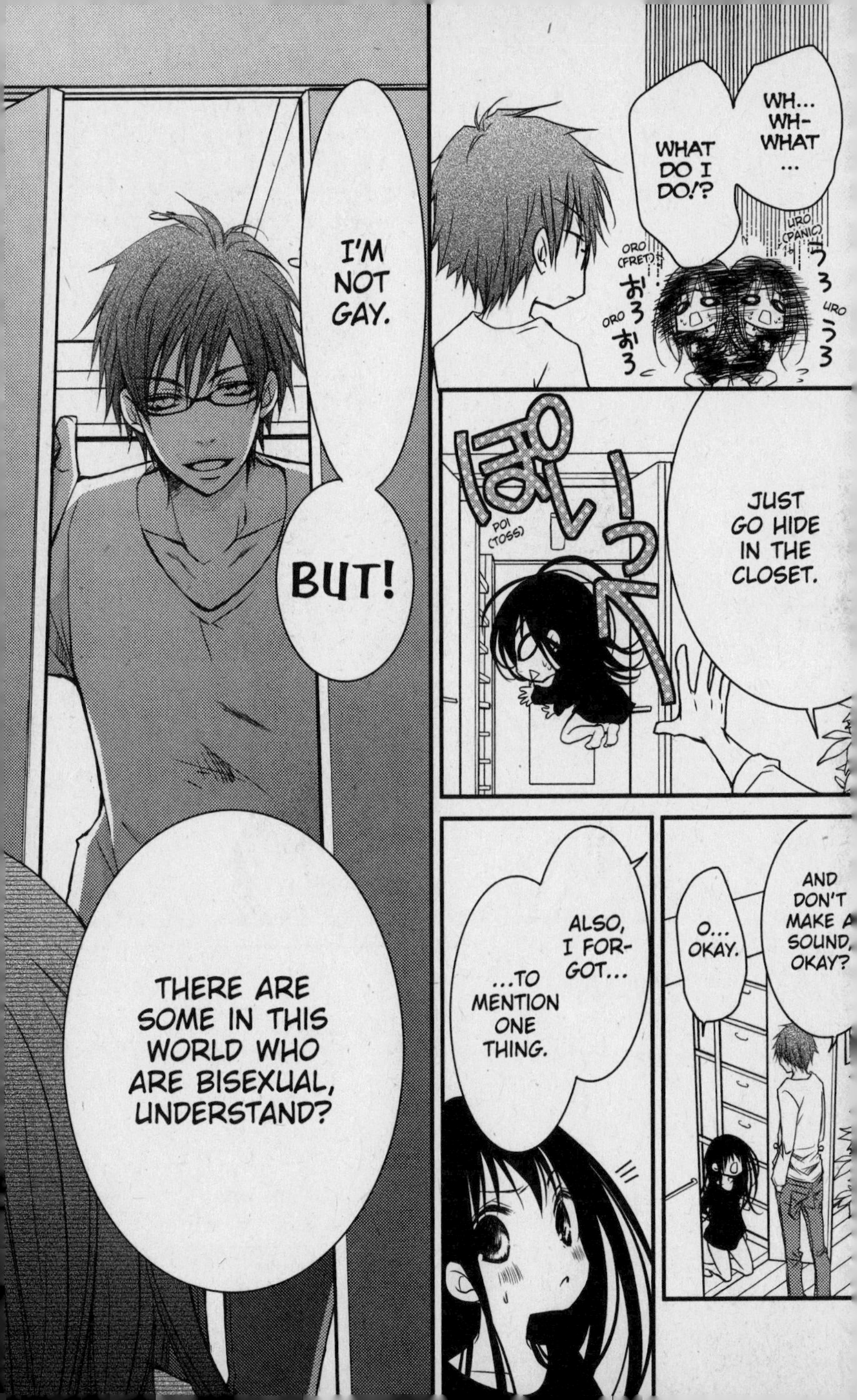

WH... WH-WHAT...
WHAT DO I DO!?
URO (PANIC)
うろ
URO
うろ
ORO (FRET)
おろ
ORO
おろ
JUST GO HIDE IN THE CLOSET.
ぽいっ
POI (TOSS)
AND DON'T MAKE A SOUND, OKAY?
O... OKAY.
ALSO, I FORGOT...
...TO MENTION ONE THING.
I'M NOT GAY.
BUT!
THERE ARE SOME IN THIS WORLD WHO ARE BISEXUAL, UNDERSTAND?

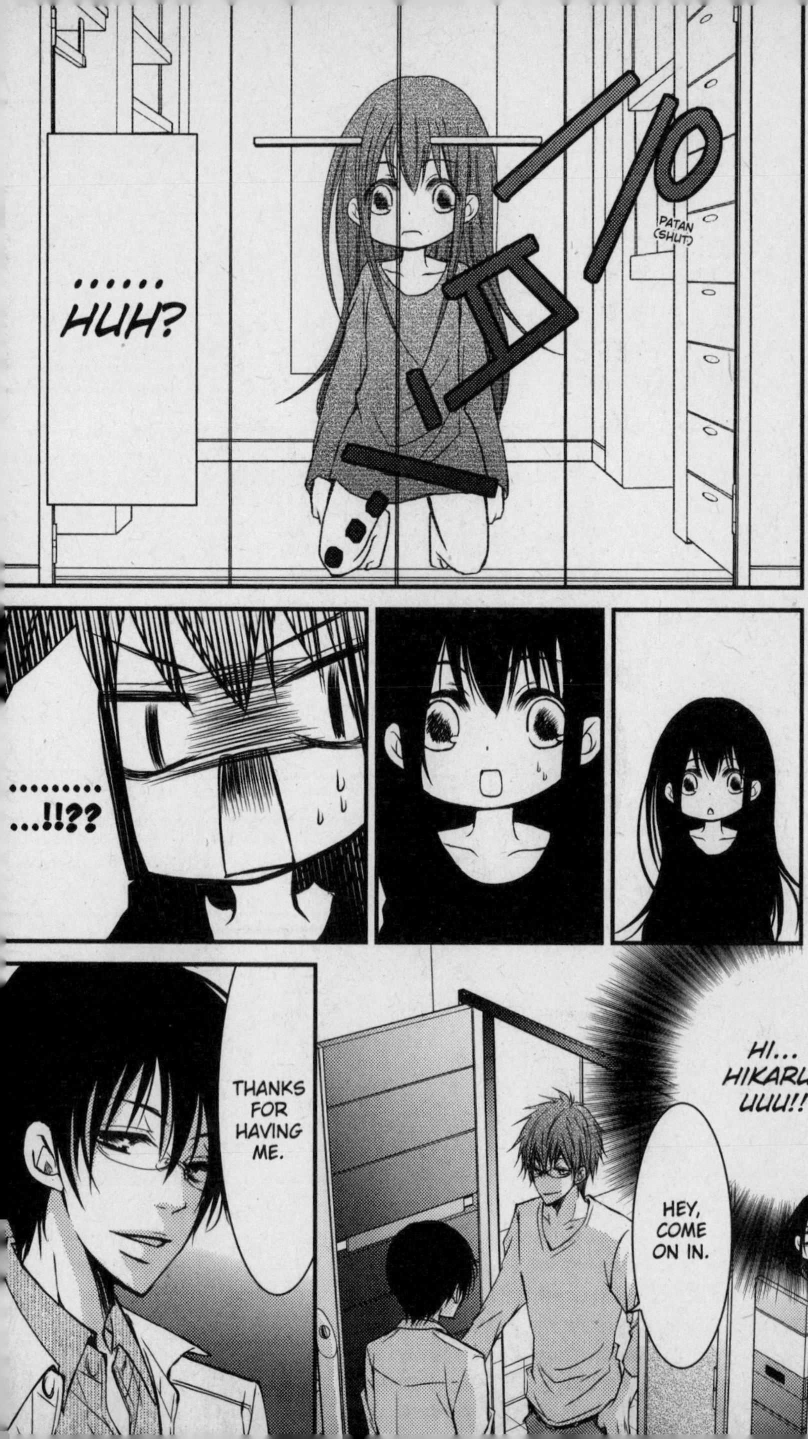
PATAN (SHUT)
......HUH?
....
...!!??
HI... HIKARU-UUU!!
HEY, COME ON IN.
THANKS FOR HAVING ME.

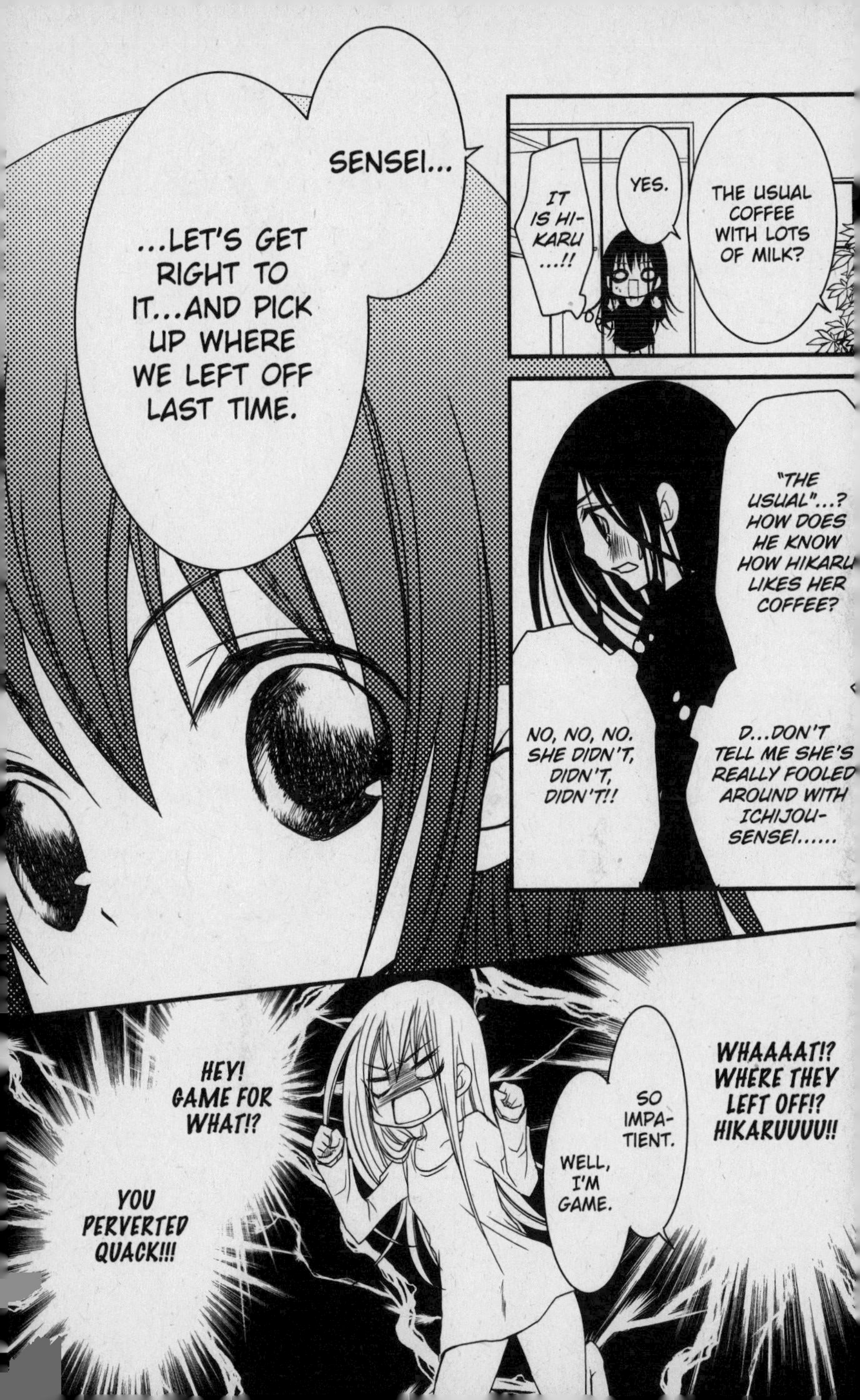
THE USUAL COFFEE WITH LOTS OF MILK?
YES.
IT IS HIKARU...!!
"THE USUAL"...? HOW DOES HE KNOW HOW HIKARU LIKES HER COFFEE?
D...DON'T TELL ME SHE'S REALLY FOOLED AROUND WITH ICHIJOU-SENSEI......
NO, NO, NO. SHE DIDN'T, DIDN'T, DIDN'T!!
SENSEI...
...LET'S GET RIGHT TO IT...AND PICK UP WHERE WE LEFT OFF LAST TIME.
WHAAAAT!? WHERE THEY LEFT OFF!? HIKARUUUUU!!
SO IMPATIENT.
WELL, I'M GAME.
HEY! GAME FOR WHAT!?
YOU PERVERTED QUACK!!!

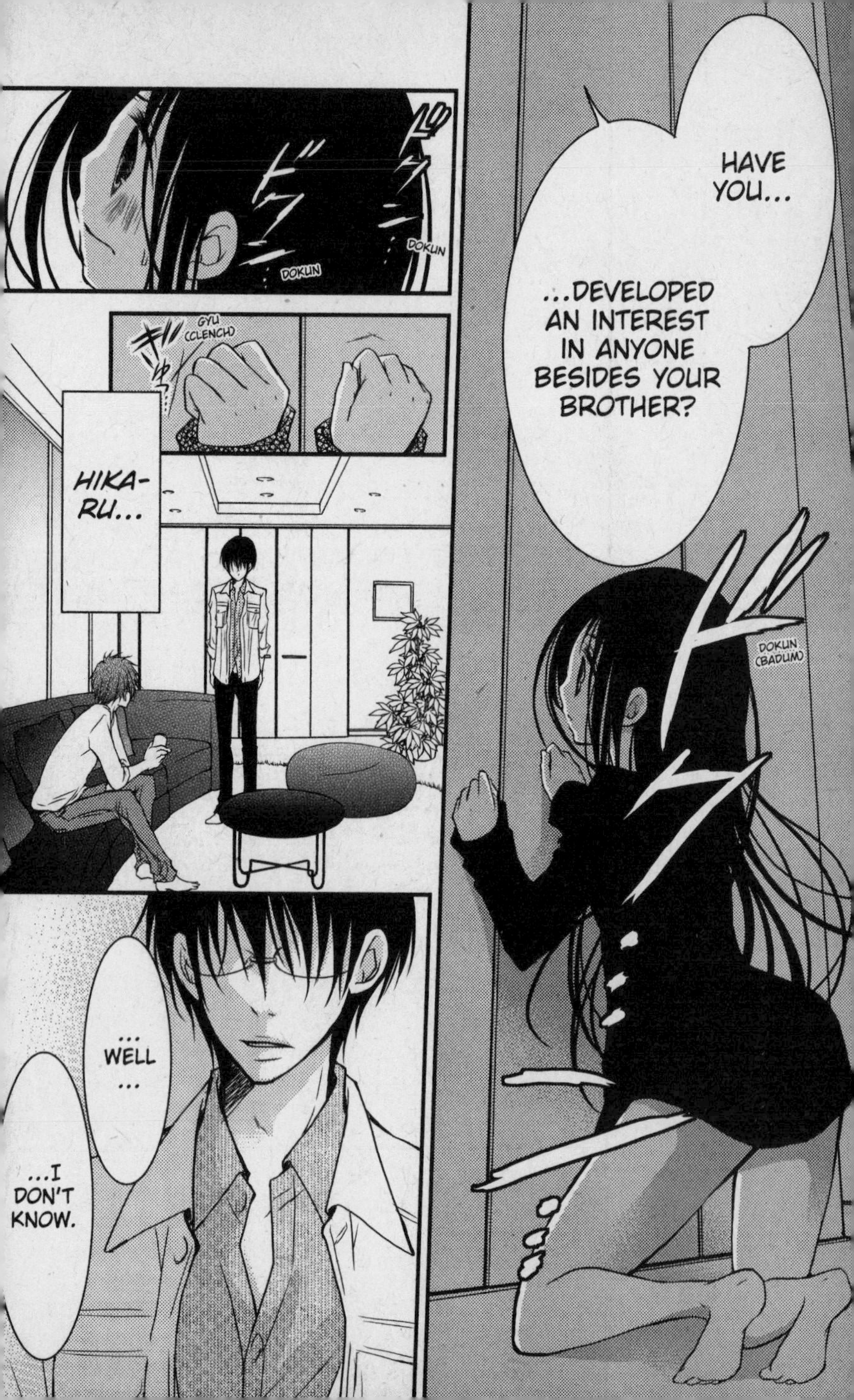
HAVE YOU...
...DEVELOPED AN INTEREST IN ANYONE BESIDES YOUR BROTHER?
DOKUN (BADUM)
DOKUN
DOKUN
GYU (CLENCH)
HIKA-RU...
...WELL...
...I DON'T KNOW.

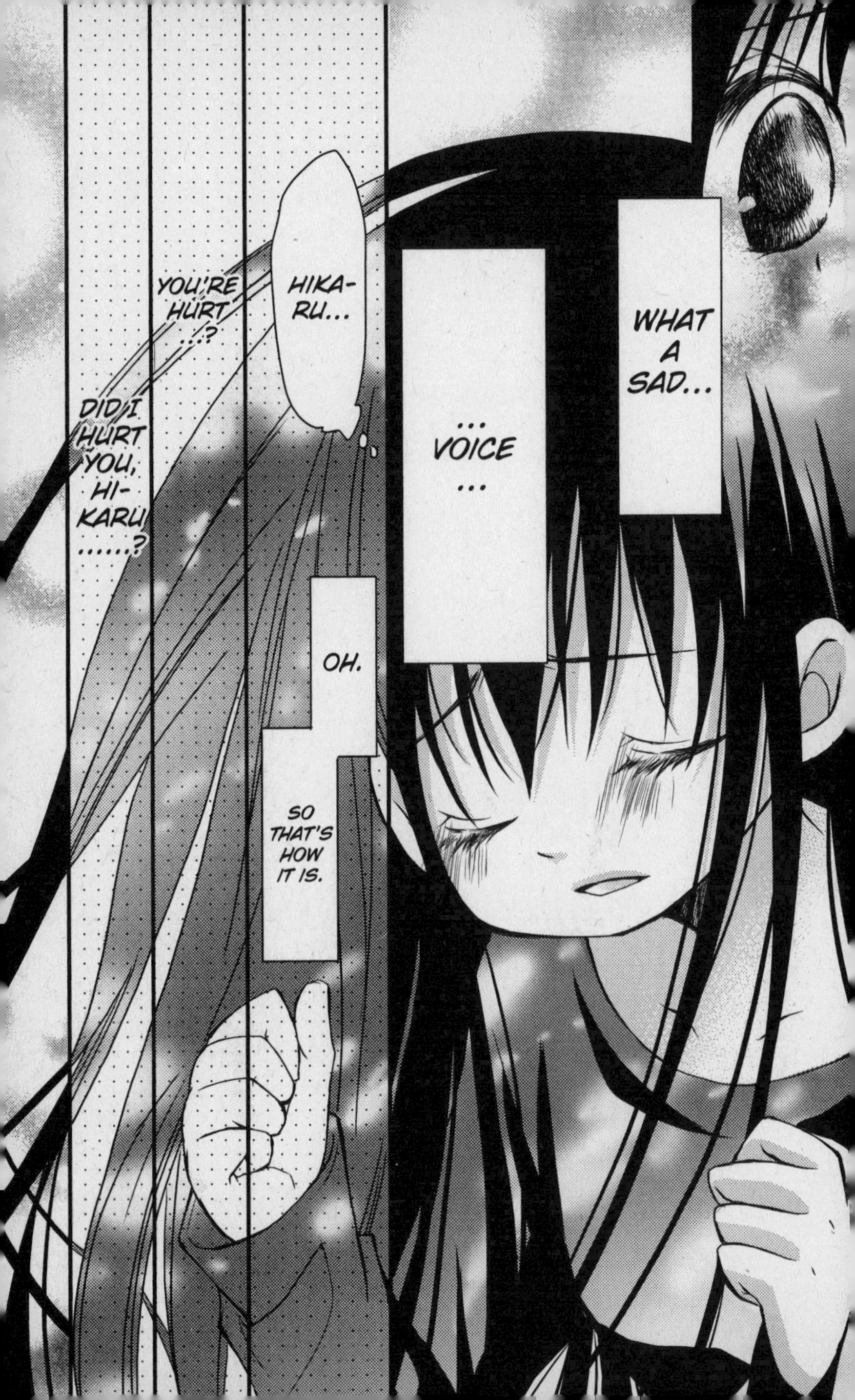
WHAT A SAD...
... VOICE ...
HIKA-RU...
YOU'RE HURT ...?
DID I HURT YOU, HI-KARU ......?
OH.
SO THAT'S HOW IT IS.

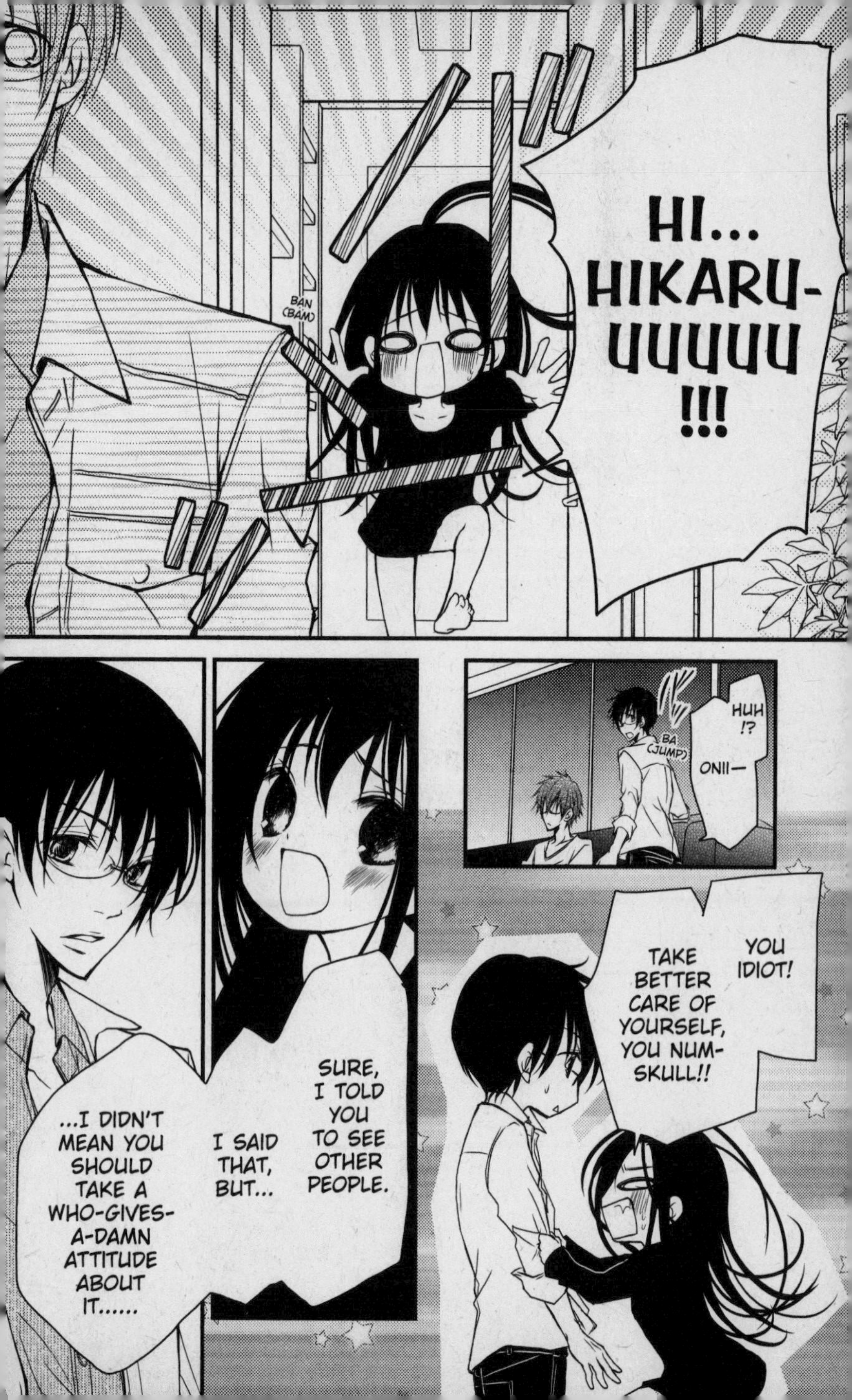
HI... HIKARU-UUUUUU!!!
BAN (BAM)
HUH!?
BA (JUMP)
ONII—
YOU IDIOT!
TAKE BETTER CARE OF YOURSELF, YOU NUM-SKULL!!
SURE, I TOLD YOU TO SEE OTHER PEOPLE.
I SAID THAT, BUT...
...I DIDN'T MEAN YOU SHOULD TAKE A WHO-GIVES-A-DAMN ATTITUDE ABOUT IT......

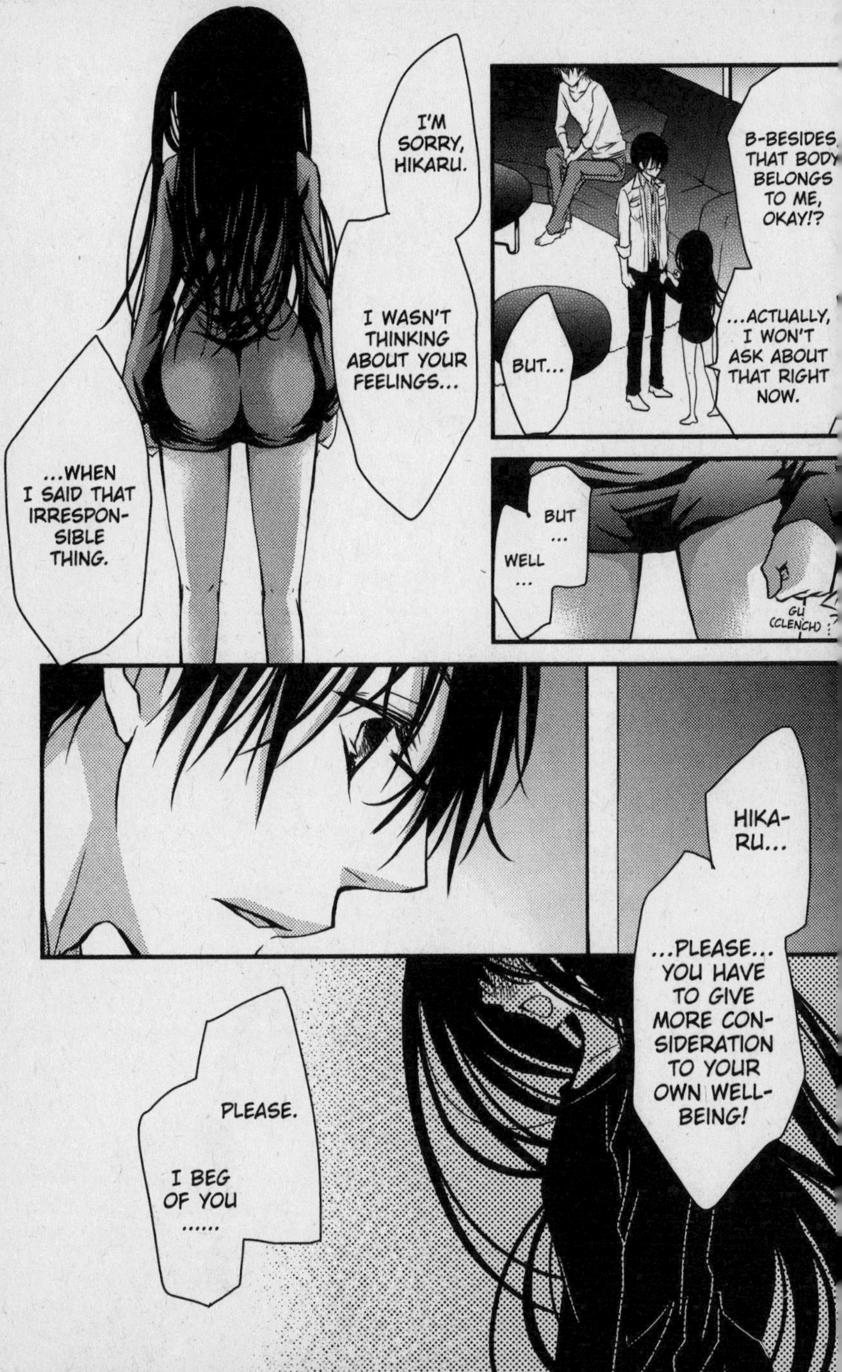
B-BESIDES, THAT BODY BELONGS TO ME, OKAY!?
...ACTUALLY, I WON'T ASK ABOUT THAT RIGHT NOW.
BUT...
BUT ... WELL ...
GU (CLENCH)
I'M SORRY, HIKARU.
I WASN'T THINKING ABOUT YOUR FEELINGS...
...WHEN I SAID THAT IRRESPON-SIBLE THING.
HIKA-RU...
...PLEASE... YOU HAVE TO GIVE MORE CON-SIDERATION TO YOUR OWN WELL-BEING!
PLEASE.
I BEG OF YOU ......

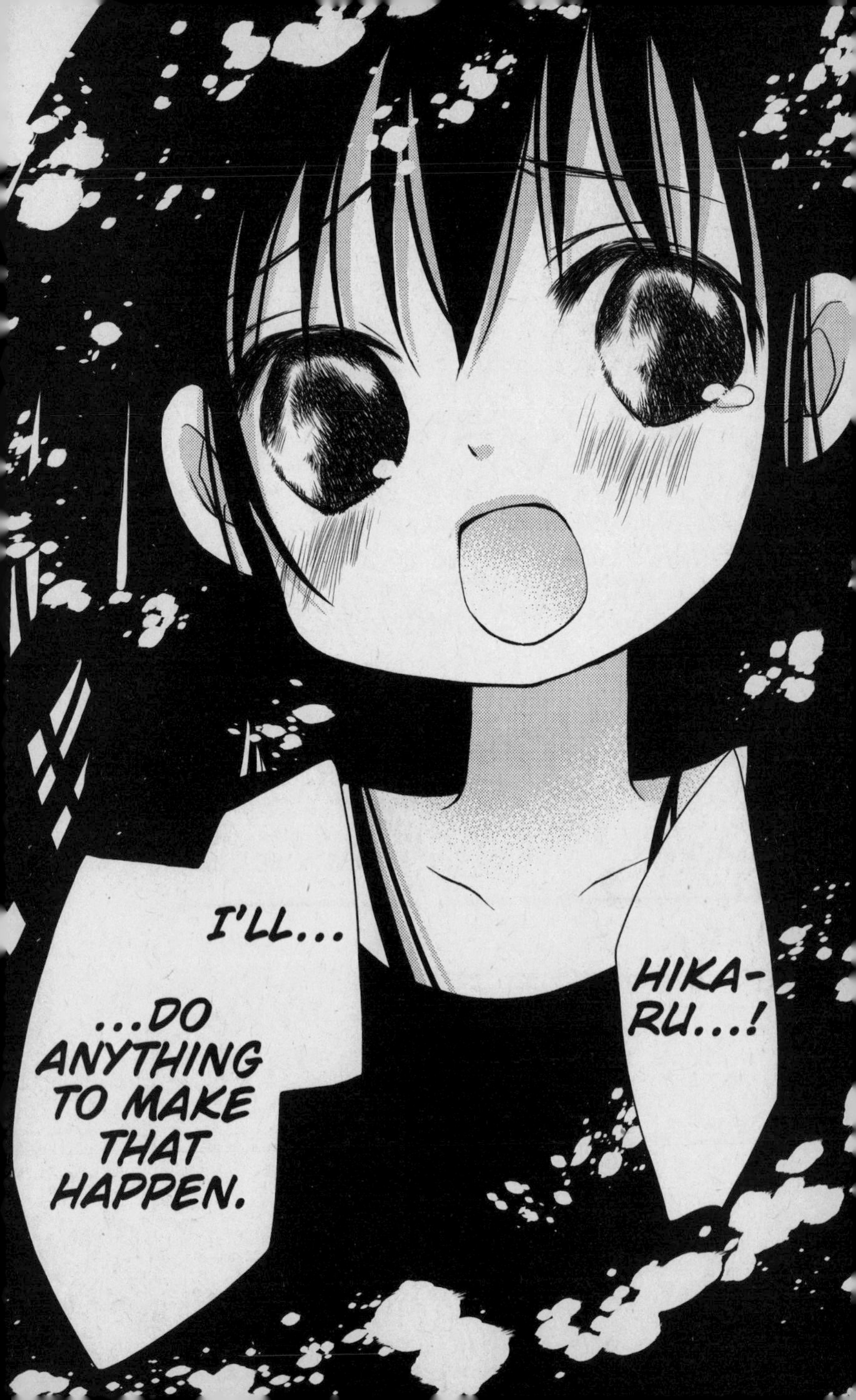
HIKA-
RU...!
I'LL...
...DO
ANYTHING
TO MAKE
THAT
HAPPEN.

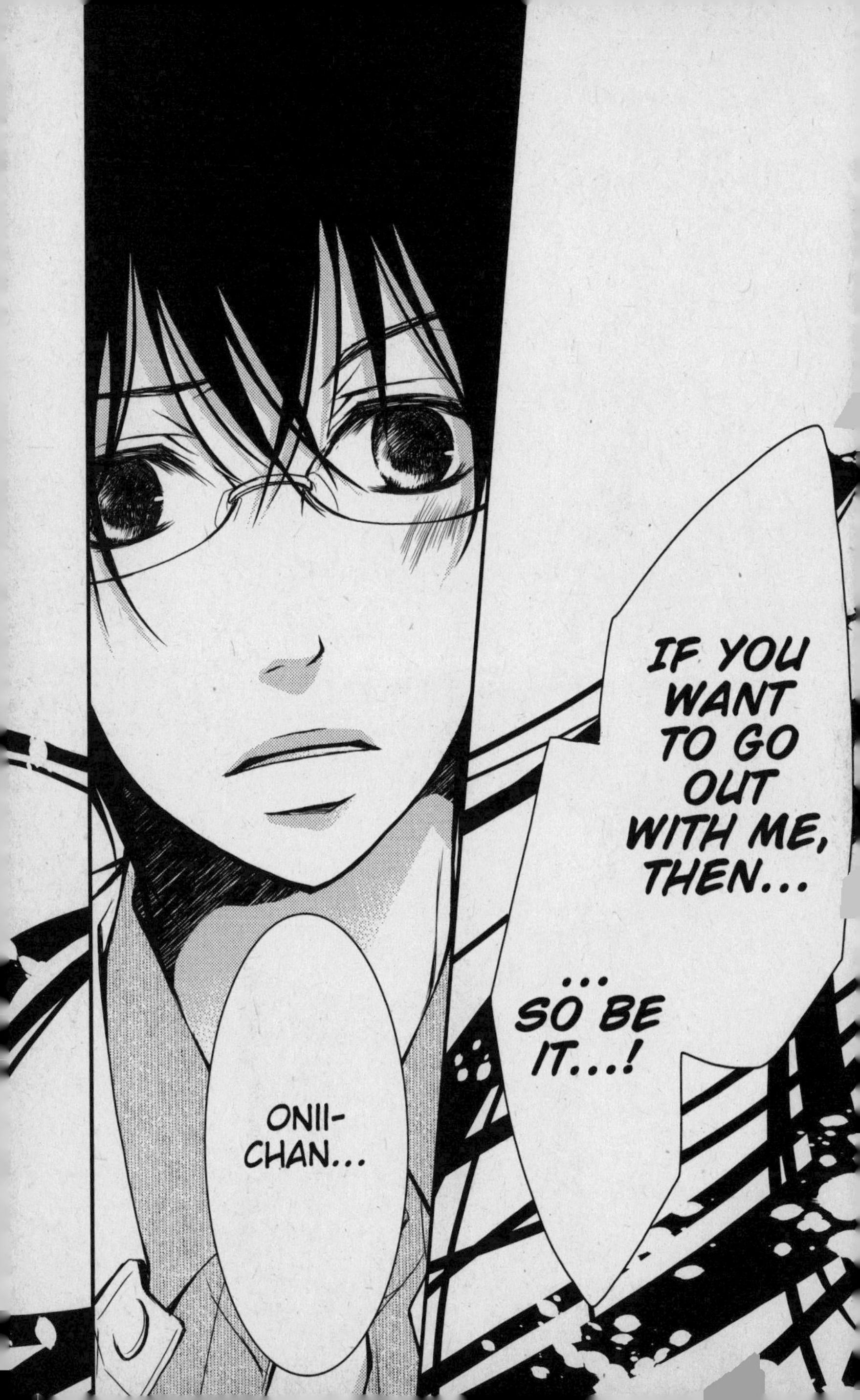
IF YOU WANT TO GO OUT WITH ME, THEN...
...SO BE IT...!
ONII-CHAN...

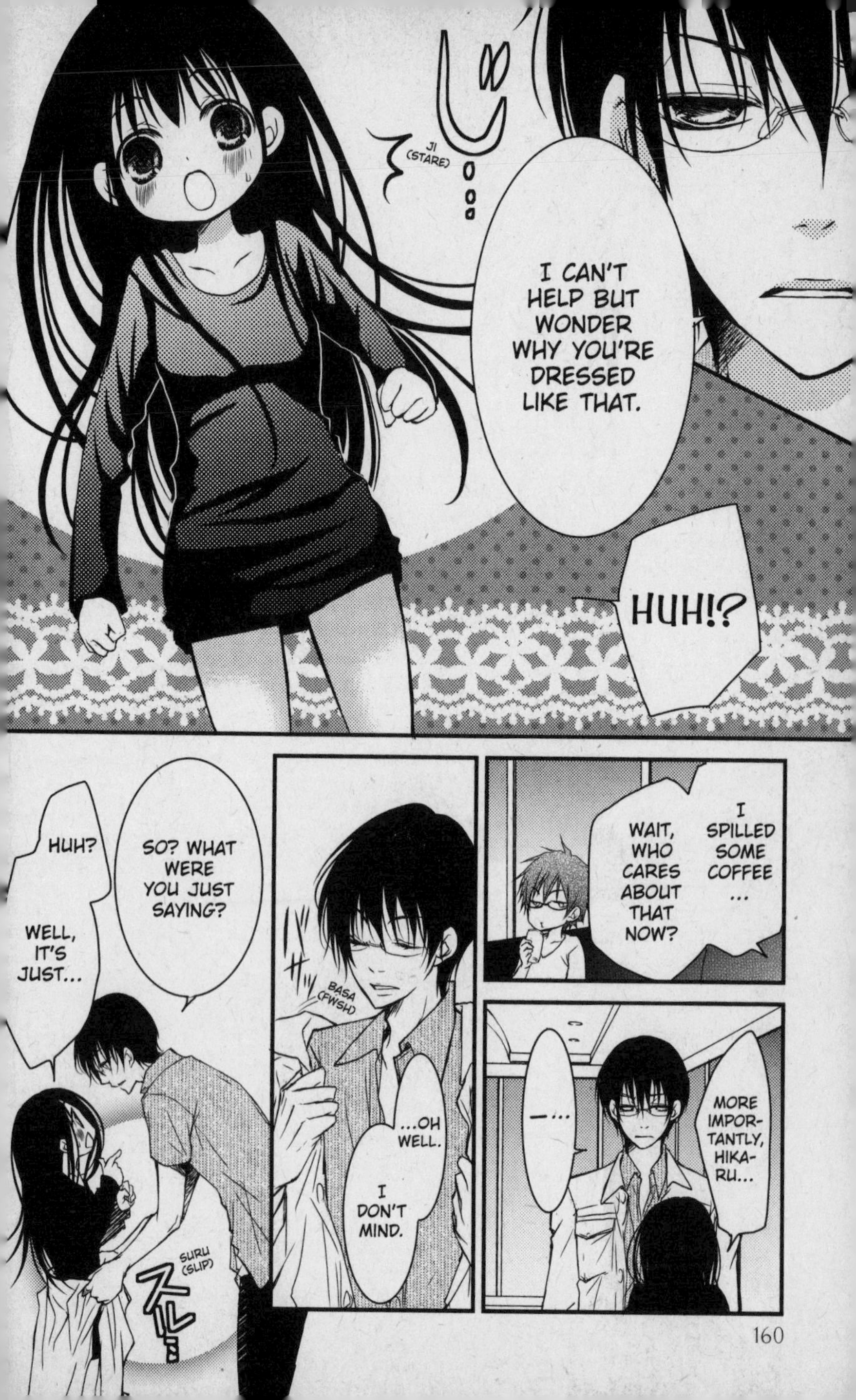
JI (STARE)
I CAN'T HELP BUT WONDER WHY YOU'RE DRESSED LIKE THAT.
HUH!?
I SPILLED SOME COFFEE...
WAIT, WHO CARES ABOUT THAT NOW?
MORE IMPORTANTLY, HIKARU...
—...
BASA (FWSH)
...OH WELL.
I DON'T MIND.
SO? WHAT WERE YOU JUST SAYING?
HUH?
WELL, IT'S JUST...
SURU (SLIP)

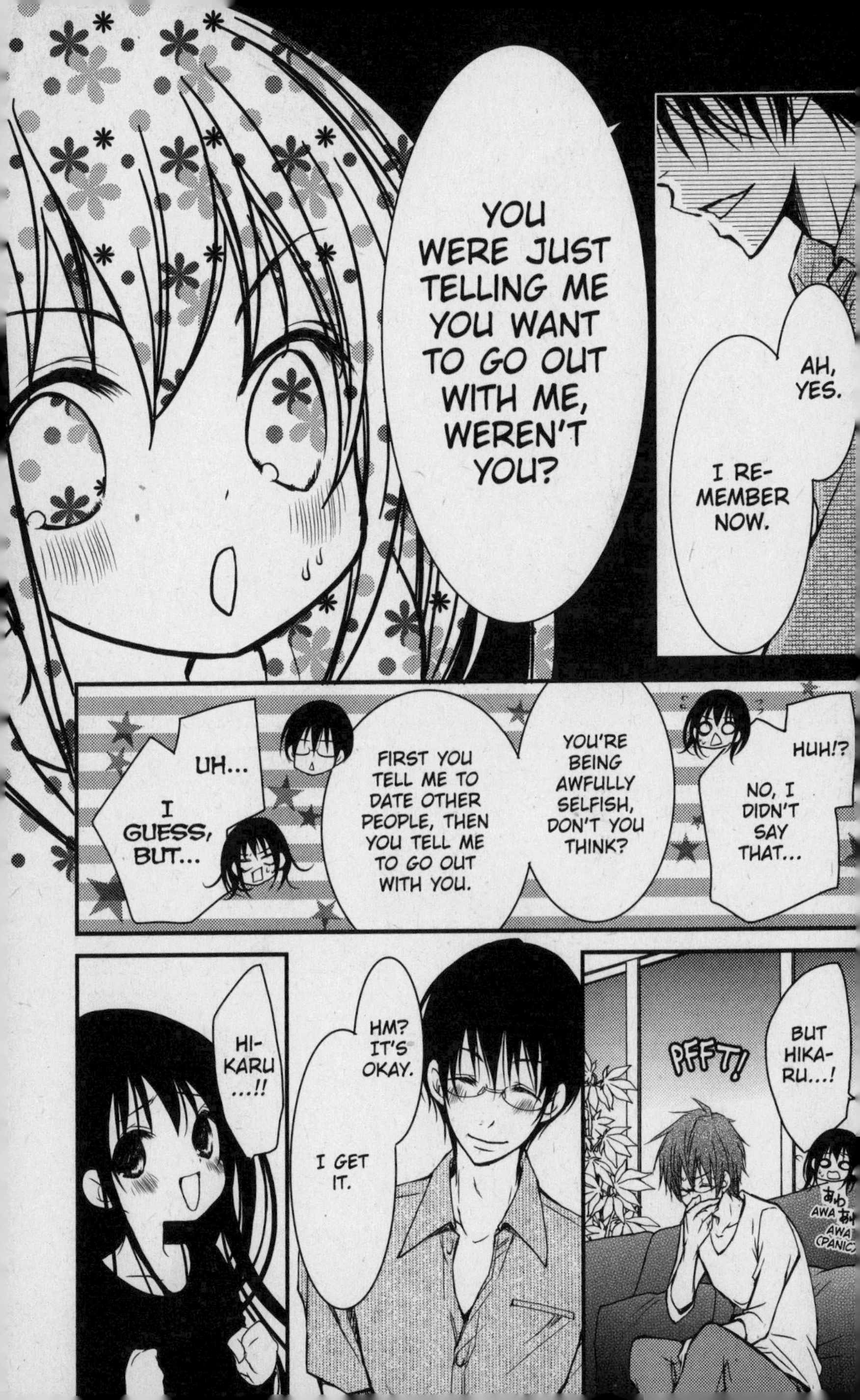
AH, YES.
I RE-MEMBER NOW.
YOU WERE JUST TELLING ME YOU WANT TO GO OUT WITH ME, WEREN'T YOU?
HUH!?
NO, I DIDN'T SAY THAT...
YOU'RE BEING AWFULLY SELFISH, DON'T YOU THINK?
FIRST YOU TELL ME TO DATE OTHER PEOPLE, THEN YOU TELL ME TO GO OUT WITH YOU.
UH...
I GUESS, BUT...
BUT HIKA-RU...!
PFFT!
AWA AWA (PANIC)
HM? IT'S OKAY.
HI-KARU...!!
I GET IT.

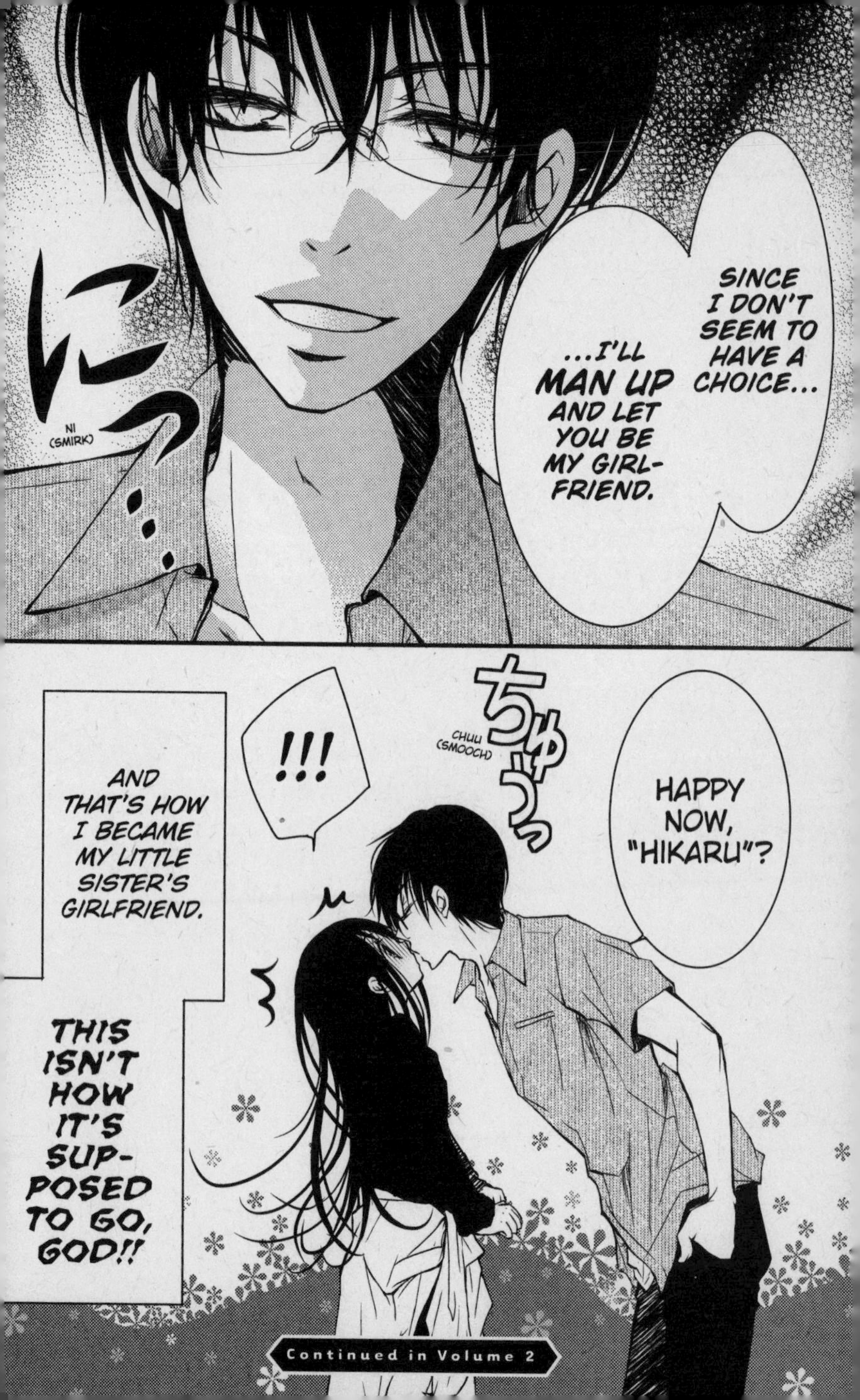
SINCE I DON'T SEEM TO HAVE A CHOICE...
...I'LL MAN UP AND LET YOU BE MY GIRLFRIEND.
NI (SMIRK)
HAPPY NOW, "HIKARU"?
CHUU (SMOOCH)
!!!
AND THAT'S HOW I BECAME MY LITTLE SISTER'S GIRLFRIEND.
THIS ISN'T HOW IT'S SUPPOSED TO GO, GOD!!
Continued in Volume 2

[Ani-Imo]

Big Brother becomes Little Sister;
Little Sister becomes Big Brother.

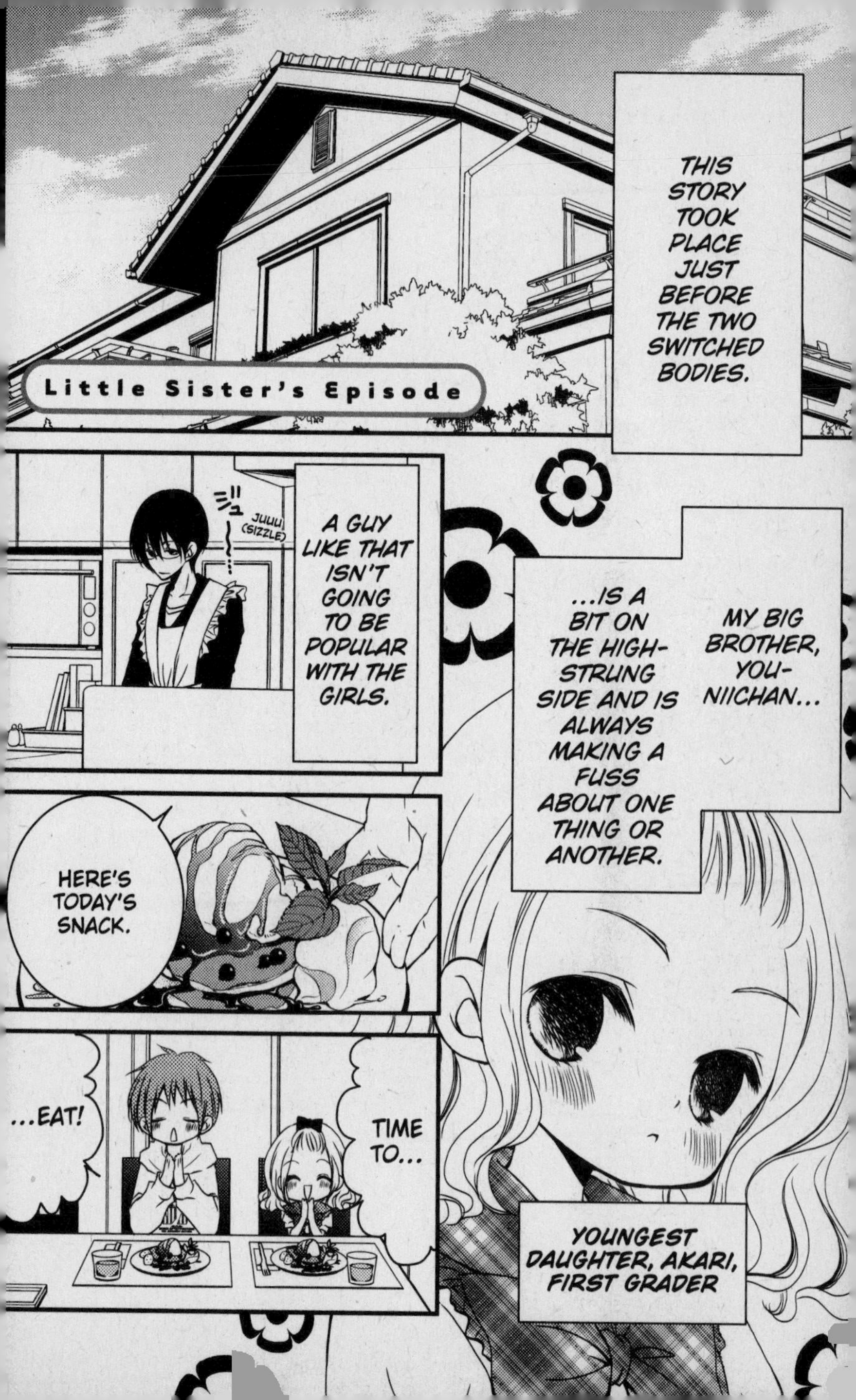
Little Sister's Episode
THIS STORY TOOK PLACE JUST BEFORE THE TWO SWITCHED BODIES.
MY BIG BROTHER, YOU-NIICHAN...
...IS A BIT ON THE HIGH-STRUNG SIDE AND IS ALWAYS MAKING A FUSS ABOUT ONE THING OR ANOTHER.
YOUNGEST DAUGHTER, AKARI, FIRST GRADER
JUUU (SIZZLE)
A GUY LIKE THAT ISN'T GOING TO BE POPULAR WITH THE GIRLS.
HERE'S TODAY'S SNACK.
TIME TO...
...EAT!

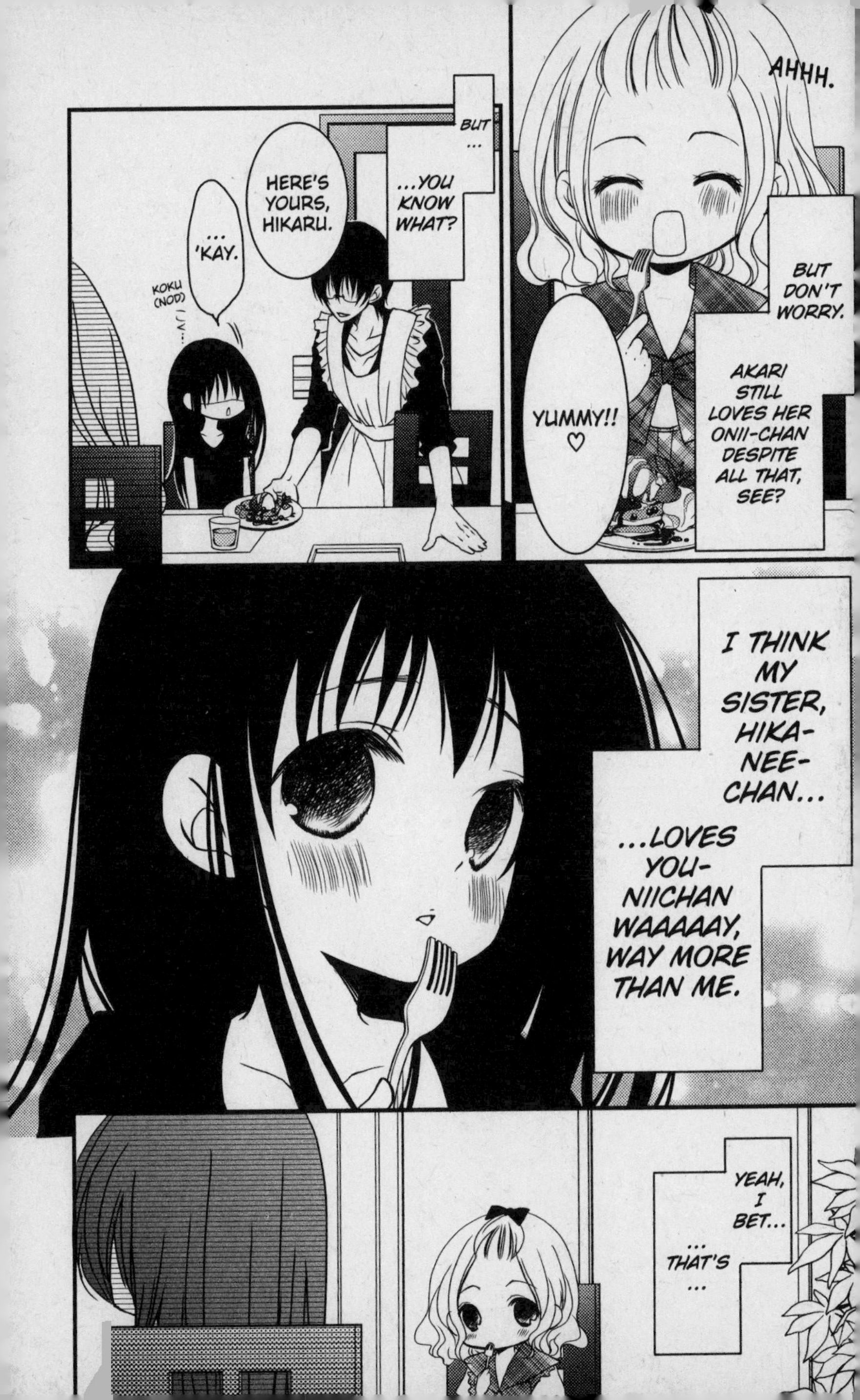
AHHH.
YUMMY!! ♡
BUT DON'T WORRY.
AKARI STILL LOVES HER ONII-CHAN DESPITE ALL THAT, SEE?
BUT ...
...YOU KNOW WHAT?
HERE'S YOURS, HIKARU.
... 'KAY.
KOKU (NOD)
I THINK MY SISTER, HIKA-NEE-CHAN...
...LOVES YOU-NIICHAN WAAAAAY, WAY MORE THAN ME.
YEAH, I BET...
... THAT'S ...

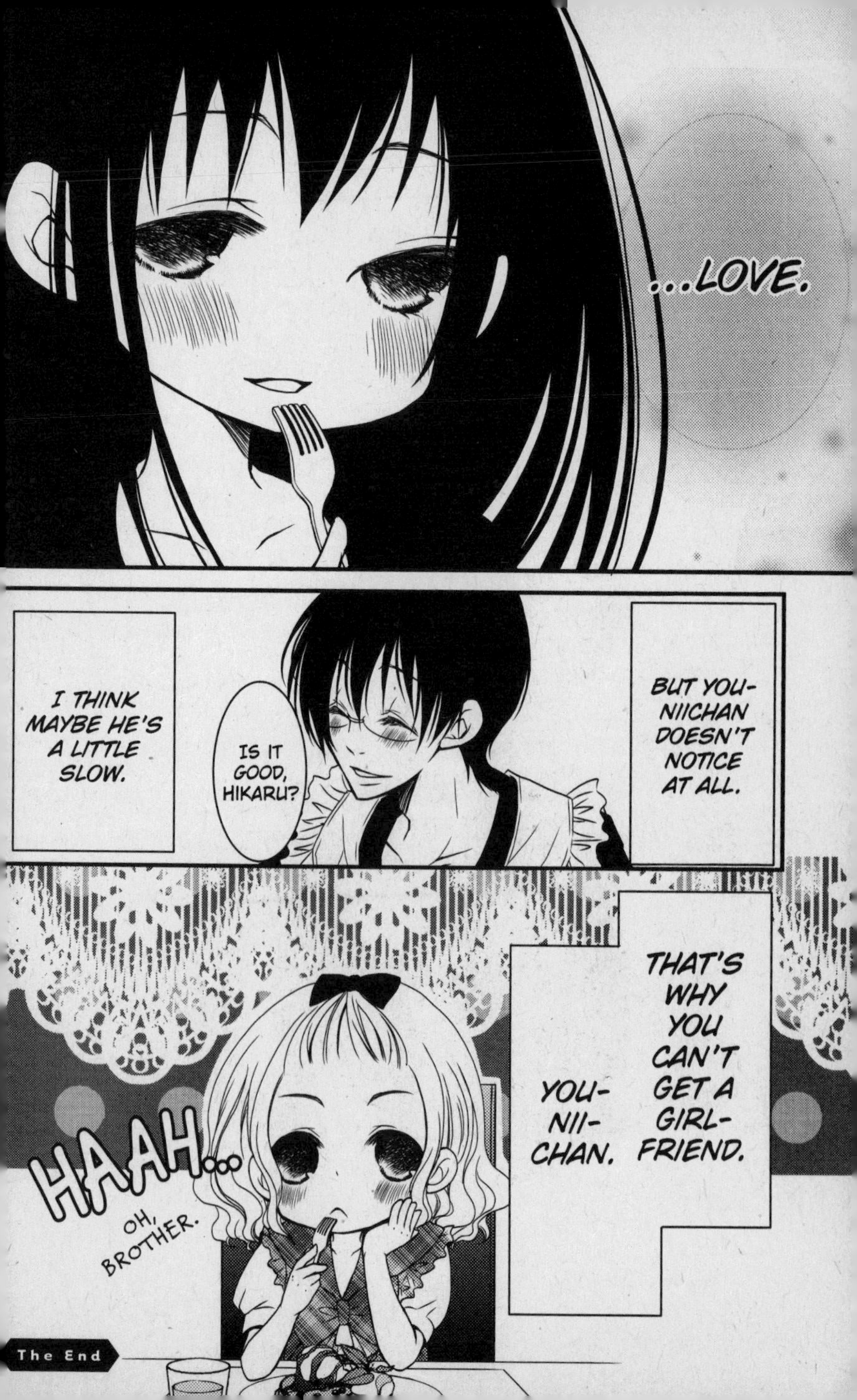
...LOVE.
BUT YOU-NIICHAN DOESN'T NOTICE AT ALL.
IS IT GOOD, HIKARU?
I THINK MAYBE HE'S A LITTLE SLOW.
THAT'S WHY YOU CAN'T GET A GIRL-FRIEND.
YOU-NII-CHAN.
HAAH...
OH, BROTHER.
The End

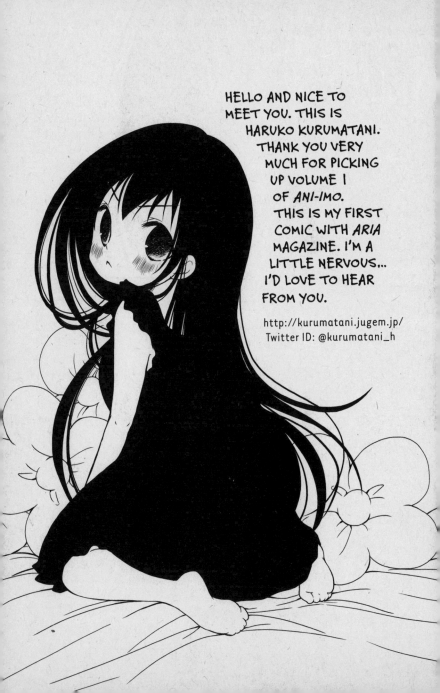

HELLO AND NICE TO MEET YOU. THIS IS HARUKO KURUMATANI. THANK YOU VERY MUCH FOR PICKING UP VOLUME 1 OF *ANI-IMO*. THIS IS MY FIRST COMIC WITH *ARIA* MAGAZINE. I'M A LITTLE NERVOUS... I'D LOVE TO HEAR FROM YOU.

http://kurumatani.jugem.jp/
Twitter ID: @kurumatani_h

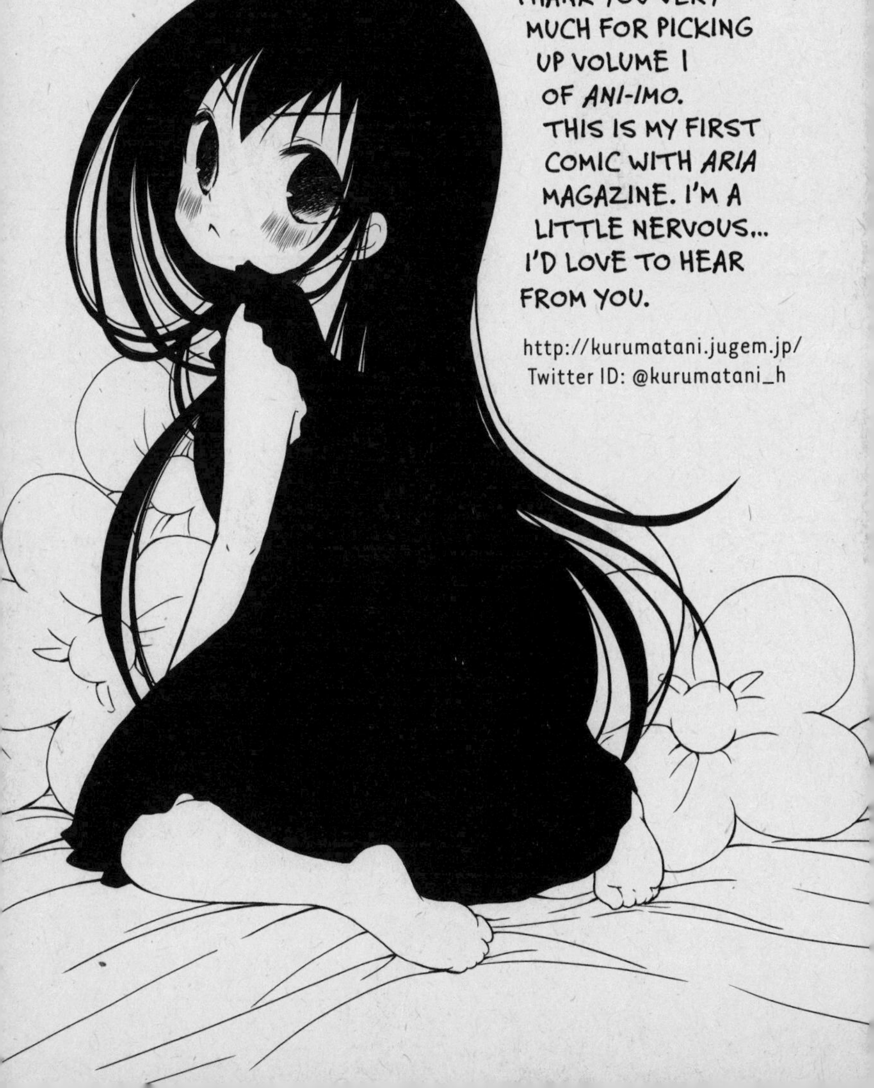

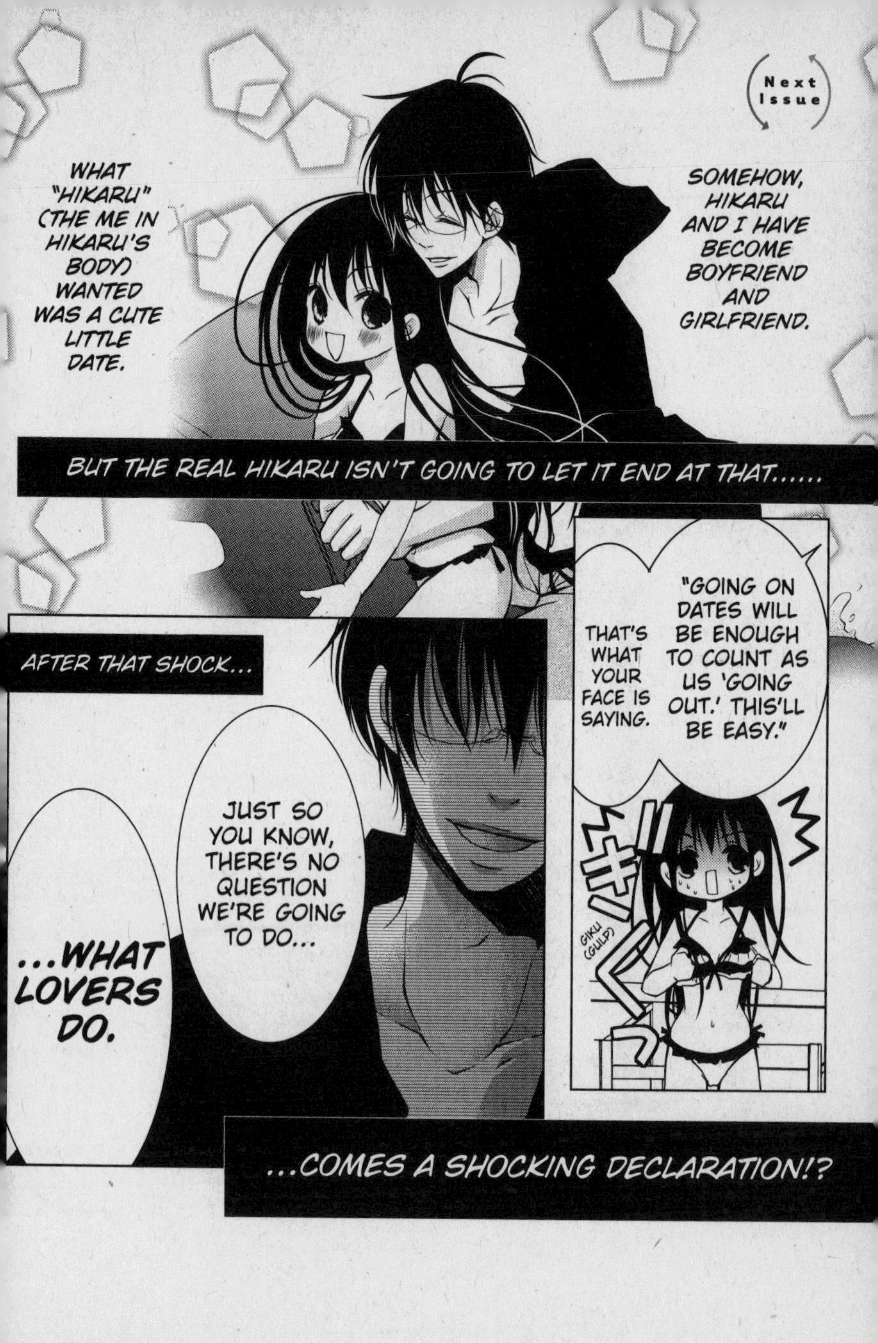
Next Issue
SOMEHOW, HIKARU AND I HAVE BECOME BOYFRIEND AND GIRLFRIEND.
WHAT "HIKARU" (THE ME IN HIKARU'S BODY) WANTED WAS A CUTE LITTLE DATE.
BUT THE REAL HIKARU ISN'T GOING TO LET IT END AT THAT......
"GOING ON DATES WILL BE ENOUGH TO COUNT AS US 'GOING OUT.' THIS'LL BE EASY."
THAT'S WHAT YOUR FACE IS SAYING.
GIKU (GULP)
AFTER THAT SHOCK...
JUST SO YOU KNOW, THERE'S NO QUESTION WE'RE GOING TO DO...
...WHAT LOVERS DO.
...COMES A SHOCKING DECLARATION!?

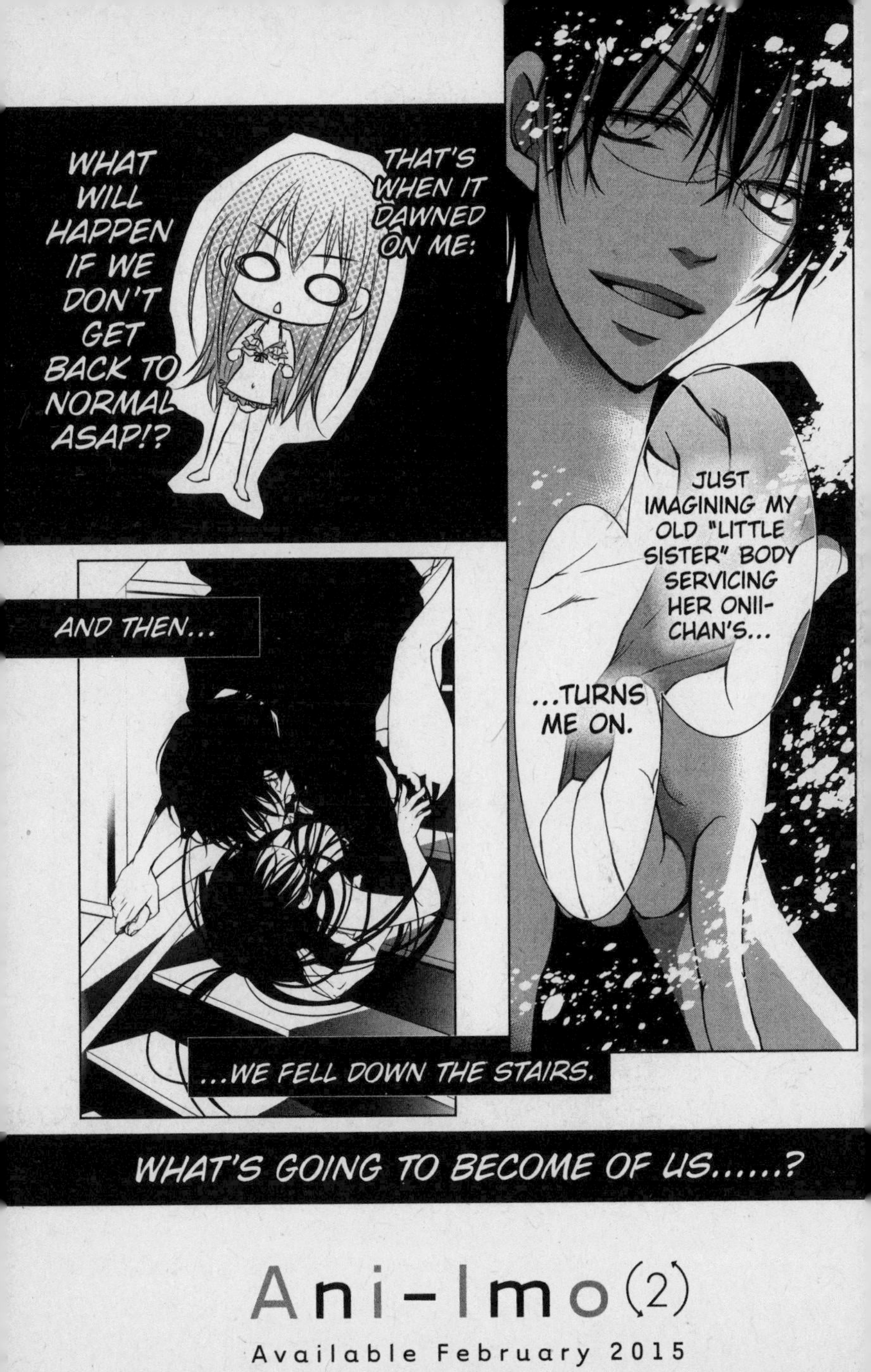
JUST IMAGINING MY OLD "LITTLE SISTER" BODY SERVICING HER ONII-CHAN'S...
...TURNS ME ON.
THAT'S WHEN IT DAWNED ON ME:
WHAT WILL HAPPEN IF WE DON'T GET BACK TO NORMAL ASAP!?
AND THEN...
...WE FELL DOWN THE STAIRS.
WHAT'S GOING TO BECOME OF US......?

Translation Notes

Common Honorifics:

no honorific: Indicates familiarity or closeness; if used without permission or reason, addressing someone in this manner would constitute an insult.

-san: The Japanese equivalent of Mr./Mrs./Miss. If a situation calls for politeness, this is the fail-safe honorific.

-sama: Conveys great respect; may also indicate that the social status of the speaker is lower than that of the addressee.

-kun: Used most often when referring to boys, this indicates affection or familiarity. Occasionally used by older men among their peers, but it may also be used by anyone referring to a person of lower standing.

-chan: An affectionate honorific indicating familiarity used mostly in reference to girls; also used in reference to cute persons or animals of either gender.

-senpai: A suffix used to address upperclassmen or more experienced coworkers.

-sensei: A respectful term for teachers, artists, or high-level professionals.

-oniisan, *onii-san*, *aniki*, etc.: Terms used to address an elder brother or brother-like figure.

-oneesan, *onee-san*, *aneki*, etc.: Terms used to address an elder sister or sister-like figure.

Page 11

Koizumi siblings' names

All the children in the Koizumi family have an element of "light" reflected in their names. *Taiyou* means "sun," and *youta* is just the reverse-order reading of the two characters that make the same word. Both *akari* and *hikaru* mean "light."

Page 12

Kyoto-style grilled fish

Fish fillets marinated overnight in Kyoto-style miso (a sweet variety of soybean paste), then grilled.

Ani-Imo

Ani-Imo (2)

Sneak Peek

Read on for an early look at Volume 2,
available February 2015

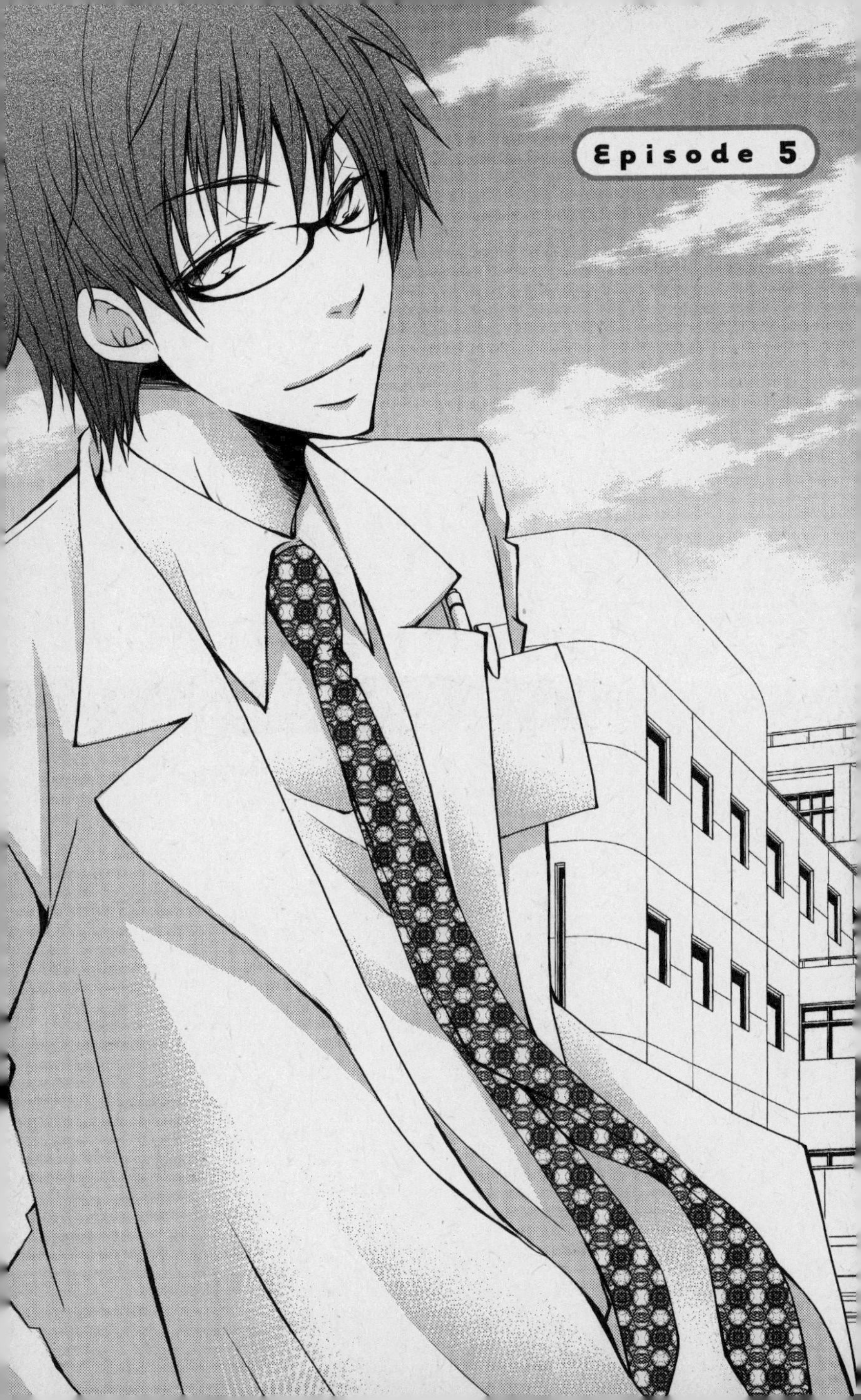
Episode 5

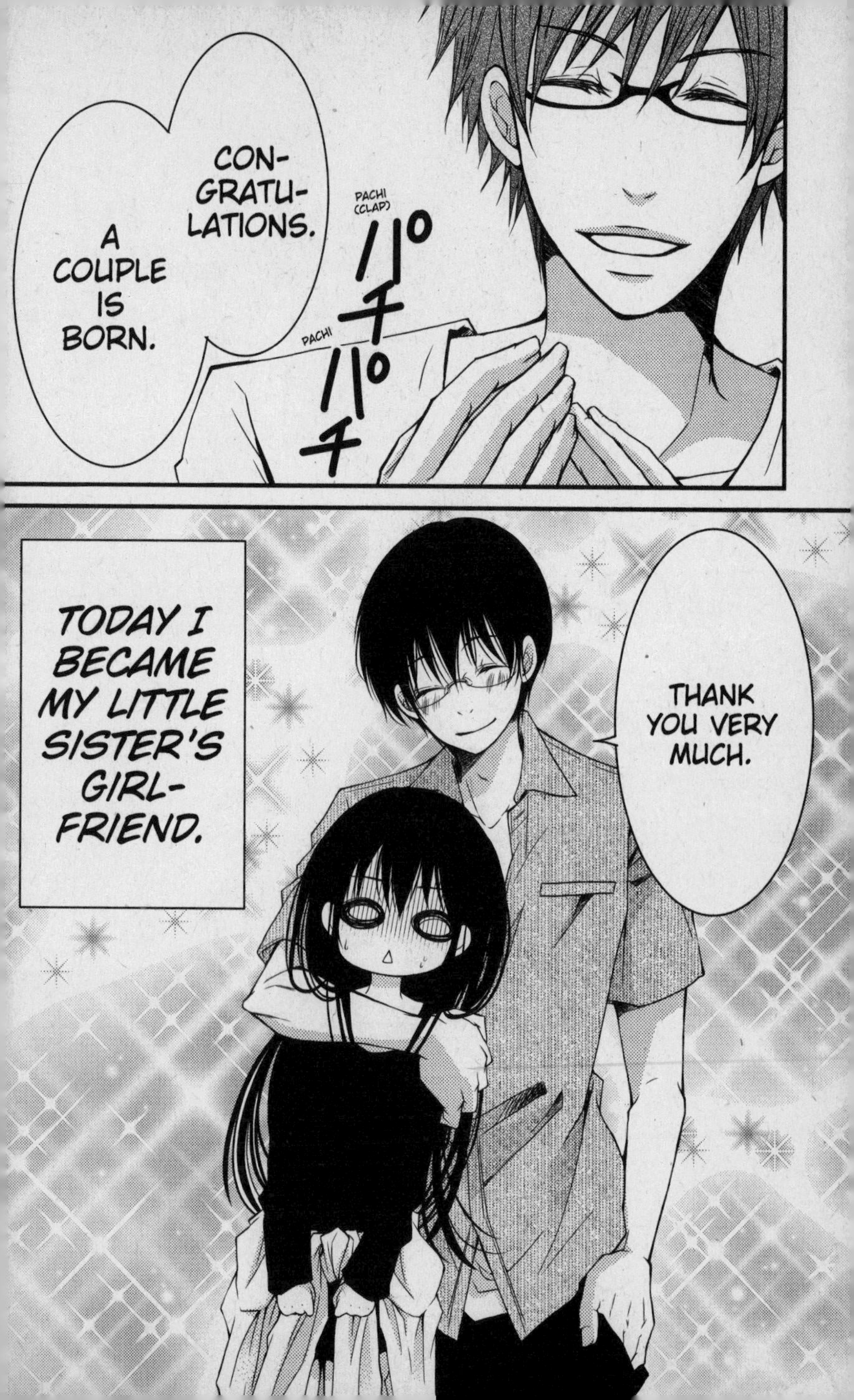
CONGRATULATIONS. A COUPLE IS BORN.
PACHI (CLAP)
パチ
PACHI
パチ
THANK YOU VERY MUCH.
TODAY I BECAME MY LITTLE SISTER'S GIRLFRIEND.

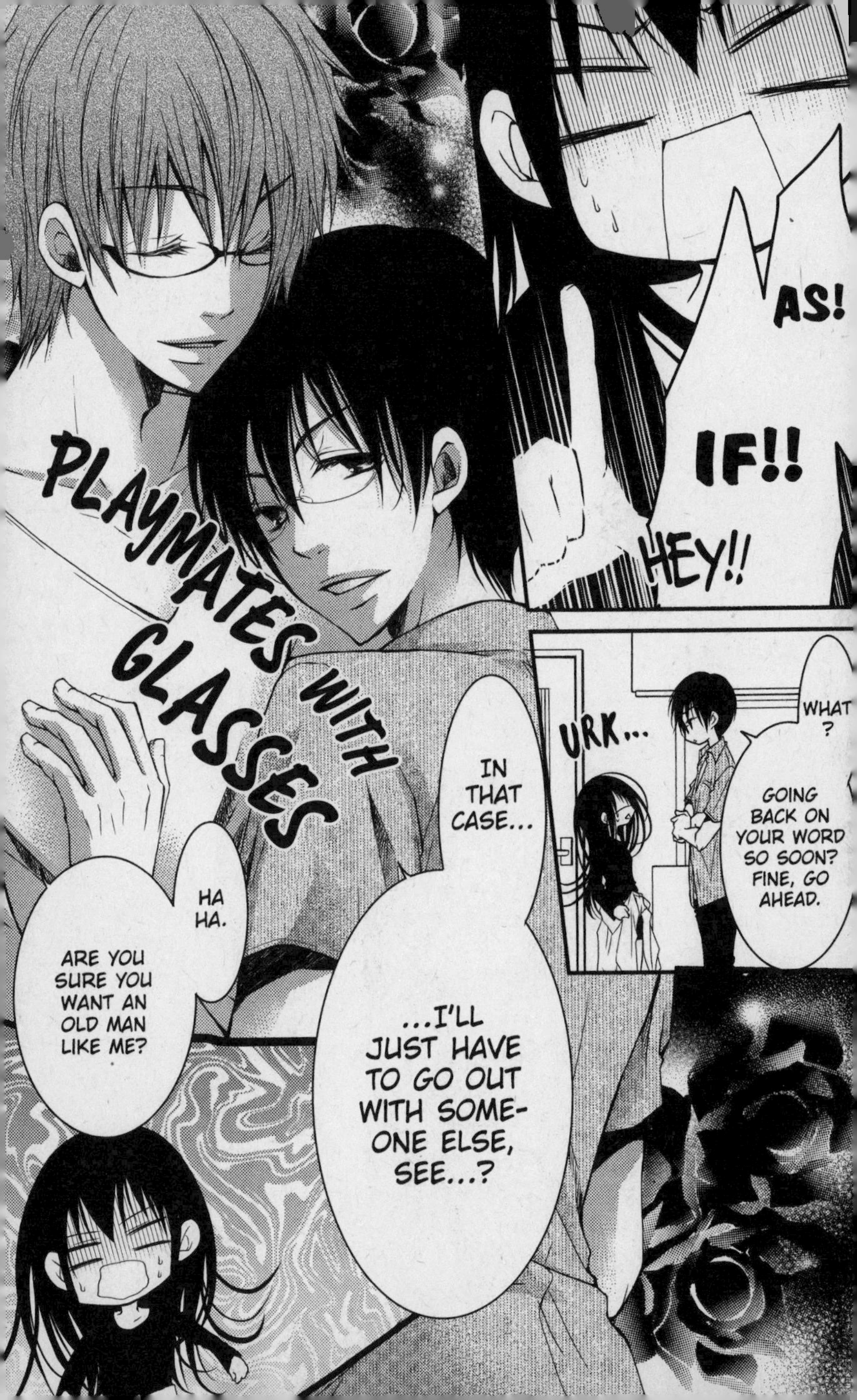
AS!
IF!!
HEY!!
WHAT?
GOING BACK ON YOUR WORD SO SOON? FINE, GO AHEAD.
URK...
IN THAT CASE...
...I'LL JUST HAVE TO GO OUT WITH SOME-ONE ELSE, SEE...?
PLAYMATES WITH GLASSES
HA HA.
ARE YOU SURE YOU WANT AN OLD MAN LIKE ME?

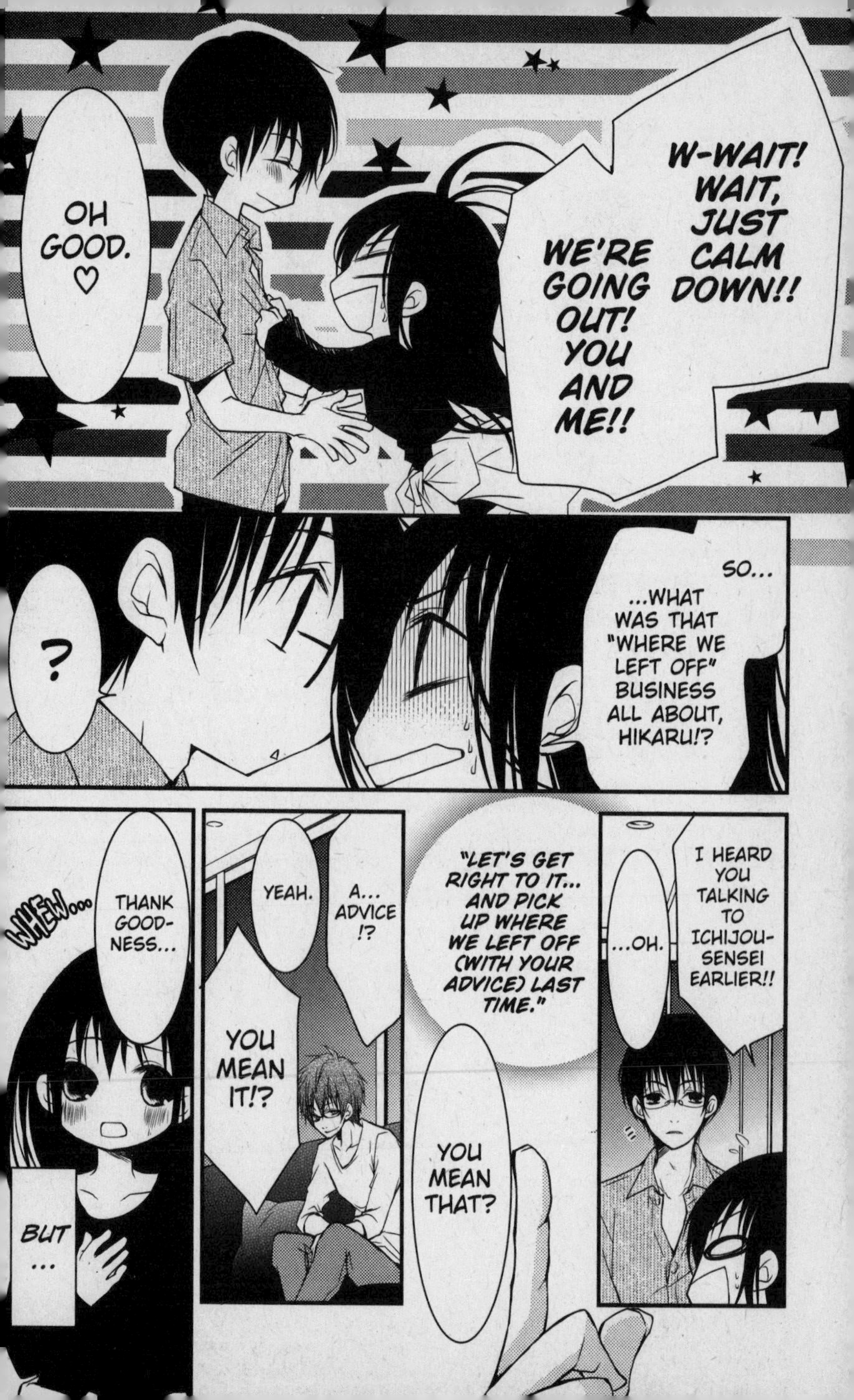
W-WAIT! WAIT, JUST CALM DOWN!!
WE'RE GOING OUT! YOU AND ME!!
OH GOOD. ♡
SO...
...WHAT WAS THAT "WHERE WE LEFT OFF" BUSINESS ALL ABOUT, HIKARU!?
?
I HEARD YOU TALKING TO ICHIJOU-SENSEI EARLIER!!
...OH.
"LET'S GET RIGHT TO IT... AND PICK UP WHERE WE LEFT OFF (WITH YOUR ADVICE) LAST TIME."
YOU MEAN THAT?
A... ADVICE!?
YEAH.
YOU MEAN IT!?
THANK GOODNESS...
WHEW...
BUT ...

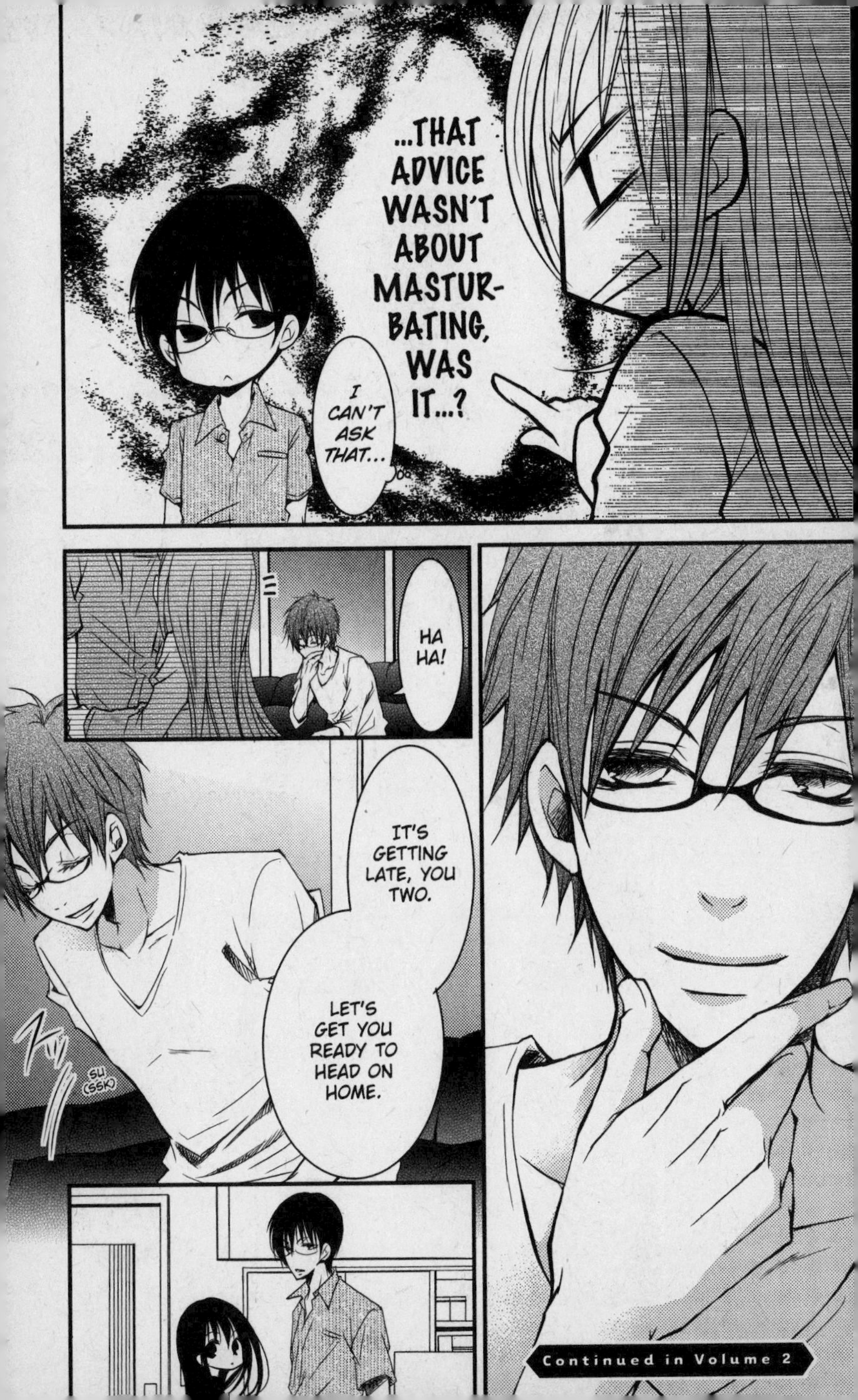
...THAT ADVICE WASN'T ABOUT MASTUR-BATING, WAS IT...?
I CAN'T ASK THAT...
HA HA!
IT'S GETTING LATE, YOU TWO.
LET'S GET YOU READY TO HEAD ON HOME.
SU (SSK)
Continued in Volume 2

ANI-IMO(1)

HARUKO KURUMATANI

Translation: Christine Dashiell

Lettering: Abigail Blackman

ANI-IMO Volume 1
© 2012 Haruko Kurumatani. All rights reserved.
First published in Japan in 2012 by Kodansha, Ltd., Tokyo.
Publication rights for this English edition arranged through Kodansha Ltd. Tokyo

Translation © 2014 by Hachette Book Group, Inc.

Yen Press
Hachette Book Group
1290 Avenue of the Americas
New York, NY 10104

www.hachettebookgroup.com
www.yenpress.com

Yen Press is an imprint of Hachette Book Group, Inc.
The Yen Press name and logo are trademarks of Hachette Book Group, Inc.

First Yen Press Edition: November 2014

ISBN: 978-0-316-37861-1

10 9 8 7 6 5 4 3 2 1

BVG

Printed in the United States of America